International Human Rights Law and Diplomacy

PRINCIPLES OF INTERNATIONAL LAW

As the issues addressed by international law become ever more complex and critical there is a greater need than ever for clear and rigorous exploration of the key principles and frameworks which underpin its working. This important series presents concise, analytical overviews of specific areas of international law, from international criminal justice and international humanitarian law to the law of treaties and the law of state responsibility.

Written by some of the best names in the field, as well as the new generation of scholars, each book uses a structured approach and an accessible style, yet also provides careful analysis and new insight. Books in the series offer an invaluable source of reference for scholars and postgraduate students, as well as for lawyers and policymakers working in the respective individual fields.

Titles in this series include:

The International Law of State Responsibility
An Introduction
Robert Kolb

International Criminal Justice
Gideon Boas and Pascale Chifflet

International Law on the Maintenance of Peace
Jus Contra Bellum
Robert Kolb

The International Law of Biotechnology
Human Rights, Trade, Patents, Health and the Environment
Matthias Herdegen

International Humanitarian Law
Rules, Controversies, and Solutions to Problems Arising in Warfare
Marco Sassòli

International Investment Law
Arnaud de Nanteuil

International Human Rights Law and Diplomacy
Kriangsak Kittichaisaree

International Human Rights Law and Diplomacy

Kriangsak Kittichaisaree

Judge of the International Tribunal for the Law of the Sea, former Ambassador and sometime Visiting Fellow at the University of Oxford, UK

PRINCIPLES OF INTERNATIONAL LAW

Edward **Elgar**
PUBLISHING

Cheltenham, UK • Northampton, MA, USA

Published by
Edward Elgar Publishing Limited
The Lypiatts
15 Lansdown Road
Cheltenham
Glos GL50 2JA
UK

Edward Elgar Publishing, Inc.
William Pratt House
9 Dewey Court
Northampton
Massachusetts 01060
USA

Paperback edition 2021

A catalogue record for this book
is available from the British Library

Library of Congress Control Number: 2019954456

This book is available electronically in the **Elgar**online
Law subject collection
http://dx.doi.org/10.4337/9781839102196

ISBN 978 1 83910 218 9 (cased)
ISBN 978 1 83910 219 6 (eBook)
ISBN 978 1 80220 509 1 (paperback)

Printed and bound by CPI Group (UK) Ltd, Croydon, CR0 4YY

Contents

Preface

Human rights is a major discipline of study in universities that offer courses in law and social science including politics and philosophy, among others. Some universities teach human rights as an interdisciplinary study. Books on human rights occupy a relatively large space in libraries and bookshops. It is difficult to be innovative offering new contributions to this already mature field of scholarship.

However, a major gap does exist amongst the excellent writings of authors from across the globe. Most of the ideals, analyses and recommendations in the existing multifarious publications may be too detailed, esoteric or technical for a large percentage of their targeted readers to digest and convey to policy decision makers and domestic constituencies who can make differences to human rights. In addition, a large percentage of them seem skewed towards a liberal, Western approach to human rights. Therefore, an easily readable book written by a non-Westerner with insights into power, diplomacy, processes and decision making in the international and domestic systems where international law and politics intersect in the matter of the peacetime rights of the human person should be more than welcome. This is especially so when the book furthers the 'de-politicization' of human rights by refuting political subterfuges utilized by States in order not to abide by their international human rights obligations – by exposing standard tactics used by States and the games that they play in the international arena, as well as acceptable approaches for responding to these tactics.

The present author used to serve as Director-General of the Department of International Organizations of Thailand's Ministry of Foreign Affairs entrusted with all aspects of international human rights, including interaction with both international and national human rights stakeholders. The author spent exactly three decades on multilateral diplomacy at various United Nations forums. Running for election to the UN International Law Commission and, subsequently, the International Tribunal for the Law of the Sea gave the author opportunities to meet face to face with permanent representatives and delegates of all UN Member States to hear their positions, concerns and demands in international affairs. Having served as a diplomat accredited to the USA, the Islamic Republic of Iran, Australia (and concurrently four Pacific Island States) and the Russian Federation (and concurrently four other members of the Commonwealth of Independent States) gives the author unique first-hand experience in the diverging traditions, religions, cultures, values and politics in these respective nations that largely mirror the diversity in today's world. Teaching part-time at law schools in four continents informs the author that for any argument to be convincing to all sides of the debate it must be objective, academically sound and practical. As an international judge, the author understands how legal arguments can win or lose a case.

Equipped with the aforesaid credentials and positions that give him a panoramic coign of vantage, the author has ventured to write this book *International Human Rights Law and Diplomacy* for pragmatists, government officials, lawyers, practitioners, scholars, students and any stakeholders interested in the real world of human rights. The book avoids presenting in-depth technical details and data in order not to be too cumbersome to read and comprehend for non-academic readers. It also aims at showing concern for non-Western perspectives on human rights, covering a wide range of material beyond the usual suspects of the European context. The approach of this book is contextual rather than overly and unselfconsciously dogmatic, where aspiration dressed in the clothing of human rights is treated as a legal right, which is a dubious political claim at best.

The author's specialization in international human rights law during his postgraduate studies at Harvard Law School forms the foundation of his knowledge of the subject. Research for this book was mostly conducted at the University of Oxford in 2018. He is beholden to the then Principal (Baroness Helena Kennedy of The Shaws, QC), fellows and staff of Mansfield College, of which he was a visiting fellow; to the Director (Professor Catherine O'Regan) and friends at the Bonarvero Institute of Human Rights, of which he was a research visitor during its first year of establishment; to Dapo Akande and other colleagues, friends and students at the university for their companionship and exchanges of ideas; and to the Bodleian Library for its excellent collections and facilities. The PhD students at the University of Hamburg's Albrecht Mendelson Bartholdy Graduate School of Law who attended the author's six-day workshop 'International Law and Politics of Human Rights' in 2019 deserve thanks for contributing some good ideas to this book.

On 28 January 2019 Maurice Kamto, who had run as a presidential candidate against the incumbent President of Cameroon, in office since 1982, was arrested on charges of sedition, insurrection and inciting violence, was put into a maximum-security prison and was not released until October 2019. Due to the alphabetical seating arrangement in the International Law Commission, Kamto and the author were 'conjoined twins', always seated together when both were ILC members. Kamto, former ILC chairman and Special Rapporteur on the topic 'Expulsion of Aliens', is a humanist aspiring for the betterment of human rights, especially in his native country. His unjust fate serves as a constant reminder that there are still unfortunate people whose human rights must be protected, and hopefully this book will make some contributions towards that end.

Ben Booth, Amber Watts, Fiona Todd, Sue Sharp and Rebecca Stowell of Edward Elgar Publishing, as well as Carolyn Fox and all those involved in the publication of this book, provided highly professional, timely and invaluable guidance, suggestions, encouragement and services that are much appreciated.

Needless to say, the views expressed in this book are the personal views of the author and do not necessarily reflect any of the organizations to which he does or has previously belonged.

Abbreviations

ACDEG	African Charter on Democracy, Elections and Governance
ACHPR	African Charter on Human and Peoples' Rights
ACHR	American Convention on Human Rights
ACRWC	African Charter on the Rights and Welfare of the Child
ACT	Accountability, Coherence and Transparency
ACtHPR	African Court on Human and Peoples' Rights
AHRD	ASEAN Human Rights Declaration
AICHR	ASEAN Intergovernmental Commission on Human Rights
AJIL	American Journal of International Law
ASEAN	Association of Southeast Asian Nations
AU	African Union
CAT	Convention against Torture and Other Cruel, Inhuman or Degrading Treatment or Punishment
CED	International Convention for the Protection of All Persons from Enforced Disappearance
CEDAW	Convention on the Elimination of All Forms of Discrimination against Women

CERD	International Convention on the Elimination of All Forms of Racial Discrimination
CESCR	Committee on Economic, Social and Cultural Rights
ch.	chapter
CMW	International Convention on the Protection of the Rights of All Migrant Workers and Members of their Families
CoE	Council of Europe
CRC	Convention on the Rights of the Child
CRPD	Convention on the Rights of Persons with Disabilities
CUP	Cambridge University Press
EBA	Everything But Arms
ECHR	European Convention for the Protection of Human Rights and Fundamental Freedoms
ECJ	Court of Justice of the European Union, or European Court of Justice
ECOSOC	United Nations Economic and Social Council
ECtHR	European Court of Human Rights
EG	Experimental governance
EJIL	European Journal of International Law
ER	English Reports
ETS	European Treaty Series
EU	European Union
FFM	Independent International Fact-Finding Mission on Myanmar
FGM	female genital mutilation
G77	Group of 77 developing States and China

GRULAC	Latin American and the Caribbean Group
Hague Recueil	Recueil des cours de l'Académie de Droit International de la Haye
HRC	Human Rights Council
Hum Rts L Rev	Human Rights Law Review
Hum Rts Quarterly	Human Rights Quarterly
IACHR	Inter-American Commission on Human Rights
IACtHR	Inter-American Court of Human Rights
ICC	International Criminal Court
ICCPR	International Covenant on Civil and Political Rights
ICESCR	International Covenant on Economic, Social and Cultural Rights
ICJ	International Court of Justice
ICLQ	International and Comparative Law Quarterly
IHDA	Institute for Human Rights and Development in Africa
IHRL	International human rights law
IIIM	International, Impartial and Independent Mechanism
ILC	International Law Commission of the United Nations
ILJ	International Law Journal
ILM	International Legal Materials
ILO	International Labour Organization
IMO	International Maritime Organization
ISIL	Islamic State of Iraq and the Levant
JIL	Journal of International Law
LJ	Law Journal
NAM	Non-Aligned Movement

NGO	Non-governmental organization
OAS	Organization of American States
OIC	Organisation of Islamic Cooperation
OSCE	Organization for Security and Cooperation in Europe
OUP	Oxford University Press
PACE	Parliamentary Assembly of the Council of Europe
PCIJ	Permanent Court of International Justice
PSC	Peace and Security Council of the African Union
R2P	Responsibility to Protect
Rev	Review
SAR	1979 International Convention on Maritime Search and Rescue
Ser	Series
SOLAS	1974 Convention on the Safety of Life at Sea
SPT	Subcommittee on Prevention of Torture and other Cruel, Inhuman or Degrading Treatment or Punishment
UDHR	Universal Declaration of Human Rights
UIDHR	Universal Islamic Declaration of Human Rights
UN	United Nations
UNCLOS	1982 UN Convention on the Law of the Sea
UNESCO	United Nations Educational, Scientific and Cultural Organization
UNGA	UN General Assembly

UNGGE	Group of Governmental Experts on Developments in the Field of Information and Telecommunications in the Context of International Security
UNHCHR	UN High Commissioner for Human Rights
UNSC	UN Security Council
UNTS	United Nations Treaty Series
UPR	Universal Periodic Review
USAID	US Agency for International Development
VCCR	Vienna Convention on Consular Relations
VCLT	Vienna Convention on the Law of Treaties
WEOG	Western European and Others Group
WGC	Working Group on Communications
WGS	Working Group on Situations

1.   Introduction to international human rights law and diplomacy

International human rights law (IHRL) is a body of legal norms, not moral or political obligations,[1] regulating human rights among nation States. IHRL and diplomacy are intertwined as States manoeuvre in international forums to achieve their goals with respect to human rights.

'Diplomacy' connotes the application of intelligence and tact to the conduct of official relations and execution of foreign policies between governments of nation States by peaceful means, applying persuasion and different forms of pressure, the success of which depends, to a great extent, on the power behind them. The power may be hard power, such as military and economic might, or soft power founded on the ability of one State or government to shape the preferences of others by co-opting instead of coercing them to agree because they appreciate its values, emulate its example and/or aspire to its level of prosperity and openness, for example.[2] There are two dimensions of diplomacy – bilateral and multilateral. Bilateral diplomacy involves interaction between two nation States, whereas multilateral diplomacy is diplomatic intercourse in international forums, such as the United Nations (UN), among States that are members of the respective forums, where they join together as groups or blocs to enhance their negotiating power and, in some cases, to get recognition of belonging to a specific group or bloc.

The UN is the world's largest, all-inclusive multilateral diplomatic forum. Within the UN system States are divided into five regional groups for the purpose of equitable geographical allocation of seats or positions: the African Group; the Asia-Pacific Group, which, strangely, includes Cyprus; the Eastern European Group; the Latin American and Caribbean Group (GRULAC); and the Western European and Others Group (WEOG), which includes the USA, Canada, Australia, New Zealand and Turkey. Beyond the aforesaid regional groups there exist numerous groupings. The Council of Europe (CoE), set up

---

[1]   Hurst Hannum, 'Reinvigorating Human Rights for the Twenty-First Century' (2016) 16 Hum Rts L Rev 409, 411, 446–51. See for the difference between ethics or moral rights and law, Amartya Sen, *The Idea of Justice* (Penguin 2010) 361–5.

[2]   Ivor Roberts (ed.), *Satow's Diplomatic Practice* (7th edn, OUP 2017) 3–4 and n. 2.

in 1949 to uphold human rights, democracy and the rule of law in Europe, has 47 Member States, including all the 28 Members of the European Union (EU) and all Eastern European States except Belarus. The Organisation of Islamic Cooperation (OIC), founded in 1969 to be the voice of the Islamic world, consists of 57 Muslim-majority States, including Albania, Azerbaijan and Turkey, which are CoE Member States. The League of Arab States, or the Arab League, set up in 1945, now comprises 22 Member States, all of which are also members of the OIC and ten of which are situated in Africa and are members of the African Union. The majority of Muslim-majority States today fall somewhere between 'purist' Saudi Arabia and 'secular' Turkey.[3] The other two important groupings are the Group of 77 (or G77, comprising 134 developing States including China) and the Non-Aligned Movement (NAM) consisting of 120 Member States that are, in theory, not formally aligned with or against any major power bloc.

According to Thomas Buergenthal, a former judge president of the Inter-American Court of Human Rights and a former judge of the International Court of Justice (ICJ), '[t]he greatest weakness of the United Nations human rights system is its susceptibility to politicization'.[4]

The terminology 'politics' derives from the fourth-century BC Greek philosopher Aristotle's work on affairs of the 'cities' or *polis* in Greek.[5] The *Collins English Dictionary* gives the modern meaning of 'politics' as 'the actions or activities concerned with achieving and using power in a country or society'. Human rights are themselves the outcome of politics in several ways. To begin with, the process of characterizing something as a right is a political one. So is the finding of the conditional exceptions to the application of certain rights. This is also the case regarding the balancing of competing rights claims.[6] For example, a decision to construct a giant dam for electricity generation to realize the right to development of one group also dislodges the

---

[3] Mashood A Baderin, *International Human Rights and Islamic Law* (OUP 2003) 8.

[4] 'A Brief History of International Human Rights Law', UN Codification Division, Office of Legal Affairs, Audiovisual Library of International Law, http://legal.un.org/avl/ls/Buergenthal_HR_video_1.html, accessed 11 Aug 2019.

[5] Aristotle, *The Politics of Aristotle* (Benjamin Jowett tr, Clarendon Press 1885).

[6] Martti Koskenniemi, *The Politics of International Law* (Hart 2011) 157–9; Elena Katselli, 'The Rule of Law and the Role of Human Rights in Contemporary International Law' in Rob Dickinson, Elena Katselli, Colin Murray and Ole W Pedersen (eds), *Examining Critical Perspectives on Human Rights* (CUP 2012) 131, 144–6; Jack Donnelly, *International Human Rights* (3rd edn, Westview Press 2007) 3–9.

right and freedom of individuals who live and earn their living on the land to be permanently submerged under the dam's water.[7]

IHRL forms part of international law, which is, to a large extent, the effect of politics involving prejudice and bias as practised by States.[8] IHRL is also part of international relations and hence international politics, particularly when some States claim justifications for human rights in other States with ulterior motives not actually related to human rights but to some kind of political gains.[9] Moreover, when it comes to the implementation and enforcement of human rights, the *realpolitik* of international relations cannot be disregarded.[10]

The ICJ, the UN's principal dispute settlement organ, has recognized on several occasions that questions submitted to it may also have political aspects which arise in international life. However, whatever its political aspects, the ICJ 'cannot refuse to admit the legal character of a question which invites it to discharge an essentially judicial task, namely, an assessment of the legality of the possible conduct of States with regard to the obligations imposed upon them by international law'.[11] Likewise, the fact that IHRL may also have political aspects does not deprive IHRL of its legal character requiring compliance by the States legally bound by this law.

In IHRL, as in any other field of international law, it is the nation State that has 'international legal personality' to act on the international plane, with individuals within the State as beneficiaries of such acts by the State.[12] It is unacceptable nowadays for nation States to assert sovereignty in defence of egregious human rights violations.[13]

Domestically, the government in each nation State needs to convince its citizens that they are not treated worse than their counterparts elsewhere;

---

[7] See, generally, Bas de Gaay Fortman, *Political Economy of Human Rights: Rights, Realities and Realization* (Routledge 2011).

[8] *Corfu Channel (United Kingdom v Albania)* Judgment [1949] ICJ Rep 4, 41 (Separate Opinion of Judge Alvarez); Koskenniemi, *The Politics of International Law* v–vi; Rein Müllerson, 'Ideology, Politics and International Law' (2016) 15 Chinese JIL 47; Tanja Aalberts and Thomas Gammeltoft-Hansen, *The Changing Practices of International Law* (CUP 2018) 26.

[9] Cf Michael Goodhart, 'Introduction: Rights in Politics and Practice' in Michael Goodhart (ed.), *Human Rights: Politics and Practice* (3rd edn, OUP 2016) 1, 5.

[10] Frans Viljoen, *International Human Rights Law in Africa* (2nd edn, OUP 2012) 40–41.

[11] *Legality of the Threat or Use of Nuclear Weapons*, Advisory Opinion [1996] ICJ Rep 226, 233–4 [13] and the cases cited therein.

[12] Robert Jennings and Arthur Watts (eds), *Oppenheim's International Law* (9th edn, OUP 2008) i (Peace) ch. 2; James Crawford, *Brownlie's Principles of Public International Law* (8th edn, OUP 2012) 115.

[13] Beth A Simmons, *Mobilizing for Human Rights: International Law in Domestic Politics* (CUP 2009) 3, 27.

or else popular discontent may unseat the government or regime in power. Internationally, every State has to defend, either on its own or in cooperation with some other States, its domestic human rights record and avert potential censure by some other States that will make it an international outcast and sow the seeds of discontent among its own population, as well as depriving it of the benefits ensuing from international trade, foreign investment and inbound tourism, among other things.

Government delegations of most States who are entrusted with human rights negotiations routinely face two unenviable assignments – one international, the other domestic. Internationally, they must try not to accept any change, imposed from abroad, to the status quo of the human rights situations at home. To this end, they must defend their State's human rights record, find allies to support their position and oppose or pre-empt any proposed change to that status quo. Domestically, after the said efforts partly or wholly fail, they must explain to their superiors at home why they fail and suggest the best possible solutions, such as becoming party to an international human rights treaty subject to reservations to the extent permissible by the treaty. Domestic resistance is to be expected from stakeholders with vested interests in maintaining the status quo and from ignorant and/or impassive actors who perceive no pressing reason to alter the status quo. Various actors, including victims of human rights violations, civil society and foreign governments, often join forces to persuade the State in question to progress in terms of human rights promotion and protection. Not infrequently, certain States take initiatives to forge ahead with progressive developments of new norms and higher standards of human rights, propelled by the maturity stage of human rights awareness, promotion and protection in these States. Also not infrequently, delegations sent by States to bilateral or multilateral human rights meetings comprise at least a few delegates who are humanistic thanks to their upbringing, education, personal experience, culture, religious belief, open-mindedness and so forth. They are 'agents of change' when they are back at home, abating the stubbornness of their State's resistance to human rights improvement as well as trying to alleviate the harshness of existing laws and measures of the State in the human rights field.

Ideally, human rights should be the rights of all persons irrespective of who or where they are, opposable against everyone and a legitimate concern of the international community. Above all, human rights should be upheld without double standards and be universal in time as well as a process.[14] But the real world is quite different.

---

[14]   Eva Brems, *Human Rights: Universality and Diversity* (Martinus Nijhoff 2001) 4, 12–15, 295, 307, 309–11.

EU and WEOG Member States are the most united of all groups in their positions on human rights issues. Although Eastern European States are members of the CoE, which also includes all EU Member States, they are the least vocal of the CoE members, being willing to give importance to the context surrounding each of the human rights issues. NAM accords significance to the right to development. Beyond the aforesaid, the rest of the groupings are quite split, depending on the particular human rights issues in question, although most GRULAC Member States tend to be very pro-human rights. Russia is close to China, Cuba and several Member States of the G77 that are frequently subjected to international censure on human rights issues.

Diverging positions among States with regard to human rights may actually reflect the underlying fact that *Homo sapiens*, by nature, is physically different, inhabits different parts of the Earth and occupies different rungs of society – and the world's human citizens seem to be generally trapped in playing a 'social Darwinism' game of 'survival of the fittest'.[15] Each group of human beings tends to have a primordial instinct for its own betterment, often at the expense of other groups. In the era of nation States, each State protects its interests vis-à-vis another State. In a domestic society, one human being in a relatively superior or better-off position tends to treat not as an equal another human being in a relatively inferior or worse-off position. Phrased differently, the 'haves' tend to protect their personal interests against any encroachment by the 'have nots', the rulers against the ruled, and one religious belief or ethnicity or race or caste against another. Even in a State priding itself on upholding the human rights of its citizens, minorities are not generally or usually accorded parallel human rights protection and this has been the case for a long time. The situation is generally worse for migrants finding themselves in a foreign State.[16] Some States face chronic national poverty that undermines their capability and willingness to protect human rights for the marginalized members of the society who happen to constitute the majority in that State. Civil wars, struggle for power to rule the nation, social instability that breeds suspicion among different groups within the nation and a legacy of past repression, with the powers-that-be striving to maintain the status quo even at the expense of those opposing it, are oft-cited causes for disregard of human rights. Although the nature of human rights abuses varies, mirroring the causes giving rise to

---

[15] See Herbert Spencer, *The Principles of Biology* (William Norgate 1864) vol I, 144, basing his conclusion on Darwin's evolutionary theory (Charles Darwin, *On the Origin of Species: By Means of Natural Selection, or the Preservation of Favoured Races in the Struggle for Life* (John Murray 1859)).

[16] Rosa Freedman, *Failing to Protect: The UN and the Politicisation of Human Rights* (C Hurst & Co 2014) 79–85.

the abuses in a particular nation and region of the world,[17] studies of deliberate human rights repression within a nation State are consistent in their conclusion that the motivation and likelihood for the repression emanate from real or imagined threats to the regime governing the State and unchecked power of government authorities, respectively.[18]

Notwithstanding the above, there is a silver lining. An in-depth analysis of ethnographic records from 60 societies has led to the discovery of seven plausible candidates for universal moral rules as a collection of tools for cooperation that are shared by communities around the world. The seven plausible candidates for universal moral rules are: (1) helping family members, (2) helping group members, (3) engaging in reciprocal cooperation, (4) being brave, (5) respecting one's superiors, (6) being fair in sharing or dividing a disputed resource, and (7) respecting others' property.[19] The challenge for IHRL is how to turn these universal moral values into tools for cooperation to improve human rights promotion and protection.

Given that humans are different in terms of, among other things, race, ethnicity, culture, traditions and religious beliefs, universal agreement on the specific contents of every human rights norm applicable in all contexts/ societies should not be expected. In fact, a reason for opposing human rights as propagated by a society or group is the perceived attitude of moral superiority and the condescending way that such society or group has been used in the past to justify colonialism, slavery and discrimination of the exploited peoples who are now the target of the human rights propagation.[20] According to an Islamic legal scholar, most Muslim proponents of the view that Islam is incompatible with IHRL are not really opposed to IHRL as such, but are disappointed with and protest against Western hegemony/ideology as well as the alleged double standards practised by the West.[21]

Double standards are often referred to in the confrontation between the West and the rest of the world, as in the Chinese reaction in response to the accusation that China has arbitrarily detained two Canadian nationals to retaliate against the Canadian authorities' arrest of a Chinese national who is the chief finan-

---

[17]   Cf Sonia Cardenas, 'Human Rights in Comparative Politics' in Goodhart (ed.), *Human Rights* 77, 79, 81.

[18]   Kathryn Sikkink, *Evidence for Hope: Making Human Rights Work in the 21st Century* (Princeton University Press 2017) 186.

[19]   Oliver Scott Curry, Daniel Austin Mullins and Harvey Whitehouse, 'Is It Good to Cooperate? Testing the Theory of Morality-as-Cooperation in Sixty Societies' (2019) 60 Current Anthropology 49.

[20]   Brooke Ackerly, 'Feminist and Activist Approaches to Human Rights' in Goodhart (ed.), *Human Rights* 28, 29–32.

[21]   Baderin, *International Human Rights and Islamic Law* 15–16, 28.

cial officer and daughter of the founder of the Chinese technology company Huawei. China considers it wrong that 'to some people, only Canadian citizens should be treated in a humanitarian manner and their freedom deemed valuable, while Chinese people do not deserve that', and that 'the laws of Canada or other Western countries are laws and must be observed, while China's laws are not and shouldn't be respected'. China questions whether 'a handful of Western countries really represent the whole international community'. It concludes: 'The reason why some people are used to arrogantly adopting double standards is due to Western egotism and white supremacy. In such a context, the rule of law is nothing but a tool for their political ends and a fig leaf for their practising hegemony in the international arena.'[22]

Another outright rejection of the legitimacy of IHRL is based on the accusation that it is 'foreign or anti-national'.[23]

This book intends to deal with IHRL and diplomacy in peacetime; it therefore does not touch upon international humanitarian law applicable in armed conflicts, which is a separate discipline of international law subject to detailed discrete international regulations[24] although historically humanity in war was a source of modern human rights law.[25]

IHRL cannot be completely separated from international criminal law.[26] The latter is an offshoot of IHRL in the sense that IHRL gradually developed a criminal law arm to prosecute the worst human rights offenders.[27] Gross

---

[22] Lu Shaye (Ambassador of China to Canada), 'China ambassador: why the double standard on justice for Canadians, Chinese?' *Hill Times* (9 Jan 2019) https://www.hilltimes.com/2019/01/09/double-standard-justice-canadians-chinese/182367, accessed 11 Jan 2019.

[23] Sikkink, *Evidence for Hope* 12.

[24] *Contra*: Hannum, 'Reinvigorating Human Rights for the Twenty-First Century' 424–5.

[25] Gerd Oberleiter, 'Humanitarian Law as a Source of Human Rights Law' in Dinah Shelton (ed.), *The Oxford Handbook of International Human Rights Law* (OUP 2013) 274.

[26] Cf the seemingly contrary view in Hannum, 'Reinvigorating Human Rights for the Twenty-First Century' 413–15, 419; Larissa van den Herik, 'Economic, Social and Cultural Rights: International Criminal Law's Blind Spot?' in Eibe Riedel, Gilles Giacca and Christophe Golay (eds), *Economic, Social and Cultural Rights in International Law: Contemporary Issues and Challenges* (OUP 2014) 343, 344–8, 365–6.

[27] Ilias Bantekas and Lutz Oette, *International Human Rights Law and Practice* (2nd edn, CUP 2016) 682; Andrew Clapham, 'Human Rights and International Criminal Law' in William A Schabas (ed.), *The Cambridge Companion to International Criminal Law* (CUP 2016) 11, 11; Christian Tomuschat, *Human Rights: Between Idealism and Realism* (3rd edn, OUP 2014) ch. 18; Robert Cryer, 'International Criminal Law' in Daniel Moeckli, Sangeeta Shah and Sandesh Sivakumaran (eds), *International Human Rights Law* (3rd edn, OUP 2018) 521. Eric A Posner (*Twilight of Human Rights Law*

human rights violations have come to be criminalized and prosecuted as international crimes under international criminal law. International criminal law is a vital international legal regime to ensure individual criminal accountability for serious human rights violations.[28] Yet the relationship between IHRL and international criminal law is a complicated one as the latter needs to comply with applicable international human rights norms such as the principle of legality requiring that a person not be subject to criminal punishment except for an act that was criminalized by law before he/she perpetrated the act (*nullum crimen sine lege*), the right to a fair trial, the right to life, the due process of criminal justice and so on.[29]

After this brief introductory chapter, Chapter 2 will critically question the claim that IHRL enjoys universalism of recognition. Chapter 3 will analyse the operation of IHRL within the UN system, where idealism clashes with international politics and international law, while Chapter 4 will discuss the role of diplomacy vis-à-vis IHRL as applied within regional human rights mechanisms across the globe. Chapter 5 questions whether everyone is protected by the nine 'core' treaties monitored by the ten existing international human rights treaty bodies, including in view of the reservations made by States Parties to such treaties. This is followed, in Chapter 6, by looking at the compliance with and enforcement of IHRL. Chapter 7 will endeavour to find reconciliation and accommodation among different perspectives and notions regarding international human rights so that international human rights norms could be 'universalized'. The final Chapter 8 will then look at two new dimensions of IHRL – in cyberspace and at sea.

(OUP 2014) 52–3) considers the 'impulses' behind IHRL to have animated international criminal law as well although the latter pre-dates the former by centuries.

[28]   Aryeh Neier, *The International Human Rights Movement: A History* (Princeton University Press 2012) 258–84, 309–11.

[29]   Clapham, 'Human Rights and International Criminal Law' 11–15.

2.   Human rights universalism: myth or reality?

1.   THE DEBATE

International human rights law (IHRL), like any other field of public international law, comprises treaties binding upon their States Parties and rules of customary international law binding on all States. When a nation State is bound by
international human rights treaty obligations, it should not have any justifiable
reason to challenge the legitimacy of the treaty by which it has consented to
be bound. However, there may be grey areas leaving some room for different
interpretations, or the treaty may allow its States Parties to make reservations
not to apply the treaty in its entirety. This has led some States to assert what
they claim to be legitimate justifications not to share the legal position taken by
other States Parties to the treaty. Certain States challenge the applicability of
rules of customary IHRL on the grounds that the rules lack normative validity
and legitimacy, including the absence of democratic representation in their
formulation.[1]

An important question is whether IHRL has now achieved universalism
– the universal consensus on acceptance and application of the substantive
and procedural norms of human rights that must be the same everywhere.
According to one view, universalism of IHRL differs from universality of
IHRL in that the latter connotes the universal acceptance that human rights
do exist and must not be violated, and this universality is now a fact since no
State today unequivocally admits that it is a human rights violator.[2] However,

---

[1]   Cf Samantha Besson, 'The Legitimate Authority of International Human Rights
Law: On the Reciprocal Legitimation of Domestic and International Human Rights' in
Andreas Føllesdal, Johan Karlsson Schaffer and Geir Ulfstein (eds), *The Legitimacy of
International Human Rights Regimes: Legal, Political and Philosophical Perspectives*
(CUP 2014) 32, 32–3, 48–51, 75–6.

[2]   Mashood A Baderin, *International Human Rights and Islamic Law* (OUP 2003)
23–4, 26; cf Antonio Cassese, 'A Plea for a Global Community Grounded in a Core of
Human Rights' in Antonio Cassese (ed.), *Realizing Utopia: The Future of International
Law* (OUP 2012) 136, 136–8.

most scholars treat universality as embracing universalism in the sense just mentioned. This book will, therefore, treat both concepts interchangeably.

The claim of the universalism or universality of human rights is asserted from two perspectives – that of the putative beneficiaries and that of those called upon to uphold human rights.[3] Challenges by the latter to the universalism of IHRL arise from the perception that IHRL embodies a 'parochial' (that is, limited or narrow) set of values or ordering of such values. The challenges may be based on 'moral relativism' in the strict sense and/or on 'epistemological relativism' deriving from the diversity of perspectives and understandings of human rights.[4]

It has been asserted, for example, that '[r]ights are a product of Western culture and history and their principal propagandists have been Western organizations, activists and academics'.[5] A frequently asked question is, therefore, whether human rights are really Western centric. In a State with a democratic system of government, laws passed by an elected parliament and policies implemented by the elected government must be accepted by all in that State even though a large percentage of them did not vote for the political party or parties that won the general election. The victors have the right, according to the principle of democracy, to govern the nation. Where a government comes into power by non-democratic means, such as a military *coup d'état*, this non-democratic 'victors' justice' is challengeable for its lack of legitimacy. A question to be asked in the context of IHRL is: do the States or entities laying down IHRL rules of universal or regional application have legitimacy to do so? If the answer is in the positive, what is or are the source(s) of such legitimacy? If a propounded IHRL norm represents a 'best practice', is it the 'best' according to which system of assessment and by whom?

Foundations for human rights came from religious as well as philosophical sources representing a value originally shared by all human societies, although with cultural variations.[6] The following are just some examples of the teach-

---

[3]   Charles R Beitz, *The Idea of Human Rights* (OUP 2009) 45.

[4]   Samantha Besson, 'Justifications' in Daniel Moeckli, Sangeeta Shah and Sandesh Sivakumaran (eds), *International Human Rights Law* (3rd edn, OUP 2018) 22, 36.

[5]   Martti Koskenniemi, *The Politics of International Law* (Hart 2011) 162. Also, Ali Allawi, 'Islam, Human Rights and the New Information Technologies' in Monroe Price and Nicole Stremlau (eds), *Speech and Society in Turbulent Times* (CUP 2018) 19, 23.

[6]   Federico Lenzerini, *The Culturalization of Human Rights Law* (OUP 2014) 32; M Christian Green and John Witte, Jr, 'Religion' in Dinah Shelton (ed.), *The Oxford Handbook of International Human Rights Law* (OUP 2013) 9; Han Yanlong, 'Legal Protection of Human Rights in China' in Peter R Bauer, Fried van Hoof, Liu Nanlai, Tao Zhenghua and Jacqueline Smith (eds), *Human Rights: Chinese and Dutch Perspectives* (Martinus Nijhoff 1996) 91, 93.

ings by religions and philosophers. Hinduism teaches the sanctity of human life, whereas Judaism preaches the value and sacredness of all God's children together with responsibility owed by one human being towards another. Christianity exhorts Christians to take care of the poor, the sick and the hungry. Buddhists are taught to observe at least the five fundamental rules including the sanctity of the life of human beings and animals. Confucianism emphasizes personal and government morality and social justice. Islam postulates absolute equality among human races and guarantees religious toleration, the sanctity of life, compassion, charity and obligations to fellow human beings. Ancient and medieval philosophers preached social justice and moral duties, which subsequently became enforceable rights. They include Mo Zi, founder of the Mohist school of moral philosophy in China almost 2,400 years ago; King Hammurabi of Babylon (circa 1811–1750 BC) whose code of laws was widely known; Plato in ancient Greece; the Roman Stoics; Thomas Aquinas (1225–74) and, on the threshold of the Age of Enlightenment in the eighteenth century, John Locke (1632–1704).[7]

The Manden Charter, inscribed in 2009 by the UN Educational, Scientific and Cultural Organization (UNESCO) on the Representative List of the Intangible Cultural Heritage of Humanity,[8] may be considered an early African counterpart of human rights ideals elsewhere.

In the early thirteenth century, circa 1236 AD, the founder of the Mandingo Empire and the assembly of his wise men orally proclaimed in Kurukan Fuga (now located in Mai, close to the border with Guinea) the Manden Charter. There are 44 edicts in the Charter, divided into four sections: social organization, property rights, environmental protection and personal responsibilities. The Charter recognizes, for example, everyone's right to life and to the preservation of physical integrity, the right of children to education, certain rights of women, prohibition of ill-treatment of slaves or foreigners, the right to divorce on certain grounds, five means of acquisition of property, and respect for kinship, marriage and the neighbourhood. The Charter warns that all those who violate these edicts will be punished. After the demise of the Mandingo Empire, the words of the Manden Charter are still transmitted orally from generation to generation within the Malinke (or Mandinka) clans, numbering 11 million at present, living in parts of West Africa, including Côte d'Ivoire,

---

[7] For more examples (such as the code of conduct of the pre-Columbian civilizations in Central and Latin America as well as that of the native Americans living in North America in the eleventh or twelfth century), see Lenzerini, *The Culturalization of Human Rights Law* 33–46; Paul Gordon Lauren, 'The Foundations of Justice and Human Rights in Early Legal Texts and Thought' in Shelton (ed.), *The Oxford Handbook of International Human Rights Law* 163–78.

[8] UNESCO, Decision of the Intergovernmental Committee: 4.COM 13.59.

Guinea, Mali, Senegal, Gambia and Guinea-Bissau. There is no record of how the Manden Charter has been upheld by public authority apart from and beyond sanctions within the clans to which the Manden Charter is upheld as a code of conduct.[9]

Although non-Western regions or cultures witnessed the existence of moral principles and movements in support of some version of human values and ethics, these principles were plausibly not premised on the idea of the rights of individuals enforceable vis-à-vis public authorities, as in the West where essential moral and legal rights of individuals were upheld by the State.[10]

John Locke deserves a special mention. In his *Two Treatises of Government* published in 1689, Locke propounds that as all men share the same common nature, faculties and powers, they ought to partake in the same common rights and privileges embodied in and protected by the law of nature.[11] He famously postulates that there shall be no interference with another person's rights as every human being in the state of nature possesses certain natural rights and since people are born in a perfect state of equality, where there can be no superiority or jurisdiction of one person over another.[12] Locke essentially posits that there be a limit on rights so as to protect the rights of others, a duty to punish those who infringe the rights of others, and the ultimate right retained by the people to overthrow a government that is destructive to liberty.[13]

Locke's works influenced the intellectual and philosophical movement during the Age of Enlightenment in Europe in the eighteenth century, driven by the reasoning of such great thinkers as Jean-Jacques Rousseau (1712–78), Voltaire (1694–1778), Montesquieu (1689–1755), David Hume (1711–76) and Immanuel Kant (1724–1804). They advance liberty, constitutional government, separation of Church and State, freedoms of speech and religion, and economic freedom/liberty, subsequently called the 'free-market economy', and so on. Kant's ethical system, in particular, propounds the inviolability of human dignity. The Enlightenment movement thus sowed the seed of 'liberal-

---

[9]   See also Bonny Ibhawoh, *Human Rights in Africa* (CUP 2018) ch. 2.

[10]   David P Forsythe, *Human Rights in International Relations* (4th edn, CUP 2018) 43–4; Olivier Roy and Pasquale Annicchino, 'Human Rights between Religions, Cultures and Universality' in Ana Filipa Vrdoljak (ed.), *The Cultural Dimension of Human Rights* (OUP 2013) 13, 14–16; Patrick Macklem, *The Sovereignty of Human Rights* (OUP 2015) 3–26; Beth A Simmons, *Mobilizing for Human Rights: International Law in Domestic Politics* (CUP 2009) 65–6; Besson, 'Justifications' 28, 35.

[11]   John W Yolton, *A Locke Dictionary* (Blackwell 1993) 243.

[12]   Ibid 244; Sabine C Carey, Mark Gibney and Stern C Poe, *The Politics of Human Rights: The Quest for Dignity* (CUP 2010) 20–21.

[13]   Aryeh Neier, *The International Human Rights Movement: A History* (Princeton University Press 2012) 30–31.

ism', the concept championing liberty and equality for all through represent-ative democracy – instead of hereditary or divine rights of sovereigns – and the rule of law. The 1776 American Declaration of Independence begins, in Lockean language, that men are evidently created equal, endowed with certain inalienable rights. Article 1 of the Declaration of the Rights of Man and of Citizens proclaimed by the French National Constituent Assembly in August 1789 after the overthrow of the monarchy reads: 'Men are born and remain free and equal in rights. ...' Thomas Paine's *Rights of Man*, published in England in 1791, alludes to natural law and rights and introduces the expression 'human rights' when he refers to man entering society to have his natural 'human rights' from the standpoint of democracy better secured.[14]

Immanuel Kant's system or principle of right derives from the innate right every human being possesses by virtue of their humanity or rational nature. Kant's *Recht* (Latin *ius*) comprises the entire body of legal obligations with corresponding legal rights that people ought to possess under an ideal legal and political system – something Western thinkers before Kant call 'natural rights'. This system of right encompasses the right to a maximal sphere of freedom or independence from other human beings' arbitrary constraints, the right of equality, the right to be one's own master and the right to be 'beyond reproach' in the sense of having done no wrong to others as long as one has not dimin-ished what is theirs by right. Kant's system of right has concomitant duties, such as the duty not to injure others and the duty to respect what belongs to each person. Kant's private right forms the basis of the 'acquired rights' with the consent of others (that is, property rights) and the guarantee of rights of all citizens forms the basis of the public right secured by the separation of powers between the legislative and the executive branches of government, with the legislature representing the people. Kant believes it is always wrong to disobey even unjust laws or an unjust ruler acting contrary to law, provided that the law and his command do not obligate one to do something that is in itself morally wrong. It is also always wrong to overthrow the existing ruler however unjust his conduct may be. The ruler and acts of legislation are restricted by the stand-ards of rights in the form of a civil constitution, 'an original contract' between the ruler and the ruled, guaranteeing the freedom, equality and independence

---

[14]   Thomas Paine, *Rights of Man: Being an Answer to Mr Burke's Attack on the French Revolution* (J Johnson 1791); Robert Lamb, *Thomas Paine and the Idea of Human Rights* (CUP 2015); Carey et al, *The Politics of Human Rights* 17–21; Immanuel Kant, *Grounding for the Metaphysics of Morals* (first published 1785, James W Ellington tr, 3rd edn, Hackett 1993); Eric A Posner, *Twilight of Human Rights Law* (OUP 2014) 9–12. See also Lauren, 'The Foundations of Justice and Human Rights in Early Legal Texts and Thought' 184–9; Lenzerini, *The Culturalization of Human Rights Law* 12–18, 29.

of citizens. A legislator should pass only such laws as could have come from the united will of the whole people who are subject to the laws.[15]

Although the 'natural law' theory is not monopolized by the West, its meaning outside Western Europe has a rather different connotation. In traditional Chinese legal thought, natural law in the sense of universal, objective, moral principles that are not human made but dependent on the nature of the universe and discoverable by reason to guide rational moral judgement did exist in ancient China during the pre-Qin dynasty (226–201 BC), as appeared in various passages and texts in Confucianism, especially in the idea of ritual propriety, or in other concepts such as Taoism (the Way). The Ming dynasty Confucian philosopher Wang Yangming (1472–1529 AD) is said to have propounded the Heavenly Principle, a coherent natural law theory whereby the natural law and its norms are discovered through reason and are clearly applicable to human-made law such as 'measures' and 'regulations'. For Wang, it suffices just to know the natural law norms based on the Heavenly Principle, without any need for a list of explicit universal principles for conduct or regulations. Founded on various sources and bases, including the eternal order of the cosmos, laws of nature, self-evident values and practical reason, Wang's natural law theory is probably the closest traditional Chinese legal thought to classical Western natural law theory. However, Wang strongly opposes litigation, even though it is permitted under human law, because litigation aims to achieve selfish benefits while breeding mistrust, something harmful to society and fundamentally contrary to the ultimate goals of unity and of seeing oneself as part of a community where each person is connected with other persons and with the universe through the Heavenly Principle. Thus, when litigation conflicts with natural law, it does not have much morally or legally binding force.[16]

Hersch Lauterpacht's seminal work entitled *An International Bill of Rights of Man*, published in 1945, which inspired the adoption of the Universal Declaration of Human Rights (UDHR)[17] in 1948 and the European Convention on Human Rights (ECHR)[18] in 1950, is historically and intellectually premised on 'the close association of the [innate rights of man pertaining to him as

---

[15] Allen W Wood, *Kant* (Blackwell Publishing 2005) 173–7; Paul Guyer, *Kant* (Routledge 2006) 262–303; Howard Williams, *Kant's Political Philosophy* (St Martin's Press 1983) 164–5.

[16] Norman P Ho, 'Natural Law in Chinese Legal Thought: The Philosophical System of Wang Yangming' (2017) 8 Yonsei LJ 1, esp 11, 27–8.

[17] Doc A/RES/217(III).

[18] ETS 5.

a human being] with the doctrine of the law of nature'.[19] The law of nature is both a spiritual basis and political inspiration to place the rights of man on 'a legal plane superior to the will of sovereign States'.[20] The natural rights of human beings propounded by Locke and his followers, with their genesis in natural law, are now enshrined in the UDHR.[21]

The UDHR, drafted by the UN Commission on Human Rights in 1947 and 1948, was adopted by the UN General Assembly (UNGA) on 10 December 1948, with 48 votes in favour, eight abstentions and two present but not voting.[22]

At the time of the drafting of the UDHR, the UN Commission on Human Rights, set up on 18 February 1946 as a subsidiary of the UN Economic and Social Council (ECOSOC), comprised delegates from Australia, Belgium, Byelorussia, Chile, China, Egypt, France, India, Iran, Lebanon, Panama, Philippines, Ukraine, USSR, USA, Uruguay and Yugoslavia. The Commission, chaired by Eleanor Roosevelt, widow of the late US President Franklin D Roosevelt, entrusted a drafting committee composed of nine members elected in their individual capacity to draft the UDHR. Eleanor Roosevelt chaired the drafting committee, with Charles Malik, a Harvard-educated Christian from Lebanon as Special Rapporteur. PC Chang, a Columbia University graduate from the Republic of China, was another drafting committee member from outside the Western hemisphere. The other members were Alexandre Bogomolov from the USSR, René Cassin who was a French Jew, Charles Duke from the UK, William Hodgson from Australia, Hernán Santa Cruz of Chile and John P Humphrey from Canada. No Muslim was in the drafting committee.

The drafting committee's product was submitted to the Commission, which debated each point therein before submitting the draft to ECOSOC, which considered it for six weeks and subsequently referred it without any change to the UNGA's Third Committee (Social, Humanitarian and Cultural Affairs),

---

[19] Hersch Lauterpacht, *An International Bill of the Rights of Man* (Columbia University Press 1945) 25.

[20] Ibid 52.

[21] Costas Douzinas, *The End of Human Rights* (Hart 2000) 9.

[22] The 48 States voting in favour of the adoption of the UDHR were: Afghanistan, Argentina, Australia, Belgium, Bolivia, Brazil, Burma, Canada, Chile, China, Columbia, Costa Rica, Cuba, Denmark, Dominican Republic, Ecuador, Egypt, El Salvador, Ethiopia, France, Greece, Guatemala, Haiti, Iceland, India, Iran, Iraq, Lebanon, Liberia, Luxembourg, Mexico, Netherlands, New Zealand, Nicaragua, Norway, Pakistan, Panama, Paraguay, Peru, Philippines, Siam (now Thailand), Sweden, Syria, Turkey, UK, USA, Uruguay and Venezuela. The eight abstaining States were: Byelorussian SSR, Czechoslovakia, Poland, Saudi Arabia, South Africa, Soviet Union, Ukrainian SSR and Yugoslavia. The two States present but not voting were Honduras and Yemen.

which is open to all UN Member States. After 80 meetings and more than 160 amendments, the Third Committee submitted the Declaration to the UNGA for adoption.[23]

The UDHR is alleged to have been 'drafted to all intents and purposes by a body dominated by Western powers with a spoiler's role for the Soviets', some of whose concerns were incorporated into the UDHR.[24] The Latin American participants in the UN Commission on Human Rights, which drafted and approved the UDHR, were perceived as essentially Western, reflecting Iberian values rather than indigenous Indian values in their respective States, while Malik was considered greatly affected by French influence and the delegate from the Philippines by US influence.[25] In short, the drafting of the UDHR has been accused of showing 'the existence of a global diplomatic elite, often schooled in Western locales, who helped tinker with the declaration at a moment of symbolic unity' and the main actors from outside the West, such as Malik of Lebanon and Romulo of the Philippines, were Christians.[26]

Some of the UDHR's Articles, such as Article 18 specifically introduced by Malik, which guarantees the right to religion, including freedom to change one's religion or belief, are problematic to Muslims.[27] The UDHR is perceived in some quarters as a victory for the US Government fighting for the global definition of human rights as enshrined in the US Constitution and Bill of Rights, contrary to Marxist doctrines propagated by the Soviet bloc. Besides, the UDHR yields to the US Department of State's opposition to the setting up of local human rights monitoring agencies around the world lest this kind of network might put pressure on governments to adopt every suggestion made by the agencies as well as allowing access by the agencies to government human rights files.[28]

---

[23]   Johannes Morsink, *The Universal Declaration of Human Rights: Origins, Drafting and Intent* (University of Pennsylvania Press 1999) 1–35.

[24]   Allawi, 'Islam, Human Rights and the New Information Technologies' 21–2.

[25]   Forsythe, *Human Rights in International Relations* 55.

[26]   Samuel Moyn, *The Last Utopia: Human Rights in History* (Harvard University Press 2010) 66 and cf ibid 62–70.

[27]   Allawi, 'Islam, Human Rights and the New Information Technologies' 25. Cf Samuel Moyn, *Christian Human Rights (Intellectual History of the Modern Age)* (University of Pennsylvania Press 2015) 67; id, *The Last Utopia* 73–7.

[28]   Olivier Barsalou, 'The Cold War and the Rise of an American Conception of Human Rights, 1945–8' in Pamela Slotte and Mia Halme-Tuomisaari (eds), *Revisiting the Origins of Human Rights* (CUP 2015) 362, 363, 373–4, 378–9. Also, Makau W Mutua, 'Politics and Human Rights: An Essential Symbiosis' in Michael Byers (ed.), *The Role of Law in International Politics: Essays in International Relations and International Law* (OUP 2000) 149, 155.

A closer look at the historical context of the drafting of the UN Charter as well as diplomatic developments up to the time of the adoption of the UDHR may give a different picture from the one the UDHR's critics want us to believe.

A study by Kathryn Sikkink of Harvard University's John F Kennedy School of Government is quite eye opening. In April 1948, eight months before the adoption of the UDHR, the American Declaration of the Rights and Duties of Man[29] had been unanimously approved by the 20 Latin American and the Caribbean States and the USA. In the 1880s there were more nation States in Latin America than in Europe that had universal male suffrage, albeit with varying restrictions, especially the requirement that voters had to be literate. Whereas the initial US drafts of the UN Charter contained no reference to human rights, the Republic of China, together with a group of Latin American States, Philippines, Lebanon, Australia and New Zealand, were in favour of the inclusion of human rights in the UN Charter. At the San Francisco Conference in 1945 each part of the UN Charter required a two-thirds majority of the total 50 States for its adoption. Thirty-one States represented at the San Francisco Conference that formed the most important bloc were the 20 Latin American States, China, Egypt, Iran, Lebanon, Philippines, Saudi Arabia, Syria, Turkey, Ethiopia, Iraq and Liberia. This group of States pressed for the inclusion in the UN Charter of the end of colonialism, which was a crucial human rights issue, while Latin American States wanted the rules of sovereignty and non-intervention in internal affairs to be subordinated to international law. India wanted the then human rights violations in South Africa not to be treated as a matter under the exclusive jurisdiction of South Africa. Three female representatives from Latin America took the lead in getting the UN Charter to recognize among the UN's purposes enumerated in Article 1 that of achieving international cooperation in promoting and encouraging respect for human rights and for fundamental freedoms 'for all without distinction as to ... sex ...'. This movement by the 'Global South' had influence on the drafting of the UDHR, and some of their representatives in San Francisco, including Malik of Lebanon, continued to play important roles in the drafting and subsequent adoption of the UDHR. Owing to Lebanon's experience of accepting persons fleeing persecution because of their religious conversions, Malik was instrumental in drafting Article 18 of the UDHR, which recognizes the freedom to change one's religion or belief.[30] It should also be noted that the opposition

---

[29] Basic Documents Pertaining to Human Rights in the Inter-American System OEA/Ser L V/II.82 Doc 6 Rev 1 at 17 (1992).

[30] Kathryn Sikkink, *Evidence for Hope: Making Human Rights Work in the 21st Century* (Princeton University Press 2017) 55–92. See also Christian Tomuschat, *Human Rights: Between Idealism and Realism* (3rd edn, OUP 2014) 51.

to this freedom coming from Afghanistan, Egypt, Saudi Arabia, Yemen and some other Muslim-majority States was defeated due to the lack of unity among Muslim-majority States themselves. Pakistan, for example, disagreed with the said opposition, arguing that Islam itself was a missionary religion striving to persuade individuals to change their faith and way of life to Islam and that Islamic teachings also recognized the same right of conversion for other religions as for itself.[31]

The significance of the contributions from non-Western States to the acceptance of human rights norms alien to the West cannot be underestimated. The following are just some examples. They succeeded in getting the UDHR to guarantee, in Article 2, the entitlement of all the rights and freedoms under the UDHR without distinction of any kind, such as race, colour, language, religion, national or social origin, property, birth or other status, or the political, jurisdictional or international status of the country or territory to which a person belongs.[32] Indeed, they achieved what Japan had failed to do at the Versailles Peace Conference in 1919 after the First World War, namely to have included in the Covenant of the League of Nations non-discrimination, either in law or in fact, of aliens on account of their race or nationality.[33] Also, the wording 'conscience' deriving from the language of the Analects of Confucius was adopted in Article 1 of the UDHR as a result of the active role of PC Chang, the Chinese member of the UDHR drafting committee, who actively promoted ideals of Chinese philosophers such as Mencius.[34] Thanks largely to the contribution of Chile's Hernán Santa Cruz and other Latin Americans, many of the social and economic rights are acknowledged as universal under the UDHR.[35]

The drafters of the UDHR also benefited from the survey by UNESCO's Committee on the Philosophic Principles of the Rights of Man, set up in 1949 and comprising leading intellectuals, philosophers and political scientists to identify a common ground and potential sources of disagreement among the various religious traditions and political ideologies for a future UDHR, with

---

[31]   Baderin, *International Human Rights and Islamic Law* 119, citing Pakistan's position in UN Doc A/PV.182 at 890 (1948).

[32]   Robin Ramcharan and Bertrand Ramcharan, *Asia and the Drafting of the Universal Declaration of Human Rights* (Palgrave Macmillan 2019) 39–64.

[33]   Naoko Shimazu, *Japan, Race and Equality: The Racial Equality Proposal of 1919* (Routledge 1998).

[34]   Hans Ingvar Roth, *P.C. Change and the Universal Declaration of Human Rights* (University of Pennsylvania Press 2018); Tae-Ung Baik, *Emerging Regional Human Rights Systems in Asia* (CUP 2012) 47; Mary Ann Glendon, *A World Made New: Eleanor Roosevelt and the Universal Declaration of Human Rights* (Random House 2001) 144.

[35]   Simmons, *Mobilizing for Human Rights* 42.

a questionnaire sent out to politicians, philosophers and scholars, such as Mohandas Gandhi or Aldous Huxley, soliciting their opinions.[36]

To be fair, the UDHR was drafted when faith in the Western Enlightenment was at its lowest ebb, with the most heinous human rights violations having occurred in Europe before and during the Second World War. The UDHR was not to be perceived as a trophy of the superiority of Western civilization, but as a warning by the West to the rest of the world that its mistakes were not to be replicated ever again.[37] Moreover, economic and social rights recognized under the UDHR were alien to Western values. At the time of drafting a legally binding international covenant on human rights, these rights were perceived by the USA and its Western allies as a socialist threat to the emerging US definition of human rights aiming at protecting individual freedoms against State oppression and the efficient functioning of a market economy. Economic and social rights were considered by their antagonists as mere statements of goals that lacked theoretical unity and judicial enforceability, with too many definitions of such rights to arrive at an international consensus as to their meaning.[38] The West's opposition to a single international covenant on human rights that also encompassed economic and social rights gave rise to two, instead of one, such covenants – the International Covenant on Civil and Political Rights (ICCPR)[39] and the International Covenant on Economic, Social and Cultural Rights (ICESCR),[40] with the Soviet bloc utilizing the majority of its members together with developing States in the UNGA to secure the adoption of these rights, albeit in a separate covenant – the ICESCR.

The UDHR might not have been 'universally' adopted since a large portion of the globe, in particular Africa and Asia, was still under colonial rule and was not represented in the process of drafting and adoption of the UDHR. At that time, the UN comprised 56 States, only three of which were from Africa (Egypt, Ethiopia and Liberia) and only 12 of which were from Asia (Afghanistan, Burma, China, India, Iran, Iraq, Lebanon, Pakistan, Philippines, Syria, Thailand and Yemen). Furthermore, eight UN Member States abstained

---

[36] UNESCO, *Human Rights: Comments and Interpretations* (A Wingate 1949); Jeffrey Flynn, *Reframing the Intellectual Dialogue on Human Rights* (Routledge 2014) 1; Mark Goodale, 'The Myth of Universality: The UNESCO "Philosophers' Committee" and the Making of Human Rights' (2018) 43 Law & Social Inquiry 596.

[37] Michael Ignatieff, *Human Rights as Politics and Idolatry* (Princeton University Press 2001) 65; Jacob Dolinger, 'The Failure of the Universal Declaration of Human Rights' in Wagner Menezes (ed.), *Bulletin of the Brazilian Society of International Law – Centenary Commemorative Edition* (Arraes Editores 2017) 953, 956–7, 985.

[38] Barsalou, 'The Cold War and the Rise of an American Conception of Human Rights' 375–6.

[39] 999 UNTS 171.

[40] 993 UNTS 3.

from voting for its adoption. The inclusion of economic and social rights in the UDHR failed to convince the Soviet bloc to vote in favour of its adoption due to the bloc's objection to the UDHR provisions on freedom of movement, as well as freedom of thought, religion and expression.[41] The other abstaining States were Saudi Arabia and South Africa. According to popular accounts, the former objected to the UDHR provision on freedom of religion that includes the right to change one's religion and to the guarantee of equal rights for men and women,[42] whereas the latter opposed Article 1 of the UDHR recognizing the equality of all persons in dignity and rights and Article 7 on equal protection of the law.

No Middle East States voted against the UDHR. Seven Muslim-majority States that were UN Member States at that time voted in favour of its adoption. They were Afghanistan, Egypt, Iran, Iraq, Lebanon, Pakistan and Syria. Pakistan and Syria even lauded the UDHR, despite the initial opposition of these two States, together with Afghanistan, Egypt, Iran, Iraq and Saudi Arabia, to Article 18 of the UDHR, which recognizes the freedom to change one's religion or belief.[43] Jamil Baroody, the Saudi delegate, was not even a Muslim but a Syrian Christian. Even though he must have taken his orders from the Saudi Government, the fact that Saudi Arabia's own delegate was of a different religious persuasion demonstrates at least a degree of religious tolerance/freedom even if only symbolically. If one discounts the personal background of the Saudi delegate, it does highlight the fact that Saudi Arabia was not overly concerned with pushing the Islamic agenda at the time and that its objections were not based on religious relativism.[44] Saudi Arabia abstained from voting to adopt the UDHR, probably because it would be inessential to include a provision on the freedom to change one's religious faith without also having an equivalent provision on the freedom to change one's thoughts, a point raised by Saudi Arabia as well as some other Middle East States regarding the UDHR.[45]

It should be noted in this connection that, as a compromise to accommodate concerns of certain Muslim-majority States, Article 18 of the ICCPR, which

---

[41] Neier, *The International Human Rights Movement* 62–3.

[42] Eg Nisrine Abiad, *Sharia, Muslim States and International Human Rights Treaty Obligations: A Comparative Study* (British Institute of International and Comparative Law 2008) 60.

[43] Mishana Hosseinioun, *The Human Rights Turn and the Paradox of Progress in the Middle East* (Palgrave Macmillan 2018) 43.

[44] Clarification given to the present author by Hosseinioun regarding her book, ibid 44.

[45] Ibid.

legally binds States Parties thereto, makes no explicit reference to the freedom to change one's religion or belief. It reads:

1. Everyone shall have the right to freedom of thought, conscience and religion. This right shall include freedom to have or to adopt a religion or belief of his choice and freedom, either individually or in community with others and in public or private, to manifest his religion or belief in worship, observance, practice and teaching.
2. No one shall be subject to coercion which would impair his freedom to have or to adopt a religion or belief of his choice.
3. Freedom to manifest one's religion or beliefs may be subject only to such limitations as are prescribed by law and are necessary to protect public safety, order, health, or morals or the fundamental rights and freedoms of others.
4. The States Parties to the present Covenant undertake to have respect for the liberty of parents and, when applicable, legal guardians to ensure the religious and moral education of their children in conformity with their own convictions.[46]

On the whole, the UDHR is, in fact, imbued with a strong sense of universalism, contrary to the view of its naysayers. Despite any shortcoming, there is no denying that the vast majority of the world's peoples today agree that the UDHR is a positive thing for them, especially in terms of the protection of the individual from oppression within a society.[47]

A next issue to be considered is the contention by some States that assertion of human rights is typically hypocritical, especially when the States cherishing human rights have profited or used to benefit from slavery and/or colonialism in the past.

2. HYPOCRISY: SLAVERY AND COLONIALISM

Slave trading and colonialism were purportedly justified as means to civilize less civilized peoples and societies for their own good.[48]

In 1550, at the height of Spanish colonization of the Americas, King Carlos V of Spain convened a debate in Valladolid, Spain, on whether the indigenous people in the colony could be enslaved. The pro-slavery debater insisted on Spain's 'perfect right to rule these barbarians of the New World and the adja-

---

[46] Cf also Heiner Bielefeldt, Nazila Ghanea and Michael Wiener, *Freedom of Religion or Belief: An International Law Commentary* (OUP 2016) 55–74.

[47] Benjamin Gregg, *Human Rights as Social Construction* (CUP 2012) 32; Ignatieff, *Human Rights as Politics and Idolatry* 70; Forsythe, *Human Rights in International Relations* 386.

[48] Upendra Baxi, *The Future of Human Rights* (3rd edn, OUP 2008) 45; Makau W Mutua, 'Savages, Victims and Saviors: The Metaphor of Human Rights' (2001) 42 Harvard ILJ 201.

cent islands, who in prudence, skill, virtues and humanity are as inferior to the Spanish'.[49] In support of his contention, he asserted that Spain had the right to rule the uncivilized people, the right to punish them for their practice of human sacrifice and idolatry akin to the right of Christians to punish the genocide of the Amorites and Perizzites mentioned in the Holy Scripture, and the right to spread Christianity by violence as Jesus would do, as evident from the Parable of the Banquet and Saint Gregory's approval of Gennadius, Exarch of Africa, who spread the faith by just war in the 600s. The anti-slavery debater fervently opposed this rationale. The debate ended without any change to the status quo of the colonized peoples.[50]

Noel Rae's book *The Great Stain: Witnessing American Slavery* narrates how, during the period of American slavery, Christian slaveholders balanced their religious beliefs with slavery by resorting to selected texts of the Old Testament indicating how slavery was common among the Israelites. The New Testament was largely ignored, except for being cited to point out that nowhere did Jesus condemn slavery and that Philemon, the runaway slave, was returned by St Paul to his master. The Latin word servus, usually translated as 'servant', was considered to really mean 'slave'. Bishop William Meade of Virginia and Bishop Stephen Elliott of Georgia were two of those who openly praised slavery as part of the English and American Churches' efforts to civilize and Christianize millions of Africans.[51]

The Fundamental Constitutions of Carolina of 1 March 1669[52] provide in Article 110: 'Every freeman of Carolina shall have absolute power and authority over his negro slaves, of what opinion or religion soever.' Article 107 adds:

> Since charity obliges us to wish well to the souls of all men and religion ought to alter nothing in any man's civil estate or right, it shall be lawful for slaves, as well as others, to enter themselves and be of what church or profession any of them shall think best and, therefore, be as fully members as any freeman. But yet no slave shall hereby be exempted from that civil dominion his master hath over him, but be in all things in the same state and condition he was in before.

---

[49]   Catherine Addington, 'Lessons from Valladolid: On Being Decent in an Indecent Age', *Mere Orthodoxy* (11 June 2018).

[50]   Lewis Hanke, *All Mankind Is One: A Study of the Disputation between Bartolomé de Las Casas and Juan Ginés de Sepúlveda in 1550 on the Intellectual and Religious Capacity of the American Indians* (Northern Illinois University Press 1994).

[51]   See the first-hand personal accounts of slavery in North America from a variety of original sources in Noel Rae, *The Great Stain: Witnessing American Slavery* (Overlook Press, Peter Mayer Publishers 2018) *passim*.

[52]   http://avalon.law.yale.edu/17th_century/nc05.asp, accessed 12 May 2018.

John Locke has been criticized for contending that 'men' were 'by nature all free, equal and independent' although he also had no qualms about accepting the inclusion of the above provisions on slavery in the Fundamental Constitutions of Carolina, which he helped author.[53] Yet the first section of the first of his *Two Treatises of Government* published in 1689 begins: 'Slavery is so vile and miserable an Estate of Man and so directly opposite to the generous Temper and Courage of our Nation' that 'tis hardly to be conceived, that an Englishman, much less a Gentleman, should plead for it'.[54] It is probable that Locke subsequently repented his earlier role in promoting and sustaining slavery. When Locke had a position on the Board of Trade and Plantations in 1696 he played a role in reforming Virginia laws and government, objecting especially to royal land grants that had rewarded those who bought 'negro servants'.[55]

The anti-slavery movement in the West in the nineteenth century came as some kind of a moral awakening, a willingness to treat all human beings as being born with natural rights and capable of reason. Followers of new Christian religious doctrines such as evangelicals (especially the Quakers) and Protestant missionaries found it difficult to reconcile their mission of converting slaves into Christians and the barbaric treatment of slaves by slave owners who were professedly Christians. Although the missionaries played an important role in the Western colonization of the African continent, whose cultures they considered vastly inferior to Western civilization, they also believed in the unity of all humankind and felt duty bound to emancipate the local population from gross oppression and injustice.[56]

A change of attitude towards slavery and slave trading took a long time to take hold. In *Somerset v Stewart*, decided by the Court of King's Bench in

---

[53] Martti Koskenniemi, 'History of Human Rights as Political Intervention in the Present' in Slotte and Halme-Tuomisaari (eds), *Revisiting the Origins of Human Rights* ix, xiii, quoting John Locke, *Two Treatises of Government and a Letter Concerning Toleration* (ed. Ian Shapiro, Yale University Press 2003), Second Treatise, 141 [95]; Yolton, *A Locke Dictionary* 258; Ann Talbot, *'The Great Ocean of Knowledge': The Influence of Travel Literature on the Work of John Locke* (Brill 2010) 279–307; David Armitage, 'John Locke, Carolina and the *Two Treatises of Government*' (2004) 32 Political Theory 602.

[54] Quoted in Yolton, *A Locke Dictionary* 258.

[55] Holly Brewer, 'Slavery, Sovereignty and "Inheritable Blood": Reconsidering John Locke and the Origins of American Slavery' (2017) 122 American Historical Rev 1038.

[56] Michael Barnett, *Empire of Humanity: A History of Humanitarianisn* (Cornell University Press 2011) 57–73; Neier, *The International Human Rights Movement* 34–6. Cf Tomuschat, *Human Rights* 20–29; Flynn, *Reframing the Intellectual Dialogue on Human Rights* 17.

1772, Lord Mansfield ruled that a person, regardless of being a slave, could not be removed from England against their will. He reasoned that slavery was 'so odious' that it was incapable of being justified by any reasons, moral or political, but only by 'positive law' (that is, an Act of Parliament) stipulating to the contrary.[57] This case gave impetus to the movement to abolish slavery, leading to the 1807 Act for the Abolition of the Slave Trade,[58] outlawing the slave trade throughout the British colonies, but without abolishing the practice of slavery itself. Before then, Great Britain was the largest carrier of slave trade to the Americas. As the then most influential maritime and political power, Great Britain succeeded in pressuring Portugal, Spain, France and Brazil to limit or terminate their participation in slave trading.[59] The 1833 Slavery Abolition Act, in force on 1 August 1834,[60] emancipated slaves below the age of six in the colonies, while former slaves over the age of six were re-designated as 'apprentices', whose servitude was to be abolished in two stages: the first set of apprenticeships to end on 1 August 1838 and the other apprenticeships on 1 August 1840. Pursuant to the Act, the British Government raised £20 million to compensate registered owners of the freed slaves for the loss of the slaves as business assets. Half of the compensation was paid to slave-owning families in the Caribbean and Africa, with the other half paid to absentee slave owners living in Britain. According to a historian of African slavery, abolition of slavery was eventually achieved not so much because of the desire to end slavery but because the modern industrial system was incompatible with a slave-based social formation, with the demise of slavery becoming inevitable in the context of absorption into a capitalist world economy.[61]

In the modern era, a large number of people in the West seem to share a genuinely altruistic, humanitarian belief that abuses of human rights abroad are prone to cause war, as in the case of Nazism prior to the Second World War, as well as national instability with deleterious effects beyond borders. Therefore, in their view, there is a need to improve the human rights of the people in foreign lands lest the violations of their rights would jeopardize the interests of the international community.[62] These well-meaning efforts may resemble the

---

[57] (1772) 98 ER 499, 510, as subsequently explained by Lord Mansfield himself in *R v Inhabitants of Thames Ditton* (1785) 99 ER 891.
[58] Stat 47 Geo III, c 36.
[59] Paul E Lovejoy, *Transformations in Slavery: A History of Slavery in Africa* (3rd edn, CUP 2011) 135–59; Posner, *Twilight of Human Rights Law* 13; Ed Bates, 'History' in Moeckli et al (eds), *International Human Rights Law* 3, 12–13; Jenny S Martinez, *The Slave Trade and the Origins of International Human Rights Law* (OUP 2012).
[60] Stat 3 & 4 Will IV, c 73.
[61] Lovejoy, *Transformations in Slavery* 244–66.
[62] Posner, *Twilight of Human Rights Law* 60–61, 68.

civilizing efforts of colonialists and missionaries in the past and may backfire, doing more harm than good, if the interests and needs of the peoples in the targeted States are not really understood.[63] However, it is not justifiable for any State to invoke the past, including slavery practised by some Western societies and a legacy of colonialism, as excuses to violate human rights today.

This is also true vis-à-vis ethnic, national, racial and other groups who now find themselves minorities in a former Western colony because of a divide-and-rule policy of the former colonial power before the independence of that colony. They are human beings whose human rights are protected under applicable rules of customary international law and human rights treaties binding on the former colony, which is now an independent sovereign State. In particular, no State is permitted to perpetrate genocide or crimes against humanity, including ethnic cleansing or persecution, torture, or any other act of the most malignant depravity proscribed by peremptory norms of general international law (*jus cogens*) from which no derogation is allowed. Any State whose agents commit the proscribed act bears State responsibility for violation of international law. Individuals responsible for the said act incur individual criminal responsibility punishable before a competent international criminal tribunal and are subject to universal jurisdiction or jurisdiction based on some other principle(s) that another State may lawfully exercise under international law to prosecute the individuals in that State's domestic court. This state of affairs partly results from the policy of international law to preserve the status quo of the frontier at the end of colonization (*uti possidetis juris*). As the Chamber of the International Court of Justice (ICJ) in *Case Concerning the Frontier Dispute (Burkina Faso/Republic of Mali)* explains, *uti possidetis* is a general principle with 'its obvious purpose ... to prevent the independence and stability of new States being endangered by fratricidal struggles provoked by the challenging of frontiers following the withdrawal of the administering power'.[64] Hence, every former Western colony has to be content with, and bears relevant international human rights obligations binding on it with regard to, the population of all races, religions, cultures and ethnicities living within its frontiers at the time of and after decolonization.

3. EXCEPTIONALISM/UNILATERALISM

Let us now consider the alleged double standards in IHRL. There appear to be two conflicting tendencies in the twenty-first century. On the one hand, human

---

[63] Ibid 122, 148; Marie-Bénédicte Dembour, 'Critiques' in Moeckli et al (eds), *International Human Rights Law* 41, 57.
[64] [1986] ICJ Rep 554, 565 [20].

rights will be more commonly accepted outside the West. On the other hand, certain non-Western States and citizens, with increasing economic and military powers, may become more critical of the fundamental global norms based on Western ideas and frameworks.[65] The former trend is sustained by the continued dominance of Western media and opinion leaders, propagating their values for democracy, market economy and human rights, which are also shared by liberal-minded leaders and intellectuals in the non-Western world.[66] The latter trend is kept alive by the perception among certain non-Western governments and ordinary citizens that the idea of human rights is merely another slogan by which Western powers rationalize their interventionist policies.[67]

The much-publicized strategy of the African Union (AU) dated 12 January 2017 for its Member States to withdraw en masse from the 1998 Rome Statute of the International Criminal Court (ICC)[68] shows the deep frustration with the perceived double standards, with Africans bearing the brunt thereof. For Africans in general, the ICC seems to have been pursuing a pattern of targeting Africans for prosecution in a manner reflective of selectivity and inequality against Africans and the 'systemic disadvantage of African nations'. The document explains that the (then) 34 African States ratified the ICC Statute with their 'moral conscience' significantly compelled by the violence in Africa in the 1980s and 1990s that 'instigated the feelings of indignity and anger' connected with the international community's inaction during the 1994 Rwandan genocide, the injustice of the South African apartheid and 'the results of the long anti-colonial struggles against European imperialism'. The AU goes on to blame the 'inherent politics' of the international decision-making processes with in-built 'systemic imbalance', particularly at the UN Security Council, whose decisions are made to further the interests of its permanent members, which are not always in line with those of Africa, 'thereby leading to a perception of a double standard against African States'. It sets out the objectives that

---

[65]   Yasuaki Onuma, *International Law in a Transcivilizational World* (CUP 2017) 361–2. See also Koskenniemi, 'History of Human Rights as Political Intervention in the Present' ix, xvii.

[66]   Onuma, *International Law in a Transcivilizational World* 415. On the vital role of the mass media in the field of human rights, see Eric Heinze, 'The Reality and Hyper-reality of Human Rights: Public Consciousness and the Mass Media' in Rob Dickinson, Elena Katselli, Colin Murray and Ole W Pedersen (eds), *Examining Critical Perspectives on Human Rights* (CUP 2012) 193.

[67]   Hosseinioun, *The Human Rights Turn and the Paradox of Progress in the Middle East* 7, 12.

[68]   2187 UNTS 90.

include ensuring that international justice is conducted in a fair and transparent method devoid of any perception of double standards.[69]

Allegations of double standards are closely related to the perception that certain influential States keep themselves outside the remit of international human rights norms although they unilaterally demand that their less influential counterparts abide by these norms. For instance, Iran's Supreme Leader Ayatollah Seyyed Ali Khamenei has prompted the Iranian Government to request the UN to condemn what he claims to be the many ongoing and endemic serious human rights violations perpetrated by and in the USA. Khamenei lists as examples:

> burning members of the Davidian cult in the USA during Bill Clinton's presidency; holding and brutally torturing inmates at Guantanamo detention centre, Abu Ghraib prison in Iraq and an American jail in Afghanistan; and not banning the sales of guns in the USA because of the profit of arms manufacturing companies.

He adds that if the UN is a truly independent international organization not affiliated with the US 'regime' it should seriously pursue these cases and make up for its past failure to do so.[70]

The US Constitution provides safeguards against human rights abuses by the US Government. For example, in relation to the Guantánamo inmates, the US Supreme Court has exerted the jurisdiction of the US federal courts over the Guantánamo Bay detention centre and ruled that the inmates had a constitutional right to habeas corpus.[71] Yet, more than half a century after the US Supreme Court's ruling in *Brown v Board of Education of Topeka* in 1954 that segregated schooling for African Americans is unconstitutional,[72] many US schools have remained segregated in fact as one-fifth of them have student populations that are at least 70 per cent Latino or African American and with disadvantaged curriculum as well as lower chances of students graduating compared with those where most students are white.[73] This is because dramatic improvements in human rights protection usually take time to materialize in

---

[69]   §§1–3, 8(a) of the document, https://www.hrw.org/sites/default/files/supporting
_resources/icc_withdrawal_strategy_jan._2017.pdf, accessed 12 Dec 2018.
[70]   'Iran Leader Asks UN to Investigate US Human Rights Violations', *Sputnik News* (28 May 2018) https://sputniknews.com/society/201805281064867348-Iran -Leader-wants-UN-to-Investigate-US/, accessed 29 May 2018.
[71]   *Rasul v Bush* 542 US 466 (2004), *Hamdan v Rumsfeld* 548 US 557 (2006) and *Boumediene v Bush* 553 US 723 (2008).
[72]   347 US 483 (1954).
[73]   Jody Heymann and Adèle Cassola, 'Achieving Equal Rights: Lessons from Global Efforts' in Jody Heymann and Adèle Cassola (eds), *Making Equal Rights Real: Taking Effective Action to Overcome Global Challenges* (CUP 2012) 1, 2.

practice. This gap between ideals and reality happens in other States championing human rights,[74] including Canada, a State often at odds with Iran and Saudi Arabia on human rights issues. Canada has a well-developed formal constitutional and legislative framework that includes constitutional and legal protections against race-related human rights violations. Yet, the gap between Canadian society's ideal of colour-blindness and the reality of racial injustice still persists in many areas of livelihood.[75] Canada itself admitted during a universal periodic review process of the UN Human Rights Council in 2009 that it had to address human rights challenges such as deficiencies in housing, poverty, racism, violence against women and especially the disadvantaged position of indigenous peoples.[76]

The result of a major survey of Jews in 12 EU Member States with the largest Jewish populations in Europe published in December 2018 reveals that anti-Semitism is rife and getting worse, with Jews becoming increasingly concerned about the risk of harassment.[77] These EU Member States are on the front line of advocating IHRL on the international plane, both bilaterally and multilaterally. The fact that they have human rights problems at home does not mean that they must stop promoting or protecting human rights abroad, provided that they are eager and willing to solve their own human rights problems.

Although the US Government's domestic human rights record is far from ideal,[78] it has been actively propagating human rights outside US soil.[79] US President Jimmy Carter, in 1977, placed human rights at the forefront of the US domestic agenda and foreign policy as part of 'the reestablishment

---

[74]   Rosa Freedman, *Failing to Protect: The UN and the Politicisation of Human Rights* (C Hurst & Co 2014) 119–26.

[75]   Grace-Edward Galabuzi, 'Equalizing Social and Cultural Rights: Approaches to Equity across Ethnic and Racial Groups' in Heymann and Cassola (eds), *Making Equal Rights Real* 149, 173–83.

[76]   Benjamin Authers, 'Representation and Suspicion in Canada's Appearance under the Universal Periodic Review' in Hilary Charlesworth and Emma Larking (eds), *Human Rights and the Universal Periodic Review: Rituals and Ritualism* (CUP 2014) 169, 178.

[77]   European Union Agency for Fundamental Rights, *Experiences and Perceptions of Antisemitism – Second Survey on Discrimination and Hate Crime against Jews in the EU* (European Union Agency for Fundamental Rights 2018).

[78]   See, eg, an argument that the Islamophobia and profiling of Muslims have stigmatized Muslim Americans by subjecting them to suspicion, surveillance and punitive action in violation of their human rights after the 11 September 2001 al Qaeda terrorist attacks on US soil (Khaled A Beydoun, 'Acting Muslim' (2018) 53 Harvard Civil Rights-Civil Liberties L Rev 1).

[79]   Forsythe, *Human Rights in International Relations* 223–37; Hurst Hannum, *Rescuing Human Rights: A Radically Moderate Approach* (CUP 2019) 135–56.

of the [US] moral and missionary credentials in the world'.[80] President Ronald Reagan, Carter's successor in 1981, assimilated human rights to the independently developed programme of 'democracy promotion' against communist regimes, while being friendly to right-wing dictators who were US allies against communism even though this led to many tragic consequences then and even now.[81] However, even Reagan subsequently changed track and supported the cause of human rights during his second term as US President, abandoning and helping to end the dictatorship regimes of Augusto Pinochet in Chile, Ferdinand Marcos in the Philippines and Jean-Claude 'Baby Doc' Duvalier in Haiti.[82]

One of the important US laws in the field of promoting human rights abroad is Section 502B of the Foreign Assistance Act Amendments of 1974, which prohibits the US Government from providing security assistance to 'any country the government of which engages in a consistent pattern of gross violations of internationally recognized human rights' including 'torture or cruel, inhuman, or degrading treatment or punishment, prolonged detention without charge and trial, causing the disappearance of persons by the abduction and clandestine detention of those persons and other flagrant denial of the right to life, liberty, or the security of the person'.[83] The US Government uses 'carrots' alongside 'sticks' to promote human rights overseas. The US Agency for International Development (USAID) is active in running assistance programmes and projects in targeted States aiming at enhancing democratic transition through the strengthening of the media, civil society and local communities in democratic reform, peace building and inter-communal harmony.

The Sergei Magnitsky Rule of Law Accountability Act of 2012[84] was enacted to impose sanctions on Russian officials accused of being responsible

[80] Moyn, *The Last Utopia* 158–9.
[81] Ibid 217. See further Jack Donnelly, *International Human Rights* (3rd edn, Westview Press 2007) 115–28, 149–71; Neier, *The International Human Rights Movement* 172–3; Baik, *Emerging Regional Human Rights Systems in Asia* 277–8.
[82] Neier, *The International Human Rights Movement* 15–16, 174–83; Ivan Manokha, *The Political Economy of Human Rights Enforcement* (Palgrave Macmillan 2008) 191–3, 213–21.
[83] Public L 93-559, 30 Dec 1974, 88 Stat 1795, now codified as 22 U.S.C. §2304(a)(2) and (d)(1). For a history and implementation of this provision, see Neier, *The International Human Rights Movement* 94, 165–9. On the compatibility with World Trade Organization law of the US Government's imposition of trade and economic sanctions against Venezuela for the latter's alleged violations of human rights, see Iryna Bogdanova, 'WTO Dispute on the US Human Rights Sanction Is Looming on the Horizon' *EJIL Talk!* (31 Jan 2019) https://www.ejiltalk.org/wto-dispute-on-the-us-human-rights-sanctions-is-looming-on-the-horizon/#more-16856, accessed 31 Jan 2019.
[84] 22 U.S.C. 5811, Public Law 112-208, 14 Dec 2012, 12 Stat 1502.

for the death of Russian tax accountant Sergei Magnitsky in a Moscow prison
in 2009. The underlying rationale for the Act is the US aspiration for 'a mutually beneficial relationship' with Russia based on respect for human rights and
the rule of law and US support for Russians in 'their efforts to realize their full
economic potential and to advance democracy, human rights and the rule of
law', based on Russia's obligations under the Convention against Torture and
Other Cruel, Inhuman, or Degrading Treatment or Punishment; the ICCPR;
the UN Convention against Corruption and the ECHR. The Act proceeds to
proclaim that owing to such voluntary commitment by a State to respect obligations and responsibilities through the adoption of international agreements
and treaties, the obligations must be observed in good faith in order to maintain the stability of the international order. Above all, '[h]uman rights are an
integral part of international law and lie at the foundation of the international
order', the protection of which 'is not left exclusively to the internal affairs of
that [State]'.[85]

In 2016 the US Congress passed the Global Magnitsky Act to allow the US
Executive branch to impose visa bans and targeted sanctions on individuals
anywhere in the world allegedly responsible for committing human rights
violations or acts of significant corruption.[86] In December 2018, building on
the Global Magnitsky Act, the US Congress enacted the Reciprocal Access
to Tibet Act[87] to promote access of diplomats, other officials, journalists and
others from the USA to 'Tibetan areas of China'. According to the latter Act's
main rationale, while Chinese citizens travel freely throughout the USA,
Chinese authorities severely restrict Americans' ability to have access to
Tibet so as to hide the true human rights situation of the Tibetan people from
them and despite US Government officials' repeated requests for diplomatic
access to Tibet. Above all, Tibetan-Americans are almost always denied the
right to visit and meet their family members in Tibet. The Act requires the
US Secretary of State to assess Americans' level of access to Tibet within 90
days of its enactment and to send a report to Congress every year thereafter
identifying the Chinese officials responsible for keeping Americans out of
Tibet. The Secretary will then ban those officials from receiving visas to enter
the USA. The Chinese Government has rebutted that this Act 'has disregarded
the facts, grossly interfered in China's domestic affairs and violated the basic
norms of international relations', and that China is resolutely opposed to it and

---

[85] Ibid s 402(a).
[86] Public Law 114-328. See also Executive Order 13818 of 20 December 2017
Blocking the Property of Persons Involved in Serious Human Rights Abuse or
Corruption, Fed Register, vol 82, No 246, Tues 26 Dec 2017, Presidential Documents
60839.
[87] HR 1872, in force on 19 Dec 2018.

has made stern representations to the USA. Besides, according to the spokes-man of the Chinese Ministry of Foreign Affairs, nearly 40,000 Americans visited Tibet between 2015 and December 2018, including the minority leader of the US House of Representatives and senators.[88] However, to ease the US pressure, in May 2019 China allowed the US Ambassador to China to visit Tibet for a week, where the Ambassador engaged with local leaders to raise long-standing concerns about restrictions on religious freedom and the preser-vation of Tibetan culture and language.

Promoting human rights abroad resonates with liberal theories of interna-tional relations that emphasize democracy, the rule of law and international cooperation based on moral values and norms, including human rights norms, in the furtherance of State interests.[89] It also finds support from those who favour promoting well-being, including human rights, in foreign nations by providing foreign aid as the carrot and coercion as the stick vis-à-vis these foreign nations.[90] They argue that it is not 'neo-imperialism' so long as the pressure is for the avowed purpose of altruistic protection of human rights of individuals and not for any ideological reason.[91] Nevertheless, rather than altruistically furthering IHRL, the US Government has for decades abided by 'prudentialism', with political and practical factors, especially its security interests, being decisive as to whether it would pursue human rights protection overseas.[92]

Exempting oneself from the ambit of IHRL can undermine the credibility of the self-exempting State's human rights agenda abroad.

---

[88]   https://www.fmprc.gov.cn/mfa_eng/xwfw_665399/s2510_665401/2511 _665403/t1622128.shtml, accessed 24 Dec 2018.

[89]   Baik, *Emerging Regional Human Rights Systems in Asia* 32–4. Similarly, Sonia Cardenas, 'Human Rights in Comparative Politics' in Michael Goodhart (ed.), *Human Rights: Politics and Practice* (3rd edn, OUP 2016) 77, 83.

[90]   Posner, *Twilight of Human Rights Law* 7–8, 141–4, 148. Posner cautions, however, that putting too much pressure on the targeted State may force that State to shift its alliance away from the targeting State; that collective action by a group of States may not work where one or more States in the group has a strong incentive to free ride, hoping other States will incur the costs of sanctioning the targeted State; and that well-meaning attempts to enforce human rights treaties on foreigners without really understanding the interests of these foreigners may do more harm than good (ibid 80–81, 122, 148). Simmons (*Mobilizing for Human Rights* 177, 374–5) is in favour of using economic incentives, including foreign aid, provided that they would not be con-sidered as 'substitutes for clear legal rights'.

[91]   Freedman, *Failing to Protect* 164–5.

[92]   Zachary D Kaufman, *United States Law and Policy on Transnational Justice: Principles, Politics and Pragmatics* (OUP 2016) *passim* and 57–8, 213–14. Similarly, Posner, *Twilight of Human Rights Law* 105–7.

The USA has pursued a 'self-exemption policy' against becoming party to most human rights treaties, while becoming party to other treaties subject to reservations, understandings and declarations, thereby limiting the domestic effects of such treaties in the USA.[93] In spite of its many good deeds in human rights protection at home and abroad, the USA has expressly refused to accept many recommendations made during the UN Human Rights Council's Universal Periodic Review process, including the setting up of a national human rights institution and ratifying key human rights treaties (such as the ICESCR and the 1998 Rome Statute of the ICC).[94] As of this writing, the Donald Trump Administration has stopped responding to official complaints from UN special rapporteurs since 7 May 2018, with at least 13 formal queries remaining unanswered. The queries include those relating to family separation of Central Americans at the US border with Mexico, death threats against a transgender activist in Seattle and allegations of anti-gay bias in the sentencing to death of a prisoner in South Dakota. This is a departure from the US practice dating back several decades, although some areas in the USA are consistently off limits to UN special rapporteurs, such as US prisons and the detention camp on Guantánamo Bay. A US Department of State spokesman affirms that the USA remains 'deeply committed to the promotion and defence of human rights around the globe' and expresses 'strong support' for UN special rapporteurs, but only in the context of their investigations into *other* States. The spokesman adds that the USA backs those mandates 'that have proven effective in illuminating the most grave human rights environments, including in Iran and [North Korea]'. It is paradoxical that the Trump Administration's decision to shun the UN special rapporteurs places the USA among a small minority of uncooperative States resisting international oversight from UN special rapporteurs, one of which is North Korea.[95]

Even when the USA becomes party to a human rights treaty, this is not necessarily the end of the matter.

The US Constitution's supremacy clause provides that the US Constitution, federal law enacted pursuant to it and treaties concluded under

---

[93]   Jamie Mayerfeld, *The Promise of Human Rights: Constitutional Government, Democratic Legitimacy and International Law* (University of Pennsylvania Press 2016) 148–51 and chs 4 and 5.

[94]   Human Rights Council, *Universal Periodic Review: Report of the Working Group on the Universal Periodic Review – United States of America*, 16th session, UN Doc A/HRC/16/11 (4 Jan 2011) 13–28.

[95]   'US halts cooperation with UN on potential human rights violations', *The Guardian* (London), 4 Jan 2019, https://www.theguardian.com/law/2019/jan/04/trump -administration-un-human-rights-violations, accessed 5 Jan 2019.

the authority of the United States shall be the supreme law of the land.[96] In *Sei Fujii v State of California*,[97] decided in 1952, the California Supreme Court, by a majority of four to three, struck down California's Alien Land Act for violating the Fourteenth Amendment of the US Constitution since it had been created and enforced as an instrument for effectuating racial discrimination, in that particular case against Japanese. However, Chief Justice Gibson, for the plurality, rejected the Plaintiff's argument that the land law had been invalidated and superseded by the preamble and Articles 1, 55 and 56 of the UN Charter in which the UN Member States pledge to promote the observance of human rights and fundamental freedoms without distinction as to race. The plurality reasoned that although the UN Charter was a treaty binding on the USA, a treaty did not automatically supersede local laws inconsistent with it unless the treaty provisions were self-executing. In determining whether a treaty was self-executing, US courts had to look to the intent of the signatory parties as manifested by the language of the instrument and, if the instrument was uncertain, recourse might be had to the circumstances surrounding its execution. For a treaty provision to be operative without the aid of implementing US legislation and to have the force and effect of a statute, the framers of the treaty must have intended to prescribe a rule that, standing alone, would be enforceable in US courts. The aforesaid provisions of the UN Charter were held not to be self-executing as they were not the type customarily employed in treaties held by US courts to be self-executing and to create rights and duties in individuals. They merely stated general purposes and objectives of the UN and did not purport to impose legal obligations on the individual UN Member States to create rights in private persons. In other words, although the UN Member States had bound themselves to cooperate with the UN in promoting respect for and observance of human rights, it was contemplated that future legislative action by them would be required to accomplish the declared objectives and there was nothing to indicate that these provisions were intended to become rules of law for US courts upon the US ratification of the UN Charter.

The US practice of making a distinction between executing and non-executing treaties, as interpreted by US courts themselves, has led to the USA failing to comply with international human rights obligations, such as when it could not comply with the *LaGrand* and *Avena* judgments of the ICJ holding the USA in violation of its obligations under the 1963 Vienna Convention on Consular Relations (VCCR).[98]

---

[96]   US Constitution, Art VI, cl 2.
[97]   38 Cal.2d 718 (1952).
[98]   596 UNTS 261.

LaGrand concerns two German nationals and the subsequent *Avena* case more than 50 Mexicans sentenced to death in certain federal states in the USA.[99] In both cases, the US authorities failed to inform these individuals of their right to have the consular post of the State of their nationality notified of their arrest and the consequential mutual rights of communication and access of consular officers and their nationals, and the right of consular officers to visit their nationals in prison and to arrange for their legal representation, as required by Article 36(1) of the VCCR. The USA was found not only to have breached its obligation to Germany and Mexico, respectively, as a State Party to the VCCR, but also to have violated the individual rights of these individuals under Article 36(1), which rights could be relied on before the ICJ by their State of nationality. Despite the ICJ's orders for the indication of the provisional measures calling upon the US Government to take all measures at its disposal to ensure that the persons named in the respective orders not be executed pending the ICJ's final decision on the merits, they were executed nevertheless. The ICJ stressed that these orders did have legally binding effect on the USA and the various competent US authorities failed to take all the steps they could have taken to implement the orders.

One of the Mexican nationals named in the ICJ's *Avena* judgment whose rights were violated was José Ernesto Medellín, convicted in the USA of capital murder and sentenced to death. After his conviction and sentence were upheld on appeal, Medellín filed a series of petitions for habeas corpus relief. US President George W Bush issued a memorandum stating that the USA would discharge its international obligations by having state courts give effect to the decision in cases filed by the Mexican nationals affected by the ICJ's judgment. The Texas Court of Criminal Appeals rejected the memorandum as a basis for overriding federal state procedural requirements governing post-conviction proceedings for convicted criminals. On appeal to the US Supreme Court, it was held that neither the ICJ's judgment nor the US President's memorandum created directly enforceable federal law because none of the relevant treaty sources relating to the case against the USA in the ICJ was self-executing and the ICJ's judgment did not create binding US

---

[99] *LaGrand (Germany v United States of America)*, Provisional Measures, Order of 3 Mar 1999 [1999] ICJ Rep 9; *LaGrand (Germany v United States of America)* [2001] ICJ Rep 466; *Avena and Other Mexican Nationals (Mexico v United States of America)*, Provisional Measures, Order of 5 Feb 2003 [2003] ICJ Rep 77; *Avena and Other Mexican Nationals (Mexico v United States of America)*, Judgment [2004] ICJ Rep 12; *Request for Interpretation of the Judgment of 31 March 2004 in the Case concerning Avena and Other Mexican Nationals (Mexico v United States of America) (Mexico v United States of America)*, Provisional Measures, Order of 16 July 2008 [2008] ICJ Rep 311.

domestic law. Moreover, ruled the Supreme Court, the US President lacked authority to create domestic law pre-empting contrary federal state law under these circumstances, since it was for Congress, not the Executive, to transform an international obligation arising from a non-self-executing treaty into domestic law.[100]

The US courts ignored the ICJ's ruling that the US obligation not to execute the persons named in the ICJ's orders and judgments was an *obligation of result* to be performed unconditionally, although the ICJ left it to the USA to choose the means of implementation, not excluding the introduction within a reasonable time of appropriate legislation, if deemed necessary under domestic constitutional law.[101]

It is odd that the USA has failed to effectuate the implementation of the ICJ's judgments because of the technically legal antinomies between US courts and international courts and tribunals that can adversely affect, and have in fact adversely affected, human rights of individuals found on US soil. The UN International Law Commission's Articles on State Responsibility for Internationally Wrongful Acts of 2001[102] provides in Article 4 that the conduct of any State organ is an act of that State under international law, whether the organ exercises legislative, executive, judicial or any other functions, whatever position it holds in the organization of the State and whatever its character as an organ of the central government or of a territorial unit of the State. In this respect, an organ includes any person or entity which has that status in accordance with the internal law of the State. This provision has been quoted with approval by the ICJ.[103]

A question may be asked: if a nation State can invoke separation of powers under its constitutional law in such a manner, why cannot other nation States use the same or similar reason or excuse? It should be noted that in July 2019 the ICJ applied its reasoning and decisions in *LaGrand* and *Avena* to the case

---

[100] *Medellín v Texas* 552 US 491 (2008). Cf Sean D Murphy, 'The United States and the International Court of Justice: Coping with Antinomies' in Cesare PR Romano (ed.), *The Sword and the Scale: The United States and International Courts and Tribunals* (CUP 2009) 46; Curtis A Bradley, 'The Supreme Court as a Filter between International Law and American Constitutionalism' (2016) 104 California L Rev 1567, 1573–4.

[101] *Request for Interpretation of the Judgment of 31 March 2004 in the Case concerning Avena and Other Mexican Nationals (Mexico v United States of America) (Mexico v United States of America)* [2009] ICJ Rep 3, 19–20.

[102] Report of the International Law Commission on the work of its fifty-third session, 23 April–1 June and 2 July–10 Aug 2001, UNGA Official Records, Fifty-sixth Sess, Supp No 10 (A/56/10) ch. IV.

[103] *Difference Relating to Immunity from Legal Process of a Special Rapporteur of the Commission on Human Rights* [1999] ICJ Rep 62, 87 [62].

of *Jadhav*, an Indian national accused of espionage and sentenced to death by Pakistan.[104]

The ramifications of the double standards and exceptionalism will be duly assessed at the end of this chapter.

4.   DEMOCRACY AND HUMAN RIGHTS

Human rights are usually advocated as a natural concomitant of democracy and vice versa. The terminology 'democracy' comes from the Greek words '*demos*' (people) and '*kratos*' (rule); therefore, it connotes rule by the people.

Reinhold Niebuhr, the renowned American anti-Soviet communism political philosopher and theologian, posits that democracy is 'the characteristic of the fruits of bourgeois civilization' since it expresses the typical viewpoints of the commercial middle classes who rose to power in Europe in the sixteenth through eighteenth centuries and reached their zenith in the nineteenth century. They used democratic ideals of equality and political liberty armed with the political power of suffrage to defeat the ecclesiastical and aristocratic rulers of the feudal-medieval world. Beyond its middle-class roots, democracy is 'a perennial form of social organization in which freedom and order are made to support, and not contradict, each other'. Ideal democracy therefore seeks unity within the conditions of freedom of individuals and maintains that freedom within the framework of order within the community. Niebuhr famously concludes: 'Man's capacity for justice makes democracy possible; but man's inclination to injustice makes democracy necessary.'[105]

The democracy described by Niebuhr is the Western liberal democracy originating from the Age of the Enlightenment in Europe. The *Oxford English Dictionary* defines 'liberal democracy' as '[a] democratic system of government in which individual rights and freedoms are officially recognized and protected and the exercise of political power is limited by the rule of law'. Similarly, the *Collins English Dictionary* defines 'liberal democracy' as 'a democracy based on the recognition of individual rights and freedoms, in which decisions from direct or representative processes prevail in many policy areas'.

---

[104] *Jadhav Case (India v Pakistan)*, Judgment of 17 July 2019. The ICJ makes it clear that the obligation to provide effective review and reconsideration is 'an obligation of result' which 'must be performed unconditionally' and, consequently, Pakistan 'shall take all measures to provide for effective review and reconsideration, including, if necessary, by enacting appropriate legislation' (ibid §146).

[105] Reinhold Niebuhr, *The Children of Light and the Children of Darkness: A Vindication of Democracy and a Critique of its Traditional Defense* (University of Chicago Press 1944) 1–6 and Preface.

It is widely believed that democracies tend to have a deep-rooted preference for human rights and better human rights records than do non-democracies because democracy enhances, among other things, the quality of the police, the prosecutor and court systems conducive to the development of the rule of law and the consequential complete enforcement of human rights.[106] However, insofar as human rights has been identified as synonymous with Western liberal democracy,[107] it is very problematic because a pluralist conception of human rights in a multipolar world should permit the pluralism of cultures and ways of life as well as 'good', or legitimate, political regimes not necessarily following the liberal democratic system of government.[108] According to an established Soviet view, despite the difference among States with different economic and social systems – be they socialist democracy or bourgeois democracy – there exists a general concept of democracy and a general democratic concept of human rights. 'Pure' democracy and 'pure' human rights do not really exist since there are varying historical types and forms of democracy. However, fascism is an example of a negation of democracy and human rights in general.[109]

The hortatory and non-binding UDHR provides in Article 21(1) and (3) that everyone has the right to take part in the government of his country, directly or through freely chosen representatives and that the basis of the authority of government shall be the will of the people expressed in periodic and genuine elections which shall be by universal and equal suffrage and shall be held by secret vote or by equivalent free voting procedures. Article 29(b) of the UDHR allows limitations on the rights and freedoms provided that such limitations are determined by law solely for the purpose of securing due recognition and respect for the rights and freedoms of others and of meeting the just requirements of morality, public order and the general welfare 'in a democratic society'.

---

[106] Courtney Hillebrecht, *Domestic Politics and International Human Rights Tribunals: The Problem of Compliance* (CUP 2014) 20, 32, 187; Baik, *Emerging Regional Human Rights Systems in Asia* 258, 263, 279; Tim Dunne and Marianne Hanson, 'Human Rights in International Relations' in Goodhart (ed.), *Human Rights: Politics and Practice* 44, 48; Freedman, *Failing to Protect* 98–117; Mayerfeld, *The Promise of Human Rights* 2. Cf Koskenniemi, *The Politics of International Law* 166 on 'Cosmopolitan Democracy' that 'sees rights as one aspect of expanding democratic international realm'.

[107] Mutua, 'Politics and Human Rights' 149–50.

[108] Chantal Mouffe, 'Democracy, Human Rights and Cosmopolitanism: An Agnostic Approach' in Costa Douzinas and Conor Gearty (eds), *The Meaning of Rights: The Philosophy and Social Theory of Human Rights* (CUP 2014) 181, 188, 191–2.

[109] GI Tunkin, *Theory of International Law* (William E Butler tr, George Allen & Unwin 1974) 82–3.

The right to vote and to be elected at genuine periodic elections by universal and equal suffrage and held by secret ballot is enshrined in Article 25(2) of the ICCPR, which binds its States Parties. Article 4 of the ICCPR, which prohibits derogation by its States Parties from some of the ICCPR obligations in time of public emergency which threatens the life of the nation, and the existence of which is officially proclaimed, does not prohibit derogation from the right in Article 25 of the ICCPR however.

The Vienna Declaration and Programme of Action[110] adopted by the World Conference on Human Rights in Vienna on 25 June 1993, which is not legally binding, postulates that democracy, development and respect for human rights and fundamental freedoms are interdependent and mutually reinforcing and that the international community should support the strengthening and promoting of democracy, development and respect for human rights and fundamental freedoms in the entire world, especially in the least developed countries committed to the process of democratization and economic reforms.[111]

A question is whether democracy is really the best available form of government, especially when the elected ones use their majority control to abuse human rights. Not infrequently, the elected government eventually turns out to be kakistocratic – one run by the worst, unqualified or unscrupulous individuals. It could be contended that since the common Article 1(1) of both the ICCPR and the ICESCR stipulates that all peoples have the right of self-determination in the sense of freely determining their political status and freely pursuing their economic, social and cultural development, once a democratically elected government is in power it may do anything it wants. Yet, election is not necessarily an end in and of itself – it is merely a means to ensure that the elected heed the will of the electorate and implement the mandate given to the former by the latter.

Elected governments not infrequently renege on their election promises. Elections may be free of cheating but the electoral system put in place by the powers that be may ensure that they remain in power and in the name of democracy.[112] A government with absolute power owing to the general election giving it the majority control over Parliament may be blind to the demands of the electorate as well as corrupt and/or prone to persecute the opposition in order to stay in power.[113] The human rights movement is often at odds with

---

[110] UN Doc A/CONF.157/23 (12 July 1993).

[111] Ibid §I(8) and (9).

[112] 'Lots of elections, little democracy: South-East Asia shows that there is more to freedom than voting', *The Economist* (26 May 2018) 57.

[113] Gregory S Kavka, *Hobbes* (Princeton University Press 1986) 228–9, disputing Thomas Hobbes' conclusion that absolute governments are unlikely to rob and perse-

democratically elected governments on human rights issues and many significant human right abuses are committed by democratic governments.[114]

A thought-provoking article in *The Economist* explains well the perils faced by democracy. In 2017 the health of democracy in 89 nation States regressed, compared with only 27 improving. The regression typically comes in four stages. First, there is a genuine popular grievance with the status quo and, frequently, with the liberal elites or technocrats in charge. Second, opportunistic populist politicians and would-be strongmen identify enemies for voters to blame. Third, after winning the election by exploiting fear or discontent, the victorious politicians set out to dismantle the opposition, including a free press, an impartial judiciary and other extant or potential threats to their agenda. The final stage is the erosion of these constitutional checks-and-balances institutions. Safeguards against such 'illiberal democracy' are through the protection of the constitutional checks-and-balances institutions as well as other watchdogs, such as the free press, that expose abuses of power and corruption by politicians in power. A freely elected government must respect individual and minority rights, the rule of law and independent institutions. The tide has turned against illiberal democracies ruled by autocrats in several parts of the world in the past few years and this bodes well for the future of liberal democracy.[115]

Defenders of liberal democracy maintain that democracy should not be seen as a utopia since it has inherent shortcomings. Democracy involves group decision making that may be relatively slow to respond to increasingly complex issues in the globalized world. By contrast, autocrats may be able to respond more expeditiously to these challenges. New technologies are double-edged swords – they can be used to promote as well as to undermine democracy. Nevertheless, it is heartening that 'even imperfect democracies can prevail over this century's new challenges' and that most of the world's most developed countries are still highly committed democracies because democracy serves as an ultimate safety valve against abuse of power by holding those in power accountable for their acts.[116]

---

cute segments of their citizenry. Cf also the 'illiberal democracy' in Fareed Zakaria, *The Future of Freedom: Illiberal Democracy at Home and Abroad* (WW Norton 2003).

[114] Neier, *The International Human Rights Movement* 175–6; Tomuschat, *Human Rights* 155–8, 432.

[115] 'How democracy dies' and 'Democracy's retreat', *The Economist* (16 June 2018) 14 and 53–5, respectively. Cf also Yascha Mounk, *The People vs. Democracy: Why Our Freedom Is in Danger & How to Save It* (Harvard University Press 2018).

[116] James Stavridis, 'Democracy Isn't Perfect, But It Will Still Prevail', *Time* (12 July 2018) http://www.time.com/5336615/democracy-will-prevail/, accessed 1 Aug 2018.

Democracy is expected to foster the rule of law. The rule of law is, in turn, intrinsically linked to the protection of human rights since it imposes constraints on the State's actions, preventing the democratically elected national leaders from abusing their power and authority. By contrast, autocratic rulers remain accountable to only narrow segments of their societies, if at all.[117] The rule of law is not unique to the West. For example, Islamic scholars find that the rule of law comports with the essential elements in the Constitution of Medina of the Prophet Mohammad circa 622 BC; namely, the existence of sufficiently precise legal rules that are publicly promulgated, accessible to all, applied by institutions that are accountable and consistent with human rights standards.[118]

The third preambular paragraph of the UDHR cogently declares: 'it is essential, if man is not to be compelled to have recourse, as a last resort, to rebellion against tyranny and oppression, that human rights should be protected by the rule of law'. This principle is also enshrined in the ECHR and is extensively referred to in the Treaty of the European Union,[119] including in Article 21(1), which limits the EU's action in the international sphere. Although the ICCPR does not expressly refer to the rule of law as such, the Human Rights Committee entrusted with interpreting the ICCPR has held that the safeguards in relation to the derogation under Article 4 of the ICCPR that allows measures in response to a public emergency are 'based on the principle of legality and the rule of law inherent in the [ICCPR] as a whole'.[120]

According to the statistics compiled by Jonathan Powell and Clayton Thyne, political scientists at the University of Central Florida and the University of Kentucky, respectively, Africa has witnessed 204 *coups d'état*, that is, illegal and overt attempts by the military or other civilian officials inside the State to oust incumbent national leaders by unconstitutional means. Of these, there

---

[117]   Elena Katselli, 'The Rule of Law and the Role of Human Rights in Contemporary International Law' in Rob Dickinson, Elena Katselli, Colin Murray and Ole W Pedersen (eds), *Examining Critical Perspectives on Human Rights* (CUP 2012) 131, 138–40, 152; Simmons, *Mobilizing for Human Rights* 24–5; Christian Tomuschat, 'Democracy and the Rule of Law' in Shelton (ed.), *The Oxford Handbook of International Human Rights Law* 469, 482, 488; Lisa Conant, 'Missing in Action? The Rare Voice of International Courts in Domestic Politics' in Marlene Wind (ed.), *International Courts and Domestic Politics* (CUP 2018) 11, 15–16; John Laws, 'Are Human Rights Undemocratic?' in Anja Seibert-Fohr and Mark E Villiger (eds), *Judgments of the European Court of Human Rights – Effects and Implementation* (Nomos 2014) 187, 187–9.

[118]   Hossein Esmaeili, Irmgard Marboe and Javid Rehman, *The Rule of Law, Freedom of Expression and Islamic Law* (Hart 2017) ch. 2.

[119]   OJEU C83/13, 30 Mar 2010.

[120]   General Comment No 29, States of Emergency (Art 4), Human Rights Committee, CCPR/C/21/Rev.1/Add.11, 31 Aug 2001.

have been 100 coups lasting longer than seven days and 104 coups not lasting that long. Sudan has had the most coups, with 14, whereas Burkina Faso has had the highest number of coups lasting more than seven days, with seven. From 1960 to 1999 there were between 39 and 42 coups in Africa every decade owing to the instability experienced by newly independent African States. Since then there has been a steady decline, with 22 coups in Africa in the 2000s and 16 in the current decade. Conditions common for coups are poverty and poor economic performance. Globally, the total number of coups stands at 475. Latin America has had 95 attempted coups, 40 of which lasted longer than seven days. However, in the past two decades there has been a decline in the number of coups in Latin America, with the last, unsuccessful, coup staged in Venezuela in 2002 against President Hugo Chavez. This decline could be attributed to the end of the Cold War and, consequently, the end of the USA's and the Soviet Union's meddling in Latin American affairs as well as to the willingness of the international community to impose sanctions on the governments that come into power by coups, such as the Government of Haiti in 1994. Asia has also had a decline in the number of coups.[121]

Article 4(m) of the 2000 Constitutive Act of the African Union[122] lists as one principle of the AU 'respect for democratic principles, human rights, the rule of law and good governance'. On 30 January 2007 the AU adopted the African Charter on Democracy, Elections and Governance (ACDEG),[123] which entered into force in February 2012 after ratification by 15 States. As of September 2017, the ACDEG has been ratified by 30 States out of the AU's 55 Member States.

Some of the ACDEG's interesting provisions include Article 14(1), providing unequivocally that States Parties shall strengthen and institutionalize constitutional civilian control over the armed and security forces to ensure the consolidation of democracy and constitutional order. Articles 17 through 22 deal with democratic elections, whereas Articles 23 through 26 cover sanctions in case of unconstitutional changes of government. Article 25 provides, inter alia, that where there has been an unconstitutional change of government in a State Party and diplomatic initiatives have failed, the said State Party shall be suspended from the exercise of its right to participate in the AU's activities until the situation leading to the suspension is resolved. However, the suspended State Party shall continue to fulfil its obligations to the AU,

---

[121] Christopher Giles, 'Gabon coup: Is Africa seeing fewer military take-over attempts?', *BBC News* (7 Jan 2019) https://www.bbc.com/news/world-africa-46783600, accessed 8 Jan 2019.

[122] OAU Doc CAB/LEG/23.15 (2001) Art 3(m).

[123] https://au.int/en/treaties/african-charter-democracy-elections-and-governance, accessed 19 Dec 2018.

in particular with regard to those relating to respect for human rights. The perpetrators of unconstitutional change of government shall not be allowed to participate in elections held to restore the democratic order or hold any position of responsibility in political institutions of their State and they may also be tried before the competent court of the AU. In addition, the Assembly of Heads of State and Government of the AU may decide to apply other forms of sanctions on perpetrators of unconstitutional change of government including punitive economic measures.

A notable outcome from the ACDEG is the development of the African Governance Architecture as the overall political and institutional framework mechanism for dialogue between stakeholders mandated to promote and strengthen democracy, good governance and human rights in Africa. According to one study published in 2017, while the ACDEG has led to changes in some AU Member States' approach to democracy and governance, in other AU Member States it has had limited impact. The level of acceptance and implementation of the ACDEG remains highly uneven across the African continent.[124]

The AU has regularly suspended Member States over *coups d'état*, readmitting them when they return to constitutional democracy. For example, it suspended Madagascar after the coup in March 2009 until January 2014 when the newly elected government was sworn in. The AU suspended Mali after the coup in March 2012 until October of that same year after the AU endorsed a roadmap for fresh elections and the return of law and order in Mali.

Things were different in relation to Egypt, an AU Member State with considerable strategic importance and diplomatic influence. The AU suspended Egypt from July 2013 after Field Marshall Abdel Fattah Al-Sissi, Egypt's then minister of defence and head of the army, had announced on 3 July 2013 that Egypt's first democratically elected president, Mohamed Morsi, had been removed from power after massive protests against the latter that had largely paralysed the government since January 2013. The AU ended Egypt's suspension in June 2014 after the presidential election had been held in Egypt in May 2014 resulting in Al-Sissi being elected president. The AU's decision was a difficult one. On the one hand, there was the need for consistency in the implementation of AU norms on unconstitutional changes of government and consolidation of the democratic advances in Africa. On the other hand, the AU had to take into account other considerations crucial to the AU and Africa, particularly the need for the AU to continue to effectively and constructively

---

[124] Chika Charles Aniekwe, Lutz Oette, Stef Vandeginste and Micha Wiebusch, *The 10th Anniversary of the African Charter on Democracy, Elections and Governance* (Institute of Development Studies 2017).

engage the Egyptian authorities and other stakeholders on the democratization process and the stabilization of the situation in Egypt. The AU thus had to find defensible justifications to end Egypt's suspension.

The AU explained that Egypt's suspension was lifted in the light of (i) the progress made and the steps taken by the Egyptian authorities to formally restore constitutional order in Egypt, (ii) the fact that the suspension of Egypt for almost one year had sent a strong signal to the Egyptian stakeholders about the AU's attachment to its principles and instruments and (iii) the need for the AU to remain engaged with Egypt and to accompany the efforts of the Egyptian authorities for the full implementation of the roadmap to restore full democracy. The AU underscored that this should not be a precedent in terms of adherence to Article 25 of the ACDEG, but 'should only be viewed in light of the unique set of circumstances'. It also suggested that Egypt be persuaded to speedily sign and ratify all relevant AU instruments on democracy, elections and governance, notably the ACDEG, and to take concrete steps towards the implementation of the provisions contained therein. Moreover, despite the lifting of the suspension, the AU would continue to keep human rights and democracy in Egypt on the agenda of the AU Peace and Security Council. In view of the difficulties encountered in applying the AU norms on unconstitutional changes of government, particularly in the context of popular uprisings, the AU adopted a guideline for determining the compatibility of popular uprisings with AU norms on unconstitutional changes of government. Taking into account recent experiences in North Africa, including in Egypt, the following elements should be considered together: (a) the descent of the government into total authoritarianism to the point of forfeiting its legitimacy; (b) the absence or total ineffectiveness of constitutional processes for effecting change of government; (c) popularity of the uprisings in the sense of attracting a significant portion of the population and involving people from all walks of life and ideological persuasions; (d) the absence of involvement of the military in removing the government; and (e) peacefulness of the popular protests.[125] Egypt's diplomatic clout and international standing as a major regional power in Africa played a crucial role in getting the AU's suspension lifted and the aforesaid guideline adopted.[126]

---

[125] Final Report of the African Union High-Level Panel for Egypt, 22 July 2014 §§75–83, http://www.peaceau.org/en/article/final-report-of-the-african-union-high -level-panel-for-egypt, accessed 23 July 2019.

[126] See, eg, Solomon Dersso, 'Egypt vs African Union: A mutually unhappy ending?', *Al Jazeera* (14 July 2014) https://www.aljazeera.com/indepth/opinion/2014/ 07/egypt-vs-african-union-mutually-u-2014714687899839.html, accessed 23 July 2019.

Earlier, in the Americas, the Organization of American States (OAS) had adopted the Inter-American Democratic Charter on 11 September 2001,[127] binding on all OAS Member States. Its preamble refers, inter alia, to the 1948 American Declaration on the Rights and Duties of Man and the 1969 American Convention on Human Rights, which contain the values and principles of liberty, equality and social justice that are intrinsic to democracy. The preamble reaffirms the promotion and protection of human rights as a basic prerequisite for the existence of a democratic society and recognizes the importance of the continuous development and strengthening of the Inter-American human rights system for the consolidation of democracy. Articles 7 through 10 of the Democratic Charter cover the issue of democracy and human rights. Article 7 stipulates that democracy is indispensable for the effective exercise of fundamental freedoms and human rights in their universality, indivisibility and interdependence, embodied in the respective constitutions of States and in Inter-American and international human rights instruments. Article 8 requires, inter alia, that OAS Member States reaffirm their intention to strengthen the Inter-American system for the protection of human rights for the consolidation of democracy in the hemisphere. Article 9 then elaborates that the elimination of all forms of discrimination (especially gender, ethnic and racial discrimination, as well as diverse forms of intolerance), the promotion and protection of human rights of indigenous peoples and migrants and respect for ethnic, cultural and religious diversity in the Americas contribute to the strengthening of democracy and citizen participation.[128] According to Article 10, the promotion and strengthening of democracy require the full and effective exercise of workers' rights, and the application of core labour standards and democracy is strengthened by improving standards in the workplace and enhancing the quality of life for workers in the hemisphere.

Pursuant to Article 21 of the OAS Democratic Charter, when a special session of the OAS General Assembly determines that there has been an unconstitutional interruption of the democratic order of a Member State and

---

[127]   40 ILM 1289.

[128]   This Article is copied, with some changes, by Art 8 of the African Union's ACDEG, which reads:

1.   State Parties shall eliminate all forms of discrimination, especially those based on political opinion, gender, ethnic, religious and racial grounds as well as any other form of intolerance.

2.   State Parties shall adopt legislative and administrative measures to guarantee the rights of women, ethnic minorities, migrants, people with disabilities, refugees and displaced persons and other marginalized and vulnerable social groups.

3.   State Parties shall respect ethnic, cultural and religious diversity, which contributes to strengthening democracy and citizen participation.

diplomatic initiatives have failed, the special session shall take the decision to suspend the said Member State, with immediate effect, from the exercise of its right to participate in the OAS by an affirmative vote of two-thirds of the Member States. However, the suspended Member State shall continue to fulfil its obligations to the OAS, in particular its human rights obligations. Notwithstanding the suspension of the Member State, the OAS will maintain diplomatic initiatives to restore democracy in that State.[129] Article 22 provides for the possibility of lifting the suspension once the situation that led to suspension has been resolved.

Since the last (and unsuccessful) coup was staged in the Americas in 2002, the OAS has not had an occasion to directly enforce its Democratic Charter.[130] Nonetheless, to their credit, several AU and OAS Member States try their best not to support candidatures of undemocratic governments for elections to international organizations. It is also common knowledge that many African and American States do not vote for these candidates irrespective of any promise or reciprocal support arrangement that precedes the undemocratic usurpation of power in the States concerned.

Ironically, the so-called 'authoritarian regime' in the People's Republic of China is considered in some quarters as being more effective in combating endemic poverty than its more democratic counterparts, thereby raising a question whether democracy, especially Western liberal democracy, is always a prerequisite for the betterment of human welfare.[131]

In China, long before the present communist regime, Confucian culture is believed to have impacted speech or deliberation and produced authoritarian deliberation. The Confucian *minben* (people-centric) ideal formed the foundation for Confucian speech, with all public discussions aiming at promoting public interests, with self-interest being subjugated by a form of discipline or control. People are to be persuaded by morality first, reason second and might as a last resort. While the freedom of speech in the West is citizen empowerment as an attribute of democracy, speech in China has been largely sanctioned to improve governance, enhance government authority and generate government legitimacy through political loyalty. In the case of remonstration, Chinese emperors heard competing arguments by remonstrating officials and those best able to demonstrate their loyalty to the emperor had the greatest influence on his decision making, even though they were severe in their criticisms of him. The official system of political consultation and deliberation in present-day

---

[129] This provision is followed in Art 25 of the AU's ACDEG.

[130] Cf Antonio F Perez, 'Democracy Clauses in the Americas: The Challenges of Venezuela's Withdrawal from the OAS' (2017) 33 Am U Int'l L Rev 391, 426–76.

[131] Beitz, *The Idea of Human Rights* 177–9.

China seems to follow the same Confucian culture in upholding the domination and leadership of the government.[132] As one commentator puts it, 'according to Chinese tradition, humanism is practised and great harmony pursued not by means of emphasizing the rights of individuals but their obligations, and not by means of the rule of law but the rule of virtue'.[133] The ultimate Confucian objective of harmony achieved through discipline and hierarchical obedience resonates well with Leninist notions of party discipline and the belief that legitimate governance can only be achieved by leaders of the nation.[134] In the era of social media and the Internet, China has consistently asserted the right to safeguard law and order and public morality against threats coming from cyberspace, including by setting up a 'Great Firewall' to prevent politically sensitive information from reaching Internet users in China, and has asserted 'national cyber sovereignty' whereby it has the right to decide how to develop and regulate the Internet and without interference by other States.

At the World Conference on Human Rights held in Vienna in June 1993, the head of the Chinese delegation opposed any one-size-fits-all perception of human rights and emphasized the priority of economic development because, in China's view, only when there is justice, order and stability in a nation State or society can its development as well as the well-being and basic human rights of its citizens be guaranteed.[135] China, in effect, uses a 'specificity' argument, invoking the specific Chinese situation due to its historical, social, economic and cultural conditions to support its contention for difference in the understanding and practice of human rights by each nation State.[136]

Singapore is another remarkable case study. It has excelled economically, its society is peaceful and its people are highly educated. Yet, several Western notions of human rights, such as the freedom of speech, are somewhat curtailed. Lee Kuan Yew, Singapore's founding father, invoked in support of Singapore's perspective of human rights the Confucian values of communitarianism or group orientation, harmony, consensus and deference to authority, which are different from those individualistic values cherished in the West.

---

[132] Baogang He, 'Confucian Speech and its Challenge to the Western Theory of Deliberative Democracy' in Price and Stremlau (eds), *Speech and Society in Turbulent Times* 59, *passim*.

[133] Xia Yong, 'Human Rights and Chinese Tradition' in Bauer et al (eds), *Human Rights: Chinese and Dutch Perspectives* 77, 79.

[134] Rogier Creemers, 'Cyber-Leninism: The Political Culture of the Chinese Internet' in Price and Stremlau (eds), *Speech and Society in Turbulent Times* 255, 257–60.

[135] Fried van Hoof, 'Asian Challenges to the Concept of Universality' in Bauer et al (eds), *Human Rights: Chinese and Dutch Perspectives* 1, 5.

[136] Eva Brems, *Human Rights: Universality and Diversity* (Martinus Nijhoff 2001) 50–51.

Lee's 'Asian values' stress good government or good governance that ensures order, justice under the rule of law and non-discrimination between peoples so as to achieve national stability, security and economic development. In relation to free speech, it must not get in the way of an elected government performing its mandate or undermine national harmony and social cohesion. This is understandable because Singapore is a small city State that depends on economic success as protection against instability, racial tension and deleterious external influences.[137]

At the 1993 Vienna Conference, the Foreign Minister of Singapore explained that Singapore does not consider human rights in the abstract, but justifies its human rights records by practical successes, as evident from Singaporeans' high standard of living, with freedom and dignity in an environment that is safe, healthy, clean and incorrupt – something not enjoyed by many of Singapore's 'well-meaning critics'. Singapore disagrees that all nations and societies can agree on the specific meanings of human rights, citing as examples the disagreement about the right to abortion, the right to a particular system of social security and the right to trials by jury, just to name a few. On the basis that every nation State must find its own way regarding human rights, Singapore is convinced that the ultimate test is whether the government succeeds in providing the order and stability necessary for development by exercising its government power to govern effectively and fairly. In Singapore's opinion, if political institutions fail to deliver a better life to their people, they will not last long and human rights will not be accepted if they are perceived as an obstacle to progress.[138]

Writing in 1999, Amartya Sen, the famous laureate of the Nobel Memorial Prize in Economic Sciences, disagrees with Lee Kuan Yew's hypothesis that non-democratic systems are better at bringing about economic development. Sen concedes that Lee is certainly correct that 'some disciplinarian States' (such as South Korea in 1999 and post-reform China) have had faster rates of economic growth than many 'less authoritarian ones'. Sen, however, criticizes Lee's hypothesis for being based on 'sporadic empiricism, drawing on very selective and limited information, rather than on any general statistical testing over the wide-ranging data that are available'. For example, Botswana, the nation State with the best record of economic growth in Africa and probably in the whole world, has been 'an oasis of democracy on that continent over the decades'. Sen argues that systematic empirical studies give no real

---

[137] Ibid 36–46; Cherian George, 'Neoliberal "Good Governance" in Lieu of Rights: Lee Kuan Yew's Singapore Experiment' in Price and Stremlau (eds), *Speech and Society in Turbulent Times* 114.

[138] Van Hoof, 'Asian Challenges to the Concept of Universality' 7–9; Yash Ghai, 'Human Rights and Governance: The Asian Debate' (1994) 15 Australian YBIL 1.

support to the claim that there is a general conflict between political rights and economic performance, as the directional linkage seems to depend on many other circumstances. Viewing all the comparative studies together, one may plausibly conclude that there is no clear relation between economic growth and democracy in either direction. Besides, there is no reason whatsoever to assume that any of the policies driving economic prosperity is inconsistent with greater democracy and has to be forcibly sustained by the elements of authoritarianism. By contrast, there is overwhelming evidence to show that it is a friendlier economic climate rather than a harsher political system that propels faster economic growth. In relation to the broader demands of economic development, including the need for economic and social security, there is a connection between political and civil rights to prompt a government to respond to the acute suffering of its people, on the one hand, and the prevention of major economic disasters, on the other.[139]

The case of South Korea, currently one of the Asian economic powerhouses, may also be cited in support of Sen's view. Its military regime during the 1970s and 1980s denounced human rights for the sake of national security and economic development. However, the eventual transformation of South Korea into a democratic society, with strong promotion and protection of human rights, has actually strengthened the national economy, without simultaneously undermining national security.[140] Sen's opinion can also find support from the example of Taiwan, which calls itself the Republic of China but which the People's Republic of China considers to be part of mainland China. Economically prosperous, Taiwan has been transformed from an authoritarian regime to a democratic one that voluntarily accepts and implements through its legislation human rights norms under international human rights treaties even though Taiwan is not party. Moreover, Taiwan's Confucian tradition has not hampered such positive transformation.[141]

Some commentators fear that those relying on the 'Asian values' exception to the universality of human rights may only use it as 'a phony basis for old-fashioned repression', whereas respect for human rights actually brings legitimacy and, therefore, stability in Asian society.[142] Nevertheless, Sen's view is disputed insofar as there is no empirical proof that the economy

---

[139] Amartya Sen, 'Democracy as a Universal Value' (1999) 10 Journal of Democracy 3, 6–7. See also id, *Development as Freedom* (OUP 1999); Neier, *The International Human Rights Movement* 89–92.

[140] Baik, *Emerging Regional Human Rights Systems in Asia* 57–8, 279–80.

[141] See Jerome A Cohen, William P Alford and Chang-Fa Lo (eds), *Taiwan and International Human Rights: A Story of Transformation* (Springer 2018).

[142] Michael Haas, *International Human Rights: A Comprehensive Introduction* (2nd edn, Routledge 2014) 516. Cf Joanne Bauer and Daniel A Bell (eds), *The East Asian*

of a nation State where human rights are respected will necessarily grow faster than that of a State where the rights are not respected.[143] Yet, this begs a question, are human rights measured in terms of economic prosperity alone? Cannot people be happy when their human rights are upheld although they remain dirt poor?

On the whole, it must be conceded that there is no 'one-size-fits-all' democratic system of government. Challenging a State that does not currently embrace Western liberal democracy is an uphill task for anyone representing a State that is materialistically worse off than the challenged State. The burden of proof should be reversed to the challenger to substantiate that by pursuing Western liberal democracy and its human rights values the challenged State can substantially enhance its national prosperity and other things it holds dear, at no risk of upheavals and unreasonable extra cost to it.

5.   ISLAM AND HUMAN RIGHTS

A major challenge for IHRL is to ensure that while recognizing diversity in religions there is a solid safeguard against human rights violations committed in the name of religion or using a religious logic.[144]

Christianity is currently the world's largest religion with approximately 2.42 billion followers in mid 2015. Islam is the world's second-largest religion, with around 1.703 billion Muslims living mainly in the Middle East, South Asia, Africa and three nation States in South East Asia. Although Hindus form the world's third-largest population, numbering roughly 984.5 million, Hindus live mainly in India. The number of about 520 million Buddhists makes Buddhism the world's fourth-largest religion.[145] While there are clashes between Buddhists and non-Buddhists in some parts of the world, this is normally not due to a religious divide but because of other factors, especially nationalism. For example, the controversy about the relations between some Buddhists and the ethnic Rohingya Muslims in Myanmar is caused by the former considering the latter 'Bengalis' who are not an indigenous ethnic group but illegal immigrants unjustifiably settled in Myanmar.

Islam is in the news the most often for its purported clash with Western values, including in the realm of human rights. Muslim-majority States have

---

Challenge for Human Rights (CUP 1999) Part I (Critical Perspectives on the 'Asian Values' Debate).

[143] Posner, *Twilight of Human Rights Law* 145–6.

[144] Roja Fazaeli, 'Human Rights and Religion' in Goodhart (ed.), *Human Rights: Politics and Practice* 163, 179.

[145] These statistics are from 'Christianity 2015: Religious Diversity and Personal Contact' (2015) 39 International Bulletin of Missionary Research 28, 29.

also organized themselves into the Organisation of Islamic Cooperation (OIC) to play active roles in global diplomacy and promote their political, and some-times religious, goals. Therefore, Islam naturally merits more attention than the other non-Christian religions in this regard.

The following narrative explains something about Islam:

> The religion of Islam was founded in the 7th century of the Christian era and spread rapidly from Arabia through the Middle East and westwards to North Africa. Arabic became the common literary language for a succession of empires stretching from Spain to India.
>
> Mathematics can be useful to a practising Muslim. Astronomy is of value in computing the Islamic calendar and in determining the proper times for prayer throughout the day. Geography can be put to work in establishing the *qibla*, the direction in which the faithful pray towards Mecca.
>
> As well as their specifically religious uses, the mathematical sciences were studied much more broadly in medieval Islam. The texts of ancient Greece were translated and developed and new approaches created. For several hundred years Islam was the world's most dynamic and innovative mathematical culture.

The above passages are not part of propaganda by faithful Muslims to glorify Islam. They appear in an exhibit under the heading 'The Islamic World' at the University of Oxford's Museum of the History of Science. The nearby exhibits of astrolabes explain that astrolabes are 'the most celebrated of all mathematical instruments', combining 'ingenuity and beauty, with a wide range of uses in time-telling, astronomy, astrology and surveying'. Originating in ancient Greece, astrolabes were developed by medieval Islamic scholars who made their use 'universal rather than restricted to particular latitudes'.

Islamic cultures must be considered one of the major civilizations of the world; otherwise, Muslims could not have invented so many scientific advances unbeknown to the ancient world, to be emulated by medieval Europe and beyond.

The normative foundations and development of Islamic law, or Sharia (meaning 'the right way or path to follow') date back to the seventh century AD. The Quran, containing 114 chapters (*surah*) divided into 6,219 verses, is understood to be the revelation of God to Mohammad, the prophet of God who conveyed God's message to his people. *Sunna* or *sunnah* denotes what the Prophet said, did, approved and disapproved of, explicitly or implicitly, which constitutes inspired prophetic guidance to give additional insight into the Quran and address those issues not covered expressly or impliedly by the Quran. The narrations of *sunna* were reported in *hadith*.[146] A *hadith* has

---

[146] Louay Fatoohi, 'The Differences between "Sunna" and "Hadith"', *Qur'anic Studies* (17 Apr 2013) http://www.quranicstudies.com/prophet-muhammad/the

two parts: the chain of transmitters (*isnad*) and the text of what the Prophet reportedly said (*matn*). The chain of transmitters is a list of all the people who conveyed the Prophet's statements across generations before the *hadith* was written down in a compiled source, many of them in the mid nineteenth century, or more than two centuries after the Prophet's demise. Subsequent generations of Muslim jurists developed methods to authenticate the *hadith*, including by a historical analysis of each member of the chain of transmission and an assessment of his reputation for truthfulness, or by analysing the textual content and its implications on other authoritative texts from the Quran or other established *hadith* sources. Inevitably, there are disputes whether some statements forming part of the *hadith* are authentically what the Prophet said, did or decided.[147] In the context of Islamic legal system, pre-modern Muslim jurists developed legal doctrines or Islamic jurisprudence of Sharia (*fiqh*) as the temporal interpretation of Islamic law, bringing together all the rules sys-temized by the end of the fifth century after the start of the Islamic calendar.

Islam is rather unique among all religions in that as the Prophet Mohammad was not just a prophet and teacher but also a government administrator, he recognized the link between religion and politics.[148]

There are now four Sunni legal schools and three Shiite schools.[149] Therefore, there is 'extensive legal pluralism', with 'multiple legal traditions' within Islamic law,[150] leaving Islamic society with no uniform understanding of Islamic law. Although the Quran is the final word of Allah or God, this may be subject to interpretation by *sunna* or Islamic traditions, with a selected group of *mufti* or Islamic experts being entrusted with such interpretation.[151] The schools of jurisprudence reflect sensitivity to the diverging cultures of the different geographical areas. The first Sunni school prevails in Turkey, Syria, Lebanon, Jordan, India, Pakistan, Afghanistan, Iraq and Libya; the second prevails in North Africa, West Africa and Kuwait; the third in southern Egypt,

---

-differences-between-sunna-and-hadith/, accessed 8 Dec 2018; Ahmed M El Demey, *The Arab Charter of Human Rights: A Voice for Sharia in the Modern World* (Council on International Law and Politics 2015) 39–41, 47.

[147] Anver M Emon, 'Shar'ia and the Modern State' in Anver M Emon, Mark Ellis and Benjamin Glahn (eds), *Islamic Law and International Human Rights Law* (OUP 2012) 52, 55–6.

[148] Carey et al, *The Politics of Human Rights* 18. See also Karen Armstrong, *Muhammad: A Biography of the Prophet* (Weidenfeld & Nicolson 2001) 211–49.

[149] Emon, 'Shar'ia and the Modern State' 56–60.

[150] Ibid 80.

[151] Baderin, *International Human Rights and Islamic Law* 32–38; Hosseinioun, *The Human Rights Turn and the Paradox of Progress in the Middle East* 22–24; Eli Grossman, 'The Human Dimension of Shari'a Law' (2018) 50 NYU J Int'l L & Pol 1021, 1023–4.

southern Arabia, East Africa, Indonesia and Malaysia; and the fourth in Saudi Arabia and Qatar. One Shiite school of jurisprudence prevails in Iran and southern Iraq, whereas another prevails in Oman and parts of North Africa, and the other in Yemen.[152]

The systems of government in Muslim-majority States vary from one to another. For instance, Bahrain and Morocco have constitutional monarchies; Iran is a Shiite Islamic republic; Saudi Arabia is a Sunni Islamic republic; whereas Malaysia comprises 13 federal states and three federal territories, some of which adopt different approaches to the application of Sharia. Lebanon, a member of the OIC and the League of Arab States, is a multi-confessional State where 18 officially recognized religious sects participate in Lebanon's overall political and constitutional structure.[153] Muslim-majority States also differ in the position that Sharia is given in their respective domestic legal systems. The national constitutions of Lebanon and Turkey do not accord Sharia a privileged position. Sharia is constitutionally acknowledged but with limited constitutional consequences in Algeria, Egypt, Jordan and Yemen. However, Sharia is acknowledged with strong constitutional consequences in the constitutions of Iran, Pakistan and Saudi Arabia. These examples reveal that there can be no generalization of the role of Sharia among Muslim-majority States.[154]

With the failure of the attempt by the OIC in 1981 to set up an Islamic Court of Justice, to be situated in Kuwait, there is no single authoritative judicial body to interpret Islamic law in a uniform way.[155]

Interpretation of Sharia can be traditionalistic or evolutionary in its approach. Traditionalists tenaciously adhere to the classical interpretation of Sharia as laid down in the tenth century in the legal treatises of the established schools of Islamic jurisprudence. By contrast, evolutionists endeavour to make the classical jurisprudence and methods of Islamic law relevant to contemporary times, convinced of the continual evolution of Islamic law to take modern developments into account. The latter, also known as Islamic liberals or moderates, adopt the 'back and forward looking approach' in interpreting Sharia

---

[152] Baderin, *International Human Rights and Islamic Law* 37–8. Cf M Cherif Bassiouni, *The Shari'a and Islamic Criminal Justice in Time of War and Peace* (CUP 2014) chs 1–3; Joshua Castellino and Kathleen A Cavanaugh, *Minority Rights in the Middle East* (OUP 2013) 29–43 (on the 'plural readings' of Islam among Muslims).

[153] Abiad, *Sharia, Muslim States and International Human Rights Treaty Obligations* xx.

[154] Ibid 34–57.

[155] Baderin, *International Human Rights and Islamic Law* 228. See also Muhammad Khalid Masud, 'Clearing Ground: Commentary to Shar'ia and the Modern State' in Emon et al (eds), *Islamic Law and International Human Rights Law* 104.

plus a contextual application of classical Islamic jurisprudence.[156] Sharia as 'liberally' interpreted treats Islam and human rights as inherently compatible in the belief that the rights recognized in Islam pre-date modern human rights norms; or treats human rights not specifically mentioned in or deriving from Sharia as existing in tandem with Sharia.[157]

Turkey, a Muslim-majority State, has separated religion from the State since 3 March 1924 when the caliphate was officially abolished and replaced by the establishment of Turkey as a constitutionally secular State. Sharia has been replaced ever since by a European civil code of law. In *Refah Partisi (the Welfare Party) and Others v Turkey*, the Grand Chamber of the European Court of Human Rights unanimously upholds the Turkish Constitutional Court's dissolution of the political party named Refah on the grounds that it was a centre of activities contrary to the principles of secularism under the Turkish Constitution. The Grand Chamber finds no violation of the freedom of association under Article 11 of the ECHR to which Turkey is party. It reasons, inter alia, that the fact that Refah's model of a State and society organized according to Islamic Sharia is incompatible with the fundamental principles of democracy, since principles such as pluralism in the political sphere and the constant evolution of public freedoms have no place in Sharia and a regime based on Sharia clearly diverges from ECHR values. Therefore, rules the Grand Chamber, ECHR Contracting States may oppose political movements based on religious fundamentalism in the light of their historical experience and, taking into account the importance of the principle of secularism in Turkey, the Turkish Constitutional Court was justified in holding that Refah's policy of establishing Sharia was incompatible with democracy.[158]

The most significant human rights instruments in the Islamic world are the Universal Islamic Declaration of Human Rights (UIDHR)[159] adopted in September 1981 by the London-based Islamic Council of Europe, set up in 1973 as a forum for Islamic statesmen and scholars to discuss contemporary issues facing Muslims living in the West; the Cairo Declaration on Human

---

[156] Baderin, *International Human Rights and Islamic Law* 44.

[157] Fazaeli, 'Human Rights and Religion' 173. Cf Abdullah Saeed, *Human Rights and Islam: An Introduction to Key Debates between Islamic Law and International Human Rights Law* (Edward Elgar Publishing 2018). For Sharia's roles in Western societies, see Rex Ahdar and Nicholas Aroney (eds), *Shari'a in the West* (OUP 2010). For an Islamic legal history in Brunei, Burma (now Myanmar), Indonesia, Malaysia, Philippines and Singapore, see MB Hooker, *Islamic Law in South-East Asia* (OUP 1984).

[158] (2003) 37 EHRR 1, nos 41340/98, 41342/98, 41343/98 and 41344/98 (Judgment of 13 Feb 2003).

[159] https://www.lawschool.cornell.edu/womenandjustice/upload/League-of-Arab -States-Universal-Islamic-Declaration-of-Human-Rights.pdf, accessed 12 Jan 2019.

Rights in Islam[160] adopted in August 1990 by the OIC; and the Arab Charter on Human Rights initially drafted by the Arab League in 1994 as revised and adopted in 2004.[161] It is uncertain whether they are meant to replace or supplement human rights norms enshrined in other international human rights instruments as Sharia is often referred to as the sole source for interpreting human rights.[162] For example, the original and authentic Arabic version of Article III(a) of the UIDHR on the equality of all persons before the law reads 'equality under Sharia',[163] and its Article XXIII discriminates between Muslims and non-Muslims by recognizing only the right of every Muslim to freely move in and out of any Muslim country.

6.   HUMAN RIGHTS DIPLOMACY AMID VARYING PERSPECTIVES

Irrespective of where human rights originate from, universalism of human rights can be considered from three perspectives. First, according to 'foundational universalism' it is undisputed that all human beings are entitled to human rights because of their status as human beings. Secondly, questions may be raised from a conceptual perspective as to whether human rights do share the same constitutive elements in all regions of the world and which rights are universally applicable. Thirdly, assuming that a given human rights norm is universally applicable, a question is whether its content is the same everywhere. For example, does the right not to be subjected to inhuman or degrading treatment or punishment or the right to life presuppose that exactly the same actions (such as corporal punishment meted out in Muslim-majority States) are proscribed with regard to all peoples in the world or whether there are exceptions varying from one community/individual to another?[164] According to this view, 'the cultural, philosophical or geographical origin of a given human rights standard is substantially irrelevant, provided that such a standard is [voluntarily and] spontaneously accepted everywhere'.[165] Universalism or universality of human rights is a goal, not a justification, for respect for international human rights norms although a convergence of different models and origins of human rights is to be welcomed.[166]

---

[160]   UN Doc A/CONF.157/PC/62/Add.18 (1993).

[161]   (2005) 12 Int'l Hum Rts Rep 893.

[162]   SI Strong, *Transforming Religious Liberties: A New Theory of Religious Rights for National and International Legal Systems* (CUP 2018) 20–3.

[163]   Castellino and Cavanaugh, *Minority Rights in the Middle East* 76–7.

[164]   Lenzerini, *The Culturalization of Human Rights Law* 31–2, 242.

[165]   Ibid 238.

[166]   Ibid 245–8.

This chapter undertakes a study of the theories and diplomatic history of universalism of human rights. It leaves aside other relevant sectoral debates such as feminist perspectives on human rights,[167] a separate analysis of which would occupy too much space for a book of this size and which are, in any event, subsumed under the theories covered by this chapter.

Allegations of double standards and discriminatory targeting of certain States for human rights censures must be taken seriously as they undercut the influence to induce the targeted State to comply with their human rights obligations.[168] However, they do not absolve these States from responsibility under IHRL. International tribunals have rejected the defence that the persons meting out criminal justice have also committed the same or similar crimes (*tu quoque*).[169] They have also rejected the argument that unless all egregious human rights abusers are held accountable, none should be selected or singled out for punishment.[170] There may be various reasons, including geo-strategic and international political ones, why some of these abusers remain unpunished, but this is no excuse not to punish those human rights abusers if and when an opportunity does arise.[171] The same logic applies to compliance with and enforcement of IHRL.

Criticisms of the purported universalism of human rights could possibly be refuted if the bases for the accusation concerning hypocrisy, double standards, exceptionalism and others that undermine the credibility of human rights universalism can be dismantled to a certain extent. This may be achieved by finding the right answers to the following questions: why and against whom is a human rights issue raised? What is the objective of raising the issue? How is the issue raised? By whom is the issue to be raised? And when is the opportune moment to raise the issue?

---

[167] Karen Engle, 'International Human Rights and Feminism: When Discourses Meet' (1992) 13 Michigan JIL 517; Gayle Binion, 'Human Rights: A Feminist Perspective' (1995) 17 Hum Rts Quarterly 509; Julie Peters and Andrea Wolper (eds), *Women's Rights, Human Rights: International Feminist Perspective* (Routledge 1995).

[168] Ryan Goodman and Derek Jinks, *Socializing States: Promoting Human Rights through International Law* (OUP 2013) 132.

[169] *In re Weizsaecker and Others*, US Military Tribunal, Nuremberg, 14 Apr 1949 (1949) 16 Ann Dig 344, 348; *Prosecutor v Zoran Kupreskic and Others* (Judgment) IT-95-16-T, International Criminal Tribunal for the former Yugoslavia Trial Chamber II (14 Jan 2000) §§ 23, 125, 162, 511, 513, 515–24, 527–35, 765.

[170] *Prosecutor v Zejnil Delalic, Zdravko Mucic, Hazim Delic and Esad Landzo* (Judgment) IT-96-21-A, International Criminal Tribunal for the former Yugoslavia Appeal Chamber (20 Feb 2001) §618.

[171] *Prosecutor v Kanyabashi* (Decision on Defence Motion on Jurisdiction) ICTR-96-15-T, International Criminal Tribunal for Rwanda Trial Chamber II (18 June 1997) §36.

Why and against whom is a human rights issue raised? The reason a foreign State or an international organization raises the issue must be sound and justifiable. Human rights in every nation State need constant monitoring for abuses. This need increases in States where the abuses are likely to take place, are taking place or have taken place. According to the ICJ in *Barcelona Traction*, a State owes the obligations towards the international community as a whole because the importance of the rights involved means that all States have a legal interest in their protection. These so-called obligations *erga omnes* derive, for example, in contemporary international law, from the outlawing of acts of genocide, as also from the principles and rules concerning the basic rights of the human person, including protection from slavery and racial discrimination.[172] With respect to human rights treaties, the ICJ in *Questions relating to the Obligation to Prosecute or Extradite (Belgium v Senegal)* interprets the object and purpose of the 1984 Convention against Torture and Other Cruel, Inhuman or Degrading Treatment or Punishment[173] 'to make more effective the struggle against torture ... throughout the world' as giving rise to 'obligations *erga omnes partes*', whereby each State Party has a 'common interest' in complying with such obligations and, consequently, each State Party is entitled to make a claim concerning the cessation of an alleged breach by another State Party.[174] International human rights treaties to which the targeted State is party may also have an object and purpose that gives rise to obligations *erga omnes partes* allowing any other State Party to the same treaties to require the targeted State to comply with the treaties' obligations.

What is the objective of raising the issue with the targeted State? The foreign State or international organization should have a purely altruistic motive in raising the issue; otherwise, it will meet strong opposition from the targeted State. Some States – for example China, Cuba, Iran, Laos and Vietnam – do not have the Western democratic system of government for historical reasons and it is for the rest of the international community to interact with them not by regime change but by finding common ground in human rights universalism and through their voluntary participation in international human rights treaties.

One apparently altruistic measure is the US Government's implementation of the Trafficking Victims Protection Act of 2000[175] to end modern-day slavery and human trafficking around the world. The US Department of State is required to submit annual trafficking in persons reports cataloguing and rating each State's efforts and success rates in combating human trafficking.

---

[172] *Barcelona Traction, Light and Power Company Limited (Belgium v Spain)* Second Phase [1970] ICJ Rep 3, 32 [33]–[34].

[173] 1465 UNTS 85.

[174] [2012] ICJ Rep 422, 449–50 [67]–[70].

[175] 22 U.S.C. 78.

States placed in Tier 1 are considered up to the international standard expected of them. Those in Tier 2 are the ones trying their best and with increasing success rates in this matter. Those in Tier 3 are the worst of all in this field and face possible US sanctions, such as the withholding of non-trade-related, non-humanitarian assistance like the US ban on their participation in international military education and training, foreign military financing and foreign military sales programmes run by the US Government. The impact of the annual reports and the classification of States into the three tiers extends beyond the aforesaid US sanctions. Goods imported into the USA from States in Tier 3 suffer bad marketing prospects because a large number of US consumers have the impression that the goods are made by victims of human trafficking. This kind of measure as adopted by the US Government is acceptable insofar as the US Government also objectively evaluates its own performance as regards human trafficking. For example, the 2019 report admits, inter alia, that, in the USA, human traffickers prey upon children in the foster care system and a large number of victims of child sex trafficking were at one time in the foster care system.[176]

The *context* in which a human rights issue is raised is also crucial. For example, Israel is perennially criticized for its treatment of Palestinians. Such criticisms would be more credible if they were isolated from the overarching Israeli–Palestinian conflicts and pinpointed precisely the human rights norms purportedly violated by Israel.

How is the human rights issue raised? Governments at times argue that external pressure exerted on them to improve human rights of persons within their respective territories, jurisdiction or effective control amounts to intervention or interference in their internal affairs. The ICJ's judgment in *Nicaragua v USA* explains that the principle of non-intervention, which represents customary international law, 'involves the right of every sovereign State to conduct its affairs without outside interference' because, between independent States, respect for territorial sovereignty is an essential foundation of international relations and international law requires political integrity also to be respected.[177] This principle of non-intervention forbids all States or groups of States from intervening directly or indirectly in internal or external affairs of other States. A prohibited intervention must accordingly be one bearing on matters in which each State is permitted, by the principle of State sovereignty, to decide freely, such as the choice of a political, economic, social and cultural system and the formulation of foreign policy. Intervention

---

[176] US Dept of State, *2019 Trafficking in Persons Report* (Dept of State 2019) 4.

[177] *Military and Paramilitary Activities in and against Nicaragua (Nicaragua v The United States of America)*, Merits, Judgment [1986] ICJ Rep 14, 106 [202].

is 'wrongful when it uses methods of coercion in regard to such choices, which must remain free ones'.[178] The ICJ backs up its conclusion by referring to the Declaration on Principles of International Law concerning Friendly Relations and Cooperation among States in accordance with the Charter of the United Nations, adopted by the UNGA without a vote in October 1970.[179]

The Declaration proclaims, inter alia, the principle concerning the duty not to intervene in matters within the domestic jurisdiction of any State, in accordance with the UN Charter, and elucidates this principle as prohibiting any State or group of States from intervening, directly or indirectly, for any reason whatever, in the internal or external affairs of any other State, as well as prohibiting any State from using or encouraging the use of economic political or any other type of measures 'to coerce another State in order to obtain from it the subordination of the exercise of its sovereign rights and to secure from it advantages of any kind'. However, the Declaration also stipulates the duty of States to cooperate with one another in accordance with the UN Charter, which includes 'the promotion of universal respect for, and observance of, human rights and fundamental freedoms for all and in the elimination of all forms of racial discrimination and all forms of religious intolerance'. The principle of sovereign equality of States means equal rights and duties and equal membership of the international community, including the duty to comply fully and in good faith with its international obligations and to live in peace with other States.

Therefore, asking or even putting pressure on a foreign government to improve its human rights record is not prohibited by international law insofar as there is no coercion exerted upon the government 'in order to obtain from it the subordination of the exercise of its sovereign rights and to secure from it advantages of any kind'. Since every sovereign State is equally bound to comply in good faith with its international human rights obligations, prompting it to do so does not violate the principle of non-interference, especially if the method(s) and manner of persuasion is not 'coercive'.

Talking points prepared even by geniuses to be used at bilateral or multilateral meetings tend to sound curt and/or assertive due to the need for them to be concise and to the point. Things likely get worse when talking points on human rights are delivered by persons such as heads of government or politicians who do not fully understand the nuances of the message to be conveyed to a foreign government, thereby making it sound like an ultimatum or unacceptable condescension. A better alternative would be for the targeted State and its foreign counterpart to engage in exchange of experiences and best practices in the

---

[178] Ibid 107–8 [205].
[179] A/RES/25/2625 (24 Oct 1970).

human rights field as well as reciprocal 'peer review' of human rights records. Exchange visits to learn more about each other's way of life and culture also help, provided that the venues to be visited are not so conspicuously pre-arranged to indoctrinate the foreign visiting party that the visitor will doubt the genuineness of what it sees and the sincerity of the inviting host.

By whom is the human rights issue to be raised? The party raising it should not be one of those who sowed the seeds of the root cause of the human rights problem faced by the targeted State. For instance, the targeted State would be exasperated and insulted if its former colonial master, which relocated an ethnic group from elsewhere in the territory of the targeted State under the then colonial master's divide-and-rule policy, now took the lead in protecting that ethnic group's human rights. This is like the former colonial State rubbing salt into the targeted State's old wound. Imagine also how the targeted State would react to a foreign government that used to support regime change by non-democratic means in the targeted State now demanding that the targeted State respects democracy, the rule of law and their consequential human rights.

In a world where no nation State is ideal or perfect, it is impossible to follow the old adage 'let him who without sin cast the first stone'. Instead, a rule of thumb in choosing a foreign State or government to interact with the targeted State on human rights matters is that neither of these States has an old score to settle with the other. Nevertheless, this consideration must be weighed against another one – whether the foreign State or government in question has the leverage to effectuate human rights betterment in the targeted State? If the foreign State or government with an old score to settle with the targeted State happens to be the only one that can make the targeted State uphold human rights, so be it.

When is the opportune moment to raise human rights issues? States may raise human rights issues during their bilateral or multilateral consultations, as long as an agenda relating to human rights can be agreed, preferably without compulsion, by the States concerned. For instance, Australia is one of the few States that has a human rights dialogue with Laos, with frank and constructive discussions on an extensive range of human rights issues, including engagement with international human rights mechanisms, protection and discrimination issues, access to justice and cases of concern, such as freedom of religion or belief, and the protection of the rights of persons with disability and people from culturally and linguistically diverse groups. Australia and Laos have also launched the 2017–21 Human Rights Technical Cooperation Programme for Australia to provide practical support to assist Laos in meeting its international human rights obligations. It is typical at the annual EU–Laos Human Rights Dialogue for the EU to offer its assistance to Laos in implementing the recommendations made to Laos by the bodies monitoring the implementation of the human rights treaties to which Laos is party and by the Human Rights Council.

The EU also encourages Laos to become party to international human rights treaties to which Laos is not yet party, and to issue invitations to UN special rapporteurs to visit Laos. For its part, the US Government raises human rights issues as one item on the agenda of its annual Comprehensive Dialogue with Laos.

Multilaterally, routine schedules for human rights scrutiny adopted by the UN Human Rights Council, human rights treaty bodies and so forth can help assuage unease of States subjected to scrutiny as they are not likely to feel specifically targeted or subjected to bias. For example, even after the withdrawal of its membership of the Human Rights Council in 2018, the USA still faces a routine universal periodic review in the Human Rights Council in the year 2020.

Notwithstanding the foregoing, when a State is adversely affected by a human rights violation in another State, the former may raise the issue when and where it considers appropriate. This occurs, for instance, when State A bears the brunt of a mass influx into its territory of refugees fleeing persecution and other gross human rights violations in State B. State A can raise the issue directly with State B and, where appropriate, in multilateral forums at the moment State A deems necessary, in the specific context of demanding State B to end the cause of the mass influx that undermines State A's national interests.

Furthermore, there are situations where a body duly established by an international organization with a human rights mandate makes a recommendation for an international sanction against a government or individuals for having abused human rights. If and when the competent international organization, such as the UN Security Council, fails to discharge its mandate in response to the recommendation due to some political reason, a State may unilaterally act upon the recommendation to impose sanctions against the government or individuals if it is in a position to do so.

3. United Nations human rights system: clash of politics, idealism and law

The United Nations, comprising almost 200 Member States, is the world's most universal multilateral diplomacy forum where all groups of States interact. It has six principal organs. The General Assembly (UNGA) comprises all Member States. The Security Council (UNSC) has five permanent members (China, France, Russia, UK and USA) and ten non-permanent members elected by the UNGA for a two-year term. The Economic and Social Council (ECOSOC) has 54 Member States elected by the UNGA for a three-year term. The International Court of Justice (ICJ) has 15 judges elected simultaneously by the UNGA and the UNSC for a nine-year term. The UN Secretariat is headed by the Secretary-General, the chief administrative UN officer appointed for a five-year term by the UNGA upon the UNSC's recommendation. The other principal organ, the Trusteeship Council, has suspended its operations since 1 November 1994, a month after the independence of Palau, the last remaining UN trust territory.

1. THE UN CHARTER: NEW DAWN OR FALSE HOPE?

The UN was founded on 24 October 1945 in response to the failure of the League of Nations to secure world peace after the First World War, culminating in the Second World War. The large-scale, systematic and heinous human rights violations before and during the Second World War, especially by the Nazis, also prompted the international community to seek a new dawn for human rights.

The UN Charter[1] provides in Article 55(c), under Chapter IX: International Economic and Social Co-operation, that the UN shall promote 'universal respect for, and observance of, human rights and fundamental freedoms for all without distinction as to race, sex, language or religion'. Article 56 adds that all UN members pledge themselves to take joint and separate action in cooperation with the UN for the achievement of the purposes set forth in Article 55.

---

[1] 1 UNTS XVI.

However, Article 2(1) of the Charter – under Chapter I: Purposes and Principles – affirms that the UN is based on the principle of the sovereign equality of all its members. Article 2(7) stipulates that nothing in the Charter shall authorize the UN 'to intervene in matters which are essentially within the domestic jurisdiction of any State or shall require the Members to submit such matters to settlement under the present Charter', except where the UNSC applies enforcement measures under Chapter VII of the Charter against threats to the peace, breaches of the peace and acts of aggression.

The provision of Article 2(7) derives from a similar provision in the eighth paragraph of Article 15 of the 1919 Covenant of the League of Nations,[2] which excludes from the competence of the Council of the League of Nations any dispute arising out of 'a matter which by international law is solely within the domestic jurisdiction' of the party challenging the League's competence to take up the dispute. The Permanent Court of International Justice (PCIJ), the forerunner of the ICJ, opined in *Tunis–Morocco Nationality Decrees* that although the matters referred to in Article 15(8) of the League Covenant might very closely concern the interests of more than one State, they were not, in principle, regulated by international law and were, therefore, left to each State as the sole judge. The PCIJ added that this was an essentially relative question and depended upon the development of international relations. As international law stood in 1923, questions of nationality at issue in *Tunis–Morocco Nationality Decrees* were in principle within this reserved domain of each State, subject to international legal obligations the State might have undertaken towards other States.[3]

The operation of Article 2(7) of the UN Charter has been increasingly limited in practice, especially in relation to human rights.[4] For example, starting from 1962 until the end of apartheid in South Africa in 1993, UN organs adopted a series of resolutions to allow intervention to end the apartheid policy, law and practice in South Africa.[5] Since the adoption by the African Union (AU) in 2002 of the Protocol Relating to the Establishment of the AU's Peace and Security Council (PSC),[6] the PSC as the standing organ of the

---

[2]   (1919) 13 AJIL Supp 128.

[3]   *Advisory Opinion No 4, Nationality Decrees Issued in Tunis and Morocco (French Zone) on 8 November 1921* [1923] PCIJ (ser B) No 4 (7 Feb 1923) 4, 23–4 [39]–[41].

[4]   Kristen Walker, 'An Exploration of Article 2(7) of the United Nations Charter as an Embodiment of the Public/Private Distinction in International Law' (1993) 26 NYU J Int'l L & Politics 173, 174–81.

[5]   Eg UNGA Resolution 1761 of 6 Nov 1962; UNGA Resolution 2624 (XX) of 13 Oct 1970 and Resolution 2671 (XXV) of 8 Dec 1970; UNSC Resolution 591 (1986) of 28 Nov 1986.

[6]   http://www.peaceau.org/uploads/psc-protocol-en.pdf, accessed 14 Dec 2018.

AU may recommend to the Assembly of Heads of State and Government of the AU to intervene in an AU Member State in respect of grave circumstances, namely war crimes, genocide and crimes against humanity, which are the most serious violations of human rights. As of this writing, the Protocol is binding on 52 AU Member States. The three AU Member States that are not party to the Protocol are Cabo Verde, DR Congo and South Sudan.

Human rights limit the sovereignty of States in the sense that their violation entails State responsibility at the international level and no excuse against external interference is permitted in case of such violation.[7] Therefore, no State can now legitimately maintain that an abuse of human rights of individuals within its territory, jurisdiction or effective control is a matter essentially within its domestic jurisdiction and is not subject to international human rights law (IHRL). It does not matter whether the victim of the human rights abuse is the State's own citizen or a foreign national present within its territory.[8]

By recognizing that human rights might be connected to international peace and security, the UN makes human rights a formal part of international relations and international politics.[9] In discharging its mandate under the UN Charter, the UNSC is implicated wherever human rights violations may lead to threats to, or breaches of, international peace and security; commission of international crimes, especially crimes proscribed under peremptory norms of international law (*jus cogens*); massive refugee outflows or internal displacements; potential humanitarian disasters and other comparable catastrophes.[10] Unfortunately, as Chapter 6 will show, the UNSC has not discharged this mandate satisfactorily, succumbing to international politics and the veto of some UNSC permanent members to shield their allies from sanctions against human rights violations.

The ICJ, as the principal dispute settlement organ of the UN, has taken up cases relating to human rights on various occasions. There were 25 cases submitted to the ICJ relating to IHRL between 1991 and 2010.[11] The ICJ's jurisprudence in the IHRL field covers a variety of important issues, including

---

[7]   John Rawls, *The Law of Peoples* (2nd edn, Harvard University Press 1999) 79; Joseph Raz, 'Human Rights without Foundations' in Samantha Besson and John Tasioulas (eds), *The Philosophy of International Law* (OUP 2010) 328–9.

[8]   Hurst Hannum, 'Reinvigorating Human Rights for the Twenty-First Century' (2016) 16 Hum Rts L Rev 409, 410.

[9]   Cf David P Forsythe, *Human Rights in International Relations* (4th edn, CUP 2018) 49.

[10]   Bertrand G Ramcharan, *The Law, Policy and Politics of the UN Human Rights Council* (Brill 2015) 68.

[11]   Gentian Zyberi, 'Human Rights in the International Court of Justice' in Mashood A Baderin and Manisuli Ssenyonjo (eds), *International Human Rights Law: Six Decades after the UDHR and Beyond* (Ashgate 2010) 303–4.

the internationalization of human rights; formulation of certain fundamental principles of IHRL; characterization of the right of peoples to self-determination as a right *erga omnes*; interpretation of the prohibition of genocide as including an obligation to prevent genocide; clarifications on the right to asylum, diplomatic and consular protection, and protection of human rights rapporteurs in order for them to fulfil their duty when in the service of the UN; applicability of international human rights instruments in situations of armed conflict; clarifications on the issue of individual criminal responsibility for serious crimes of international concern; extraterritorial application of IHRL treaties; and some significant pronouncements on environmental issues as part of human rights.[12]

In the past, ECOSOC had primary responsibility for human rights matters. Article 62 of the UN Charter entrusts ECOSOC with making or initiating studies and reports with respect to international economic, social, cultural, educational, health and related matters and ECOSOC may make recommendations with respect to any such matters to the UNGA, to UN Member States and to the specialized agencies concerned. It may make recommendations for the purpose of promoting respect for, and observance of, human rights and fundamental freedoms for all. It may prepare draft conventions for submission to the UNGA, as well as convening international conferences on matters falling within its competence. Pursuant to Article 68 of the Charter, ECOSOC shall set up commissions in economic and social fields and for the promotion of human rights and such other commissions as may be required for the performance of its functions.

ECOSOC set up the UN Commission on Human Rights in 1946 as its functional ancillary body on human rights. The membership of the Commission kept expanding from 18 mostly Western States in 1946 to 21 in 1962, 32 in 1967, 43 in 1980 and 54, from all geographical regions, in 1993. In its early years, the Commission's primary focus was on human rights standard setting and its achievements included the drafting of the 1948 Universal Declaration of Human Rights (UDHR), the 1966 International Covenant on Civil and Political Rights (ICCPR)[13] and the 1966 International Covenant on Economic, Social and Cultural Rights (ICESCR).[14] From 1967, ECOSOC authorized the Commission to deal with human rights violations. The Commission discharged

---

[12] Ibid 289; Ralph Wilde, 'Human Rights beyond Borders at the World Court: The Significance of the International Court of Justice's Jurisprudence on Extraterritorial Application of International Human Rights Law Treaties' in Wagner Menezes (ed.), *Bulletin of the Brazilian Society of International Law – Centenary Commemorative Edition* (Arraes Editores 2017) 1035.

[13] 999 UNTS 171.

[14] 993 UNTS 3.

this new mandate by, inter alia, monitoring and investigating – through a confidential complaints procedure open to States, NGOs and individuals – human rights violations in individual States even without their permission and cooperation, culminating in annual public debates among States on country-specific human rights violations. The Commission, meeting in regular sessions for six weeks each year, also created thematic mandates to examine human rights issues across a number of States/regions or within a specific State.[15]

The human rights idealism and international law enshrined in the UN Charter collided head on with international politics conducted through multilateral diplomacy exploiting loopholes in ECOSOC's Human Rights Commission. A lack of membership criteria apart from equitable geographical representation[16] allowed States with dubious human rights reputations to be elected members of the Commission thanks to their political alliances. These States shielded themselves from the Commission's censure as well as returned the favour to their political allies by taking no action on alleged human rights violations by the latter. Country-specific issues were often biased and selective, reflecting the political and partisan purposes of some of the States that were members of the Commission. The Commission had insufficient time and resources allocated to it to deal with human rights issues, which kept expanding in their scope. Inter-sessional meetings were convened on only four occasions – in 1992 to consider the situation in the former Yugoslavia, in 1994 to deliberate on the situation in Rwanda, in 1999 to discuss the situation in East Timor and in 2000 to consider the situation of the Palestinian people.[17]

Having failed to discharge its mandate satisfactorily, the Commission has been abolished and replaced by the Human Rights Council since 2006.

2. HUMAN RIGHTS COUNCIL'S UNFULFILLED PROMISES

The Human Rights Council (HRC) is set up as a subsidiary organ of the UNGA, and not of ECOSOC, pursuant to UNGA Resolution 60/251 of 15 March 2006.[18] The HRC is responsible for promoting universal respect for the protection of all human rights and fundamental freedoms for all individuals,

---

[15] Rosa Freedman, *The United Nations Human Rights Council: A Critique and Early Assessment* (Routledge 2013) 9–17.

[16] In 2005, the final year of the Commission, the Commission's members were as follows: 15 from the African Group, 12 from the Asian Group, five from the Eastern European Group, 11 from the Latin American and Caribbean Group and ten from the Western European and Others Group.

[17] Freedman, *The United Nations Human Rights Council* 1, 18–35.

[18] UN Doc A/RES/60/251 (3 Apr 2006).

without distinction of any kind and in a fair and equal manner.[19] It 'should' address situations of violations of human rights, including gross and systematic violations and make recommendations thereon as well as promote the effective coordination and the mainstreaming of human rights within the UN system.[20] The HRC's work 'shall be guided by the principles of universality, impartiality, objectivity and non-selectivity, constructive international dialogue and cooperation, with a view to enhancing the promotion and protection of all human rights, civil, political, economic, social and cultural rights, including the right to development'.[21]

The HRC shall, inter alia, promote human rights education and learning as well as advisory services, technical assistance and capacity building, to be provided in consultation with and with the consent of Member States concerned. It shall also serve as a forum for dialogue on thematic issues on all human rights, make recommendations to the UNGA for the further development of IHRL, and promote the full implementation of human rights obligations undertaken by States and follow-up to the goals and commitments related to the promotion and protection of human rights emanating from UN conferences and summits. In addition, the HRC shall undertake a universal periodic review (UPR), based on objective and reliable information, of the fulfilment by each State of its human rights obligations and commitments in a manner which ensures universality of coverage and equal treatment with respect to all States. The UPR shall be a cooperative mechanism, based on an interactive dialogue, with the full involvement of the State concerned and with consideration given to its capacity-building needs. As a cooperative mechanism, the UPR shall complement and not duplicate the work of treaty bodies. Further, the HRC shall contribute, through dialogue and cooperation, towards the prevention of human rights violations and respond promptly to human rights emergencies. It shall assume the role and responsibilities of the UN Commission on Human Rights relating to the work of the Office of the UN High Commissioner for Human Rights (UNHCHR) as well as working in close cooperation in the field of human rights with governments, regional organizations, national human rights institutions and civil society. The HRC shall make recommendations with regard to the promotion and protection of human rights and submit an annual report to the UNGA.[22]

The fourth preambular paragraph of the resolution reaffirms that 'while the significance of national and regional particularities and various historical, cul-

---

[19] Ibid §2.
[20] Ibid §3.
[21] Ibid §4.
[22] Ibid §5.

tural and religious backgrounds must be borne in mind, all States, regardless of their political, economic and cultural systems, have the duty to promote and protect all human rights and fundamental freedoms'.

The HRC consists of 47 UN Member States, elected directly and individually by secret ballot by the majority of the members of the UNGA. The membership is based on equitable geographical distribution, with the seats distributed among regional groups as follows: Group of African States, 13; Group of Asian States, 13; Group of Eastern European States, six; Group of Latin American and the Caribbean States, eight; and Group of Western European and Other States, seven. The members of the HRC shall serve for a period of three years and shall not be eligible for immediate re-election after two consecutive terms.[23] When electing HRC members, UN Member States shall take into account the contribution of candidates to the promotion and protection of human rights and their voluntary pledges and commitments made in this regard. The UNGA, by a two-thirds majority of the members present and voting, may suspend the rights of membership in the HRC of an HRC member that commits gross and systematic violations of human rights.[24] In 2011 Libya became the first HRC member to be suspended due to alleged crimes against humanity committed in Libya, which had been condemned by the UNSC, the League of Arab States and the Organisation of Islamic Cooperation (OIC), among others. After their election to the HRC, HRC members shall uphold the highest standards in the promotion and protection of human rights and shall fully cooperate with the HRC and be reviewed under the UPR mechanism during their term of membership.[25]

Apart from the members of the HRC, every four-and-a-half years, on a rotational basis, all UN Member States undergo an interactive review of the human rights situation in their respective States. The UPR review sessions are held for two weeks, three times a year. Fourteen States are reviewed in each session, totalling 42 each year. The human rights issues under review are those arising from the UN Charter, the UDHR, the human rights treaties to which the reviewed State is party and international humanitarian law. Any UN Member State may participate in the discussions held during a UPR led by groups of three randomly selected States ('troikas'). During each State review lasting three-and-a-half hours, special independent experts ('Special Rapporteurs') present information and evidence as well as pose questions. Any UN Member State and NGO can also submit questions and evidence. The State under review then explains the actions already taken or that it plans

---

[23] Ibid §7.
[24] Ibid §8.
[25] Ibid §9.

to take to address the issues raised. The troika subsequently prepares a report with the involvement of the reviewed State and technical assistance from the Office of the UNHCHR, providing a summary of the discussion, questions and comments. It also sets out recommendations officially made and any necessary technical assistance suggested, as well as the reviewed State's responses. The HRC, meeting in plenary a few days after the review, discusses and adopts the report. The reviewed State has the primary responsibility to implement the recommendations in the final report and keep the HRC updated on developments in this regard. If the reviewed States fail to implement the recommendations in the final report, the HRC may pursue a series of measures, such as specific investigations and the setting up of committees to put pressure on the non-cooperating States and shaming them by drawing the world's attention to their non-implementation of the recommendations.

The HRC must meet regularly throughout the year and schedule no fewer than three sessions per year, including a main session, for a total duration of no less than ten weeks and shall be able to hold special sessions, when needed, at the request of an HRC member with the support of one-third of the HRC membership.[26] The HRC's methods of work must be transparent, fair and impartial and must enable genuine dialogue, be results oriented and allow for subsequent follow-up discussions to recommendations and their implementation. They must also allow for substantive interaction with special procedures and mechanisms.[27]

A confidential complaint procedure has been set up by the HRC since 19 June 2007 to deal with allegations of consistent patterns of gross and reliably attested violations of all human rights and fundamental freedoms anywhere

---

[26]   Ibid §10.

[27]   Ibid §11. For succinct accounts of the background and rules of the UPR, see Hilary Charlesworth and Emma Larking, 'Introduction: The Regulatory Power of the Universal Periodic Review' in Hilary Charlesworth and Emma Larking (eds), *Human Rights and the Universal Periodic Review: Rituals and Ritualism* (CUP 2014) 1, 1–10; Christian Tomuschat, 'Universal Periodic Review: A New System of International Law with Specific Ground Rules?' in Ulrich Fastenrath, Rudolf Geiger, Daniel-Erasmus Khan, Andreas Paulus, Sabine von Schorlemer and Christoph Vedder (eds), *From Bilateralism to Community Interest: Essays in Honour of Judge Bruno Simma* (OUP 2011) 609. On the importance of special procedures, see Elvira Domínguez-Redondo, 'Human Rights through the Backdoor: The Contribution of Special Procedures to the Normative Coherence and Contradictions of International Human Rights Law' in Carla M Buckley, Alice Donald and Philip Leach (eds), *Towards Convergence in International Human Rights Law Approaches of Regional and International Systems* (Brill Nijhoff 2016) 543. According to Freedman, States cooperate with special procedures because they need assistance and support in the implementation of human rights obligations (Rosa Freedman, *Failing to Protect: The UN and the Politicisation of Human Rights* (C Hurst & Co 2014) 138).

in the world and under whatever circumstances. To be admissible, the alleged violation must not be already subject to a special procedure or a treaty body, or other UN or similar regional human rights complaints procedure. Two working groups are set up to examine the communications and to bring to the attention of the HRC such human rights violations. The working groups should, to the greatest possible extent, work on the basis of consensus, failing which decisions shall be taken by simple majority of the votes. The Working Group on Communications (WGC) consists of five members chosen from the 18 independent experts of the HRC Advisory Committee, a think tank to the HRC, appointed for three years with the possibility of one renewal. The WGC screens the communications received to ensure their admissibility, assess their merits and eliminate manifestly ill-founded or anonymous communications. The Working Group on Situations (WGS), consisting of one representative from each of the five regional groups of the HRC members serving in their personal capacity, shall, on the basis of the information and recommendations provided by the WGC, present the HRC with a report on such human rights violations and recommend to the HRC the course of action to take, with due justifications. Decisions of the WGS to discontinue consideration of a situation should be taken by consensus, if possible, or by simple majority of the votes. The WGC and the WGS shall meet at least twice a year, for five working days each period, to examine the communications, including replies of States thereto, as well as the situations which the HRC has already taken up under the complaints procedure.[28]

A former acting UNHCHR lauds the HRC for drawing attention to problems affecting the enjoyment of human rights of peoples and for advancing recommendations to address them. Besides, the HRC has affirmed the importance of effective preventive measures as a part of overall strategies to promote and protect human rights. It has also urged States to create and maintain, in law and in practice, a safe and enabling environment where civil society can operate free from hindrance and insecurity. It has recognized that cultural diversity and the pursuit of cultural development by all peoples and nations are a source of mutual enrichment for the cultural life of humankind. It has urged the integration of human rights education and training into school and training curricula. The UPR, together with the UN treaty bodies, have become important mechanisms for the promotion and protection of human rights, especially in the light of the HRC's efforts to attain effective follow-ups to UPR recommendations accepted by the States concerned.[29] The HRC's strongest

---

[28] Cf Ramcharan, *The Law, Policy and Politics of the UN Human Rights Council* 5–6.

[29] Ibid 64.

contribution to protection has been in the area of 'structural protection', high-lighting structural international factors having an impact, actual or potential, on the universal realization of human rights. However, the HRC gives generic treatment of this issue, as in the case of the right to peace, rather than target-ing a particular State. The HRC also pursues structural measurement at the national level vis-à-vis the voluntary goals regarding human rights pledged by the State concerned. The HRC has laid down some building blocks in other areas, such as the right to food, the protection of human rights of civilians in armed conflict and combating impunity.[30] On the other hand, the HRC's failure to discharge its responsibility to protect is its Achilles heel. This is due to the diplomatic and political decision of the majority in the HRC to opt for dialogue and cooperation instead of condemnatory actions against governments guilty of gross violations of human rights (except Israel).[31]

Indeed, the HRC has been criticized as being 'political from the outset', with States advancing and protecting their allies from the HRC's scrutiny as well as from politically motivated attacks by other States. The HRC has achieved greater cross-regional cooperation on human rights issues when there is disunity within regional blocs like the OIC. In country-specific situations, the HRC often plays politics by excessively and discriminatorily scrutinizing some States while entirely ignoring others and/or shielding others from action being taken against them. Five of the first 12 of the HRC's special sessions convened at short notice to enable the HRC to respond expeditiously to serious and escalating violations of human rights taking place outside regular HRC sessions centred on Israel and the Occupied Palestinian Territory. By contrast, there was only one such session on Darfur in Sudan, four on Syria, which had been expelled from the Arab League, but none on the alleged violent govern-ment suppression and grave human rights violations during the Arab Spring uprisings starting in December 2010 and other comparable serious human rights situations elsewhere. In the special session on Darfur, Sudan's allies blamed non-State actors for the atrocious human rights violations that had occurred and supported providing capacity-building and technical assistance to the Sudanese Government so that it could prevent and suppress such viola-tions by the non-State actors in the future.[32]

The replacement of the UN Commission on Human Rights with the HRC is, therefore, not really a radical reform of the central UN body responsible for

---

[30]   Ibid 245–50.

[31]   Ibid 250, 253–66.

[32]   Freedman, *Failing to Protect* 50–54, 62–6, 69–76. Cf also id, *The United Nations Human Rights Council* 282–97; Rosa Freedman and Ruth Houghton, 'Two Steps Forward, One Step Back: Politicisation of the Human Rights Council' (2017) 17 Hum Rts L Rev 753, 753–61, 765–8.

human rights since there are so many similarities between the two, especially when global politics and regional political blocs continue to protect allies and shame foes in the HRC using all sorts of subterfuge.[33] It is a truism that an international human rights body such as the HRC is as effective as the States establishing it actually intend it to be.[34] The majority of the States have always wanted the HRC to be just like it is now.

On 27 September 2018 the HRC adopted a resolution on the situation of human rights of Rohingya Muslims and other minorities in Myanmar[35] by a vote of 35 in favour, three against, seven abstentions, with two either not voting or being absent. The resolution was an outcome of joint efforts by all Member States of the European Union (EU) and those of the OIC.

The resolution expresses grave concern at the findings of an independent international fact-finding mission (FFM) that there is sufficient information to warrant the investigation and prosecution of senior officials in Myanmar's military chain of command so that a competent court may determine their liability for genocide in relation to the situation regarding the Rohingya Muslims in Myanmar's Rakhine state. The FFM also finds that crimes against humanity and war crimes have been committed in Kachin, Rakhine and Shan states. The resolution, therefore, strongly condemns all violations and abuses of human rights in Myanmar as set out in the FFM's report.[36] It takes an unprecedented step for the HRC by setting up an ongoing independent mechanism to collect, consolidate, preserve and analyse evidence of the most serious crimes and violations of international law committed in Myanmar since 2011, in order to facilitate and expedite fair and independent criminal proceedings, in accordance with international law standards, in national, regional or international courts or tribunals that have or may in the future have jurisdiction over these crimes, in accordance with international law. The resolution also takes note of the International Criminal Court (ICC) Pre-Trial Chamber's ruling that it may exercise jurisdiction over the deportation of the Rohingya Muslims from Myanmar to Bangladesh and requests that the mechanism cooperate closely with any of the ICC Prosecutor's future investigations pertaining to human rights violations in Myanmar.

---

33 Freedman, *The United Nations Human Rights Council* 84, 119–290.
34 Cf Eric A Posner, *Twilight of Human Rights Law* (OUP 2014) 103–4, 115.
35 A/HRC/39/L22 (25 Sept 2018).
36 A/HRC/39/64. The FFM subsequently concludes in its report of 22 August 2019 that the Myanmar security forces committed crimes against humanity and war crimes in Rakhine state, as well as genocide against the Rohingya, and that Myanmar's civilian authorities, including State Counsellor Aung San Suu Kyi, have not met their responsibility to protect the civilian population, thereby enabling the commission of these crimes.

The mechanism is similar to the International, Impartial and Independent Mechanism (IIIM) set up by the UNGA in 2016 to assist in investigation and prosecution of those responsible for human rights atrocities in Syria.[37] While the IIIM for Syria is financed by voluntary contributions, the mechanism established by the HRC will be financed by UN budgets, initially estimated at approximately US$2.77 million. In December 2018, the Administrative and Budgetary Committee approved without a vote approximately US$28 million for the independent mechanism to perform its task.

China, Philippines and Burundi voted against the HRC resolution. China, one of Myanmar's immediate neighbouring States, is the largest foreign investor in Myanmar and China has its own problems with the Uighur Muslim minorities living in China's Zinjiang Province. Since 8 February 2018, the ICC Prosecutor has been conducting preliminary investigations regarding crimes allegedly committed in the Philippines from at least 1 July 2016 in the context of the 'war on drugs' campaign launched by the Philippine Government in which thousands of persons have been subject to extrajudicial killings in the course of police operations to suppress narcotic drug trafficking. The Philippines deposited its written notification of withdrawal from the Rome Statute of the ICC[38] in March 2018. Burundi has ceased to be a State Party to the Rome Statute since 27 October 2017, in response to a preliminary investigation launched in April 2016 by the ICC Prosecutor into possible crimes against humanity in Burundi.

The abstaining HRC members were Angola, Ethiopia, Japan, Kenya, Mongolia, Nepal and South Africa. Kenya used to campaign hard for AU Member States to withdraw en masse from the Rome Statute of the ICC following the then pending prosecution of Kenya's President and his deputy before the ICC. Although Japan is not the largest foreign investor in Myanmar, it has provided more than US$7 billion in foreign aid to Myanmar since 2016. Japan considers the Rohingya crisis a complicated and serious issue on which it will work bilaterally with Myanmar and will support the Myanmar Government's efforts to resolve it. Japan has been providing humanitarian aid to Rakhine state, from where the Rohingya Muslims have been displaced, giving US$3 million to Myanmar in January 2018 to assist displaced Rohingya Muslims returning from Bangladesh. The Independent Commission of Enquiry on Rakhine set up by the Government of Myanmar to investigate alleged human rights violations concerning the Rohingya Muslims has two foreign members, one of whom is a former Japanese career diplomat who once served as UN Under-Secretary-General for Humanitarian Affairs and

---

[37]   UNGA Resolution 71/248 of 21 Dec 2016 (A/Res/71/248, 11 Jan 2017).
[38]   2187 UNTS 3.

Emergency Relief Coordination.[39] Japan's stance echoes the long-established non-confrontational diplomacy practised by Japan in international arenas, except vis-à-vis North Korea, whose nuclear weapon capability is considered by Japan to be a serious threat to the stability of East Asia. Japan has also been urging Bangladesh, another State receiving huge foreign aid from Japan, to cooperate with Myanmar in repatriating the more than 730,000 Rohingya living in overcrowded camps in Bangladesh since August 2017. In other words, Japan pursues a win–win policy for all sides, with Japan getting the credit and increasing influence in Myanmar. It is a mystery why the other States abstained, however.

Those absent or not voting were Cuba and Venezuela. On the same day of the adoption of the HRC resolution, the ICC Prosecutor received a referral from a group of States Parties to the Rome Statute – Argentina, Chile, Colombia, Paraguay, Peru and Canada – requesting her to initiate an investigation into crimes against humanity allegedly committed in Venezuela since 12 February 2014, with a view to determining whether one or more persons should be charged with the commission of such crimes. This is the ninth referral received by the ICC Prosecutor since the Rome Statute came into force on 1 July 2002 and the first referral submitted by a group of States Parties concerning a situation on the territory of another State Party. The ICC Prosecutor herself has already initiated a preliminary examination of the situation in Venezuela to analyse crimes allegedly committed in Venezuela since at least April 2017, in the context of mass demonstrations and related political unrest.

Ironically, multinational corporations as well as human rights NGOs have urged the EU not to suspend its trade preferences for Myanmar; otherwise hundreds of thousands of jobs in Myanmar would be jeopardized while leaving the targeted Myanmar military leaders unaffected. The concern revolves around Myanmar's garment industry, which employs more than 500,000 workers, about 300,000 of whom are young women. Myanmar exports approximately 70 per cent of its garment products to the EU.[40]

The example of the HRC's response to the alleged violations of the human rights of the Rohingya Muslims in Myanmar shows how the HRC actually operates. The HRC's members vote mostly as dictated by their respective national interests, as well as domestic and foreign policies on a particular issue. This is also the case, for example, for India's overall role and voting pattern in the HRC. India either dilutes or abstains from adopting draft human rights

---

[39] Nan Lwin, 'Abe Vows Further Support for Gov't on Democracy, Rakhine', *Irrawaddy*, 10 Oct 2018, https://www.irrawaddy.com/news/abe-vows-support-govt-democracy-rakhine.html, accessed 11 Oct 2018.

[40] John Reed, 'Rohingya rights: EU urged to keep Myanmar trade preferences', *Financial Times* (19 Oct 2018) 4.

resolutions submitted to the HRC on civil and political rights, such as those on the roles of civil society and those on human rights defenders. In relation to country-specific resolutions, India has been either hostile or indifferent, except in the cases of Sri Lanka and Palestine. Apropos socio-economic rights, India has been more proactive, especially as regards resolutions on access to medicine and human rights and those on transnational corporations. As regards emerging human rights issues such as sexual orientation and gender identity, India either abstains or votes for a number of hostile amendments to dilute the content of the relevant draft resolutions.[41]

Yet, with the UNSC failing to end ongoing mass atrocities around the world, the HRC has recently been active in passing resolutions in response to such atrocities. For instance, the HRC's 41st regular session in June and July 2019 adopted such resolutions concerning Eritrea, DR Congo and Syria. On 11 July 2019 the HRC adopted its first resolution on the Philippines to entrust the UNHCHR to submit a detailed report by June 2020 on allegations of extrajudicial killings, forced disappearances and arbitrary arrests during the Philippine Government's war on drugs. The resolution, tabled by Iceland, was adopted mainly along the human rights ideological divide and in the light of each HRC Member State's bilateral relation with the Philippines, with 18 States voting in favour, 14 against and 15 abstentions.[42] Interactive dialogues were also held with the international commissions of inquiry on Burundi and Syria as well as with the Special Rapporteur on the human rights situation in Myanmar. The HRC thus provides an avenue to raise international awareness regarding ongoing human rights violations in the targeted States and galvanize the international community to try to do something about them.

With regard to the HRC's UPR process, it has both successes and shortcomings.

On the positive side, the UPR is inclusive in terms of participation by all States, human rights issues regardless of the ratification of the human rights treaties in question, and 360-degree human rights reviews among States in public. According to one piece of research, published in 2012, two years after their first review States acted on 40 per cent of all the recommendations

---

[41]   Arvid Narrin, 'India's Role in the Human Rights Council: Is There a Constitutional Vision in its Foreign Policy' (2017) 57 Indian JIL 87, 91–118.

[42]   Those HRC members voting in favour were Argentina, Australia, Austria, Bahamas, Bulgaria, Croatia, Czech Republic, Denmark, Fiji, Iceland, Italy, Mexico, Peru, Slovakia, Spain, Ukraine, UK and Uruguay. Those voting against were Angola, Bahrain, Cameroon, China, Cuba, Egypt, Eritrea, Hungary, India, Iraq, Philippines, Qatar, Saudi Arabia and Somalia. The abstaining HRC members were Afghanistan, Bangladesh, Brazil, Burkina Faso, Chile, DR Congo, Japan, Nepal, Nigeria, Pakistan, Rwanda, Senegal, South Africa, Togo and Tunisia.

addressed to them during the review, and 15 per cent of the rejected recommendations triggered action from the States under review. International human
rights norms stipulated in various instruments, both binding and non-binding
on the States concerned, are reaffirmed during the process. It also gives States
an opportunity to promote rights not yet universally recognized. Several States
recommend other States to uphold human rights that are disregarded by the
recommending States themselves within their own respective territories and
jurisdictions. These recommending States are, therefore, estopped from reject-
ing these same rights when the rights are invoked against them in the future.
Furthermore, the UPR provides a unique learning experience to the relevant
government agencies and other stakeholders responsible for human rights protection and promotion so that a consensus on international human rights standards may be built or reinforced at the domestic level. On the negative side, the
modalities of national consultations and national implementation of past cycle
recommendations are, among other things, weak, insufficiently inclusive and
neither timely nor transparent. There is a lack of a follow-up mechanism to
examine the implementation of recommendations, which are the most visible
outcome of the UPR process at the HRC. The average number of 111 specific
or broad recommendations per State under review causes difficulties for their
implementation and for assessing the successes or failures in implementation.[43]

The UPR process has also been criticized as lapsing into ritualism. Certain
States may participate without the intention of accepting any of the recommendations. Some other States may accept all of them so as to claim that they are
dedicated to human rights, but without the ability or intention to implement
these recommendations. Some States may accept just a few of the recommendations while failing to give answers to others. For their part, the recommending States merely repeat their previous recommendations without concrete
follow-ups of the recommendations previously made by them to the targeted
States and the recommending States tend to focus on relatively non-confrontational issues such as ratification of human rights treaties, women's rights and
the rights of the child.[44]

The HRC has utilized FFMs, such as the one on the Gaza Conflict set up in
April 2009 and headed by Judge Richard Goldstone, the first Chief Prosecutor
of the International Criminal Tribunal for the former Yugoslavia and that for

---

[43] Roland Chauville, 'The Universal Periodic Review's First Cycle: Successes and
Failures' in Charlesworth and Larking (eds), *Human Rights and the Universal Periodic
Review* 87, 88–99, 100–103; Walter Kälin, 'Ritual and Ritualism at the Universal
Periodic Review: A Preliminary Appraisal' in ibid 25, 31–41. Cf Freedman, *The United
Nations Human Rights Council* 253–82.

[44] Kälin, 'Ritual and Ritualism at the Universal Periodic Review' 25, 31–41;
Chauville, 'The Universal Periodic Review's First Cycle' 100–103.

Rwanda, to investigate alleged violations of IHRL and international humanitarian law in the Palestinian territories, particularly the Gaza Strip. The ensuing report, known as the Goldstone Report, was not well received by Israel and its allies.[45] This is probably because the missions were not welcomed by the host States in the first place. In comparison, the fact-finding missions authorized by the HRC at the initiative of Sri Lanka – which wants to utilize the weight of international actors to promote reconciliation, accountability and human rights in Sri Lanka after decades of internecine conflicts – have been well received.[46]

On 19 June 2018 the USA announced its decision to withdraw from the HRC. What might have helped prompt this decision was the oral report to the HRC on 1 June 2018 by Philip Alston, UN Special Rapporteur on extreme poverty and human rights, on his fact-finding mission to the USA. The Special Rapporteur reports, under the agenda item 'Promotion and protection of all human rights, civil, political, economic, social and cultural rights, including the right to development', that millions of Americans already struggling to make ends meet are facing severe deprivation of food and almost no access to health care. The report chastises US President Donald Trump and the Republicans in Congress for enacting a tax bill that 'overwhelmingly benefited the wealthy and worsened inequality' and is apparently 'deliberately designed to remove basic protections from the poorest, punish those who are not in employment and make even basic health care into a privilege'. As one of the world's wealthiest societies, the USA is called a 'land of stark contrasts', being home to one in four of the world's 2,208 billionaires, while 40 million Americans live in poverty, over 5 million of them eking out an existence in absolute deprivation normally associated with the developing world. Americans are said by the report to experience shorter and sicker lives than nationals of other wealthy democracies, increasing tropical diseases that thrive in conditions of poverty, and the world's highest incarceration rate. Alston has also found US voter registration levels to be among the lowest in industrialized nations – 64 per cent of the voting-age population, compared with 91 per cent in Canada and the UK and 99 per cent in Japan.[47]

The US decision to withdraw from the HRC explains that US calls for HRC reform were unheeded; human rights abusers continue to serve on, and be elected to, the HRC; 'the world's most inhumane regimes' continue to escape its scrutiny; the HRC continues 'politicizing scapegoating of countries with

---

[45] An abridged version appears in Adam Horowitz, Lizzy Ratner and Philip Weiss (eds), *The Goldstone Report: The Legacy of the Landmark Investigation of the Gaza Conflict* (Nation Books 2011).

[46] HRC Resolution 34/1, A/HRC/RES/34/1 of 3 Apr 2017.

[47] The official report by the Special Rapporteur is published as UN Doc A/HRC/38/33/Add.1 (4 May 2018).

positive human rights records in an attempt to distract from the abusers in its ranks', thereby making the HRC 'a cesspool of political bias'; and the HRC has been making a mockery of itself, its members and its mission – for years, the HRC has engaged in 'ever more virulent anti-American and anti-Israel invective'.[48]

An article by two members of a US conservative think tank, the Heritage Foundation, rebuts Special Rapporteur Alston's report as being based essentially on 'faulty information' deriving from the US Census Bureau's statistics. In particular, the said statistics purportedly consider only the cash income each family reports in an annual survey while excluding 'substantial off-the-books earnings among low-income households' and omitting roughly 95 per cent of the US$1.1 trillion US taxpayers provide in means-tested cash, food, housing and medical benefits for low-income persons each year. The article argues that 'at most 25.9 million Americans live in poverty, based on reported spending less than the official poverty threshold', which, in any event, is 'far higher than the living standard for most of the world's population'.[49]

Are criticisms of the HRC well founded? An extensive survey of the views of various stakeholders at the HRC was conducted between June and December 2015 on the politicization, or the pursuit of political objectives unrelated to human rights, at the HRC, using three indicators to measure the politicization: country bias, issue bias and instrumental use of cultural relativism. Country bias was perceived to be prevalent within the HRC's UPR mechanism, whereas it was perceived to exist to a much smaller extent in the treaty bodies comprising experts serving in their individual capacity than in the UPR. In relation to issue bias, a vast majority of those surveyed believed that some human rights issues were frequently given more attention than others in the UPR process, whereas they considered treaty bodies gave more attention to some issues than others at a frequently slightly, but not markedly, lesser level than that of the UPR process. With respect to the instrumental use of cultural relativism in the UPR process, about half of the survey respondents found frequent contradiction with the cultural, religious or ideological values of reviewed States, while a substantial minority of the survey respondents thought this contradiction seldom occurred. Interestingly, all the respondents affirmed that government delegates of reviewed States often used, more or less explicitly,

---

[48] Laura Quran, 'US leaving Human Rights Council – "a cesspool of political bias"', *CNN* (20 June 2018) https://edition.cnn.com/2018/06/19/politics/haley-pompeo -human-rights-bias/index.html, accessed 20 June 2018.

[49] Jamie Bryan Hall and Robert Rector, 'Don't Believe the UN Propaganda about "Extreme Poverty" in the US' (17 July 2018) https://www.heritage.org/poverty-and -inequality/commentary/dont-believe-the-uns-propaganda-about-extreme-poverty-the -us, accessed 25 July 2018.

the existence of different cultural sensitivities to justify non-fulfilment of their human rights obligations or to argue for divergent interpretations of certain human rights provisions. Those invoking cultural relativism as a reason for the non-compliance considered human rights to be a Western construct. Most controversies arose when States gave recommendations to Arab and African States on issues related to the rights of sexual orientation and gender identity. Recommendations from treaty bodies were perceived to be less culturally controversial than those issued by State representatives in the UPR process. However, all the survey respondents also affirmed that cultural relativism was invoked by State representatives as well as by all regional groups before treaty bodies to justify non-compliance with human rights obligations. Regarding the credibility of these two mechanisms in the light of the perceived level of politicization in each of them, treaty bodies were perceived to be less politically motivated than the UPR. Nonetheless, the process of election of experts to treaty bodies that involved other States, including those subjected to review by treaty bodies, engaged in exchanging reciprocal support with the States nominating candidates for treaty bodies somewhat undermined the genuine credibility of the experts in such bodies.[50]

Some unexpected positive consequences of the politicization in the UPR process is the increased willingness of States that accept a recommendation in the UPR to seriously commit to it so as to avoid 'losing face' with political allies, thereby raising the stakes for non-compliance. This kind of commitment seems lacking in the treaty body process, which uses a follow-up procedure to put pressure on States to comply with its recommendations but it is entirely up to the States to decide to what extent they will implement such recommendations. Since it is not reasonable to expect the UPR process to be free of political bias, States have lower expectations of its impartiality than they do of treaty bodies. Therefore, when treaty bodies do not live up to the expectation of independence, the frustration with the bodies is clearly manifest.[51]

Several proposals for reforming the HRC have been made. In essence, they look forward to the elimination of the existing fundamental flaws of the HRC by, inter alia, rigorously enforcing HRC membership criteria to allow only those States with impeccable or at least near impeccable human rights records to be members; elimination of bloc voting to support political allies; ending selectivity and bias in addressing human rights; increased participation of non-State actors in the process of assessing a State's human rights

---

[50] Valentina Carraro, 'The United Nations Treaty Bodies and Universal Periodic Review: Advancing Human Rights by Preventing Politicization?' (2017) 39 Hum Rts Quarterly 943, 947–66.

[51] Ibid 967–8. For a similar view, see Posner, *Twilight of Human Rights Law* 41–3.

records; replacing States' delegates with independent human rights experts; and strengthening the compliance procedure, at least by increasing the HRC's ability to put pressure on States to comply with their human rights obligations and commitments.[52]

Any reform of the HRC is unrealistic as long as States with candidacies for elections to international organizations still enter into reciprocal support arrangements, promising to vote for each other's candidate(s). There are countless such elections each year, not only at the UN, but also at specialized bodies like the International Maritime Organization, the Appellate Body of the World Trade Organization and so forth. Candidacies are normally announced at least a few years in advance of the election date in order for the States concerned to campaign for support. The standard formula for exchange of support is to exchange support between one State's candidature with another State's candidature to the same body or another body of equal importance, if the former and the latter are from different regional groups or are not competing with one another at the same election. A two-year non-permanent membership of the UNSC is a top priority for any State aspiring to be recognized as a 'front bencher' in international political affairs. Therefore, a State running for election to the UNSC usually has to agree to support two or more candidacies of another State in return (eg UNSC = HRC + 1 or more). Because voting is by secret ballot, it is widely believed that approximately 85–90 per cent of written commitments are honoured, compared with 40 per cent or less for oral promises not confirmed in writing. Hence, States with candidatures for election have every incentive to enter into reciprocal support arrangements with as many States as possible. The most relevant factor in choosing a candidate to support, be it by a reciprocal support arrangement or an unconditional support where the voting State has no candidacy for any election, is the bilateral relationship between the States concerned, including past support given to the voting State in multilateral forums. This factor is strengthened if the regional group or organization to which the voting State belongs has endorsed that particular candidate for election. Only if all other things are equal among the candidates for a particular election do the voting States consider as decisive the better qualifications one candidate has over the other(s). At times and unless otherwise committed, certain States consider themselves free to vote for the candidate(s) with the best individual qualifications during the second and subsequent rounds of voting when these rounds are necessary after the first round

---

[52] Cf Miloon Kothari, 'From Commission to the Council: Evolution of UN Charter Bodies' in Dinah Shelton (ed.), *The Oxford Handbook of International Human Rights Law* (OUP 2013) 587, 614–17; Freedman, *The United Nations Human Rights Council* 297–302.

fails to fill the vacancy or vacancies in accordance with the applicable election procedure. The USA is the only one not engaged in vote swapping. Neither does the USA indicate which State's candidate(s) the USA will support or not support. The USA explains that it considers a candidate's qualifications to be of utmost importance to its decision whether to support the candidate. At the same time, the USA has so many friends and does not want to alienate some of them by not supporting their candidates. Thanks to the USA's clout, its candidates are usually elected although where there is more than one vacancy for the regional group to which the USA belongs the US candidate rarely garners the highest number of votes among those elected. This shows the impact of vote swapping even when a superpower like the USA is running for election.

States aspiring to be members of the HRC have been exploiting this reciprocal support arrangement practice to their advantage. States frequently subjected to international criticisms for their human rights records are willing to exchange support with any candidature of any State, preferably a friendly one, for their successful election to the HRC. Once elected, why should a State Member of the HRC make enemies of those whose support has made it possible for it to be in the HRC in the first place – unless this is absolutely necessary and unavoidable?

As long as the HRC cannot be realistically reformed, its members must be put under the spotlight for the international community to see whether they are up to the highest standards of human rights expected of them. In addition, HRC members must fully cooperate with the HRC as well as have their human rights records reviewed during their three-year HRC membership. By being elected an HRC member, the State forfeits the right to challenge an issue of human rights being raised against it, the ulterior motive and the manner of raising the issue in the HRC by anyone duly authorized under the HRC's rules of procedures to raise it and the timing for raising the issue.

The work of the HRC is closely linked to that of the Third Committee (Social, Humanitarian and Cultural Affairs) of the UNGA.

3.   THIRD COMMITTEE OF THE UN GENERAL ASSEMBLY: DUPLICATOR PAR EXCELLENCE?

The Third Committee is open to all UN Member States. This is where human rights issues within the UN system are scrutinized before draft resolutions on human rights are submitted to the UNGA for further action. Therefore, the Third Committee also considers reports and proposals from the HRC, which is a subsidiary body of the UNGA. As a result, there is duplication of efforts in human rights matters in both the HRC in Geneva and the Third Committee in New York, including the tabling of repetitive and duplicative human rights resolutions, repetitive interactive dialogues with thematic special procedures mandate-holders, and the challenges in the Third Committee to the HRC's annual report to the UNGA.[53]

Through their participation in the Third Committee's work, some States can help ensure that human rights are best protected and promoted, whereas other States want to dilute or even eliminate, where possible, the harshness of the HRC's criticisms of their human rights records. The Third Committee is, in effect, an important UN forum for non-members of the HRC to press their cases, as well as for HRC members to have another chance to get what they have failed to achieve at the HRC. Nevertheless, those aspiring to be elected to the HRC in the future have an incentive to 'behave themselves' lest they will be considered human rights pariahs with their odds of being elected to the HRC unnecessarily lessened.

Universal Rights Group (URG), a Geneva-based human rights NGO, has discovered that between 2012 and 2013, approximately 27 per cent of all human rights resolutions adopted by the Third Committee were functionally identical, elaborative or significantly overlapping with resolutions adopted by the HRC, and that when including resolutions by the HRC with lesser degrees of overlap, there was an overlap of more than 40 per cent with all human rights resolutions passed by the Third Committee. At the end of the annual session of the Third Committee in 2017, some 17.3 per cent of the texts were functionally identical, elaborative or significantly overlapping with the HRC's equivalent text, but when including resolutions with a lesser degree of overlap, this figure rose to more than 41 per cent of all human rights resolutions passed by the Third Committee in 2017. A silver lining seems to be that the Third Committee has become more careful not to reopen the HRC's annual report in order to 'suspend' resolutions adopted by vote in the HRC.[54]

URG's comparative analysis of the texts adopted in the 2018 calendar year by the HRC and the Third Committee finds that the HRC passed 86 resolutions compared with the Third Committee's passing 57 resolutions, 39 of which were human rights related. Like previous calendar years, there remained significant overlap/duplication between the resolutions of the two bodies. Fifty-four per cent of the Third Committee's 39 human rights resolutions in 2018 appeared to be the same (judging by the resolution titles) as those adopted by the HRC that year. Eight per cent were functionally identical in the sense of having the same content, another 8 per cent elaborated upon corresponding HRC texts, and another 5 per cent had a significant overlap. In total,

---

[53]   Universal Rights Group, 'Strengthening coherence between the Human Rights Council and the Third Committee' (5 Dec 2017) https://www.universal-rights.org/blog/strengthening-coherence-human-rights-council-third-committee/, accessed 24 Aug 2018.
[54]   Ibid.

21 per cent of the Third Committee's human rights texts in 2018 had a high degree of overlap/duplication with corresponding HRC texts. The percentage of the corresponding HRC/Third Committee texts sharing the same content of 10 per cent or more was 66 per cent. Overall, compared with previous years, in 2018 the Third Committee adopted the same proportion of resolutions with a high degree of overlap with corresponding HRC texts (21 per cent) as it did during the years 2014 and 2015 and somewhat less than the 27 per cent in 2012 and 2013. However, if texts with some degree of overlap were considered, 2018 was worse in terms of duplication, at 66 per cent, than either 2012–13 (at 40 per cent) or 2014–15 (at 48 per cent). URG also finds that some States decided to 'stagger' the tabling of resolutions on the same subjects between the HRC and the Third Committee (that is, the text is tabled one year in the HRC and next year in the Third Committee). Where States had not staggered the tabling of resolutions, the practice of 'copying and pasting' HRC wording into UNGA texts as drafted by the Third Committee remained prevalent, causing a waste of time and resources. Nonetheless, the 2018 HRC annual report to the UNGA was adopted without a vote as there was no attempt to 'reopen' the report although some States in the Third Committee did complain or express doubts about aspects of the HRC's work in 2018, especially the HRC's country-specific resolutions, which are the usual target of criticisms in the Third Committee.[55]

A meaningful solution to the duplication/overlap between the work of the HRC and that of the Third Committee may be achieved in 2021 when UN Member States will start reviewing and considering the HRC's status. Ideally, UN Member States should elevate the HRC to become a main body of the UN, on a par with ECOSOC, so that the HRC may report directly to the UNGA. It is doubtful whether this can be accomplished because States may prefer to keep the status quo so long as those who are not members of the HRC can assert their position in the open-ended Third Committee.

One of the HRC's mandates is to promote the full implementation of human rights treaty obligations undertaken by States. Failure to implement these obligations is also subject to debate in the Third Committee. Therefore, the work of human rights treaty bodies is closely linked to the work of the HRC and the Third Committee.

---

[55]   Danica Damplo, 'Duplication or Complementarity? A Comparative Analysis of Human Rights Council and Third Committee Resolutions', *Universal Rights Group* (11 Dec 2018) https://www.universal-rights.org/blog-nyc-3/duplication -or-complementarity-a-comparative-analysis-of-human-rights-council-and-third -committee-resolutions/, accessed 18 Dec 2018.

4.   TREATY BODY MECHANISMS AND THEIR
      SHORTFALLS

The International Covenant on Civil and Political Rights sets up the Human
Rights Committee to monitor the implementation of the ICCPR by the States
Parties thereto.

A majority of States Parties to the ICCPR have become parties to the
Optional Protocol to the ICCPR[56] by a separate expression of consent to be
bound. The Optional Protocol was adopted and opened for signature, ratification or accession by the UNGA's Resolution 2200 A (XXI) of 16 December
1966, which adopted the ICCPR itself. Both the ICCPR and the Optional
Protocol entered into force on 23 March 1976. The Optional Protocol enables
the Human Rights Committee to receive and consider communications from
individuals claiming to be victims of violations of any of the rights under the
ICCPR. In its General Comment No 33 on the Obligations of States Parties
under the Optional Protocol to the ICCPR,[57] the Human Rights Committee
opines that although its function in considering individual communications is
not, as such, that of a judicial body, the views issued by the Committee under
the Optional Protocol 'exhibit some important characteristics of a judicial
decision', having been arrived at 'in a judicial spirit, including the impartiality
and independence of Committee members, the considered interpretation of
the language of the ICCPR and the determinative character of the decisions'.
Therefore, the said views represent 'an authoritative determination' by the
integral organ established under the ICCPR charged with the interpretation of
that instrument. These views derive their character, and the importance which
attaches to them, from the integral role of the Committee under both the ICCPR
and the Optional Protocol. The Committee alludes to its decision in 1997 to
appoint a member of the Committee as Special Rapporteur for the Follow-Up
of Views, to urge compliance with the Committee's views and discuss factors
that may be impeding their implementation. Through the Special Rapporteur's
written representations and personal meetings with diplomatic representatives
of the State Party concerned, in a number of cases this procedure has led to
acceptance and implementation of the Committee's views where previously
the transmission of those views met with no response.[58] Apart from this procedure, the Committee also issues General Comments and recommendations on
matters of a general nature, addressed to all States Parties, as well as findings

---

[56]   999 UNTS 302.
[57]   CCPR/C/GC/33, 5 Nov 2008.
[58]   Ibid §§11, 13 and 16.

in the form of concluding observations and comments addressed to a particular State after the consideration of that State's report.[59]

The ICJ notes that the Human Rights Committee has, since its inception, built up a considerable body of interpretative case law, in particular through its findings in response to the individual communications which may be submitted to it in respect of States Parties to the first Optional Protocol and in the form of its General Comments. Although the ICJ is in no way obliged, in the exercise of its judicial functions, to model its own interpretation of the ICCPR on that of the Committee, the ICJ believes it should ascribe great weight to the interpretation adopted by this independent body set up specifically to supervise the application of the ICCPR. The point here is to achieve the necessary clarity and the essential consistency of international law, as well as legal security, to which both the individuals with guaranteed rights and the States obliged to comply with treaty obligations are entitled.[60]

Several other human rights treaties have similar monitoring mechanisms, collectively known as 'the human rights treaty body system'. As of this writing, there are ten human rights treaty bodies that monitor implementation of the nine core human rights treaties. In addition to the Human Rights Committee of the ICCPR, there are the Committee on Economic, Social and Cultural Rights (CESCR), which monitors the implementation of the ICESCR; the Committee on the Elimination of Racial Discrimination, monitoring the implementation of the 1965 International Convention on the Elimination of All Forms of Racial Discrimination (CERD);[61] the Committee on the Elimination of Discrimination against Women, which monitors the implementation of the 1979 Convention on the Elimination of All Forms of Discrimination against Women (CEDAW);[62] the Committee against Torture, monitoring the implementation of the 1984 Convention against Torture and Other Cruel, Inhuman or Degrading Treatment or Punishment (CAT);[63] the Committee on the Rights of the Child, which monitors the implementation of the 1989 Convention on the Rights of the Child (CRC);[64] the Committee on Migrant Workers, monitoring the implementation of the 1990 International Convention on the Protection of the Rights of All Migrant Workers and Members of their Families (CMW);[65]

---

[59]   Machiko Kanetake, 'UN Human Rights Treaty Monitoring Bodies before Domestic Courts' (2018) 67 ICLQ 201, 207.

[60]   *Ahmadou Sadio Diallo (Republic of Guinea v Democratic Republic of the Congo)*, Merits, Judgment [2010] ICJ Rep 639, 664 [66].

[61]   660 UNTS 195.

[62]   1249 UNTS 13.

[63]   1465 UNTS 85.

[64]   1577 UNTS 3.

[65]   2220 UNTS 3.

the Committee on the Rights of Persons with Disabilities, monitoring the 2006 Convention on the Rights of Persons with Disabilities (CRPD);[66] and the Committee on Enforced Disappearances, monitoring the 2006 International Convention for the Protection of All Persons from Enforced Disappearance (CED).[67] Unlike the nine treaty bodies just mentioned, the Subcommittee on Prevention of Torture and other Cruel, Inhuman or Degrading Treatment or Punishment (SPT) does not examine individual complaints or periodic reports by States Parties. The SPT discharges its preventive mandate pursuant to the 2002 Optional Protocol to CAT[68] by visiting places of detention and advising National Preventive Mechanisms of States Parties to CAT.

For ease of reference, the monitoring procedures utilized by several of these treaty bodies appear in the Appendix to this book.

Treaty bodies have played an important role in interpreting the treaties under their respective mandates in a dynamic way in the light of changing circumstances. This is the case of, for example, the CEDAW Committee, which has alleviated CEDAW's main limitations such as its lack of any reference to violence against women, its assumption of normative married heterosexuality and its limited acknowledgement of multiple and intersectional forms of discrimination.[69]

The practical and lasting impact on States Parties scrutinized by the respective human rights treaty bodies cannot be underestimated. The case of Thailand in relation to the Human Rights Committee is one example.

In the summer of 2005, Thailand was to appear before the Human Rights Committee for the first time to explain its report on the measures Thailand had adopted to give effect to the rights recognized in the ICCPR. The timing was not opportune. From February to April 2003, the Thai Government had launched a 'war on drugs' to suppress illicit drug trafficking and prevent illicit drug abuse. This 'war' allegedly resulted in 2,873 extrajudicial killings of suspected drug traffickers and some innocent bystanders inadvertently caught in the line of fire. The UN Special Rapporteur on Extrajudicial, Summary or Arbitrary Executions sent an urgent communication to the Thai Government in 2003 to raise serious concerns and demand that due process of law be strictly followed. On 12 March 2004 a prominent Thai Muslim lawyer and human rights activist disappeared without trace. On 28 April 2004 Thai soldiers shot to death all the 32 Thai Muslim militants who had barricaded themselves inside the Krue Se mosque in Pattani Province in the south of Thailand after

---

[66]   2515 UNTS 3.
[67]   2716 UNTS 3.
[68]   2375 UNTS 237.
[69]   Dianne Otto, 'Women's Rights' in Daniel Moeckli, Sangeeta Shah and Sandesh Sivakumaran (eds), *International Human Rights Law* (3rd edn, OUP 2018) 309, 317.

the latter had carried out armed attacks against military and police checkpoints resulting in the death of three officers and the injury of 18 other officers. On 25 October 2004 seven Thai Muslims were shot to death while the Thai authorities were trying to disperse the unruly crowd of approximately 1,500 Thai Muslims protesting in front of the Tak Bai police station, Narathiwat Province, against the police detention of six men believed by the protesters to be innocent. Seventy-eight more protesters died from suffocation or organ collapse after being stacked on top of one another in trucks and transported to a military camp in another province, five hours' drive away. The present author was deputy secretary of the independent commission of inquiry set up by the Thai Government into the Krue Se mosque incident and, at the time of preparing and presenting Thailand's report to the Human Rights Committee, Ambassador attached to the Thai Ministry of Foreign Affairs responsible for legal affairs and counter-international terrorism, who was also assigned the task of being the editor-in-chief of the report.

The Thai delegation to the Human Rights Committee's session on Thailand was jointly headed by the Vice Minister of Foreign Affairs and the Vice Minister of Justice. It comprised approximately 30 delegates from all relevant ministries and agencies, who would individually report to the Committee on the implementation of the ICCPR within their respective areas of responsibility and explain to their constituencies when they returned home the Committee's recommendations for further action. Before going to Geneva, the delegation had a plenary meeting with the then Thai Prime Minister to explain its mission and to request future policy approval from him. The Premier was informed that Thailand was not specifically targeted by the Committee since it was Thailand's turn to explain Thailand's implementation of the ICCPR. The mass death incidents in 2004 had raised concerns in the OIC and among the three Muslim-majority States that are members of the Association of Southeast Asian Nations (ASEAN) to which Thailand also belongs. Instead of merely giving explanations on what had happened, Thailand would have to give commitments to the international community that any shortcomings in this regard would never happen again, by reforming law enforcement procedures and by bringing *all* those responsible for human rights violations to justice under the due process of law. In the end, the Prime Minister concurred with the delegation's submissions, authorized the start of the criminal prosecution against those accused of wrongdoing in the aforesaid incidents, and ordered reform of the rules and standard of policing so as to measure up to international standards. The Human Rights Committee, therefore, served as a major catalyst for human rights awakening in Thailand, especially among Thai Government agencies. The Committee achieved what Thailand's very own National Human Rights Commission had failed to do in prompting the Thai Government to act. The ensuing reform may be time consuming and justice to victims of human rights violations may be slow, but at least Thailand now understands that it is always subject to international human rights scrutiny, with Thailand's international reputation and stature at stake.

Due to the continued growth of such treaty bodies, the UNGA adopted a resolution on 9 April 2014

> to consider the state of the human rights treaty body system no later than six years from the date of adoption of the present resolution, to review the effectiveness of the measures taken in order to ensure their sustainability and, if appropriate, to decide on further action to strengthen and enhance the effective functioning of the human rights treaty body system.[70]

To help UN Member States prepare for this review, the Geneva Academy of International Humanitarian Law and Human Rights, an academic think tank, has collected ideas emerging from consultations with its partners across the globe. Its report[71] identifies the main challenges confronting the treaty body system as ones relating to its effectiveness, efficiency and coordination.

The Geneva Academy is concerned that the number of treaty bodies, which has doubled in the last decade, still keeps on increasing, resulting in a considerable overload and backlog for treaty bodies although their respective resources in terms of the number of staff and level of expertise remain inadequate. The ten existing treaty bodies – composed of 172 independent, part-time, unpaid experts – have developed their own working methods and procedures and some of them even work on similar issues without much coordination. National selection procedures and UN election processes for these experts lack the openness and transparency required to secure a suitably qualified and competent membership that is independent of government. Meanwhile, non-compliance with reporting obligations is widespread, with only 16 per cent of the reports due to treaty bodies in 2010 and 2011 being submitted on time and merely 13 per cent of States Parties to human rights treaties with treaty bodies having fully met their reporting obligations by 19 January 2016. The weakness of the diverse follow-up procedures adopted by treaty bodies, lack of access to treaty bodies' work and their low visibility might contribute to this failure.[72]

It is suggested that the following measures be adopted for meaningful reforms of the treaty body system. Reforms must accord universal protection

---

[70]   UNGA Res 60/262 on 'Strengthening and enhancing the effective functioning of the human rights treaty body system', Doc A/RES/68/268 (21 Apr 2014) operative §41.
[71]   Claire Callejon, Kamelia Kemileva, Felix Kirchmeier and Domenico Zipoli, *Optimizing the UN Treaty Body System: Academic Platform Report on the 2020 Review* (Geneva Academy of International Humanitarian Law & Human Rights 2018).
[72]   Ibid 11–12.

of human rights by placing human rights-holders at the centre, being victim oriented and upholding the essential integrity of the system. The system must be fair to all States Parties and accessible as well as visible to stakeholders (including through the medium of civil society organizations and a consistent level of predictability). The system must be economically viable, with adequate resources. The integrity of the human rights treaties must be upheld, with incremental change within the existing legal framework, which should not cause amendment of the treaties. The reform process should be open to bold reform initiatives, short term and long term. Lastly, the system must be fit for purpose in the sense of being designed and equipped to cope with its growing workload.[73] It should be added that IHRL must actually deliver adequate justice to victims of human rights violations, either as individual victims or as a class of victims, be it in the form of compensation, restitution, rehabilitation and/or any other type of satisfaction such as apologies or assurance of non-repetition.[74]

The Geneva Academy recommends two options for State Party reports. First, under the 'single State report combined with a consolidated State review' model, States Parties would be reviewed by all relevant treaty bodies during the same week every seven to eight years on the basis of a single State report containing a general section that covers all the treaties to which a State is party, followed by sections that are treaty specific. The outcome of the review would include distinct concluding observations from the treaty body of each treaty to which the State is party. In practical terms, this option would require all but one of the ten treaty bodies to sit simultaneously in Geneva in different meeting rooms for a week.[75] States under review would meet each relevant treaty body in turn. The other option is for a semi-consolidated State report combined with a clustered State review. This would also consolidate State reviews but would not require all treaty bodies to sit simultaneously every seven to eight years. States would be reviewed twice, by different treaty bodies, at four-year intervals. Clustering the reviews by treaty bodies of the ICCPR and the ICESCR and treaty bodies of the treaties that address specific groups and themes could strengthen follow-up and reinforcement while avoiding unnecessary and unintended overlaps. In addition, the report suggests incremental changes in working methods to achieve synergies in the treaty body system, such as aligning working methods, sharing information or establishing a joint working

---

[73] Ibid 14–15.
[74] Fiona McKay, 'What Outcomes for Victims?' in Shelton (ed.), *The Oxford Handbook of International Human Rights Law* 921.
[75] The only exception is the SPT.

group on follow-up, as well as by interacting with other UN human rights mechanisms and regional ones.[76]

5.   UN HIGH COMMISSIONER FOR HUMAN RIGHTS: IMPOSSIBLE MANDATES?

UN agencies and partners involved in the promotion and protection of human rights and which interact with the main human rights bodies include the UN High Commissioner for Refugees, Office for the Coordination of Humanitarian Affairs, Inter-Agency Internal Displacement Division, International Labour Organization, World Health Organization, UNESCO, Joint UN Programme on HIV/AIDS, Inter-Agency Standing Committee, Department of Economic and Social Affairs, Commission on the Status of Women, Office of the Special Adviser on Gender Issues and the Advancement of Women, Division for the Advancement of Women, UN Population Fund, UN Children's Fund, UN Entity for Gender Equality and the Empowerment of Women, UN Development Programme, Food and Agriculture Organization, UN Human Settlements Programme, and UN Mine Action.

ECOSOC still retains its role on human rights insofar as these fall within its direct mandate, as in the case of the agenda item entitled 'Economic and social repercussions of the Israeli occupation on the living conditions of the Palestinian people in the Occupied Palestinian Territory, including East Jerusalem and the Arab population in the occupied Syrian Golan'. On 23 July 2019, for example, ECOSOC adopted a resolution on the situation of and assistance to Palestinian women by a vote, mostly along the international political divide, of forty to two with nine abstentions and three absent, which, inter alia, reaffirms the obligations of States and all parties to armed conflict to comply with international humanitarian law and IHRL, including CEDAW, as applicable and the need to end all violations of these bodies of law. It also calls upon Israel

> to immediately cease all measures contrary to international law, as well as dis-
> criminatory legislation, policies and actions in the Occupied Palestinian Territory,
> including East Jerusalem, that violate the human rights of the Palestinian people and

---

[76] Callejon et al, *Optimizing the UN Treaty Body System* 6–8, 17–44. For some earlier similar proposals, see Kelisiana Thynne, 'Reform of United Nations Human Rights Institutions: Current Developments – Enhancing the Rule of Law in International Human Rights Treaty Bodies' (2007) 9 World Legal Information Institute 7. Cf Nigel S Rodley, 'The Role and Impact of Treaty Bodies' in Shelton (ed.), *The Oxford Handbook of International Human Rights Law* 621, 642–7.

stresses that Palestinian civilians, particularly women and children, account for the vast majority of those adversely affected by the conflict.[77]

Out of 20 agenda items on ECOSOC's 2018–19 agenda, this agenda item focuses on condemning a specific State. All the other focus areas concern global topics such as disaster relief assistance and the use of science and technology for development.

It is the Office of the UNHCHR that serves as the principal human rights coordinating body of the UN to spearhead the UN's human rights efforts by offering leadership, working objectively, educating and taking action to empower individuals and assist States in upholding human rights.

The Office of the UNHCHR is a part of the UN Secretariat, with its own headquarters in Geneva. The Office's thematic priorities are strengthening international human rights mechanisms, enhancing equality and countering discrimination, combating impunity and strengthening accountability and the rule of law, integrating human rights in development and in the economic sphere, widening the democratic space and early warning, and protection of human rights in situations of conflict, violence and insecurity. It also supports the work of the UN human rights mechanisms, including the treaty bodies and the HRC's special procedures. It promotes the right to development, coordinates UN human rights education and public information activities and strengthens human rights across the UN as well as working to ensure the enforcement of universally recognized human rights norms, including through promoting both the universal ratification and implementation of the major human rights treaties and respect for the rule of law. As of 31 December 2013, the Office had 1,085 staff based in Geneva, New York and in 13 country offices and 13 regional offices or centres around the world, as well as a workforce of 689 international human rights officers serving in UN peace missions or political offices. The Office is financed by the UN regular budget and from voluntary contributions from UN Member States, intergovernmental organizations, foundations and individuals.

The UNGA's resolution setting up the post of the UNHCHR stipulates that the UNHCHR shall be a person of high moral standing and personal integ-

---

[77] Doc E/2019/L.25 (17 July 2019). Those voting in favour were: Andorra, Angola, Armenia, Azerbaijan, Belarus, Benin, Cambodia, China, Colombia, Denmark, Ecuador, Egypt, El Salvador, Ethiopia, France, Ghana, India, Iran, Ireland, Japan, Kenya, Luxembourg, Mali, Malta, Morocco, Netherlands, Norway, Pakistan, Paraguay, Philippines, South Korea, Russia, St Vincent and the Grenadines, Saudi Arabia, Sudan, Turkey, Turkmenistan, Uruguay, Venezuela and Yemen. The USA and Canada voted against it, whereas Brazil, Cameroon, Germany, Jamaica, Mexico, Romania, Togo, Ukraine and UK abstained. Chad, Eswatini and Malawi were absent.

rity and shall possess expertise, including in the field of human rights, and the general knowledge and understanding of diverse cultures necessary for impartial, objective, non-selective and effective performance of the duties of the UNHCHR. He or she shall be appointed by the UN Secretary-General and approved by the UNGA, with due regard to geographical rotation, and have a fixed term of four years with a possibility of one renewal for another fixed term of four years.[78] The resolution does not specify how the UNHCHR is to be selected for appointment by the Secretary-General.

To date, there have been seven UNHCHRs, four of whom have been female. All of them are individuals who have had internationally recognized human rights roles. José Ayala-Lasso, a career diplomat and former Foreign Minister of Ecuador, became the first UNHCHR on 5 April 1994, appointed by the UN Secretary-General with the unanimous approval of the UNGA. He was chosen after having chaired, in 1993, the working group that considered establishing the post of UNHCHR and implementing other aspects of the 1993 Vienna Declaration and Programme of Action, adopted at the World Conference on Human Rights that year. He resigned as UNHCHR on 15 March 1997 to become Minister of Foreign Affairs of Ecuador once again.

Mary Robinson, a lawyer and former President of Ireland, became the second UNHCHR on 12 September 1997. Sergio Vieira de Mello, a Brazilian, was appointed UNHCHR on 12 September 2002 after his long and distinguished career in humanitarian and peacekeeping operations as well as other UN bodies, including as UN Under-Secretary-General for Humanitarian Affairs and Emergency Relief Coordinator. After his untimely death in August 2003, Bertrand Ramcharan, Deputy UNHCHR, became acting UNHCHR until July 2004, when Louise Arbour, a Canadian former Chief Prosecutor for the International Criminal Tribunals for the former Yugoslavia and for Rwanda, was appointed UNHCHR. She was succeeded by Navi Pillay, a South African former judge of the International Criminal Tribunal for Rwanda and the ICC.

Zeid Ra'ad Al Hussein, a Jordanian career diplomat, became UNHCHR on 1 September 2014, being the first Asian, Muslim and Arab to assume this post. He had served as the first President of the Assembly of States Parties to the Rome Statute of the ICC.

On 10 August 2018 the UNGA approved Michelle Bachelet as the new UNHCHR. A medical doctor by training and a torture victim during the Pinochet military dictatorship, she served as President of Chile twice, from 2006 to 2010 and from 2014 to 2018. At the time of her appointment as UNHCHR, she was the first executive director of the newly established UN Entity for Gender Equality and the Empowerment of Women.

---

[78] A/RES/48/141 (7 Jan 1994).

The practice in the selection and appointment of the UNHCHR as explained by the UN Secretary-General in 2018 is as follows. The position is advertised through a diplomatic note to all UN Member States, a vacancy announcement on the website of the Secretary-General and distribution in various media, civil society and other relevant networks. The Secretary-General also makes a specific request to UN Member States, NGOs, national human rights institutions and regional organizations for the nomination of women candidates and to the public to encourage women candidates to apply for the vacancy. Shortlisted candidates will be interviewed by a panel of internal and external experts and finalists will be recommended to the Secretary-General for consideration. The Secretary-General strives to ensure that the candidate fully meets the profile for the position and that the selection decision enhances the UN's objectives for gender parity and geographic diversity.[79] This explanation has failed to placate a coalition of civil society actors who believe that the UNHCHR is a person handpicked by the Secretary-General without following a process that is fully meritocratic and transparent and that involves conducting wide and inclusive consultations, including with civil society.[80]

In any case, the UNHCHR must command general acceptance among UN Member States for she/he to be approved by the UNGA. Once appointed, if she/he wishes to seek the renewal of the mandate for another four-year term she/he must have the necessary support of UN Member States. As such, she/he cannot antagonize the majority of them, especially the influential ones, with criticisms of their human rights records, however appalling they may be. UNHCHR Al Hussein went public, telling the media he did not seek a renewed mandate lest he would have to bend a knee in supplication, mute a statement of human rights advocacy and lessen the independence and integrity of his role in exchange for the support of UN Member States.[81] One quick fix would be having a single extended term for the UNHCHR, who may still be removed from office by an independent mechanism in the case of the UNHCHR's

---

[79] Letter from the Chef de Cabinet of the UN Secretary-General dated 8 June 2018 addressed to Mr Ben Donaldson, Head of Campaigns, United Nations Association – UK, https://www.una.org.uk/file/12579/download?token=ctOoCKA_, accessed 17 Aug 2019.

[80] Marc Limon (Executive Director, Universal Rights Group), 'The selection and appointment of the next High Commissioner for Human Rights: Right person, shame about the process' (14 Aug 2018) https://www.universal-rights.org/blog/the-selection -and-appointment-of-the-next-high-commissioner-for-human-rights-right-person -shame-about-the-process/, accessed 17 Aug 2019.

[81] Somini Sengupta and Nick Cumming-Bruce, 'Zeid Ra'ad al-Hussein, Top Human Rights Official, Won't Seek a Second Term', *New York Times* (20 Dec 2017) https://www.nytimes.com/2017/12/20/world/un-human-rights-al-hussein.html, accessed 25 Aug 2018.

incompetence, incapacity, abuse of power or position or neglect of duty. Even so, the question may be asked whether it is, in fact, impossible for the UNHCHR to do more to protect and promote human rights. The UNHCHR is a coordinator on international human rights issues with high standing in the eyes of the international community of nations. Unfortunately, the post does not endow the UNHCHR with any legal power or authority to compel governments to abide by their human rights obligations. The UNHCHR must act within the rules of the game jointly established by States to protect their respective interests.

It seems that the UNHCHR usually succeeds with 'soft targets' but not hard ones. For instance, the UNHCHR's criticism of and objection to Brunei's imposing capital punishment on those convicted of gay sex led to Brunei's moratorium on the implementation of this controversial Sharia law barely a month after its promulgation in April 2019. Brunei is a soft target because Brunei and its government have a respectable standing among the international community of nations and this issue is not so critical to Brunei's overall national interests that it cannot back off. Compare this to the UNHCHR's denunciation of serious human rights abuses in Syria, Sudan under the then President Al-Bashir, and other 'hard' cases. Here, the UNHCHR faces four interconnected denials by the targeted person(s). First, no such human rights violation happened. Second, even if it did happen, it was not perpetrated by the person(s) subjected to the UNHCHR's censure. Third, if indeed the aforesaid person(s) did the act(s) in question, this, for some reason, is not prohibited under international law. Finally, if such act(s) is or are proscribed by international law, the appropriate procedure or mechanism that must be followed to punish the human rights abuser(s) has not been used. Where hard-core human rights abusers are protected by powerful States, their aforesaid denials can be effectively refuted only with the cooperation of all the five UNSC permanent members acting collectively. Where this is the case, the UNHCHR is straight-jacketed and must rely on UN bodies as well as treaty body mechanisms to fully and honestly discharge the respective human rights mandates expected of her/him.

6.   REALISM

Criticisms against the UN human rights system should not overlook the reality of international diplomacy. The system gives States internationally justifiable and legitimate opportunities to deal with human rights issues faced by other States. Its ground rules as to who can raise the issues, what issues can be raised, against whom and why, enable the international community to protect and promote human rights within the real-life constraints of international relations.

Multilateral diplomacy follows a consistent pattern, including in the realm of human rights. The Western European and Others Group (WEOG) is the most well coordinated of all regional groups. The WEOG's meetings are regular and well attended by its members. By contrast, only a few delegates normally turn up at coordinating meetings of the Group of 77, comprising developing States, because of lack of human resources and, often, lack of financial resources to finance attendance by delegates from their respective capital cities. Although the UN does have some financial support arrangements funded mostly by voluntary contributions, they are not sufficient to sponsor attendance by all those who should be there. The G77 also faces a serious dilemma – the longer an international diplomatic conference on a particular issue drags on, especially with more sessions or inter-sessional meetings, the fewer delegates/delegations from the G77 attend it and, frequently, those who attend are newcomers to the issue since the previous ones are assigned to other duties. Institutional memories among members of the G77 are, thus, not as good as those of their financially better endowed counterparts. This is why the better coordinated and informed WEOG has an upper hand in getting its positions accepted by the plenary more often than those of other groups of States. Also, this is possibly why the Western liberal democratic version of human rights has dominated UN forums.

In any diplomatic conference that requires consensus for adopting decisions or resolutions, beware of hard-line States with an agenda to protect their hard-line stances. Without their concurrence, there can be no consensus. Their delegates always attend coordinating and plenary meetings to propagate their positions and/or to oppose the attainment of consensus unless their positions – sometimes in unrelated matters and at another multilateral forum – are accepted by the State(s) pressing for the consensus.

Compared to the UNHCHR, the UN Secretary-General has much greater clout and stature. Yet, it is common knowledge that the latter is 'Secretary' rather than 'General' of the UN, where Member States, especially the five permanent members of the UNSC, wield influence and leverage over the UN's roles and direction. The appointment of the Secretary-General must receive the approval of all the five permanent members of the UNSC and he/she needs support from UN Member States to fulfil his/her mandate. How to strike the right balance between ensuring continued cooperation from governments and bringing abusive ones to account is quite problematic. Therefore, the Secretary-General is often criticized for not doing enough after quiet diplomacy has failed, such as by not publically naming and shaming governments that abuse human rights so as to galvanize the international community to make the governments liable for, or at least terminate, their acts.[82]

Nevertheless, as Chapter 6 will explain, even within the aforesaid restraints, compliance with IHRL and enforcement of that law against States are essentially enhanced by the existence and operation of the UN human rights system discussed in this chapter.

---

[82]　Eg, Kenneth Roth, 'UN Chief Guterres Has Disappointed on Human Rights: New Strategy Needed for Second Half of Term', *Human Rights Watch* (22 July 2019) https://www.hrw.org/news/2019/07/22/un-chief-guterres-has-disappointed-human -rights, accessed 23 July 2019.

4. Regional human rights mechanisms: tailor-made for the locals?

1. UNIVERSAL HUMAN RIGHTS NORMS AS LOCALLY APPLIED?[1]

As Judge James Crawford of the International Court of Justice (ICJ) has rightly pointed out, although 'human rights are expressly based on putative universal values ... [and] despite common aims and similar legal and philosophical genealogy, the specific content of human rights and of the mechanisms to enforce those rights, is nuanced between regional regimes – to the point of significant variation'.[2]

The second World Conference on Human Rights was held in Vienna, Austria, from 14 to 25 June 1993.[3] It was attended by representatives of 171 States and approximately 800 NGOs. In preparing for the Vienna Conference, three key regional meetings were convened in Tunis, San José and Bangkok, producing declarations outlining particular concerns and perspectives of Africa, Latin America and the Caribbean, and Asia Pacific, respectively, which should shed light on what States in these three regions actually think

---

[1]   See further, Ilias Bantekas and Lutz Oette, *International Human Rights Law and Practice* (2nd edn, CUP 2016) 235–94; David P Forsythe, *Human Rights in International Relations* (4th edn, CUP 2018) ch. 5; Malcolm D Evans, 'The Future(s) of Regional Courts on Human Rights' in Antonio Cassese (ed.), *Realizing Utopia: The Future of International Law* (OUP 2012) 261; Christoff Heyns and Magnus Killander, 'Universality and the Growth of Regional Systems' in Dinah Shelton (ed.), *The Oxford Handbook of International Human Rights Law* (OUP 2013) 670; Başak Çali, 'Regional Protection' in Daniel Moeckli, Sangeeta Shah and Sandesh Sivakumaran (eds), *International Human Rights Law* (3rd edn, OUP 2018) 411.

[2]   James Crawford, 'Chance, Order, Change: The Course of International Law' (2013) 365 Hague Recueil 9, 244.

[3]   The first World Conference on Human Rights was convened in Tehran, Iran, during the Cold War, from 22 April to 13 May 1968 to review the progress made and to formulate a programme for the future. It was attended by representatives of 84 States, four regional organizations and 57 NGOs. The Proclamation issued after the conference is rather modest and largely reaffirms the principles in the 1948 Universal Declaration of Human Rights (UN Doc A/Conf. 32/41 (1968) 3).

about international human rights norms, as will be elucidated in sections 3, 4 and 6 below.

In the global diplomatic context, States from all regions could join the consensus at the Vienna Conference in adopting the Vienna Declaration and Programme of Action of the World Conference on Human Rights,[4] which is almost 30 pages in length. Among other things, its preamble recognizes and reaffirms that 'all human rights derive from the dignity and worth inherent in the human person, and that the human person is the central subject of human rights and fundamental freedoms and consequently should be the principal beneficiary and should participate actively in the realization of these rights and freedoms'. It also emphasizes the responsibilities of all States, in conformity with the UN Charter, to develop and encourage respect for human rights and fundamental freedoms for all, without distinction as to race, sex, language or religion. The 1948 Universal Declaration of Human Rights (UDHR)[5] is considered to constitute 'a common standard of achievement for all peoples and all nations' as well as 'the source of inspiration' that has been the basis for the UN in making advances in standard setting as contained in the existing international human rights instruments, in particular the 1966 International Covenant on Civil and Political Rights (ICCPR)[6] and the 1966 International Covenant on Economic, Social and Cultural Rights (ICESCR).[7] The Vienna Declaration and Programme of Action covers, inter alia, the right of self-determination, the right to development, the rights of women and the girl child, the rights of persons belonging to minorities, the rights of indigenous peoples, the rights of the child, the rights of disabled persons, and the freedom from torture. Its operative paragraph I(1), (5) and (32) deals with universalism or universality of human rights as follows:

1. The World Conference on Human Rights reaffirms the solemn commitment of all States to fulfil their obligations to promote *universal* respect for, and observance and protection of, all human rights and fundamental freedoms for all in accordance with the Charter of the United Nations, other instruments relating to human rights and international law. The *universal* nature of these rights and freedoms is beyond question.

...

5. All human rights are *universal*, indivisible and interdependent and interrelated. The international community must treat human rights globally in a fair and equal manner, on the same footing and with the same emphasis. While the significance of national and regional particularities and various historical, cultural

---

4   UN Doc A/Conf.157/23 (12 July 1993).
5   Doc A/RES/217(III).
6   999 UNTS 171.
7   993 UNTS 3.

and religious backgrounds must be borne in mind, it is the duty of States, regardless of their political, economic and cultural systems, to promote and protect all human rights and fundamental freedoms.

...

32. The World Conference on Human Rights reaffirms the importance of ensuring the *universality*, objectivity and non-selectivity of the consideration of human rights issues. (Emphasis added.)

Despite the different systems of government among the participating States, they declare that democracy, development and respect for human rights and fundamental freedoms are interdependent and mutually reinforcing, and that the international community should support the strengthening and promoting of democracy, development and respect for human rights and fundamental freedoms in the entire world.[8] Regional arrangements have a fundamental role in promoting and protecting human rights and they should 'reinforce *universal human rights standards*, as contained in international human rights instruments and their protection'.[9] The Conference reaffirms the important and constructive role played by national human rights institutions and NGOs for the promotion and protection of human rights, in particular in their advisory capacity to the competent authorities, in remedying human rights violations, in the dissemination of human rights information and in education in human rights.[10] It encourages the increased involvement of the media, for whom freedom and protection should be guaranteed within the framework of national law.[11]

The Vienna Conference's conclusion that the promotion and protection of human rights must be treated as a priority objective of the UN as well as its recognition of the link between that objective and the maintenance of international peace and security was then novel and provided impetus for the strengthening of UN work in preventive diplomacy, peacemaking and peacekeeping.[12]

The Vienna Declaration and Programme of Action is not a legally binding human rights instrument and its provisions were an outcome of diplomatic compromises that need not reflect the legal position and/or policy of some of the States joining the consensus in adopting it in order to court global respect

---

[8] Ibid §I(8).
[9] Ibid §I(37) (emphasis added).
[10] Ibid §I(36), (38).
[11] Ibid §I(39).
[12] Kevin Boyle, 'Stock Taking on Human Rights: The World Conference on Human Rights, Vienna 1993' (1995) 43 Political Studies 79, 80.

and recognition. Notably absent from the Declaration is the idea of having a discrete 'world court of human rights'.[13]

Regional human rights mechanisms have been set up in the belief that they will better reflect human rights values of heterogeneous States in particular regions having similar governance, cultures and legal norms and are tied to one another through geography, politics and economics.[14] The larger a regional or subregional grouping, the more likely that it can afford to leave behind those whose positions the majority cannot accommodate. For a grouping with relatively few Member States, consensus is the rule – no State is left behind and all must accept the lowest common denominator attainable by consensus within the grouping.

A study undertaken in 1999 on the impact of the international human rights system on 20 States in the five UN regions shows a widespread preference for regional systems above the UN system.[15] The rest of this chapter will proceed to consider regional human rights mechanisms in a chronological order according to the date when modern international human rights law (IHRL) first set its roots in the respective regions of the world.

2.   EUROPE

All the 47 members of the Council of Europe (CoE)[16] are parties to the 1950 European Convention for the Protection of Human Rights and Fundamental Freedoms, or the European Convention on Human Rights (ECHR)[17] for short.

The ECHR is probably part of the conservatives' efforts to set up new supranational mechanisms to protect the West against communism and fascism both

---

[13]   The present author finds unrealistic such suggestion in Gerd Oberleitner, 'Towards an International Court of Human Rights?' in Mashood A Baderin and Manisuli Ssenyonjo (eds), *International Human Rights Law: Six Decades after the UDHR and Beyond* (Ashgate 2010) 359, 370.

[14]   Cf Rosa Freedman, *Failing to Protect: The UN and the Politicisation of Human Rights* (C Hurst & Co 2014) 142–8, 160.

[15]   Christoff Heyns and Frans Viljoen, 'The Impact of the United Nations Human Rights Treaties on the Domestic Level' (2001) 23 Hum Rts Quarterly 483, 521.

[16]   As of this writing, they are Albania, Andorra, Armenia, Austria, Azerbaijan, Belgium, Bosnia and Herzegovina, Bulgaria, Croatia, Cyprus, Czech Republic, Denmark, Estonia, Finland, France, Georgia, Germany, Greece, Hungary, Iceland, Ireland, Italy, Latvia, Liechtenstein, Lithuania, Luxembourg, Malta, Moldova, Monaco, Montenegro, Netherlands, Norway, Poland, Portugal, Republic of North Macedonia, Romania, Russia, San Marino, Serbia, Slovak Republic, Slovenia, Spain, Sweden, Switzerland, Turkey, Ukraine and UK.

[17]   ETS 5. See further Martyn Bond, *The Council of Europe and Human Rights: The European Convention on Human Rights* (Council of Europe Publishing 2018); William A Schabas, *The European Convention on Human Rights: A Commentary* (OUP 2015).

at home and abroad in Europe. Human rights enshrined in the ECHR resonate with traditional Christian European values/civilization upholding democratic freedom.[18] Transnational movements for European unity comprising non-State actors were the driving force behind the ECHR, determining the ECHR's out-lines prior to the start of intergovernmental negotiations on the ECHR itself.[19] The last preambular paragraph of the ECHR makes it clear that the ECHR was born out of the resolve of 'the governments of European countries which are like-minded and have a common heritage of political traditions, ideals, freedom and the rule of law, to take the first steps for the collective enforce-ment of certain of the rights stated in the [UDHR]'. Social rights are omitted from the ECHR because it was doubted whether they were justiciable in courts of law and would be difficult or impossible to enforce, or because European conservatives were opposed to such rights, which they perceived to reflect socialist or communist values.[20] The First Protocol to the ECHR dated 20 March 1952[21] adds the right of property, the right to education (including the right of parents to ensure such education and teaching in conformity with their own religious and philosophical conviction) and the undertaking by parties to the First Protocol to hold free elections at reasonable intervals by secret ballot, under conditions which will ensure the free expression of the opinion of the people in the choice of the legislature.

The CoE has also taken steps to supplement international human rights instruments, for example by adopting the 1987 European Convention for the Prevention of Torture and Inhuman or Degrading Treatment or Punishment[22] to effectuate the implementation of the 1984 Convention against Torture and Other Cruel, Inhuman or Degrading Treatment or Punishment (CAT),[23] adopted by the UN General Assembly (UNGA) in December 1984 and in force on 26 June 1987. The 1987 European Convention sets up the European Committee on the Prevention of Torture and Inhuman or Degrading Treatment or Punishment, composed of a number of members equal to that of the States Parties to the 1987 European Convention. The Committee visits States Parties to the 1987 Convention in order to examine the treatment of persons deprived of their liberty with a view to strengthening, if necessary, the protection of such persons from torture and from inhuman or degrading treatment or

[18] Marco Duranti, *The Conservative Human Rights Revolution: European Identity, Transnational Politics and the Origins of the European Convention* (OUP 2017) 3, 330–32, 403.
[19] Ibid 322.
[20] Ibid 326–7.
[21] ETS No 9.
[22] ETS No 126.
[23] 1465 UNTS 85.

punishment. The Committee also interacts closely with the Subcommittee on Prevention of Torture and Other Cruel, Inhuman or Degrading Treatment or Punishment set up by CAT.

The European Court of Human Rights (ECtHR), based in Strasbourg, France, is empowered to interpret the ECHR. The ECtHR has jurisdiction over applications by individuals against States party to the ECHR and inter-State disputes between States party to the ECHR. Pursuant to Protocol No 16 to the ECHR, open for signature on 2 October 2013 and in force on 1 August 2018 in respect of the States that have signed and ratified it,[24] the ECtHR may give non-binding advisory opinions to the highest national courts and tribunals of States party to the Protocol on questions of principle relating to the interpretation or application of the rights and freedoms defined in the ECHR or the protocols thereto. The requesting court or tribunal may seek an advisory opinion only in the context of a case pending before it. A panel of five judges of the Grand Chamber of the ECtHR shall decide whether to accept the request for an advisory opinion and shall give reasons for any refusal to accept the request. If the panel accepts the request, the Grand Chamber shall deliver the advisory opinion. The said panel and the Grand Chamber shall include *ex officio* the judge elected in respect of the State Party to which the requesting court or tribunal pertains. If there is none or if that judge is unable to sit, a person chosen by the President of the ECtHR from a list submitted in advance by that State Party shall sit in the capacity of judge.

Applications by individuals constitute the majority of cases before the ECtHR. It has a very heavy workload. For example, at the end of 2018 the ECtHR had more than 4,000 individual applications before it that were apparently related solely to the events in Crimea or the hostilities in Eastern Ukraine, including allegations of the detention of individuals by Russia or Ukraine, by the self-proclaimed Donetsk and Luhansk People's Republics and about the destruction of housing during hostile action. In addition, there was a related inter-State case of *Ukraine v Russia (re Eastern Ukraine)*, in which the Government of Ukraine raised various complaints against the Russian Government, alleging violations of the ECHR by the latter.[25]

All the members of the European Union (EU)[26] are also members of the CoE, whose membership includes non-EU Member States. The EU itself

---

[24] ETS No 214. As of this writing, these States are Albania, Armenia, Estonia, Finland, France, Georgia, Lithuania, San Marino, Slovenia and Ukraine.

[25] App No 8019/16; ECtHR Press Release 423 (2018) 17.12.2018.

[26] As of this writing, the 28 EU Member States are Austria, Belgium, Bulgaria, Croatia, Cyprus, Czech Republic, Denmark, Estonia, Finland, France, Germany, Greece, Hungary, Ireland, Italy, Latvia, Lithuania, Luxembourg, Malta, Netherlands, Poland, Portugal, Romania, Slovakia, Slovenia, Spain, Sweden and UK.

adopted, in 2000, the Charter of Fundamental Rights of the EU.[27] Article 52(3) of the Charter provides that insofar as the EU Charter contains rights which correspond to rights guaranteed by the ECHR, the meaning and scope of those rights shall be the same as those stipulated in the ECHR, but this shall not prevent EU law from providing more extensive protection than that accorded by the ECHR. It is the Court of Justice of the EU, or European Court of Justice (ECJ), in Luxembourg that interprets the EU Charter as well as EU law and intra-EU agreements, many of which have a direct bearing on human rights.

Europe is the most homogeneous geographical region of the world in terms of culture and values. However, inside Europe as well as inside a European nation State opinions are divided on such human rights issues as the right to abortion – perceived either as a facet of the right of the pregnant woman or the right to life of the unborn foetus – religious symbols, and treatment of marginalized groups like the Roma.[28] The sharp divisions about abortion 'signal the complexity of the value and the markedly different ways that different cultures, different groups and different people, equally committed to [the sanctity or inviolability of every stage of every human life], interpret its meaning'.[29] While an overwhelming majority of nation States legally allow abortion to save women's lives, drastically fewer States allow it for the protection of women's physical and mental health, even fewer again permit abortion for the protection of victims of rape or incest, and the fewest number of States permit abortion for 'social or economic' reasons.[30] This is despite the Human Rights Committee's General Comment No 28 in the context of the right to life protected by Article 6 of the ICCPR that States Parties to the ICCPR should give information on any measures taken by them to help women prevent unwanted pregnancies and to ensure that they do not have to undergo life-threatening clandestine abortions.[31] To assess compliance with Article 7 of the ICCPR on the right not to be subject to torture or to cruel, inhuman or degrading treatment or punishment as well as with Article 24 of the ICCPR,

---

[27]   OJ C 326/391 of 26.10.2012.

[28]   Freedman, *Failing to Protect* 153–4.

[29]   Ronald Dworkin, *Life's Dominion: An Argument about Abortion and Euthanasia* (HarperCollins 1993) 238. Dworkin concludes that each individual should have the right to decide for herself (ibid 238–9). Cf Elizabeth Wicks, 'International Trends in the Recognition of Abortion Rights' in Carla M Buckley, Alice Donald and Philip Leach (eds), *Towards Convergence in International Human Rights Law Approaches of Regional and International Systems* (Brill Nijhoff 2016) 103.

[30]   Patricia Londono, 'Redrafting Abortion Rights under the Convention: A, B and C v Ireland' in Eva Brems (ed.), *Diversity and European Human Rights: Rewriting Judgments of the ECHR* (CUP 2013) 95, 96–7.

[31]   General Comment No 28 (2000): Article 3 (The Equality of Rights between Men and Women) 29 Mar 2000, CCPR/C/21/Rev.1/Add.10 §10.

which mandates special protection for children, the Human Rights Committee asks for information from ICCPR States Parties on whether they give access to safe abortion to women who have become pregnant as a result of rape.[32]

The Eighth Amendment of the Irish Constitution recognizing the right to life of an unborn child was adopted by the referendum held in 1983. In 2013 the Protection of Life During Pregnancy Act[33] was enacted to permit abortions if the mother's life was immediately threatened, including by suicide. The issue of the right to abortion in Ireland was put to a referendum on 25 May 2018, resulting in 66.4 per cent (or a majority of 706,349) in a turnout of 64.1 per cent of those eligible to vote voting in favour of the repeal of the Eighth Amendment. However, except where a woman's life is at risk or there is a risk of permanent and serious damage to a woman's mental or physical health, abortion is still illegal in Northern Ireland, which is part of the UK. The UK's Abortion Act of 1967, as amended by the Human Fertilization and Embryology Act of 1990,[34] which generally legalizes abortion on numerous grounds up to 24 weeks of gestation in all of Great Britain, does not extend to Northern Ireland.

In order to accommodate the differences among cultures and societies in Europe, the ECtHR has invented and applied the doctrine of margin of appreciation since the 1950s, despite the absence of any express reference to this doctrine in the ECHR or its drafting history.[35]

Because ECHR States Parties have primary responsibility in protecting the human rights under the ECHR within their respective territories or jurisdiction or effective control, the ECtHR, which is subsidiary to the national systems safeguarding human rights, exercises judicial restraint by deferring to the States Parties to strike a balance between competing ECHR rights as well as to determine whether there is a 'pressing social need' capable of justifying interference with one or more of the ECHR rights.[36] However, the ECtHR retains

---

[32] Ibid §11.

[33] Act No 35 of 2013.

[34] 190 c 37. See Sally Sheldon, 'The Decriminalization of Abortion: An Argument for Modernization' (2016) 36 Oxford J Legal Studies 334.

[35] Steven Greer, 'Universalism and Relativism in the Protection of Human Rights in Europe: Politics, Law and Culture' in Peter Agha (ed.), *Human Rights between Law and Politics: The Margin of Appreciation in Post-National Contexts* (Hart 2017) 18, 27–36; Ben Golder, 'On the Varieties of Universalism in Human Rights Discourse' in Agha (ed.), ibid 37, esp 53; Jiří Přibáň, 'Anything to Appreciate?: A Sociological View of the Margin of Appreciation and the Persuasive Force of their Doctrines' in Agha (ed.), ibid 89, 109–10.

[36] Dominic McGoldrick, 'Affording States a Margin of Appreciation: Comparing the European Court of Human Rights and the Inter-American Court of Human Rights' in Buckley et al (eds), *Towards Convergence in International Human Rights Law*

strong elements of supervision as national authorities may not be always better placed, capable or willing to provide the optimal solution to human rights clashes.[37] The Copenhagen Declaration adopted by the High Level Conference of the 47 CoE Member States meeting in Copenhagen on 12 and 13 April 2018[38] refers to the ECtHR's jurisprudence on the margin of appreciation as recognition that in applying certain ECHR provisions there may be a range of different but legitimate solutions which could each be compatible with the ECHR depending on the context. The Declaration considers the margin of appreciation as going hand in hand with supervision under the ECHR system, and the decision as to whether there has been a violation of the ECHR ultimately rests with the ECtHR.[39] The Declaration, therefore, welcomes the further development of the principle of subsidiarity and the doctrine of the margin of appreciation by the ECtHR in its jurisprudence.[40]

The ECtHR most commonly applies the doctrine of margin of appreciation in the context of limits of rights under the ECHR. With respect to positive obligations under the ECHR, the ECtHR gives each State Party to the ECHR a wide margin of appreciation in determining the steps to be undertaken to ensure compliance with the ECHR with due regard to the needs and resources of the community and individuals concerned. In balancing between the relevant competing interests and in respect of which the State may enjoy a margin of appreciation, the ECtHR determines whether there is a pressing social need for the measure in question and whether the interference by the measure is proportionate.[41] Although the nature of the right and the type of case are not in themselves grounds for deference by the ECtHR, they do affect reasons for deference or non-deference to the margin of appreciation. One piece of research concludes that absolute rights (right to life and prohibition of torture) allow

---

Approaches of Regional and International Systems 325, 326; Stijn Smet, 'When Human Rights Clash in the "Age of Subsidiarity": What Roles for the Margin of Appreciation' in Agha (ed.), *Human Rights between Law and Politics* 55, 58–66, citing, inter alia, *Faber v Hungary* App No 40721/08 (ECHR 24 July 2012) §42 and *Eweida v The United Kingdom* App No 48420/10 et al (ECHR 15 Jan 2013) §106. Also, Dimitrios Tsarapatsanis, 'The Margin of Appreciation as an Underenforcement' in Agha (ed.), *Human Rights between Law and Politics* 71, 72.

[37]   Smet, 'When Human Rights Clash in the "Age of Subsidiarity"' 67–8; Eva Brems, *Human Rights: Universality and Diversity* (Martinus Nijhoff 2001) 418–22; Frans Viljoen, *International Human Rights Law in Africa* (2nd edn, OUP 2012) 21; Andrew Legg, *The Margin of Appreciation in International Human Rights Law: Defence and Proportionality* (OUP 2012) 38–49, 223–4.

[38]   https://rm.coe.int/copenhagen-declaration/16807b915c, accessed 1 Sept 2018.

[39]   Ibid §28(d).

[40]   Ibid §31.

[41]   Legg, *The Margin of Appreciation in International Human Rights Law* 175 et seq.

limited scope for the margin of appreciation; strong rights (fair trial, liberty and derogable rights) allow a little more scope for deference; qualified rights (privacy, freedoms of religion, assembly and speech and non-discrimination) anticipate a role for the margin of appreciation, and 'weak' rights (property, education and free elections) give a wide measure of diversity to States.[42]

The ECtHR is criticized for the largely unpredictable and subjective way in which it applies this doctrine by balancing the relevant interests.[43] One suggestion is to confine the application of the doctrine to the situation where there is no 'European consensus' on how to resolve the human rights clash in question or where the issue is a sensitive or ethical one.[44] The ECtHR has, in fact, taken into account the consensus or common value emerging from the practices among States Parties to the ECHR – a stronger consensus will likely narrow the margin of appreciation whereas a weaker consensus will likely broaden such margin.[45]

How the ECtHR has dealt with margin of appreciation in the context of the abortion issue in Ireland is extensively debated.[46] For those opposed to the Irish anti-abortion law, the Grand Chamber of the ECtHR's judgment in *A, B and C*[47] does not adequately protect the human rights of women with unwanted pregnancies. By contrast, those lauding the judgment deem it to have rightly taken cognizance of the delicate balance within Irish society as incorporated into Irish law. In the final analysis, all depends on the subjective assessment of different commentators and the margin of appreciation doctrine is not one and the same as the objective test of 'the man in the street' applied by most legal systems of the world.

There is also some concern that the wide margin of appreciation during emergencies undermines the ECtHR's role as the ultimate protector of human rights under the ECHR.[48]

The doctrine is also criticized for its potential to 'empower a majoritarian, or dominant, political order to consolidate itself against minority claims', as manifested in the ECtHR's series of rulings denying the right of Muslim

---

[42] Ibid 200–217.

[43] Fried van Hoof, 'The Stubbornness of the European Court of Human Rights' Margin of Appreciation Doctrine' in Yves Haeck, Brianne McGonigle Leyh, Clara Burbano-Herrera and Diana Contreras-Garduño (eds), *The Realisation of Human Rights: When Theory Meets Practice* (Intersentia 2013) 125.

[44] Smet, 'When Human Rights Clash in the "Age of Subsidiarity"' 69.

[45] McGoldrick, 'Affording States a Margin of Appreciation' 326–37.

[46] Eg, Londono, 'Redrafting Abortion Rights under the Convention' 100–113; Legg, *The Margin of Appreciation in International Human Rights Law* 220–23.

[47] (2011) 53 EHRR 13.

[48] McGoldrick, 'Affording States a Margin of Appreciation' 337–40.

women to wear Islamic headscarves.[49] This is where Europe has a diplomatic hurdle when it wishes to assert the moral high ground regarding human rights for the rest of the world to emulate. Europe needs to prove that universal human rights norms exist and are duly upheld in Europe; otherwise, Europe will not be in a justifiable position to challenge human rights records of non-European governments, especially those of Muslim-majority States – at least not diplomatically.

In 2011 France became the first European nation State to ban the wearing in public places of a *niqab* (a veil covering the person's face and showing only that person's eyes). Act No 2010-1192 of 11 October 2010 stipulates in Article 1 that '[n]o one may, in a public space, wear any apparel intended to conceal the face'. Article 2 defines 'a public space' as 'public streets and walkways and places open to the public or designated for a public service'. It excludes from the prohibition clothing authorized by law or justified for health or professional reasons, sports practices, festivities or artistic or traditional manifestations. Article 3 sets out the penalties for this minor offence: 'a fine corresponding to offences of category 2' and/or 'mandatory attendance at a citizenship course'. Forcing a person to conceal the face is a serious offence under the Act, pursuant to Article 225-4-10 of the French Criminal Code, which reads:

> The act, by any person, of forcing one or several other persons to conceal the face, by means of threats, violence, coercion, abuse of authority or of power, by reason of their sex, shall be punishable by one year of prison and a fine of €30 000. When such an act is committed against a minor, the penalties shall be increased to two years' imprisonment and a fine of €60 000.

Some other European States have followed France's lead.[50] The Danish law passed by the Danish Parliament on 31 May 2018, by a vote of 75 to 30, effective as of 1 August 2018, stipulates that anyone who wears a garment

---

[49]   Roja Fazaeli, 'Human Rights and Religion' in Michael Goodhart (ed.), *Human Rights: Politics and Practice* (3rd edn, OUP 2016) 163, 177–8. For some early cases, see Tawhida Ahmed and Anastasia Vakulenko, 'Minority Rights 60 Years after the UDHR: Limits on the Preservation of Identity?' in Baderin and Ssenyonjo (eds), *International Human Rights Law* 155, 161–71. For a critique of these rulings, see Nehal Bhuta, 'Rethinking the Universality of Human Rights: A Comparative Historical Proposal for the Idea of "Common Ground" with Other Moral Traditions' in Anver M Emon, Mark Ellis and Benjamin Glahn (eds), *Islamic Law and International Human Rights Law* (OUP 2012) 123, 136–42; Ahmed M El Demey, *The Arab Charter of Human Rights: A Voice for Sharia in the Modern World* (Council on International Law and Politics 2015) 298–306.

[50]   Eva Brems (ed.), *The Experiences of Face Veil Wearers in Europe and the Law* (CUP 2014); SI Strong, *Transforming Religious Liberties: A New Theory of Religious Rights for National and International Legal Systems* (CUP 2018) 172–8; Neville

that hides the face in public shall be punished with a fine. Wearing a *burqa* (a one-piece veil covering the face and body, often leaving only a mesh screen to see through) or a *niqab*, only showing a person's eyes, in public will be fined up to 1,000 kroner (or €134). A person wearing other accessories that hide the face such as balaclavas and false beards shall also be fined. Repeated violations shall be fined up to 10,000 kroner. By virtue of a Dutch law enacted in June 2018, effective as of 1 August 2019, face-covering clothing, such as a *burqa* or *niqab*, is prohibited in educational facilities, public institutions and buildings, hospitals and public transport. Security officials shall ask people with face-covering clothing to show their faces. If they refuse, they can be denied access to public buildings and fined €150.

The latest judgments of the ECtHR regarding Islamic headscarves as of this writing are *Belkacemi and Oussar v Belgium*[51] and *Dakir v Belgium*,[52] both decided on 11 July 2017 and concerning the Belgian ban on Islamic headscarves. The ECtHR ruled that the decision on whether or not to proscribe the wearing of full-face veil in public places is a choice of society and that the Belgian law at issue aims to protect a form of interaction which is necessary and proportionate to assure the functioning of a democratic society; hence, there is no violation of either the right to respect for private or family life under Article 8 or the right of thought, conscience and religion under Article 9 of the ECHR.[53]

European Council Directive 2000/78/EC of 27 November 2000[54] aims at laying down a general framework for combating discrimination on the grounds of religion or belief, disability, age or sexual orientation as regards employment and occupation, with a view to putting into effect in the EU Member States the principle of equal treatment. Discrimination is defined in Article 2 as direct or indirect discrimination on any of the aforesaid grounds. Article 4 (Occupational Requirements) stipulates, inter alia, that notwithstanding Article 2, EU Member States may treat a difference of treatment which is based on a characteristic related to any of the listed grounds of discrimination as not constituting discrimination where, by reason of the nature of the particular occupational activities concerned or of the context in which they are carried out, such a characteristic constitutes a genuine and determining

---

Cox, *Behind the Veil: A Critical Analysis of European Veiling Laws* (Edward Elgar Publishing 2019).

[51] App No 37798/13 (ECHR 11 July 2017).

[52] [2017] ECHR 656.

[53] Cf Eva Brems, Corina Heri, Saïla Ouald Chaib and Lieselot Verdonck, 'Head-Covering Bans in Belgium: Headscarf Persecution and the Complicity of Supranational Courts' (2017) 39 Hum Rts Quarterly 882, 882–98.

[54] OJ L 303 of 2.12.2000.

occupational requirement, provided that the objective is legitimate and the requirement is proportionate. Likewise, in the case of occupational activities within churches and other public or private organizations the ethos of which is based on religion or belief, a difference of treatment based on a person's religion or belief shall not constitute discrimination where, by reason of the nature of these activities or of the context in which they are carried out, a person's religion or belief constitutes a genuine, legitimate and justified occupational requirement, having regard to the organization's ethos. In interpreting this Directive, the ECJ has held there is no discrimination against Islamic headscarf wearers where the workplace imposes a general rule against its employees wearing visible signs of their political, philosophical or religious beliefs in the workplace and/or from engaging in any observance of such beliefs.[55] However, the ECJ has found indirect discrimination on the grounds of religion where the prohibition of the wearing of headscarves is not part of a general neutral policy of the workplace, but is a result of the wish of a customer that female employees of that workplace not wear Islamic headscarves, thereby placing employees of a particular religious group in a more disadvantaged position than others.[56]

From an Islamic law perspective, dress requirements for Muslim women in public places aim at enhancement of human dignity by shielding their sensuous private parts from public eyes, which might cause some seductive temptation for adultery or fornication prohibited by Islamic law. Specifically, the Quran requires women to 'draw their veils over their bosoms' and not to publicly expose their beauty 'except for what must ordinarily appear' (Quran 24: 30–31). However, there are different interpretations about the meaning of the said exception and Muslim women should be able to choose voluntarily between a traditionalist/conservative interpretation or a liberal interpretation regarding the scope of this exception.[57] From the perspective of the ICCPR, the Human Rights Committee emphasizes that any specific regulation of clothing to be worn by women in public may involve a violation of a number of rights guaranteed by the ICCPR, such as Article 26, on non-discrimination; Article 7, if corporal punishment is used to enforce such a regulation; Article 9, when failure to comply with the regulation is punished by arrest; Article 12, if liberty of movement is subject to such a constraint; Article 17, which guarantees all persons the right to privacy without arbitrary or unlawful interference; Articles 18 and 19, when women are subjected to clothing requirements that are not

---

[55] *Achbita & Anor v G4S Secure Solutions NV* [2017] CJEU C-157/15 §37.
[56] *Bougnaoui and ADDH v Micropole SA* [2015] CJEU C-188/15. Both decisions are criticized in Brems et al, 'Head-Covering Bans in Belgium' 904–6.
[57] Mashood A Baderin, *International Human Rights and Islamic Law* (OUP 2003) 64–6.

in keeping with their religion or their right of self-expression; and Article 27, when the clothing requirements conflict with the culture to which the woman can lay a claim.[58]

On 23 October 2018 the Human Rights Committee, in two decisions considered concurrently due to their identical legal questions, found that France had violated the human rights of two women by fining them for wearing a *niqab*.[59] The Committee received the two complaints in 2016 after two French women were prosecuted and convicted in 2012 for wearing the *niqab* in violation of the French law proscribing the wearing in a public space of any article of clothing intended to conceal the face.

The Committee recalls its General Comment No 22, according to which the freedom to manifest religion or belief may be exercised either individually or in community with others and in public or private and that the observance and practice of religion or belief may include not only ceremonial acts, but also such customs as the wearing of distinctive clothing or head coverings.[60] The wearing of the full veil is customary for a segment of the Muslim faithful and it unquestionably concerns the performance of a rite and practice of a religion. Accordingly, the Committee considers the ban under the Act to constitute a restriction or limitation of the individual's freedom to manifest the complainants' beliefs or religion – by wearing the *niqab* – within the meaning of Article 18(1) of the ICCPR. Article 18(3) of the ICCPR permits restrictions on the freedom to manifest religion or belief only if limitations are prescribed by law and are necessary to protect public safety, order, health or morals or the fundamental rights and freedoms of others.[61] Article 18(3) is to be strictly interpreted: restrictions are not allowed on grounds not specified therein, even if they would be allowed as restrictions to other rights protected in the ICCPR, such as national security. Limitations may be applied only for those purposes for which they are prescribed and must be directly related and proportionate to the specific need on which they are predicated. Restrictions may not be imposed for discriminatory purposes or applied in a discriminatory manner. In the Committee's opinion, the Act comprehensively prohibits the wearing of certain face coverings in public at all times and France has failed to demonstrate how wearing the full-face veil in itself represents a threat to public order and safety that would justify such an absolute ban. Nor has France provided

---

[58] Human Rights Committee General Comment No 28 (2000): Article 3 (The Equality of Rights between Men and Women) 29 March 2000, CCPR/C/21/Rev.1/Add.10 §13.
[59] *Sonia Yaker v France*, CCPR/C/123/D/2747/2016, 17 October 2018; *Miriana Hebbadj v France*, CCPR/C/123/D/2807/2016, 17 Oct 2018.
[60] General Comment No 22 on Article 18 (CCPR/C/21/Rev.1/Add.4) §4.
[61] Ibid §8.

any public safety justification or explanation why covering the face for certain religious purposes – that is, the *niqab* – is prohibited, while covering the face for numerous other purposes, including sporting, artistic and other traditional and religious purposes, is allowed. Moreover, France has not described any context, or provided any example, in which there was a specific and significant threat to public order and safety that would justify such a blanket ban on the full-face veil. Even if France could demonstrate the existence of a specific and significant threat to public order and safety in principle, it has failed to demonstrate that the prohibition contained in Act No 2010-1192 of 11 October 2010 is proportionate to that objective, in view of its considerable impact on the individual as a woman wearing the full-face veil. Nor has France attempted to demonstrate that the ban was the least restrictive measure necessary to ensure protection of the freedom of religion or belief.[62] The Committee concludes that France has not discharged the burden of proving why the ban is necessary and proportionate for attaining the goal of 'living together' in society, either.

The French law is held by the Human Rights Committee to be also in violation of Article 26 of the ICCPR, which prohibits any discrimination and guarantees to all persons equal and effective protection against discrimination on any ground such as race, colour, sex, language, religion, political or other opinion, national or social origin, property, birth or other status. The Committee takes note of the drafting history of the French law in which the French National Assembly considered the wearing of a full-face veil to be 'contrary to the values of the [French] Republic' and wanted 'the fight against discrimination and the promotion of equality between men and women to be priorities of public policy'. Furthermore, while Act No 2010-1192 was drafted in general terms, it includes exceptions for most contexts of face covering in public, thus limiting the applicability of the ban to little more than the full-face Islamic veil and the Act has been primarily enforced against women wearing the full-face veil as a form of religious observance and identification for a minority of Muslim women. A violation of Article 26 of the ICCPR may, therefore, result from the discriminatory effect of a rule or measure that is apparently neutral or lacking any intention to discriminate.[63] The Committee then proceeds to determine whether the differential treatment of the petitioners vis-à-vis other forms of face covering authorized under the exceptions established by Article 2 of Act No 2010-1192 meets the criteria of reasonableness, objectivity and legitimacy of the aim. It answers in the negative. France has

---

[62]   The Human Rights Committee refers, in this connection, to the report of the Special Rapporteur on freedom of religion or belief, Asma Jahangir (E/CN.4/2006/5) §58.

[63]   The Human Rights Committee cites *Althammer et al v Austria* (CCPR/C/78/D/998/2001) §10.2.

provided no explanation why the blanket prohibition is reasonable or justi-fied, in contrast to the exceptions allowable under the Act. Furthermore, the blanket ban on the full-face veil introduced by the Act appears to be based on the assumption that the full veil is inherently discriminatory and that women who wear it are forced to do so. While acknowledging that some women may be subject to family or social pressures to cover their faces, the Committee observes that the wearing of the full veil may also be a choice – or even a means of staking a claim – based on religious belief, as in the petitioners' case.[64] The prohibition under the Act, rather than protecting fully veiled women, could have the opposite effect of confining them to their homes, impeding their access to public services and exposing them to abuse and marginalization. In fact, the Human Rights Committee has already expressed its concern at the time of its consideration of France's fifth periodic report submitted to it that the Act's ban on face coverings in public places infringes the freedom to express one's religion or belief and has a disproportionate impact on the members of specific religions and on girls and that the Act's effect on certain groups' feeling of exclusion and marginalization could run counter to the Act's intended goals.[65] The Committee further notes that a separate provision of the Act, Article 225-4-10 of the Criminal Code, criminalizes as a serious offence forcing an individual to conceal the face and thus specifically addresses that stated concern. Finally, the penalties under the Act have a criminal nature and have been applied against some women, including the petitioners, on multiple occasions, thereby necessarily and negatively impacting their right to manifest their religion through wearing the veil and potentially other rights.

According to the Chairperson of the Human Rights Committee, these deci-sions are not directed against the notion of secularity, nor are they an endorse-ment of a custom regarded by many members of the Committee, including the Chairperson, as a form of oppression of women. Rather, the decisions reflect the Committee's position that a general criminal ban does not allow for a reasonable balance between public interests and individual rights. France has to report to the Human Rights Committee within 180 days on the action taken to implement the Committee's decisions, including compensation of the

---

[64] The Human Rights Committee takes note of the ECtHR's ruling that 'a State Party cannot invoke gender equality in order to ban a practice that is defended by women – such as the applicant – in the context of the exercise of the rights enshrined in those provisions, unless it were to be understood that individuals could be protected on that basis from the exercise of their own fundamental rights and freedom ...' (*S.A.S. v France* [2014] ECHR 695 §119).

[65] Concluding observations on the fifth periodic report of France (CCPR/C/FRA/CO/5) §22.

two petitioners and measures taken to prevent similar violations in the future, including by reviewing the law in question.

Beyond the Islamic veil issue, the ECtHR has dealt with the applicability of Sharia in Europe. In *Molla Sali v Greece*,[66] decided on 19 December 2018, the Grand Chamber of 17 judges of the ECtHR notes that in general Sharia law is applied in CoE Member States as a foreign law within the framework of private international law. Outside that framework, only France applied Sharia law to the population of the territory of Mayotte, an overseas territory of France in the Indian Ocean, but that practice ended in 2011 when Mayotte became a department of the French Republic and had its judicial system re-organized based on ordinary law instead of Sharia. As regards the UK, the application of Sharia law by the Sharia councils is accepted only insofar as recourse to it remains voluntary. Greece itself, as of 15 January 2018, has abol-ished the special regulations imposing recourse to Sharia law for the settlement of family law cases within the Muslim minority. Recourse to a mufti in matters of marriage, divorce or inheritance is now only possible in Greece with the agreement of all those concerned.[67]

The abolition of that Greek law preceded the events in *Molla Sali v Greece*. On the death of her husband, the applicant inherited her husband's whole estate under a will drawn up by her husband before a notary. Subsequently, her husband's two sisters challenged the validity of the will, arguing that as their brother had belonged to the Thrace Muslim community any question relating to inheritance was subject to Islamic law (Sharia) and the jurisdiction of the mufti, not the provisions of the Greek Civil Code. The Greek courts considered the will devoid of effect because the law applicable to the case was Islamic inheritance law and that, in Greece, the latter law applied specifically to Greeks of Muslim faith. Relying on Article 6(1) (right to a fair trial) read separately and in conjunction with Article 14 (prohibition of discrimination) of the ECHR, the applicant complained before the ECtHR about the application of Sharia law to her inheritance dispute instead of the ordinary law applicable to all Greek citizens, despite the fact that her husband's will had been drawn up in accordance with the provisions of the Greek Civil Code. She also claimed to have suffered discriminatory treatment on the grounds of religion because had her husband not been of Muslim faith, she would have inherited the whole estate instead of only one-third thereof.

The Grand Chamber of the ECtHR ruled, unanimously, that there had been a violation of Article 14 (prohibition of discrimination) of the ECHR, read in conjunction with Article 1 of Protocol No 1 (protection of property) to the

---

[66]   App No 20452/14.
[67]   Ibid §§159–60.

ECHR. It finds, in particular, that the difference in treatment suffered by the applicant as the beneficiary of a will drawn up under the Civil Code by a Greek testator of Muslim faith, as compared with a beneficiary of a will drawn up under the Civil Code by a Greek testator not of Muslim faith, has not been objectively and reasonably justified.[68] The Grand Chamber points out, inter alia, that freedom of religion does not require the ECHR's Contracting States to create a particular legal framework in order to grant religious communities a special status entailing specific privileges. Nevertheless, a State which has created such a status has to ensure that the criteria established for a group's entitlement to it are applied in a non-discriminatory manner.[69] Furthermore, refusing members of a religious minority the right to voluntarily opt for and benefit from ordinary law amounts not only to discriminatory treatment but also to a breach of the right to free self-identification, which is the 'corner-stone' of international law on the protection of minorities in general and this applies especially to the negative aspect of the right – no bilateral or multi-lateral treaty or other instrument requires anyone to submit against his or her wishes to a special regime in terms of protection of minorities.[70] Lastly, the Grand Chamber notes that Greece was the only country in Europe which, up until the material time, applied Sharia law to a section of its citizens against their wishes and this is particularly problematic in the instant case because the application of Sharia law has led to a situation detrimental to the individual rights of the applicant.[71]

On 22 January 2019, the Parliamentary Assembly of the Council of Europe (PACE), comprising 324 members from the national parliaments of CoE Member States and entrusted with enforcing human rights in the Member States, adopted a resolution on Sharia, the Cairo Declaration and the ECHR.[72]

The resolution, inter alia, expresses concern about the 'judicial' activities of 'Sharia councils' in the UK. Although they are not considered part of the British legal system, Sharia councils attempt to provide a form of alternative dispute resolution, whereby members of the Muslim community, sometimes voluntarily, often under considerable social pressure, accept their religious jurisdiction mainly in marital and Islamic divorce issues, but also in matters relating to inheritance and Islamic commercial contracts. The rulings of the Sharia councils clearly discriminate against women in divorce and inheritance cases. PACE specifically asks the UK Government to ensure that Sharia councils operate within the law, especially as it relates to the prohibition of discrim-

---

[68] Ibid §161.
[69] Ibid §155.
[70] Ibid §157.
[71] Ibid §158.
[72] PACE Res 2253 (2019) of 22 Jan 2019.

ination against women, and respect all procedural rights. The UK's Marriage Act should be reviewed to make it a legal requirement for Muslim couples to civilly register their marriage before or at the same time as their Islamic ceremony, as is already stipulated by law for Christian and Jewish marriages. In this connection, the UK Government is to take appropriate enforcement measures to oblige the celebrant of any marriage, including Islamic marriages, to ensure that the marriage is also civilly registered before or at the same time as celebrating the religious marriage. The barriers to Muslim women's access to justice are to be removed and measures to provide protection and assistance to those who are in a situation of vulnerability are to be enhanced. The UK is to put in place awareness campaigns to promote knowledge among Muslim women of their rights, especially in the areas of marriage, divorce, custody of children and inheritance and to work with Muslim communities, women's organizations and other NGOs to promote gender equality and women's empowerment. Lastly, the UK is to conduct further research on 'judicial' practice of Sharia councils and on the extent to which such councils are used voluntarily, particularly by women, many of whom would be subject to intense community pressure in this respect. PACE notes that informal Islamic courts such as the Sharia councils in the UK may exist in other CoE Member States too. It calls on these CoE Member States to protect human rights regardless of religious or cultural practices or traditions, on the principle that where human rights are concerned 'there is no room for religious or cultural exceptions'. PACE also calls on these States to promote, within the multilateral organizations of which they are members or observers, 'the universal values of human rights without any discrimination based inter alia on sex, gender, sexual orientation, gender identity and religious faith or the lack of it'.

By also calling upon CoE Member States to engage in the process of revision of the Organisation of Islamic Cooperation's (OIC) Cairo Declaration on Human Rights in Islam to ensure that the future OIC Declaration on Human Rights is 'compatible with universal human rights standards and the [ECHR]', PACE directly encroaches into the realm of international diplomacy and assigns to itself the right to determine which are the universal standards of human rights norms. The revision of the Cairo Declaration as demanded by PACE is a diplomatically impossible task to accomplish, as will be shown in section 5 below.

3.   THE AMERICAS

Central and South America, as well as the Caribbean nation States, used to be under Western colonization. Many of the States share a common history of military dictatorships, socialist revolutions and common social problems such as poverty, illiteracy and marginalization of indigenous peoples. The Americas are racially, ethnically, politically and economically less homogeneous than their European counterparts.[73]

The Organization of American States (OAS) is one of the world's oldest regional governmental organizations, dating back to the adoption of the OAS Charter[74] by the Ninth International Conference of American States, held in Bogota, Colombia, in April 1948. The following 21 States participated in the Conference and signed the OAS Charter immediately after its adoption: Argentina, Bolivia, Brazil, Chile, Colombia, Costa Rica, Cuba, Dominican Republic, Ecuador, El Salvador, Guatemala, Haiti, Honduras, Mexico, Nicaragua, Panama, Paraguay, Peru, USA, Uruguay and Venezuela. The US Government considered the OAS as a Cold War instrument to fight communist penetration into the Western hemisphere. At that same Conference, the participating American States also adopted the American Declaration on the Rights and Duties of Man,[75] eight months prior to the adoption of the UDHR by the UNGA.

The first preambular paragraph of the American Declaration shows the imprint of the natural law of the Western human rights tradition, declaring that '[a]ll men are born free and equal, in dignity and in rights and, being endowed by nature with reason and conscience, they should conduct themselves as brothers one to another'. This is hardly surprising since the USA was taking the lead in setting up the OAS, and the ruling class in the other participating States, except Haiti, were of Spanish or Portuguese ancestry and all the participating States had Christians as the majority of their populations.

The American Declaration, containing 38 Articles and divided into two chapters, is more detailed than the UDHR, which has 30 relatively concise Articles.

Chapter One postulates the right to life, liberty and personal security; right to equality before law; right to religious freedom and worship; right to freedom of investigation, opinion, expression and dissemination of ideas; right to protection of honour, personal reputation and private and family life; right to a family and to protection thereof; right to protection for mothers and children; right to residence and movement; right to inviolability of the home; right to the inviolability and transmission of correspondence; right to the preservation of health and to well-being; right to education; right to the benefits of culture;

---

[73] Freedman, *Failing to Protect* 155–7; Thomas M Antkowiak, 'The Americas' in Moeckli et al (eds), *International Human Rights Law* 425; Jo M Pasqualucci, 'The Inter-American Regional Human Rights System' in Baderin and Ssenyonjo (eds), *International Human Rights Law* 253.

[74] 119 UNTS 3.

[75] Basic Documents Pertaining to Human Rights in the Inter-American System OEA/Ser L V/II.82 Doc 6 Rev 1 at 17 (1992).

right to work and to fair remuneration; right to leisure time and to the use thereof; right to social security; right to recognition of juridical personality and civil rights; right to a fair trial; right to nationality; right to vote and to participate in government; right of assembly; right of association; right to property; right of petition; right of protection from arbitrary arrest; right to a due process of law; and right of asylum. The final Article of Chapter One provides that these rights of man are limited by the rights of others, by the security of all and by the just demands of the general welfare and the advancement of democracy.

Chapter Two elaborates the duties of man to society, towards children and parents, to acquire at least an elementary education, to vote, to obey the law, to serve the community and the nation, to cooperate with the State and the community with respect to social security and welfare in accordance with his ability and with existing circumstances, to pay taxes, to work, and to refrain from political activities in a foreign State that are reserved exclusively to the citizens of the State in which he is an alien. The last-mentioned duty echoes the widespread concern among the governments south of the US border about foreigners engaged in political activities in their respective States for the purpose of unconstitutional regime change.

The American Declaration is not a legally binding instrument.[76] The American Convention on Human Rights (ACHR)[77] was adopted in November 1969, some three years after the UNGA's adoption of the ICCPR and the ICESCR. The ACHR, which entered into force in 1978, draws on the ICCPR and is supplemented by the 1988 Additional Protocol to the ACHR in the Area of Economic, Social and Cultural Rights,[78] in force in November 1999. There are 23 States Parties to the ACHR as of this writing: Argentina, Barbados, Bolivia, Brazil, Chile, Colombia, Costa Rica, Dominica, Dominican Republic, Ecuador, El Salvador, Grenada, Guatemala, Haiti, Honduras, Jamaica, Mexico, Nicaragua, Panama, Paraguay, Peru, Suriname and Uruguay. Of the 23 States Parties, 20 of them (that is, except Dominica, Grenada and Jamaica) have accepted the contentious jurisdiction of the Inter-American Court of Human Rights (IACtHR). Trinidad and Tobago denounced the ACHR on 26 May 1998 over a death penalty issue, while Venezuela did so on 10 September 2012, alleging that the IACtHR and the Inter-American Commission on Human Rights (IACHR) set up by the ACHR had been undermining the Venezuelan Government's stability by interfering in the domestic affairs of Venezuela.

---

[76]   Cf Christina M Cerna, 'Reflections on the Normative Status of the American Declaration on the Rights and Duties of Man' (2009) 30 U Pa JIL 1211.

[77]   1144 UNTS 123.

[78]   OAS Treaty Ser No 69.

The regional meeting for Latin America and the Caribbean held in San José, Costa Rica, in January 1993 as part of the preparations for the Vienna Conference on Human Rights in June of that year came up with a Declaration[79] containing 31 brief paragraphs. It, inter alia, expresses the hope that the Vienna Conference would be 'based on the unconditional and indissoluble link between human rights, democracy and development'. The San José Declaration affirms the interdependence and indivisibility of civil, political, economic, social and cultural rights. These States stress that respect for human rights and fundamental freedoms, the strengthening of development, democracy and pluralism in international relations with full respect for the sovereignty, territorial integrity and political independence of States, and the sovereign equality and self-determination of peoples are the pillars of their regional system. The defence and strengthening of representative democracy are considered the best guarantee of the effective enjoyment of all human rights. The rupture of democratic order threatens human rights in the State concerned and has negative repercussions on the other States in the region, particularly neighbouring States. The Declaration draws attention to the need to protect the rights of the child, women, indigenous peoples, vulnerable groups, the disabled, migrant workers, the elderly and those infected with HIV/AIDS. It expresses concern about and condemns acts of terrorism that threaten democracy and seriously impede the full realization of all human rights and fundamental freedoms in the region. These States emphasize that the UN must give priority to the protection and promotion of human rights, with appropriate budgetary resources allocated therefor.

On the whole, the human rights vision of States in Latin America and the Caribbean is not much different from what is to be expected in Europe, except for its frequent reference to democracy and a mention of the rights of indigenous peoples. The emphasis on democracy is a clear reminder of the numerous undemocratic changes of government that had taken place in the Americas. The rights of indigenous peoples must be reckoned with, given that there are more than 800 different indigenous peoples, accounting for nearly 45 million women and men or around 8 per cent of the region's population.

The human rights regime in Latin America and the Caribbean is supervised by the IACHR and the IACtHR, respectively.

The IACHR, set up in 1959, comprises seven members elected by the OAS General Assembly for a four-year term, renewable only once, to serve in their individual capacity. It monitors compliance with human rights obligations by

---

[79] Reprinted in *San José Declaration on Human Rights, 22 January 1993: World Conference on Human Rights, Regional Meeting for Latin America and the Caribbean, San José, Costa Rica, 18–22 January 1993* (United Nations 1993).

States Parties to the ACHR. The IACHR may consider petitions from individuals alleging violations of their human rights by the State after the exhaustion of available local remedies in that State. The IACHR convenes meetings between the petitioner and the State to explore a friendly settlement, failing which the IACHR may recommend specific measures, or may report the case to the IACtHR, provided that the State has accepted the IACtHR's competence. In urgent cases, the IACHR can call upon a State to take precautionary measures to prevent irreparable harm to a petitioner. The IACHR may also undertake on-site visits to assess and report on the human rights situation of the State and issue recommendations after the visits. The IACHR may appoint rapporteurs on human rights issues deserving priority, such as the rights of children, women, indigenous peoples, Afro-descendants, migrant workers, prisoners and displaced persons, and on freedom of expression.[80]

The IACtHR, established in 1979 and based in San José, Costa Rica, is the judicial organ that interprets the ACHR. It is composed of seven judges elected by the OAS General Assembly for a term of six years and who may be re-elected only once. The IACtHR decides on contentious cases as well as rendering advisory opinions sought by the IACHR. It is hailed as 'the only international body with binding jurisdiction that has consistently ordered [the] full range of reparations [of restitution, rehabilitation, satisfaction and guarantees of non-repetition, in conjunction with pecuniary and non-pecuniary damages]'.[81] The IACtHR has developed an innovative judicial penalty of non-pecuniary collective reparations seeking to preserve the name of the victim and to offer some form of recognition of the wider community affected by human rights violations, including public acts of apology, renaming of streets and so forth.[82] It also generally responds to victims' preferences for restoration and even contemplates the complex situations of certain marginalized populations.[83] In a region ravaged by the phenomenon of enforced disappearances for many decades, the IACtHR has pioneered the conceptual development of the crime of enforced disappearance.[84]

---

[80]   Thomas M Antkowiak and Alexandra Gonza, *The American Convention on Human Rights: Essential Rights* (OUP 2017) 5–11; David J Padilla, 'The Inter-American Commission on Human Rights of the Organization of American States: A Case Study' (1993) 9 Amer U Int'l L Rev 95; Stephen Vasciannie, 'The Inter-American Commission on Human Rights: Reform and the Question of Universality' (2014) 21 ILSA J of Int'l & Comp L 409.

[81]   Antkowiak and Gonza, *The American Convention on Human Rights* 19 and also 285–316.

[82]   Crawford, 'Chance, Order, Change' 245.

[83]   Antkowiak and Gonza, *The American Convention on Human Rights* 20.

[84]   Ibid 21.

In August 2001 the IACtHR applied 'an evolutionary interpretation of international instruments for the protection of human rights' to uphold the existence of an indigenous people's collective right to their land. It construes the right to property under Article 21 of the ACHR to encompass 'the rights of members of the indigenous community within the framework of communal property' in view of the concept of property in indigenous communities. That concept recognizes a communitarian tradition among indigenous peoples regarding a communal form of collective property in the land, whereby the land ownership is not centred on an individual but rather on the group and its community, and the close ties of the group with the land form the fundamental basis of its cultures, spiritual life, integrity and economic survival, as well as a material and spiritual element to be fully enjoyed, preserved and transmitted to future generations.[85]

In another case decided in November 2007, the IACtHR reaffirms the special relationship that members of indigenous and tribal peoples have with their territory and the need to protect their right to that territory in order to safeguard the physical and cultural survival of such peoples.[86] That case involves the Saramaka people, a tribal community of descendants of African slaves forcibly taken to Suriname during European colonization in the seventeenth century, whose social, cultural and economic characteristics are different from other sections of the national community, particularly because of their special relationship with their ancestral territories and because they regulate themselves, at least partially, by their own norms, customs and/or traditions. The IACtHR ruled that in ensuring the effective participation of members of the Saramaka people in development or investment plans within their territory, the State has a duty to actively consult with the said community according to their customs and traditions. This duty requires the State to both accept and disseminate information and entails constant communication between the parties. These consultations must be in good faith, through culturally appropriate procedures and with the objective of reaching an agreement. Furthermore, the Saramaka people must be consulted, in accordance with their own traditions, at the early stages of a development or investment plan, not only when the need arises to obtain approval from the community, if such is the case, since early notice provides time for internal discussion within communities and for proper feedback to the State. The State must also ensure that members of the Saramaka people are aware of possible risks, including environmental

---

[85] *Mayagna (Sumo) Awas Tingni Community v Nicaragua*, IACtHR (2001) Ser C, No 79, 31 Aug 2001 §§148–9. See also *Saramaka People v Suriname*, IACtHR (2007) Ser C, No 172, 28 Nov 2007, esp §158.

[86] *Saramaka People v Suriname* §90.

and health risks, in order that the proposed development or investment plan is accepted knowingly and voluntarily. Finally, consultation should take account of the people's traditional methods of decision making. Additionally, in the case of large-scale development or investment projects that would have a major impact within their territory, the State has a duty not only to consult with the potentially affected people, but also to obtain their free, prior and informed consent, according to their customs and traditions.[87]

On 15 November 2017 the IACtHR became the first international human rights court to recognize a new extraterritorial jurisdictional link based on control over domestic activities with extraterritorial effect as well as the substantive meaning of the right to a healthy environment. This advisory opinion was rendered in response to a request submitted by Colombia on 14 March 2016 to address the scope of Articles 1(1) (obligation to respect rights), 4(1) (right to life) and 5(1) (right to humane treatment/personal integrity) of the ACHR and the interpretation of Articles 4(1) and 5(1) in relation to Article 1(1) and 'in the light of international environmental law'.[88] In addressing these issues, the IACtHR refers to the relevant documents of the OAS, its own jurisprudence, decisions and other statements or reports by other human rights bodies such as the ECtHR, the African Commission on Human and Peoples' Rights and experts including the UN Special Rapporteur on human rights and the environment.

The IACtHR considers the protection of the environment to be critical to the enjoyment of other human rights due to the existence of an undeniable relationship between them since environmental degradation and the adverse effects of climate change affect the effective enjoyment of human rights.[89] The human right to a healthy environment is both an individual right and a collective right; it is a collective right in the sense that the right to a healthy environment constitutes a universal interest owed to the present as well as future generations. The right to a healthy environment as a human right creates an obligation for States to protect the human rights impacted by a degraded environment.[90]

The exercise of jurisdiction by the State of origin over transboundary harms is based upon the understanding that it is the State in whose territory or under

---

[87] Ibid §§133–4.

[88] *Environment and Human Rights (State Obligations in Relation to the Environment in the Context of the Protection and Guarantee of the Rights to Life and to Personal Integrity – Interpretation and Scope of Arts 4(1) and 5(1) of the American Convention on Human Rights)*, Advisory Opinion OC-23/18, IACtHR (2017) Ser A, No 23, 15 Nov 2017.

[89] Ibid §47.

[90] Ibid §55.

whose jurisdiction these activities are carried out that has effective control over the activities and is in a position to prevent a transboundary harm affecting the enjoyment of the human rights of individuals outside its territory. The possible victims of the negative consequences of such activities are deemed to be within the jurisdiction of the State of origin for the sake of that State's potential liability for the failure to fulfil its obligation to prevent transboundary harms. Therefore, the obligation to prevent transboundary environmental harms is an obligation recognized in international environmental law, for which States may be liable for significant harms affecting persons outside their boundaries due to activities originating in their territory or under their authority or effective control. This obligation does not depend on the lawful or unlawful character of the conduct causing the harm because States must provide relief immediately, adequately and effectively to the persons and States that are victims of a transboundary harm resulting from activities carried out in their territory or under their jurisdiction, independently of whether the activity that caused said harm is prohibited by international law. However, there must be a causal relationship between the harm caused and the action or omission of the State of origin of the harm with respect to activities in its territory or under its control.[91]

In the IACtHR's opinion, the right to life creates the duty to prohibit impacts to the right to life. States also have a positive duty to protect this right by guaranteeing the creation of the conditions required for their full enjoyment and exercise, including the access to and quality of water, food and health and a healthy environment.[92]

In *López Soto v Venezuela*[93] the IACtHR holds Venezuela responsible for the act of a private actor because States have a positive duty under the ACHR to prevent human rights abuses, including those committed by private individuals. Article 1 of the ACHR requires its States Parties to undertake to respect the rights and freedoms recognized therein and to ensure to all persons subject to their jurisdiction the free and full exercise of those rights and freedoms. In addition, Article 7 of the 1994 Inter-American Convention on the Prevention, Punishment and Eradication of Violence against Women,[94] to which all OAS Member States except Canada and the USA are party, obligates its States Parties to, inter alia, undertake to apply due diligence to prevent, investigate

---

[91] Ibid §§102–3. Cf Tilmann Altwicker, 'Transnationalizing Rights: International Human Rights Law in Cross-Border Contexts' (2018) 29 EJIL 581, where the author discusses the obligation arising out of effective control over situations with extraterritorial effects (ibid 590–4) and transnational activities by non-State actors (ibid 597–604).

[92] Advisory Opinion OC-23/18 §109.

[93] Judgment of 26 Sept 2018, http://www.corteidh.or.cr/docs/casos/articulos/seriec _362_esp.pdf, accessed 21 Jan 2019.

[94] (1994) 33 ILM 1534.

and impose penalties for violence against women as well as adopt such legislative or other measures as may be necessary to give effect to this Convention.
The IACtHR rules that the report of an abduction or disappearance of a woman
is, in itself, sufficient to trigger the State's due diligence duty to act. This is
the IACtHR's first-ever ruling on State responsibility for acts of sexual torture
and sexual slavery by a private actor. Subsequently, in *Women Victims of
Sexual Torture in Atenco v Mexico*[95] the IACtHR rules that a State can be held
liable for the excessive use of force by security forces when it fails to prevent
abuses. In this latter case, the IACtHR finds that Mexican authorities could
have exercised due diligence to prevent the violence by adequately regulating
the use of force by the police; training police officers to behave profession-
ally; monitoring developments on the ground and taking immediate action
to stop the abuses as they happened; and putting proper verification, control
and accountability measures in place to address abuses. The IACtHR orders
various forms of reparations, including financial compensation, psychosocial
support, a public recognition of responsibility, proper investigations into the
crimes and measures to prevent their repetition.[96]

The IACtHR's judgments in contentious cases are final and binding. It
monitors compliance with its own judgments and this primarily involves scrutinizing periodic written submissions of reports by States on compliance with
the judgments. Where there is a situation of delay or complexity, the IACtHR
may summon the parties to private or, exceptionally, public hearings and issue
binding instructions to them. Non-compliance is reported annually to the OAS
General Assembly, with cases of repeated failures to comply highlighted in the
IACtHR's annual reports to the OAS General Assembly.[97]

The IACtHR's judgment in *Molina Theissen v Guatemala*[98] has shown that
the IACtHR can serve as a catalyst for significant breakthroughs in the domestic system of protection of human rights. The case involves alleged atrocities

---

[95] Judgment of 28 Nov 2018, http://www.corteidh.or.cr/docs/casos/articulos/seriec
_371_esp.pdf, accessed 21 Jan 2019.

[96] Both cases are analysed in Daniela Kravetz, 'Holding States to Account for
Gender-Based Violence: The Inter-American Court of Human Rights' Decisions in
López Soto vs Venezuela and Women Victims of Sexual Torture in Atenco vs Mexico',
EJIL Talk! (21 Jan 2019) https://www.ejiltalk.org/holding-states-to-account-for-gender
-based-violence-the-inter-american-court-of-human-rights-decisions-in-lopez-soto-vs
-venezuela-and-women-victims-of-sexual-torture-in-atenco-vs-mexico/#more-16824,
accessed 21 Jan 2019.

[97] Antkowiak and Gonza, *The American Convention on Human Rights* 308–12.

[98] *Molina Theissen v Guatemala*, Merits, Judgment, IACtHR (2004) Ser C, No 106,
4 May 2004; *Molina Theissen v Guatemala*, Reparations and Costs, Judgment, IACtHR
(2004) Ser C, No 108, 3 July 2004. See also the case report in [2014] 36 Loyola LA Int'l
& Comp L Rev 1889–912.

perpetrated by Guatemala's military junta's counterinsurgent operations to detain, torture for information and then kill or make 'disappear' suspected communists, critics of the military dictatorship and human rights activists. Having found Guatemala to be in breach of the applicant's rights under the ACHR, the IACtHR's Order of Monitoring and Compliance of 16 November 2009 deems it essential for Guatemala to comply with the judgment as well as incorporate the case of Molina Theissen into the studies and actions carried out by the National Follow-Up and Support Commission for the Strengthening of Justice in order to better coordinate its schedule for moving the investigation of the facts of the case; to identify, try and punish the perpetrators and master-minds behind the forced disappearance; and to further search for the remains of the applicant's brother. This eventually led to the conviction by the Court in May 2018 of four of the five former high-ranking Guatemalan military officers, once considered untouchable, for high-risk crimes in Guatemala City. The five were accused of illegal detention, torture and sexual violation of Emma Molina Theissen, one of a small number of civilians who escaped army custody during Guatemala's 36-year civil war, as well as separate charges for aggravated sexual assault against her. Four of them were convicted as charged. Three (the former head of the armed forces Benedicto Lucas García, former intelligence chief Manuel Antonio Callejas y Callejas and local commander Hugo Ramiro Zaldaña Rojas) were also found guilty of the forced disappearance of Emma Molina Theissen's 14-year-old brother, missing since 6 October 1981, and sentenced to 58 years' imprisonment. Francisco Luis Gordillo Martínez, the then commander of the secret military barracks where the crimes against Emma were committed, was sentenced to 33 years' imprisonment, whereas his then deputy at the barracks was acquitted of all charges for lack of evidence.[99]

It can be said that the IACtHR has tried to deny any excuses governments may invoke, both domestically and internationally, not to comply with their human rights obligations. For example, the IACtHR has refused to recognize Uruguay's amnesty law, which has already been confirmed in a plebiscite but which the IACtHR considers to have given rise to serious violations of

---

[99] 'Guatemala: ex-military officers convicted of crimes against humanity', *The Guardian* (23 May 2018) https://www.theguardian.com/world/2018/may/23/guatemala-ex-military-officers-convicted-of-crimes-against-humanity, accessed 1 Sept 2018. See also Paola Limón, 'What Implementation of Judgments Looks Like – or Doesn't?: The Case of the Molina Theissen Family in Guatemala', *EJIL Talk!* (2 July 2018) https://www.ejiltalk.org/what-implementation-of-judgments-looks-like-or-doesnt-the-case-of-the-molina-theissen-family-in-guatemala/, accessed 4 Aug 2019.

non-revocable norms of IHRL that constitute 'an impassable limit to the rule of the majority'.[100]

At the national level, starting from the late 1990s national judges in Latin America started to investigate human rights violations, adopting an attitude against impunity for the violations that had occurred in the past. The passage of time was crucial since it overcame the recalcitrance and opposition to criminal prosecution of human rights abusers before domestic courts. Peruvian courts, Costa Rican courts and Argentinian courts came first, second and third, respectively, of Latin American domestic courts citing the largest number of IACtHR cases in their judgments.[101]

'Margin of appreciation' has been expressly alluded to in one decision of the IACHR[102] and two advisory opinions of the IACtHR.[103] In its more recent advisory opinion in *Proposed Amendments of the Naturalization Provisions of the Constitution of Costa Rica*, rendered in 2014, the IACtHR opines that the relevant proposed amendments to the Costa Rican Constitution do not violate the ACHR because States have a margin of appreciation in the matter of granting naturalization, including by determining whether and to what extent applicants for naturalization comply with the conditions to ensure an effective link between them and the value system and interests of the society to which they wish to belong. However, the doctrine of margin of appreciation is not generally applied in the Inter-American human rights system, presumably because of a lack of trust in decisions made by States Parties to the ACHR.[104] The IACtHR has expressly rejected the argument about a lack of consensus in relation to human rights protection. In *Atala Piffo and Daughters v Chile*, the IACtHR rules that the absence of a regional consensus regarding full respect for the rights of sexual minorities cannot be a valid argument to deny or restrict their human rights or to perpetuate and reproduce the historical and structural discrimination these minorities have suffered. The alleged lack of consensus on this controversial issue cannot lead the IACtHR to abstain from issuing a decision, in which it has to 'refer solely and exclusively to the stipulations of

---

[100] *Gelman v Uruguay*, Merits and Reparations, IACtHR (2004) Ser C, No 110, 24 Feb 2011, §§238–9.

[101] Ezequiel A Gonzále-Ocantos, *Shifting Legal Visions: Judicial Change and Human Rights Trials in Latin America* (CUP 2016) chs 1, 2 and 6.

[102] *Jose Efrain Ríos Montt v Guatemala*, Case 10.804, Report No 30/93 (1993) §31.

[103] *Proposed Amendments to the Naturalization Provisions of the Constitution of Costa Rica*, OC-4/84, IACtHR (1984) Ser A, No 4, 19 Jan 1984, §58; *Rights and Guarantees of Children in the Context of Migration and/or in Need of International Protection*, OC-21/14, IACtHR (2014) Ser A, No 21, 19 Aug 2014, §39.

[104] McGoldrick, 'Affording States a Margin of Appreciation' 344.

the international obligations arising from a sovereign decision by the States to adhere to the American Convention'.[105]

4. AFRICA

Africa is a continent rich in natural resources. Paradoxically, a number of African nation States are mired in poverty, suffer unhealthy environments and have been ravaged by internal armed conflicts, at times with foreign military intervention, as well as proxy wars, especially during the Cold War when some of the world's major powers supported their 'puppet' dictators who abused human rights. Up to 30 August 2011, 23 of the 34 resolutions adopted by the UN Security Council dealt with Africa.[106] Due to armed conflicts and other upheavals, Africa hosts approximately 23 million refugees as of February 2019.[107] African States thus aspire to the right to development, the right to peace and security and the right to a satisfactory environment.[108]

A new dawn came with the adoption of the African Charter on Human and Peoples' Rights (ACHPR)[109] by the Organization of African Unity, the predecessor of the African Union (AU), in 1981, not long after the collapse in 1979 of the dictatorship regimes in Idi Amin's Uganda, Francisco Marcías Nguema's Equatorial Guinea and Jean-Bédel Bokassa's Central African Republic.[110]

The Tunis Declaration,[111] adopted in November 1992 at the end of the preparatory meeting of African States before the 1993 Vienna Conference on Human Rights, contains only 11 paragraphs. It reaffirms the African States'

---

[105] IACtHR (2012) Ser C, No 239, 24 Feb 2012, §92. Cf Legg (*The Margin of Appreciation in International Human Rights Law* 4) who maintains that because most cases before the IACtHR have largely involved findings of fact, there are far fewer examples of cases employing concepts of deference compared with the ECtHR.

[106] Viljoen, *International Human Rights Law in Africa* 50.

[107] 'UNECA chief urges concerted efforts as Africa hosts close to 23 mln refugees', *Xinhua News* (2 Feb 2019) http://www.xinhuanet.com/english/2019-02/09/c _137808693.htm; Cf Hamza Mohamed and Alia Chughtai, 'What you need to know about Africa's refugees', *Al Jazeera* (9 Feb 2019) https://www.aljazeera.com/indepth/ interactive/2019/02/africa-refugees-190209130248319.html, accessed 12 Aug 2019.

[108] Luis Gabriel Franceshi, *The African Human Rights Judicial System: Streamlining Structures and Domestication Mechanisms Viewed from the Foreign Affairs Power Perspective* (Cambridge Scholars Publishing 2014) 89–124. See also Christoff Heyns and Magnus Killander, 'Africa' in Moeckli at al (eds), *International Human Rights Law* 465. On the right to peace, see Nsongura J Udombana, 'The Right to a Peaceful World Order' in Baderin and Ssenyonjo (eds), *International Human Rights Law* 137.

[109] (1982) 21 ILM 58.

[110] Viljoen, *International Human Rights Law in Africa* 158–9.

[111] A/Conf.157/AFRM/14; A/Conf.157/PC/57 (24 Nov 1992).

commitment to the principles set forth in the UDHR, the ICCPR, the ICESCR and the ACHPR. The proper administration of justice and an independent judiciary are crucial to the full realization of human rights but the attainment of these objectives is impossible without substantial investment in capacity building in this area. Although responsibility for the implementation and promotion of human rights devolves primarily on governments, the component institutions, organizations and structures of society also play an important role in safeguarding and disseminating these rights and they should be strengthened and encouraged.

The Tunis Declaration touches on universalism of human rights, positing that the universal nature of human rights is beyond question and that their protection and promotion are the duty of all States, regardless of their political, economic or cultural systems. However, no ready-made *model* can be prescribed universally since the historical and cultural realities of each nation, and the traditions, standards and values of each people, cannot be disregarded.

The Tunis Declaration treats civil and political rights as indivisible from economic, social and cultural rights and considers none of these rights to take precedence over the others. According to the Declaration, the right to development is inalienable, and human rights, development and international peace are interdependent. Lasting progress towards the implementation of human rights implies, at the national level, effective development policies and, at the international level, a more equitable economic relationship as well as a favourable economic environment. Racism, particularly its new forms, extremism and fanaticism, whether of religious or other origin, poses serious threats to the protection and promotion of universal human rights values and all stakeholders are to exert their efforts, take the necessary steps and cooperate in tackling these threats. Africa, finding itself particularly exposed to internal tensions deriving from the failure to meet the basic needs of populations and from the rise of extremism, calls upon the international community, in particular through an intensification of international solidarity, to provide an adequate increase in development assistance and an appropriate settlement of the debt problem. Africa, while committed to respecting individual human rights, reaffirms the importance of the collective rights of peoples, particularly the right to determine their own future and to control their own resources. Africa also reaffirms the right of all peoples to self-determination and free choice of their political and economic systems and institutions, on the basis of respect for national sovereignty and non-interference in the internal affairs of States.

The 2000 Constitutive Act of the AU[112] refers extensively to human rights, and its Article 3(h) stipulates as one of the AU's objectives the promotion

---

[112] 2158 UNTS 3.

and protection of human and peoples' rights in accordance with the ACHPR and other relevant human rights instruments. However, the AU, as a multilateral diplomatic forum, has played a modest role in improving human rights in Africa, leaving it to the African Court on Human and Peoples' Rights (ACtHPR) and its successor to uphold IHRL in Africa.[113]

The ACHPR pioneers the right to development by stipulating in Article 22 'the right to ... economic, social and cultural development' together with the 'duty' of States, individually or collectively, 'to ensure the exercise of the right to development'. Although Articles 22, 23, 25 and 26 of the UDHR mention the right to social security, the right to work, the right to a standard of living adequate for health and well-being and the right to education, these UDHR provisions do not specifically provide for the right to development as a discrete right. The right to development was subsequently recognized, in 1986, by the UNGA in its Declaration on the Right to Development,[114] adopted by 146 votes in favour, eight abstentions and one (USA) against. This right is repeatedly affirmed in multilateral forums thereafter, including in Article 10 of the 1993 Vienna Declaration and Programme of Action, where the right is considered to be 'a universal and inalienable right and an integral part of fundamental human rights'. Article 11 of the Vienna Declaration provides that the right to development should be fulfilled so as to meet equitably the developmental and environmental needs of present and future generations. Extreme poverty is referred to in Article 14 of the Vienna Declaration, mentioning that the existence of widespread extreme poverty inhibits the full and effective enjoyment of human rights, and the immediate alleviation and eventual elimination of poverty must remain a high priority for the international community. Article 25 of the Vienna Declaration adds that extreme poverty and social exclusion constitute a violation of human dignity and that urgent steps are necessary to achieve better knowledge of extreme poverty and its causes, including those related to the problem of development, in order to promote the human rights of the poorest, to end extreme poverty and social exclusion and to promote the enjoyment of the fruits of social progress. In essence, the right to development shares the same objective as 'pro-poor development', which is a process of economic empowerment, including developing the full potential and creating a conducive environment, for all peoples to enable them to lead a life they desire in order to enhance their well-being and to achieve social progress and

---

[113] Viljoen, *International Human Rights Law in Africa* 164–7, 209.
[114] UN Doc A/RES/41/128 (4 Dec 1986). Cf Arjun Sengupta, 'Simple Analysis of the Right to Development' in Baderin and Ssenyonjo (eds), *International Human Rights Law* 107.

better standards of life.[115] How to realize this right to development is a daunting challenge for all States. Are wealthier States obliged to provide development assistance to poorer States?[116]

The right to national and international peace and security is enshrined in Article 23 of the ACHPR, pursuant to which the principles of solidarity and friendly relations implicitly affirmed by the UN Charter and reaffirmed by the Organization of African Unity shall govern relations between States. For the purpose of strengthening peace, solidarity and friendly relations, State Parties to the ACHPR shall ensure that any individual enjoying the right of asylum under Article 12 of the ACHPR shall not engage in subversive activities against his State of origin or any other State Party to the ACHPR and that their territories shall not be used as bases for subversive or terrorist activities against the people of any other State Party to the ACHPR.

Article 24 of the ACHPR briefly stipulates the right of all peoples to a general satisfactory environment favourable to their development. Articles 27, 28 and 29 impose duties on every individual towards his family and society, the State, 'other legally recognized communities' and the international community. Communitarianism and the idea that rights have reciprocal duties are not unique to Africa since Western societies also conformed to these notions at some stage in the past.[117] Article 7(2) provides, inter alia, that '[p]unishment is personal and can be imposed only on the offender'. This is in response to the situations in Africa where not only the offender, but also his family or community was also punished for allegedly giving him moral support for the commission of his offence.[118]

Article 18 of the ACHPR takes an innovative step in recognizing the right of the family, something not singled out for recognition in other human rights instruments at that time.

The ACHPR has no derogation clause even in time of emergencies or war.

The ACHPR expressly enumerates a limited number of economic and social rights since its drafters did not intend to overburden newly independent African nation States. It provides for the right to property, the right to work under equitable and satisfactory conditions, the right to enjoy the best attainable state of physical and mental health, the right to education, and the protection of the family and vulnerable groups in Articles 14 through 18, respectively.

---

[115] Stephen P Markus, 'Poverty' in Moeckli et al (eds), *International Human Rights Law* 597, 616. Cf Brems, *Human Rights* 450–75.

[116] As suggested by Patrick Macklem, *The Sovereignty of Human Rights* (OUP 2015) 221–2.

[117] Viljoen, *International Human Rights Law in Africa* 284.

[118] Brems, *Human Rights* 131.

The right to an adequate standard of living (including adequate food and clothing, water and sanitation, housing, social security, rest and leisure and the right to form and join trade unions) under the ICESCR[119] is absent from the ACHPR. Other omissions from the African Charter include the protection of private life, the right of free choice of a marriage partner and other marriage-related rights, the right to nationality and the prohibition of arbitrary deprivation of nationality, the prohibition of forced or compulsory labour, and the rights of minorities.[120]

Some 90 per cent of the African States are party to the ICESCR, making them a significant majority of States Parties to the ICESCR. However, very few African States are also party to the Optional Protocol to the ICESCR,[121] which recognizes the competence of the Committee on Economic, Social and Cultural Rights (CESCR) – a panel of 18 independent experts that meets twice a year – to receive complaints from persons within their jurisdiction alleging violations of their rights under the ICESCR.

One study finds the important influence the ICESCR has on the regional and, to a certain extent, domestic legal protection of economic, social and cultural rights across Africa, with the explicit protection of these rights embodied in many national constitutions. Increasingly, these rights have become justiciable in courts or at least part of the principles to be upheld in government policy. Yet they have still not achieved the same level of protection given to civil and political rights in the constitutions of several African States and, compared to the ICCPR, the ICESCR has more limited influence on the jurisprudence of national courts. The study attributes such shortcomings to non-compliance with domestic court judgments upholding these rights, political authoritarianism, high levels of corruption, poverty, armed conflict, limited roles of NGOs and civil society, and lack of respect for the rule of law and international and regional judicial and quasi-judicial organs. It suggests enhancing the ICESCR's influence by African States party thereto enacting implementing domestic legislation to give effect to the ICESCR; training and awareness raising on the ICESCR and the justiciability of the rights thereunder; reducing poverty via strategies that fully integrate these rights; ensuring accountability and transparency in combating corruption; becoming party to the Optional Protocol to the ICESCR; increasing use of strategic litigation to achieve political recognition of the rights irrespective of the outcome or the actual implementation of court rulings; and timely submission of periodic reports to the

---

[119] See Asbjørn Eide, 'Adequate Standard of Living' in Moeckli et al (eds), *International Human Rights Law* 186; Viljoen, *International Human Rights Law in Africa* 215.

[120] Brems, *Human Rights* 126–31.

[121] A/RES/63/117 (5 Mar 2009).

CESCR, including a compilation of case summaries and decisions of domestic courts and tribunals on the justiciability of these rights.[122]

Due to its direct relevance to Africa, African States are more eager to become party to the 1990 International Convention on the Protection of All Migrant Workers and Members or their Families (CMW)[123] than States in other global regions. As of this writing, there were 54 States Parties to the CMW, 24 of which are from Africa; namely, Algeria, Benin, Burkina Faso, Cabo Verde, Congo, Egypt, Gambia, Ghana, Guinea, Guinea-Bissau, Lesotho, Libya, Madagascar, Mali, Mauritania, Morocco, Mozambique, Niger, Nigeria, Rwanda, Sao Tome and Principe, Senegal, Seychelles and Uganda.

Shortcomings or omissions in the ACHPR are partially supplemented by subsequent 'opt-in' African human rights instruments for those States willing and able to assume the obligations thereunder, as well as by the interpretation of the ACHPR by the African Commission on Human and Peoples' Rights to cover the rights to adequate housing, food, social security, water and sanitation.[124]

The following are some examples of the supplementing instruments. The African Charter's 2003 Protocol on the Rights of Women in Africa (Maputo Protocol)[125] expands the rights of women under the ACHPR to include respect for dignity (Article 3), freedom from discrimination (Article 2), the right to physical and emotional security (Article 4), the right to participate in the political process (Article 9), the right to peace (Article 10), economic and social welfare rights (Article 13), health and reproductive rights (Article 14), environmental rights (Article 18) and the right to sustainable development (Article 19). The Maputo Protocol introduces some new rights not contained in the ACHPR, including governments' duty to integrate a women's perspective in policy development (Article 2); the rights of vulnerable groups of women, including elderly women, widows, disabled women and women in distress (Articles 20, 21, 22 and 24); the rights to food security and housing (Articles 15 and 16); the right to live in a positive cultural environment (Article 17); prohibition of female genital mutilation (Article 5) and the reproductive rights

---

[122] Manisuli Ssenyonjo, 'The Influence of the International Covenant on Economic, Social and Cultural Rights in Africa' (2017) 64 Netherlands IL Rev 259.

[123] 2220 UNTS 3.

[124] Olufemi Amao, 'The African Regional Human Rights System' in Baderin and Ssenyonjo (eds), *International Human Rights Law* 235, 240–41; Manisuli Ssenyonjo, 'The Development of Economic, Social and Cultural Rights under the African Charter on Human and Peoples' Rights by the African Commission on Human and Peoples' Rights' (2015) 4 Int'l Hum Rts L Rev 147, 151, 153–4, 186–8.

[125] OAU Doc CAB/LEG/66.6 (13 Sept 2000) adopted by the 2nd Ordinary Session of the Assembly of the Union, Maputo, on 11 July 2003.

of women (Article 14). The 1991 African Convention on the Ban on the Import into Africa and the Control of Transboundary Movement of Hazardous Waste in Africa (Bamako Convention)[126] complements the provisions of the ACHPR on the right to a general satisfactory environment (Article 24), the right to life (Article 4), the right to security of the person (Article 6) and the right to health (Article 16).

The 1990 African Charter on the Rights and Welfare of the Child (ACRWC)[127] is very similar to the 1989 Convention on the Rights of the Child (CRC)[128] but provides a higher level of protection in some instances in the belief that the CRC fails to reflect important socio-cultural and economic realities peculiar to Africa.[129] The ACRWC adds to the CRC in at least seven important respects. The ACRWC completely outlaws the use of child soldiers (Article 22(2)). Unlike the CRC, the ACRWC expressly prohibits child marriages (Article 21(2)). The ACRWC extends the protection of child refugees to 'internally displaced children' (Article 23(4)). States Parties to the ACRWC are obligated under Article 11(6) to create opportunities for children who become pregnant before completing their education to continue with their education. Article 30 of the ACRWC requires States Parties to undertake to provide special treatment in the form of non-custodial punishment to expectant mothers and to mothers of infants and young children who have been accused or found guilty of infringing the penal law. Article 29(b) requires States Parties to take appropriate measures to prevent the use of children in all forms of begging. Article 26 requires State Parties to individually and collectively undertake to accord the highest priority to the special needs of children living under apartheid and in States subject to military destabilization by the apartheid regime and to children living under regimes practising racial, ethnic, religious or other forms of discrimination as well as in States subject to military destabilization.[130]

The African Commission on Human and Peoples' Rights, set up in 1987, promotes and protects human and peoples' rights under the ACHPR, as well as interpreting the Charter. It is composed of 11 human rights experts, elected by secret ballot at the Assembly of Heads of State and Government of the AU for six-year renewable terms. The Commission discharges its protective mandate

---

[126] (1991) 30 ILM 773.

[127] OAU Doc CAB/LEG/24.9/49 (1990).

[128] 1577 UNTS 3.

[129] Osifunke Ekundayo, 'Does the African Charter on the Rights and Welfare of the Child (ACRWC) only Underlines and Repeats the Convention on the Rights of the Child (CRC)'s Provisions?: Examining the Similarities and the Differences between the ACRWC and the CRC' (2015) 5 Int'l J Humanities & Soc Sci 143.

[130] Viljoen, *International Human Rights Law in Africa* 393.

through scrutinizing individual and inter-State communications as well as on-site protective and fact-finding missions. It carries out its promotional mandate by scrutinizing State reporting; establishing special mechanisms in the forms of special rapporteurs, working groups or committees to investigate and report on specific human rights issues; conducting promotional visits and outreach to national human rights institutions, the general public and human rights NGOs. The Commission may also refer violations to the ACtHPR for legally binding judgments.[131] The ICJ has held that when it is called upon to apply a regional instrument for the protection of human rights, it must take due account of the interpretation of that instrument adopted by the independent bodies specifically created to monitor the sound application of the treaty in question, such as the interpretation of the ACHPR by the African Commission set up by Article 30 of the ACHPR.[132]

Since its inception in 1987 up to the year 2010, the African Commission witnessed very limited State compliance with its recommendations. This was due not only to the unwillingness of States, but also to the Commission's own failure to give effect to its Resolution on Implementation and follow up by obtaining more accurate data and exerting additional pressure on States.[133]

One major accomplishment of the African Commission is in the field of the protection of the rights of indigenous peoples. Most African governments have been reluctant to recognize indigenous peoples as beneficiaries of the rights under the ACHPR lest recognition of their right to self-determination might entail secession uprooting the stability and territorial integrity of African States and lest indigenous peoples might impede the government's actions to develop land and natural resources.[134]

The African Commission's advisory opinion rendered in 2007 assures African States that the right of indigenous peoples to freely determine their political status and freely pursue their economic, social and cultural develop-ment as well as the exercise of the right to self-determination by the indigenous peoples, including the right to autonomy or self-government in everything that concerns their internal and local affairs as well as ways and means to finance

---

[131]   Ibid 300–390.

[132]   *Ahmadou Sadio Diallo (Republic of Guinea v Democratic Republic of the Congo)*, Merits, Judgment [2010] ICJ Rep 639, 664 [67].

[133]   Frans Viljoen, 'State Compliance with the Recommendations of the African Commission on Human and Peoples' Rights' in Baderin and Ssenyonjo (eds), *International Human Rights Law* 411, 429–30.

[134]   Derek Inman, Dorothée Cambou and Stefaan Smis, 'Evolving Legal Protections for Indigenous Peoples in Africa: Some Post-UNDRIP Reflections' (2018) 26 African J Int'l & Comp L 339, 340–41, 352, 363–4; Tilahun Weldie Hindeya, 'Indigeneity of Peoples in the Context of Ethiopia: A Tool in the Pursuit of Justice against Land Dispossessions' (2019) 27 African J Int'l & Comp L 1, 4–7.

their autonomous activities, must be in conformity with the respect for sovereignty, inviolability of the borders acquired at independence of AU Member
States and respect for their territorial integrity.[135] The Commission adds that
in Africa the term indigenous populations or communities is not aimed at protecting the rights of a certain category of citizens over and above others or at
creating a hierarchy between national communities. Rather, this notion tries to
guarantee the equal enjoyment of the rights and freedoms on behalf of groups
that have historically been marginalized.[136]

In 2010, the African Commission ruled in favour of the Endorois people,
a traditional pastoralist community who were evicted from their homes in
central Kenya between the years 1973 and 1986, with minimal compensation
by the government, in order to make way for a national reserve and tourist facilities. The Commission finds the violation of their right as an indigenous people
to property, health, culture, religion and natural resources. It ordered Kenya to
compensate them.[137] The Commission follows the IACtHR's reasoning in the
Saramaka case in identifying the Endorois as an indigenous community and
thus able to benefit from the provisions of the ACHPR that protect collective
rights. The African Commission has even expanded the requirement to obtain
consent as part of the right to free, prior and informed consent to cover 'any
development or investment projects that would have a major impact within the
indigenous community',[138] and not just in the case of large-scale developments
as propounded by the IACtHR in the *Saramaka* case.

The ACtHPR was created by a protocol to the ACHPR of 9 June 1998 and
entered into force on 25 January 2004.[139] The ACtHPR is composed of 11
judges who are nationals of AU Member States elected in their individual
capacity for a term of six years, renewable only once. It meets four times a year

---

[135] *Advisory Opinion of the African Commission on Human and Peoples' Rights on the United Nations Declaration on the Rights of Indigenous Peoples*, 41st Ordinary Sess (adopted May 2007) §18, http://www.achpr.org/files/special-mechanisms/indigenous-populations/un_advisory_opinion_idp_eng.pdf, accessed 27 Jan 2019.

[136] Ibid §19. See also Hindeya, 'Indigeneity of Peoples in the Context of Ethiopia' 12–16.

[137] *Centre for Minority Rights Development and Minority Rights Group International (on behalf of the Endorois Welfare Council) v Kenya* [2010] ACHPR Communication 276/2003.

[138] Ibid §298. See also the detailed analysis of this case in Inman et al, 'Evolving Legal Protections for Indigenous Peoples in Africa' 345–63. Cf George N Barrie, 'International Law and Indigenous Peoples: Self-Determination, Development, Consent and Co-Management' (2019) 51(2) Comparative and Int'l L J of Southern Africa 171, 177–9.

[139] OAU/LEG/MIN/AFCHPR/PROT.1 rev.2 (1997). For a detailed introduction to the ACtHPR, see Viljoen, *International Human Rights Law in Africa*, ch. 10.

in Ordinary Sessions and may hold Extraordinary Sessions. The ACtHPR met for the first time in July 2006 and delivered its first judgment on 15 December 2009.

Since the adoption of the 1998 Protocol, 30 of the 55 AU Member States have ratified it. The following nine States Parties to the Protocol have made the declaration under Article 34(6) to allow individuals and NGOs to have direct access to the ACtHPR: Benin, Burkina Faso, Côte d'Ivoire, Gambia, Ghana, Malawi, Mali, Tanzania and Tunisia. As of July 2019, the Court had received 220 applications, of which it had finalized 62 cases.

One study on the ACtHPR's work between 2006 and 2016 finds that the ACtHPR rendered merits decisions in eight contentious cases, finding violations in all of them, while it declared two cases inadmissible and gave one advisory opinion. This 'extremely modest' contribution by the ACtHPR is mainly attributed to the socio-economic and cultural context of most African States, in which only a small percentage of sociological 'problems' are ever conceptualized as 'legal disputes'. Although the IACtHR gave judgments on three contentious cases in the first ten years of its existence (1979–89) and the ECtHR only seven cases on merits during its first ten years (1959–69), IHRL had greatly advanced by 2006, the first year of the ACtHPR's establishment. The IACtHR even gave 11 advisory opinions during the first decade after its creation. Moreover, it may be recalled that only nine out of the 30 African States Parties to the ACHPR have accepted the Protocol allowing direct access to the ACtHPR. The African Commission infrequently referred cases to the ACtHPR, apparently because of a lack of referral criteria, deficiencies in accurately establishing (non-)implementation, and uncertainty about the Commission's role, know-how and experience in presenting such cases before the ACtHPR.[140]

A major challenge is for the ACtHPR to serve as the appellate court and the highest court on human rights matters for all subregional judicial bodies in Africa such as the Economic Community of West African States Court of Justice, the Court of Justice of the East African Community, the Southern African Development Community Tribunal, the Court of Justice of the Common Market of East and Southern African States and the Court of Justice of the Economic Community of Central African States.[141] On 1 July 2008 the AU resolved to merge the ACtHPR with the African Court of Justice to become the African Court of Justice and Human Rights by means of the Protocol on the Statute of the African Court of Justice and Human Rights (the

---

[140] Frans Viljoen, 'Understanding and Overcoming Challenges in Accessing the African Court on Human and Peoples' Rights' (2018) 67 ICLQ 63, 64, 95–7.

[141] Cf Franceshi, *The African Human Rights Judicial System* 141–226, esp 191.

Single Protocol).[142] As of this writing, the Single Protocol, as further amended on 27 June 2014, has been signed by 32 and ratified by seven AU Member States,[143] still short of the requisite 15 ratifications for it to enter into force and the African Court of Justice and Human Rights to be set up. Pending the eventual merger, the ACtHPR will continue with its current mandate.

The ACtHPR can make a difference to human rights in Africa. An example is the ACtHPR's judgment of 11 May 2018 in the case of *Association Pour le Progrès et la Défense des Droits des Femmes Maliennes (APDF) and the Institute for Human Rights and Development in Africa (IHDA) v Mali*,[144] the ACtHPR's first ruling on the rights of women and the rights of the child in Africa.

In August 2009 there were mass demonstrations in Mali, more than 90 per cent of whose population are Muslims, to protest against the new Family Code passed by the National Assembly that would reform Mali's family law by, for example, giving women and men equal family rights, including greater inheritance rights for women and raising the minimum age for girls to marry in most circumstances to 18. The protesters also objected to the provision defining marriage as a secular institution. Mali's President yielded to the protests by not promulgating into law the Family Code passed by the National Assembly. As a compromise, the National Assembly enacted a new version of the Family Code that adhered to most of the demands of the protesters and this was promulgated into law on 30 December 2011.[145] Mali is party to the ACHPR, the 1998 Protocol to the ACHPR, the Maputo Protocol and the African Charter on the Rights and Welfare of the Child. Mali deposited the declaration prescribed under Article 34(6) of the 1998 Protocol to the ACHPR, allowing individuals and NGOs to directly seise the ACtHPR. Mali is also party to the 1979 Convention on the Elimination of All Forms of Discrimination against Women (CEDAW).[146]

Mali argued before the ACtHPR, among other things, that its Family Code of 2011 was the outcome of efforts to garner consensus and avert the huge threat of social disruption, disintegration of the nation and an upsurge in violence, the consequence of which could have been detrimental to peace,

---

[142] https://www.refworld.org/docid/4937f0ac2.html, accessed 18 Aug 2019. See also Fatsah Ouguergouz, 'The African Court of Justice and Human Rights' in Abdulqawi A Yusuf and Fatsah Ouguergouz (eds), *The African Union Legal and Institutional Framework: A Manual on the Pan-African Organization* (Martinus Nijhoff 2012) 119.

[143] Benin, Burkina Faso, Congo, Gambia, Libya, Liberia and Mali.

[144] App No 046/2016.

[145] Law No 11-080/AN-RM, http://www.demisenya.org/wp-content/uploads/2013/03/mali-code-personnes-famille-2-decembre-2011.pdf, accessed 1 Aug 2018.

[146] 1249 UNTS 13.

harmonious living and social cohesion. In its view, the mobilization of religious forces against the version of the Code in 2009 was at such a level that no amount of resistance action could contain it. Mali therefore submitted that it did not violate international obligations or maintain practices that should be discouraged – rather Mali adapted the said obligations to reflect social, cultural and religious realities in Mali.[147] Mali maintained that its laws had to reflect the 'social, cultural and religious realities' of life within Mali and that it would be pointless to pass legislation that would be difficult or impossible to implement. It also argued that the 2011 Family Code was flexible since people were free to administer their inheritance in other ways in accordance with religious or customary law if they so chose.

The ACtHPR rejected all of Mali's arguments. By adopting the 2011 Family Code and maintaining therein discriminatory practices undermining the rights of women and children, Mali was held to have violated its international commitments.[148] Additionally, the inheritance right of the child was made illusory by the application of the customary or religious regime.[149] The ACtHPR ordered Mali to amend its legislation to bring it into line with the relevant provisions of the applicable international instruments.[150]

The ACtHPR has, thus, not adopted the doctrine of margin of appreciation as in the case of its European counterpart.[151] The Malian episode also gives some food for thought as to whether it is traditional belief or Sharia that actually demands discrimination among women and men in relation to inheritance entitlement as well as some other forms of unequal treatment between the two genders. It should be noted that in August 2018 Tunisia's President promised to submit draft legislation to Parliament to amend the code of personal status by granting women and men equal inheritance rights. The President clarified that families wishing to continue observing the existing laws on inheritance might continue doing so, apparently to calm the opposition to the draft legislation from Muslim conservatives in Tunisia.[152]

Violations of provisions of the ACHPR can be litigated in the ICJ, where the parties accept the ICJ's jurisdiction, as in *Ahmadou Sadio Diallo (Republic of Guinea v Democratic Republic of the Congo)*. In that case, Guinea instituted proceedings against DR Congo in respect of a dispute concerning 'serious

---

[147]   Judgment §§64–7.

[148]   Ibid §124.

[149]   Ibid §102.

[150]   Ibid §130.

[151]   See also McGoldrick, 'Affording States a Margin of Appreciation' 360.

[152]   'Tunisia's President vows to give women equal inheritance rights', *Al Jazeera* (13 Aug 2018) https://www.aljazeera.com/news/2018/08/tunisia-president-vows-give -women-equal-inheritance-rights-180813172138132.html, accessed 23 Aug 2018.

violations of international law' alleged to have been committed upon the person of a Guinean national. The ICJ found a violation of that person's rights under Article 13 of the ICCPR as well as Article 12(4) of the ACHPR, which protect aliens or non-nationals from arbitrary and unlawful expulsions. It also found a violation of Article 9(1) and (2) of the ICCPR and Article 6 of the ACHPR, which protect the right to liberty and security of the person.[153] The ICJ awarded the amount of compensation to be paid by DR Congo to Guinea for non-material injury suffered by the national of Guinea at US$85,000 and the amount of compensation due from the former to the latter for the material injury suffered by the latter's national in relation to his personal property at US$10,000, to be paid by a specific date.[154]

Beyond the context of regional human rights instruments and mechanisms, African States' compliance with international human rights treaties to which they are party varies from one treaty to another. With respect to the 1965 International Convention on the Elimination of All Forms of Racial Discrimination (CERD),[155] the issue of respect for the rights of indigenous peoples in African States Parties is often a cause of concern to the CERD Committee. So is ethnicity-based discrimination. African States are even more reluctant to meet their obligation to report under the ICESCR than under other treaties because of the continent-wide conditions of poverty, illiteracy and general underdevelopment. The CRC is a treaty to which a very high number of African States make reservations or declarations. The grounds for the declarations/reservations range from the Islamic religion, age of majority, religion and traditional values, provisions of national legislation, inability to ensure free primary education, children seeking refugee status and so forth. The areas identified by the CRC Committee as failing to provide the protection required by the CRC include discrimination against girls, especially female genital mutilation; absence of compulsory and free primary education; the unsatisfactory quality of education; the high drop-out rate before pupils finish primary school; alarmingly low rates of birth registration owing to exclusion from basic services; socio-economic issues such as birth rates, health and welfare; the position of working children that turns them into child labour; and the position of juvenile offenders.[156]

In both bilateral and multilateral diplomatic forums, African States understand each other's multifarious constraints in implementing their human rights obligations. They also prefer to find among themselves the appropriate solu-

---

[153] [2010] ICJ Rep 639, 662–70 [63]–[85].
[154] [2012] ICJ Rep 324.
[155] 660 UNTS 195.
[156] Viljoen, *International Human Rights Law in Africa* 87–136.

tions to 'African problems'. In their diplomatic intercourse with non-African governments, they expect from the latter respect for the dignity of African States as independent sovereign States, rectification of past wrongs by former colonial powers and altruistic capacity-building assistance to help them fully realize their economic potential, which will enable them better to fulfil their human rights obligations.

5.   THE MIDDLE EAST AND THE ARAB WORLD

Muslim-majority States in the Middle East are members of the OIC and most of them are also members of the League of Arab States. Membership of these two bodies also encompasses Arab States in Africa. The OIC's membership includes Turkey; the South East Asian nation States of Brunei, Indonesia and Malaysia; Bangladesh and Pakistan in South Asia; Albania in Europe; and, in Eurasia, several Member States of the Commonwealth of Independent States.

Iranians do not consider themselves Arabs but Persians, originally part of a people known as the Arayans. Iran is therefore not a member of the Arab League, although it is an OIC member. In a world where at least 85 per cent of Muslims are Sunnis, Shiites are the majority in Iran, with less than ten per cent of its population being Sunnis. Shiites are also the majority in Iraq and comprise large minority communities in Azerbaijan, Bahrain, Syria, Lebanon and Yemen. Iran and Saudi Arabia are locked in a power struggle for political dominance in the Middle East, exacerbated by their religious differences. This lack of unity within the OIC can undermine efforts to have common OIC positions at multilateral forums, including in the area of human rights.

The OIC has adopted the Cairo Declaration on Human Rights in Islam,[157] whereas the Arab League concluded the Arab Charter on Human Rights in 2004.[158]

The Cairo Declaration of 5 August 1990 emphasizes the connection between Sharia and human rights. Its preamble mentions the protection of human rights 'in accordance with the Islamic Sharia' and pursuant to the 'binding divine commandments' contained in the Quran and 'sent through the last of His Prophets to complete the preceding divine messages'. Article 1 refers to human beings as God's subjects whose true faith is the guarantee for enhancing their dignity along the path to human perfection. Article 2 alludes to

---

[157] 5 Aug 1990, UN GAOR, World Conference on Human Rights, 4th Sess Agenda Item 5, UN Doc A/CONF.157/PC/62/Add.18 (1993).

[158] (2005) 12 Int'l Hum Rts Rep 893. For a history of the Arab Charter on Human Rights, see El Demey, *The Arab Charter of Human Rights* 130–37.

the right to life as 'a God-given gift' to every human being and prohibits any violation of this right except for a reason prescribed by Sharia.

Article 5 of the Cairo Declaration recognizes the right of men and women to marriage without restriction stemming from race, colour or nationality. It omits to include religion as a prohibited ground of restriction because Sharia does not recognize the right of a Muslim woman to marry a non-Muslim man. Article 6 recognizes the right of women to be equal to men although the husband is responsible for the support and welfare of the family. Article 7 stipulates, inter alia, that both parents are entitled to certain rights from their children and relatives are entitled to rights from their kin, in accordance with the tenets of Sharia. Article 10 prohibits any form of compulsion on a man or exploiting his poverty or ignorance in order to convert him from Islam to another religion or to atheism. Article 22 recognizes the right of everyone to express his opinion freely in such manner as would not be contrary to the principles of Sharia; as well as to advocate what is right and propagate what is good and warn against what is wrong and evil according to the norms of the Islamic Sharia. It adds that information is a vital necessity to society that may not be exploited or misused in such a way as may violate the sanctity and dignity of prophets, undermine moral and ethical values or disintegrate, corrupt or harm society or weaken its faith.

The Cairo Declaration ends by propounding, in Article 24, that all the rights and freedoms encapsulated therein are subject to the Islamic Sharia and, in Article 25, that the Islamic Sharia is the only source of reference for the explanation or classification of any of the Articles of this Declaration.

The Cairo Declaration is criticized, inter alia, for its omission of several essential rights under the ICCPR and the ICESCR.[159] Moreover, as mentioned in section 2, PACE's resolution on Sharia, the Cairo Declaration and the ECHR call upon CoE Member States to engage in the process of revision of the OIC's Cairo Declaration so as to ensure that the future OIC Declaration on Human Rights is compatible with universal human rights standards and the ECHR.[160] It specifically calls on Albania, Azerbaijan and Turkey – the three CoE Member States that are also OIC members – to consider distancing themselves from the Cairo Declaration by considering withdrawing from it; to make use of all available means to make declarations, so as to ensure that the Cairo Declaration has no effect on their domestic legal orders that may be inconsistent with their obligations as Parties to the ECHR; or to consider

---

[159] Baderin, *International Human Rights and Islamic Law* 229.

[160] See further the report by PACE's Committee on Legal Affairs and Human Rights entitled 'Compatibility of Sharia Law with the European Convention on Human Rights: Can States Parties to the Convention be signatories of the "Cairo Declaration"?', Doc AS/Jur (2016) 28 of 7 Oct 2016.

performing some formal act which clearly establishes the ECHR as a superior source of obligatory binding norms. PACE concludes by calling on the States addressed in the resolution to report back to PACE by June 2020 on the actions they have taken as a follow-up to this resolution.

According to PACE, CoE Member States are obligated to protect the right to freedom of thought, conscience and religion as enshrined in Article 9 of the ECHR, which represents one of the foundations of a democratic society. The right to manifest one's religion is a qualified right the exercise of which may be limited in response to certain specified public interests and, under Article 17 of the ECHR, may not aim at the destruction of other ECHR rights or freedoms. PACE further reiterates its support for the principle of the separation of State and religion as one of the pillars of a democratic society. It recalls that the ECtHR has already stated in *Refah Partisi (The Welfare Party) and others v Turkey* that the institution of Sharia law and a theocratic regime were incompatible with the requirements of a democratic society. In PACE's view, Sharia law rules on, for example, divorce and inheritance proceedings are clearly incompatible with the ECHR, in particular its Article 14, which prohibits discrimination on grounds such as sex or religion, and Article 5 of Protocol No 7 to the ECHR,[161] which establishes equality between marital partners. Sharia law is also in contradiction with other provisions of the ECHR, including Article 2 (right to life), Article 3 (prohibition of torture or inhuman or degrading treatment), Article 6 (right to a fair trial), Article 8 (right to respect for private and family life), Article 9 (freedom of religion), Article 10 (freedom of expression) and Article 12 (right to marry) of the ECHR, as well as Article 1 of Protocol No 1 (protection of property)[162] and Protocols Nos 6[163] and 13[164] prohibiting the death penalty.

While PACE may hold sway over the practice of CoE Member States and States Parties to the ECHR, its resolution, which is not legally binding, is unlikely to compel Albania, Azerbaijan and Turkey to confront the other signatories to the 1990 Cairo Declaration, especially since these three States also need support from OIC Member States in international arenas on numerous pressing issues. It is more realistic to expect them to abide by their obligations under the ECHR while, at the same time, showing their deference to the OIC's non-binding Cairo Declaration, for the sake of their 'having the best of both worlds'.

---

[161] ETS No 117.
[162] ETS No 9.
[163] ETS No 114.
[164] ETS No 187.

Despite the OIC's endorsement of the non-binding Cairo Declaration, several Articles of the Cairo Declaration have not been faithfully observed by the States adopting it.[165] In particular, there is no unified stance among OIC Member States regarding international human rights treaties and they have not taken steps to amend their laws to reflect the purportedly uniform Islamic standards set forth in the Cairo Declaration, which in many cases are far below the human rights standards already stipulated in their domestic laws and constitutions.[166]

The 2004 Arab Charter on Human Rights entered into force on 16 March 2008, two months after its ratification by the seventh Member State of the Arab League. The current status of ratification is not available although the latest information from various sources indicates that as of November 2013 the Arab Charter had been ratified by Algeria, Bahrain, Iraq, Jordan, Kuwait, Lebanon, Libya, Palestine, Qatar, Saudi Arabia, Syria, UAE and Yemen.

The Arab Charter encompasses four groups of rights: individual rights; rule of law and justice; civil and political rights; and economic, social and cultural rights. Apart from the rights that are also incorporated into other global and/or regional human rights treaties, the following are the salient points of the Arab Charter especially relevant to the discussion in this book.

The preamble of the Arab Charter commences by referring to

> the faith of the Arab nation in the dignity of the human person whom God has exalted ever since the beginning of creation and in the fact that the Arab homeland is the cradle of religions and civilizations whose lofty human values affirm the human right to a decent life based on freedom, justice and equality.

It proceeds to refer to 'the eternal principles of fraternity, equality and tolerance among human beings consecrated by the noble Islamic religion and the other divinely revealed religions', the right to self-determination, the rejection of 'all forms of racism and Zionism, which constitute a violation of human rights and a threat to international peace and security'. The Arab Charter recognizes the close link between human rights and international peace and security and reaffirms the principles of the UN Charter, the UDHR and the provisions of the ICCPR and the ICESCR, as well as having regard to the Cairo Declaration on Human Rights in Islam.

---

[165] Ali Allawi, 'Islam, Human Rights and the New Information Technologies' in Monroe Price and Nicole Stremlau (eds), *Speech and Society in Turbulent Times* (CUP 2018) 19, 28–9.

[166] Ann Elizabeth Mayer, 'Universal Versus Islamic Human Rights: A Clash of Cultures or a Clash with a Construct?' (1994) 15 Michigan JIL 307, 348–50.

Article 1 of the Arab Charter stipulates the aims of, inter alia, placing human rights at the centre of the key national concerns of Arab States; instilling in the human person in the Arab States a culture of human brotherhood, tolerance and openness towards others, in accordance with universal principles and values and with those proclaimed in international human rights instruments; preparing the new generations in Arab States for a free and responsible life in a civil society characterized by solidarity, founded on a balance between awareness of rights and respect for obligations and governed by the values of equality, tolerance and moderation; and entrenching the principle that all human rights are universal, indivisible, interdependent and interrelated. Both the preamble and Article 1 seem to highlight the Arab Charter's respect for universalism of human rights, albeit in the context of Arab identity and Islamic values.

Article 3 of the Arab Charter obligates each State Party to undertake to ensure to all individuals subject to its jurisdiction the enjoyment of the rights and freedoms set forth therein, without distinction on the grounds of race, colour, sex, language, religious belief, opinion, thought, national or social origin, wealth, birth or physical or mental disability. The States Parties to the Arab Charter have a positive obligation to take the requisite measures to guarantee effective equality in the enjoyment of all the rights and freedoms enumerated in the Arab Charter in order to ensure protection against all forms of discrimination based on any of the aforementioned grounds. Article 3 states unequivocally that men and women are equal in respect of human dignity, rights and obligations within the framework of the positive discrimination established in favour of women 'by the Islamic Sharia',[167] other divine laws and by applicable laws and legal instruments.

Article 4 permits derogation in exceptional situations of emergency which threaten the life of the nation and the existence of which is officially proclaimed. However, no derogation from the following Articles is permitted: Articles 5, 8, 9, 10, 13, 14(6), 15, 18, 19, 20, 22, 27, 28, 29 and 30. In addition, the judicial guarantees required for the protection of the aforementioned rights may not be suspended.

While Article 5 stipulates that every human being has the inherent right to life protected by law, Article 6 permits the death penalty for the most serious crimes in accordance with the laws in force at the time of commission of the crime and pursuant to a final judgment of a competent court. However, anyone sentenced to death shall have the right to seek pardon or commutation of the sentence. Article 7 prohibits the death sentence for persons under 18, unless otherwise stipulated in the laws in force at the time of the commission of the crime. It also prohibits the carrying out of a death penalty on a pregnant woman

---

[167] See also El Demey, *The Arab Charter of Human Rights* 114–20.

prior to her delivery or on a nursing mother within two years from the date of her delivery. Article 8 proscribes physical or psychological torture or cruel, degrading, humiliating or inhuman treatment. Article 9 prohibits medical or scientific experimentation or the use of one's organs without one's free consent and full awareness of the consequences. It also prohibits trafficking in human organs in all circumstances. Article 10 proscribes all forms of slavery and trafficking in human beings, slavery or servitude under any circumstances. Forced labour, trafficking in human beings for the purposes of prostitution or sexual exploitation, the exploitation or the prostitution of others or any other form of exploitation or the exploitation of children in armed conflict are also forbidden under Article 10.

Article 11 provides that all persons are equal before the law and have the right to enjoy its protection without discrimination. Article 12 adds that all persons are equal before courts and tribunals.

Articles 14(6), 15, 18, 19, 20, 22, 27 and 28, which are non-derogable, incorporate the right to habeas corpus, the protection under the principle of legality (no crime or no punishment without a prior provision of the law), the prohibition of imprisonment for violation of a contractual obligation, the prohibition of double jeopardy, the requirement for humane treatment of persons in detention, the right to recognition as a person before the law, the prohibition of arbitrary or unlawful deprivation of the right to leave or reside in any country or any part of that country and the right to seek political asylum, respectively. The Arab Charter does not have any provision similar to Article 12 of the ICCPR, which permits the imposition of restrictions on freedom of movement, choice of residence and the right to leave any country.

Article 25 of the Arab Charter protects the rights of persons belonging to minorities to enjoy their own culture, to use their own language and to practise their own religion. The exercise of these rights 'shall be governed by law', however.

Article 29 provides that everyone has the right to nationality and that no one shall be arbitrarily or unlawfully deprived of his nationality. States Parties shall take such measures as they deem appropriate, in accordance with their domestic laws on nationality, to allow a child to acquire the mother's nationality, having due regard, in all cases, to the best interests of the child. No one shall be denied the right to acquire another nationality, having due regard for the domestic legal procedures in his country.

Article 30 recognizes the right of everyone to freedom of thought, conscience and religion, without any restriction on the exercise of such freedoms 'except as provided for by law'. The freedom to manifest one's religion or beliefs or to perform religious observances, either alone or in community with others, 'shall be subject only to such limitations as are prescribed by law and are necessary in a tolerant society that respects human rights and freedoms for the protection of public safety, public order, public health or morals or the fundamental rights and freedoms of others'. Parents or guardians have the freedom to provide for the religious and moral education of their children.

Although Article 32 guarantees the right to information and to freedom of opinion and expression, as well as the right to seek, receive and impart information and ideas through any medium, regardless of geographical boundaries, 'such rights and freedoms shall be exercised in conformity with the fundamental values of society and shall be subject only to such limitations as are required to ensure respect for the rights or reputation of others or the protection of national security, public order and public health or morals'.

Article 34 recognizes the right to work as a natural right of every citizen, male or female. There shall be no discrimination between men and women in their enjoyment of the right to benefit effectively from training, employment, job protection and the right to receive equal remuneration for equal work.

Article 37 stipulates that the right to development is a fundamental human right and 'all States', not just States Parties to the Arab Charter, are required to establish the development policies and to take the measures needed to guarantee this right. They also have a duty to give effect to the values of solidarity and cooperation among them and at the international level with a view to eradicating poverty and achieving economic, social, cultural and political development. By virtue of this right, every citizen has the right to participate in the realization of development and to enjoy the benefits and fruits thereof.

Article 38 recognizes the right of every person to an adequate standard of living for himself and his family, which ensures their well-being and a decent life, including food, clothing, housing, services and the right to a healthy environment. In this regard, States Parties 'shall take the necessary measures commensurate with their resources to guarantee these rights'. Article 39 adds that States Parties recognize the right of every member of society to the enjoyment of the highest attainable standard of physical and mental health and the right of the citizen to free basic health-care services and to have access to medical facilities without discrimination of any kind. The measures taken by States Parties shall include development of basic health-care services and the guaranteeing of free and easy access to the centres that provide these services, regardless of geographical location or economic status, as well as combating environmental pollution and providing proper sanitation systems.

Article 40 imposes a positive obligation on States Parties to undertake to assure persons with mental or physical disabilities a decent life that guarantees their dignity and to enhance their self-reliance and facilitate their active participation in society. States Parties shall provide social services free of charge for all persons with disabilities, shall provide the material support needed by those persons, their families or the families caring for them and shall do whatever is needed to avoid placing those persons in institutions. They shall, in all cases, take account of the best interests of the disabled person.

Article 43 stipulates that nothing in the Arab Charter may be interpreted as impairing the rights and freedoms protected by the domestic laws of States Parties or those set forth in the international and regional human rights instruments which States Parties have adopted or ratified, including the rights of women, the rights of the child and the rights of persons belonging to minorities. Article 44 requires States Parties to undertake to adopt, in conformity with their constitutional procedures and with the provisions of the Arab Charter, whatever legislative or non-legislative measures that may be necessary to give effect to the rights in the Arab Charter.

The Arab Human Rights Committee, comprising seven experts elected to serve in their individual capacity for a four-year term and eligible for re-election only once, has been established since 2009, pursuant to Article 45 of the Arab Charter, to oversee its implementation. As stipulated in Article 48 of the Arab Charter, the Committee has no enforcement mechanism or special procedure. It monitors States Parties' human rights performance, interprets the Arab Charter, submits annual reports to the Arab League Council, requests information from Arab League bodies and Arab institutions and reviews reports by States Parties to the Arab Charter.

The League of Arab States adopted the Statute of the Arab Court of Human Rights[168] in September 2014, in the wake of the Arab Spring uprisings that had spread across the Arab world since early 2011. The Statute is a stand-alone, 'opt-in' agreement separate from the 2004 Arab Charter on Human Rights. The Arab Court of Human Rights is to be situated in Manama, Bahrain, and composed of seven judges who are citizens of States Parties to the Statute elected by secret ballots for a four-year term and eligible for re-election only once. There can be no more than one judge of the same nationality. The number of judges can be increased to 11 if required by the said Court and approved by the Assembly of States Parties to the Statute.

The Arab Court of Human Rights shall have jurisdiction over all cases and disputes arising from the implementation and interpretation of the Arab Charter of Human Rights or any other Arab treaty in the field of human rights involving a State Party to the Statute that is also party to the Arab treaty in question. The Court's jurisdiction is 'complementary' to the national judiciary and does not supplant it. The Court may hear a case only after the exhaustion of local remedies in the State concerned, if a case having the same subject matter has not been filed before another regional human rights court and the case is submitted to the Court six months after the applicant was notified of the final

---

[168] https://acihl.org/texts.htm?article_id=44&lang=ar-SA, accessed 18 Aug 2019.

judgment rendered by the domestic court. The Statute does not specifically bar lodging complaints with UN treaty bodies, though.

The Court's competence is confined to inter-State cases. The Statute makes clear that only a State Party to the Statute whose citizen claims to be a victim of human rights violation in another State Party to the Statute has the right to have access to the Court for judicial remedies on behalf of the citizen. However, when ratifying or acceding to the Statute or at any time thereafter, a State can allow one or more NGOs accredited or working in the field of human rights in the State whose citizen claims to be a victim of a human rights violation to have access to the Court. A Member State of the Arab League that is not party to the Statute may declare at any time its acceptance of the Court's jurisdiction whether in a specific case or in general and on the basis of reciprocity, unconditionally or for a limited duration. The Court may give advisory opinions on any legal question related to the Arab Charter on Human Rights at the request of the League of Arab States' Assembly or any of the Arab League's subsidiary organizations or authorities. The Court may, at any stage of the proceedings, embark on a confidential conciliation between the parties to a dispute before it in order to assist them in reaching an amicable settlement based on human rights principles and values and the rules of justice. A brief report on the amicable settlement achieved is to be submitted to the Assembly, which shall monitor its implementation. The Court's judgment shall be delivered within 60 days after the end of the Court's deliberation on the case. The Court's judgments are final and binding on the parties and are enforceable immediately. The Court shall submit its annual report to the Assembly of the Arab League, listing, among others, cases where its judgments are not complied with. The Statute does not provide for the Court to order compensatory damages or provisional measures against serious and urgent threats of irreparable or irreversible damage or injury, however.[169]

The 2004 Arab Charter on Human Rights is criticized for falling below international standards in certain areas and omitting crucial rights and guarantees. To its credit, the Charter builds on developments in international law and takes into consideration the general comments and recommendations of human rights treaty bodies, as well as recognizing certain rights not yet enshrined in the then existing UN human rights treaties, such as the right to own private property. A strong criticism is levelled at the unsatisfactory treatment of women under the Arab Charter, for example by requiring that rights and duties of spouses in marriage and upon its dissolution be regulated by national legislation. In addition, the Charter requires that the right to marry and 'to

---

[169] Konstantinos D Magliveras, 'Completing the Institutional Mechanism of the Arab Human Rights System' (2017) 6 Int'l Hum Rts L Rev 30, 48, 51.

found a family' should be according to the rules and conditions of marriage, a concept derived from Islamic law that is not clearly defined and is based on differing interpretations, some of which could undermine equality between the genders. Article 29 of the Charter is inconsistent with requirements of international law that do not make the passing of the nationality of the mother to her children subject to national legislation. Article 3 of the Charter allowing positive discrimination 'established in favour of women by the Islamic Sharia' in effect permits such positive discrimination only to the extent permissible by Sharia. Article 7 of the Charter, prohibiting the imposition of the death penalty on children under the age of 18, 'unless otherwise stipulated in the law in force at the time of the commission of the crime', aims to accommodate Saudi Arabia and Yemen, whose laws at the time of the adoption of the Arab Charter still imposed the death sentence on children under 18. Article 30 of the Charter permits the imposition of restrictions on the exercise of freedom of thought, conscience and religion as provided for 'by law' – something not generally recognized under international law – and this is consistent with Article 18 of the ICCPR only insofar as such restrictions by law are necessary to protect public safety, order, health or morals or the fundamental rights and freedoms of others. Article 43 of the Arab Charter is criticized for being largely vague compared with international instruments, including Article 24 of the ICESCR, Article 46 of the ICCPR, Article 23 of CEDAW and Article 16 of CAT, which all tend to be more specific.[170] It is pointed out that equality in Islam is equated with 'equivalence' rather than formal equality. Therefore, although men and women may be 'equal' under the law, they may not be 'equivalent' in their duties and roles in a patriarchal society, especially in family matters, which are regulated in detail under Sharia law, including the law governing polygamy, inheritance and divorce.[171]

The International Commission of Jurists, an international human rights NGO composed of 60 eminent human rights lawyers from all over the world, is critical of the Arab League's human rights system.[172] It considers that the Arab Charter of Human Rights generally falls short of international human rights standards – including those relating to the right to life; equality between men and women; the prohibition of cruel, inhuman or degrading treatment; and the right to freedom of thought and conscience. It deplores that justice for victims, including access to effective remedies and reparation, continues to be largely unavailable. In addition, the Arab Human Rights Committee has no mandate

---

[170] The criticisms alluded to are from Mervat Rishmawi, 'Arab Charter on Human Rights (2004)', *Max Planck Encyclopedia of Public International Law* (June 2008).

[171] El Demey, *The Arab Charter of Human Rights* 200–228.

[172] International Commission of Jurists, *The Arab Court of Human Rights: A Flawed Statute for an Ineffective Court* (International Commission of Jurists 2015).

and competence to receive and adjudicate individual complaints, to receive and consider alternative reports or to address urgent human rights situations in the Member States of the Arab League. The Statute of the Arab Court of Human Rights is criticized as manifestly deficient, particularly in relation to the Court's jurisdiction; the guarantees of the Court's independence, including the independence of its judges; admissibility of cases and access to the Court for victims of human rights violations, bearing in mind decades of experience of existing regional human rights courts and UN human rights treaty bodies showing that States, typically for diplomatic and political reasons, almost never make use of inter-State complaints procedures regarding human rights issues.

The International Commission of Jurists therefore suggests that the Statute be amended to permit direct access to the Court for all individuals within the territory of a State Party, or subject to its jurisdiction, when they claim to be victims of a violation of a right that comes under the Court's jurisdiction. Moreover, impediments to NGOs' access to the Court should be removed, including the requirement that the States themselves accept such access by NGOs. Legal standing to bring a complaint should not be restricted only to NGOs accredited in a respondent State. Other avenues to access the Court should also be provided, including for individuals or NGOs to join proceedings as interested parties or to submit amicus curiae briefs, third-party interventions or expert opinions. The Court must have competence to prescribe interim or provisional measures where the applicant faces an imminent risk of serious, irreversible or irreparable harm. The protection of victims, witnesses and other participants in proceedings before the Court by States Parties must be stipulated in the Statute of the Court. Furthermore, it is recommended that mechanisms be put in place to ensure that the Court's judgments are executed, including providing for an independent and effective monitoring mechanism and enabling the Court to prescribe specific measures to be adopted by States to execute its judgments.

In order to adequately ensure the independence and impartiality of the Court and its judges, it is suggested that the nomination of candidates and election of judges be based on transparent and non-discriminatory procedures that protect against undue, inappropriate or unwarranted State interference and that take full account of appropriate personal and legal qualifications, gender balance and a fair representation of different legal systems. Judges should sit in their individual capacity, not as representatives of their home State, and serve for a single, lengthy term with a guaranteed pension. Judges should only be suspended or removed from office for reasons of incapacity or behaviour that makes them unfit to discharge their duties, following an appropriate procedure established in advance that guarantees the rights of the judge concerned to a fair hearing with all due process guarantees.[173]

It is doubtful whether the International Commission of Jurists' recommendations can be fully, or even partially, accepted by the Arab League. Even as it is, just over half of the Member States of the Arab League are party to the Arab Charter on Human Rights, which is supposed to encapsulate the lowest common denominator of the positions of its Member States. The Statute of the Arab Court of Human Rights has been ratified only by Saudi Arabia as of this writing.

It may be rewarding for a State in this region to project its good image on human rights at the international level, provided that its domestic constituencies can be kept satisfied that local religious and traditional norms and practices will remain intact as much as possible – unless changes are unavoidable after carefully considering all the pros and cons. Becoming party to international human rights treaties that allow reservations to some of their provisions, as will be seen in Chapter 5, may serve this purpose.

6. ASIA BEYOND THE MIDDLE EAST[174]

In the rest of Asia, beyond the Middle East, religions and philosophical or cultural traditions have recognized humanism and human dignity for centuries. Abusive feudal systems turned Asian intellectuals and newer generations of Asians to embrace various Western ideals, including human rights, democracy and legal concepts, during the early period of modernization in the nineteenth and twentieth centuries in the belief that modernization in line with the West would effectively strengthen their hands in the struggles against colonialism or authoritarian regimes. The local legal systems of many Asian States have incorporated civil or constitutional norms in their respective domestic laws since the mid nineteenth century. These Western ideals were adapted and synchronized with Asian moral and ethical traditions rather than totally supplanting them.[175]

The 34 Asian States[176] meeting in Bangkok, Thailand, from 29 March to 2 April 1993, to prepare for the World Conference on Human Rights, endorsed

---

[173] See also Konstantinos D Magliveras and Gino Naldi, 'The Arab Court of Human Rights: A Study in Impotence' (2016) 29 Revue québécoise de droit international 147.

[174] See, generally, Hitoshi Nasu and Ben Saul (eds), *Human Rights in the Asia-Pacific Region: Towards Institution Building* (Routledge 2011).

[175] Tae-Ung Baik, *Emerging Regional Human Rights Systems in Asia* (CUP 2012) 4, 48–51, 61–4.

[176] Bahrain, Bangladesh, Bhutan, Brunei, China, Cyprus, Fiji, India, Indonesia, Iran, Iraq, Japan, Kiribati, Kuwait, Lao PDR, Malaysia, Maldives, Mongolia, Myanmar,

'The Bangkok Declaration'[177] containing their human rights aspirations and commitments.

The first preambular paragraph stresses 'the universality, objectivity and non-selectivity of all human rights and the need to avoid the application of double standards in the implementation of human rights and its politicization'. The rest of the preamble declares that the promotion of human rights should be encouraged by cooperation and consensus and not through confrontation and the imposition of incompatible values. It then reiterates the interdependence and indivisibility of economic, social, cultural, civil and political rights and the inherent interrelationship between development, democracy, universal enjoyment of all human rights and social justice, which must be addressed in an integrated and balanced manner. For them, the right to development is a universal and inalienable right and an integral part of fundamental human rights. Efforts to move towards the creation of uniform international human rights norms must go hand in hand with endeavours to work towards a just and fair world economic order. They are convinced that economic and social progress facilitates the growing trend towards democracy and the promotion and protection of human rights.

The operative paragraphs of the Bangkok Declaration commence by reaffirming the Asian States' commitment to the principles contained in the UN Charter and the UDHR as well as the full realization of all human rights throughout the world. It is deemed essential to create favourable conditions for effective enjoyment of human rights at both the national and international levels. The UN system is to be democratized urgently, eliminating selectivity and improving procedures and mechanisms in order to strengthen international cooperation based on principles of equality and mutual respect and to ensure a positive, balanced and non-confrontational approach in addressing and realizing all aspects of human rights. Any attempt to use human rights as a conditionality for extending development assistance is discouraged. These Asian States emphasize the principles of respect for national sovereignty and territorial integrity as well as non-interference in the internal affairs of States and the non-use of human rights as an instrument of political pressure. All countries, large and small, must have the right to determine their political systems, control and freely utilize their resources and freely pursue their economic, social and cultural development.

Nepal, North Korea, Oman, Pakistan, Papua New Guinea, Philippines, Samoa, Singapore, Solomon Islands, South Korea, Sri Lanka, Syria, Thailand, UAE and Vietnam.

[177] UN Doc A/CONF.157/ASRM/8.

Paragraph 7 repeats the wording of the first preambular paragraph but adds that no violation of human rights can be justified. Paragraph 8 recognizes that 'while human rights are universal in nature, they must be considered in the context of a dynamic and evolving process of international norm-setting, bearing in mind the significance of national and regional particularities and various historical, cultural and religious backgrounds'. According to paragraph 9, States have the primary responsibility for the promotion and protection of human rights, including by providing remedies, through appropriate infrastructure and mechanisms. Paragraph 10, once again, repeats what the preamble has already said about the interdependence and indivisibility of economic, social, cultural, civil and political rights but adds that there is a need to give equal emphasis to all categories of human rights. Paragraph 11 emphasizes the importance of guaranteeing the human rights and fundamental freedoms of vulnerable groups such as ethnic, national, racial, religious and linguistic minorities, migrant workers, disabled persons, indigenous peoples, refugees and displaced persons. Paragraph 17 reiterates the right to development mentioned in the preamble and adds that this right must be realized through international cooperation, respect for fundamental human rights, the establishment of a monitoring mechanism and the creation of essential international conditions for the realization of such right. Paragraph 18 declares that the main obstacles to the realization of the right to development lie at the international macroeconomic level, as reflected in the widening gap between the North and the South, the rich and the poor. Paragraph 19 affirms that poverty is one of the major obstacles hindering the full enjoyment of human rights, whereas paragraph 20 affirms the need to develop the right of humankind regarding a clean, safe and healthy environment. The rights of women and the rights of the child are recognized in paragraphs 22 and 23, respectively.

By and large, the Bangkok Declaration asserts the 'Asian value' approach to human rights, as explained in Chapter 2. It stresses economic development and advances the primary role of each nation State to take care of human rights within its territorial borders with as little external interference as possible, bearing in mind also national and regional particularities and various historical, cultural and religious backgrounds. This was made clear, for example, by the Foreign Minister of Indonesia, the nation State with the world's largest population of Muslims, who asked the Vienna Conference to also understand and appreciate 'the historical formation and experiences of non-Western societies and the attendant development of [their] cultural and social values and traditions'. Indonesia was against any linkage between human rights and economic/development aid on the grounds that such linkage would be 'political conditionalities'. While accepting the universal character of human rights, Indonesia contended that the expression and implementation of human rights at the national level remained the competence and responsibility of each government in accordance with the principle of sovereignty of States as well as a logical consequence of the principle of self-determination.[178]

Not all of the provisions of the hortatory Bangkok Declaration are accepted as legally enforceable human rights by every one of the 34 participating States. For example, at the time of the Declaration's adoption only eight of them[179] were party to the 1951 Convention Relating to the Status of Refugees[180] and its 1967 Protocol.[181] Only two of them have become party to these treaties since then.[182] The rest have consistently objected to recognizing the notion of 'refugees' and its concomitant rights although this appears in paragraph 11 of the Bangkok Declaration.

The Association of Southeast Asian Nations (ASEAN) is the only intergovernmental organization in Asia beyond the Middle East that has some form of regional intergovernmental human rights arrangement or mechanism comparable to those in other regions or subregions.

The ten Member States of ASEAN[183] adopted the ASEAN Charter[184] in November 2007, in force on 15 December 2008, with the subsequent establishment of the ASEAN Intergovernmental Commission on Human Rights (AICHR) on 23 October 2009, comprising one representative appointed by each ASEAN Member State to serve for a three-year term that is renewable. The AICHR's mandate is to promote human rights and uphold international human rights standards as stipulated in the UDHR, the Vienna Declaration and Programme of Action, and applicable international human rights instruments. It works by means of consultation and consensus and it reports to the ASEAN Foreign Ministers.

On 19 November 2012 the Heads of State or Government of the ASEAN Member States approved the ASEAN Human Rights Declaration[185] drafted by the AICHR. The Declaration refers to civil and political rights; economic, social and cultural rights; the right to development and the right to peace. However, operative paragraphs 6, 7 and 8 of the Declaration read:

---

[178] Fried van Hoof, 'Asian Challenges to the Concept of Universality' in Peter R Bauer, Fried van Hoof, Liu Nanlai, Tao Zhenghua and Jacqueline Smith (eds), *Human Rights: Chinese and Dutch Perspectives* (Martinus Nijhoff 1996) 1, 5–7.

[179] China, Cyprus, Fiji, Iran, Japan, Papua New Guinea, Philippines and South Korea.

[180] 189 UNTS 137, in force on 22 Apr 1954.

[181] 606 UNTS 267, in force on 4 Oct 1967.

[182] Samoa in 1994 and the Solomon Islands in 1995.

[183] Brunei, Cambodia, Indonesia, Laos, Malaysia, Myanmar, Philippines, Singapore, Thailand and Vietnam.

[184] https://www.asean.org/storage/images/archive/21069.pdf, accessed 12 Aug 2019.

[185] http://asean.org/asean-human-rights-declaration, accessed 12 Aug 2019.

6. The enjoyment of human rights and fundamental freedoms must be *balanced with* the performance of corresponding duties as every person has responsibilities to all other individuals, the community and the society where one lives. It is ultimately the primary responsibility of all ASEAN Member States to promote and protect all human rights and fundamental freedoms.
7. *All human rights are universal, indivisible, interdependent and interrelated.* All human rights and fundamental freedoms in this Declaration must be treated in a fair and equal manner, on the same footing and with the same emphasis. *At the same time, the realization of human rights must be considered in the regional and national context bearing in mind different political, economic, legal, social, cultural, historical and religious backgrounds.*
8. The human rights and fundamental freedoms of every person shall be exercised with due regard to the human rights and fundamental freedoms of others. The exercise of human rights and fundamental freedoms shall be subject only to such limitations as are determined by law solely for the purpose of securing due recognition for the human rights and fundamental freedoms of others and to meet the just requirements of national security, public order, public health, public safety, public morality, as well as the general welfare of the peoples in a democratic society. (Emphasis added.)

The ASEAN Declaration bears several striking similarities to the 1993 Bangkok Declaration and may be seen as an instrument of a political nature comparable to the OIC's Cairo Declaration. Despite numerous positive statements about human rights in the ASEAN Declaration, there is no supervisory mechanism or enforcement machinery to ensure their observance, thereby undermining their credibility.[186] Above all, the rights declared in the ASEAN Declaration must be subject to the regional and national relativism enunciated in paragraph 7 thereof.[187] For example, since 1971 Malaysia has pursued the *bumiputera* (meaning 'sons of the soil') policy, which reserves education and job opportunities for Malays and other indigenous races, as well as the primacy of Islam in Malaysia. In late 2018, even after a landslide general election victory, the newly elected Malaysian Government conceded it would be almost impossible to amend the federal Constitution to end this policy so that Malaysia could become party to CERD, as this would need the support of two-thirds of Members of Parliament, including support from the members of the opposition, especially when public resistance to this change was too strong.

ASEAN works on the basis of the 'comfort level' of the ASEAN Member States concerned, bearing in mind their different political systems, religions and cultures. ASEAN's collective approach to human rights mirrors the

---

[186] Gino J Naldi and Konstantinos D Magliveras, 'The ASEAN Human Rights Declaration' (2014) 3 Int'l Hum Rts L Rev 183, 184, 190–203, 204, 208.

[187] Cf Jaclyn L Neo, 'Realizing the Right to Freedom of Thought, Conscience and Religion: The Limited Normative Force of the ASEAN Human Rights Declaration' (2017) 17 Hum Rts L Rev 729.

Table 4.1   *ASEAN Member States and core human rights treaties*

	ICESCR	ICCPR	CEDAW	CAT	CRC	CMW	CRPD	CED	CERD
Brunei			Yes		Yes		Yes		
Cambodia	Yes	Yes	Yes	Yes	Yes		Yes	Yes	Yes
Indonesia	Yes	Yes	Yes	Yes	Yes	Yes	Yes		Yes
Lao PDR	Yes	Yes	Yes	Yes	Yes		Yes		Yes
Malaysia			Yes		Yes		Yes		
Myanmar	Yes		Yes		Yes		Yes		
Philippines	Yes	Yes	Yes	Yes	Yes	Yes	Yes		Yes
Singapore			Yes		Yes		Yes		Yes
Thailand	Yes	Yes	Yes	Yes	Yes		Yes		Yes
Vietnam	Yes	Yes	Yes	Yes	Yes		Yes		Yes

traditional ASEAN way of respect for sovereignty, non-interference in internal affairs of another Member State, settlement of disputes through consultation to achieve consensus on the way forward, which does not include punitive measures such as sanctions, and giving priority to economic developments rather than human rights of individuals.[188] Therefore, ASEAN does not have either a subregional human rights court or an international mechanism to hear individual complaints about human rights violations. The ASEAN consensus has, in effect, resulted in not naming and shaming or censuring any ASEAN Member State or government, but in trying instead to help it find a way out of the problem without losing face.

Individuals in ASEAN Member States have to rely on human rights treaty bodies to protect their human rights. The latest overall picture of ratification/accession/acceptance of the core human rights treaties among ASEAN Member States appears in Table 4.1.

Table 4.1 shows that all the ten ASEAN Member States are party to CEDAW, the CRC and the 2006 Convention on the Rights of Persons with Disabilities (CRPD).[189] This should come as no surprise since women, children and the disabled are members of every society and their good treatment earns support for political parties at the time of elections. Every UN Member State is party to the CRC. The same cannot be said of the other six international human rights treaties listed in the table. Indonesia and the Philippines are the only two ASEAN Member States party to the CMW because they are among the world's

---

[188] Daniel Aguirre and Irene Pietropaoli, 'Human Rights Protection the ASEAN Way: Non-Intervention and the Newest Regional Human Rights System' (2012) 1 Int'l Hum Rts L Rev 276.
[189] 2515 UNTS 3.

largest suppliers of migrant workers. Enforced disappearance is still a politically sensitive issue in all ASEAN Member States, so the 2006 Convention for the Protection of All Persons from Enforced Disappearance (CED)[190] has just one State Party from the ASEAN region, although, as of this writing, Thailand is in the process of enacting domestic legislation to implement CED so that it can become party to CED. CERD has seven States Parties in ASEAN, equal to the ICESCR.

Brunei, Malaysia, Philippines, Singapore, Thailand and Vietnam are party to the Optional Protocol to the CRC on the involvement of children in armed conflict.

Brunei, Malaysia, Myanmar, Philippines and Thailand are party to the Optional Protocol to the CRC on the sale of children, child prostitution and child pornography.

Cambodia and Thailand have accepted the individual complaints procedure under the Optional Protocol to CEDAW.

Cambodia and Philippines have accepted the inquiry procedures under the Optional Protocol to CEDAW.

Cambodia has accepted the inquiry procedures under CED.

Cambodia, Indonesia, Philippines and Thailand have accepted the inquiry procedures under CAT.

The Philippines has become party to the Optional Protocol to CAT and the Second Optional Protocol to the ICCPR aiming at the abolition of the death penalty. It has accepted the individual complaints procedure under the Optional Protocol to the ICCPR and the one under the Optional Protocol to CEDAW.

Thailand has accepted individual complaints procedures under the Optional Protocol to the CRC. It has also accepted the inquiry procedures under the Optional Protocol to CEDAW and the CRPD, respectively.

Brunei, Lao PDR, Malaysia, Myanmar, Singapore and Vietnam have not accepted any individual complaints procedure or inquiry procedure.

ASEAN Member States' acceptance of human rights treaty obligations should be seen in the overall context that Asia generally lags behind other regions in becoming party to international human rights treaties. As of 2011, the overall ICCPR ratification ratio for the 23 East Asian States was 74 per cent, compared with the world ratio of 86 per cent. The overall ICESCR ratification ratio globally was 82 per cent, compared with 78 per cent of the East Asian States and 67 per cent of Asia-Pacific States. The overall CAT ratification ratio globally was 77 per cent, while 61 per cent of the East Asian States and 51 per cent of Asia-Pacific States had become party to it. With respect to CERD, the overall ratification ratio globally was 90 per cent, compared with

---

[190] 2716 UNTS 3.

74 per cent of the East Asian States and 74 per cent of Asia-Pacific States.[191] This pattern shows that East Asian States are less likely to become party to politically sensitive human rights treaties than the global average and if they are party thereto they formulate a broad range of reservations or declarations to limit the effective implementation of the treaties. They are also less likely to be advocates for human rights treaties in multilateral forums than their counterparts elsewhere, probably because of their own respective shortcomings and/or lack of commitments to human rights and/or lack of faith in the selectivity or double standards in the global human rights system.[192] According to one commentator, the human rights challenges in Asia are also due to the existence in the various Asian States of authoritarian regimes, poverty and the economy-first policy, the legacy of past human rights abuses, cultural hurdles against the implementation of certain categories of human rights and weak civil society, among others.[193] Few Asian States have accepted the optional protocols to the various human rights treaties that permit individual communications/complaints/petitions to international human rights institutions relating to alleged human rights violations by States Parties.[194]

Asia also comprises the following Pacific Island States: Fiji, Kiribati, Marshall Islands, Micronesia, Nauru, Palau, Papua New Guinea, Samoa, Solomon Islands, Tonga, Tuvalu and Vanuatu. In addition to these States, there are non-self-governing territories, such as Tokelau, the Cook Islands and Niue, which are represented by New Zealand in their external affairs; and Guam, American Samoa and the Northern Mariana Islands, which are US territories.

During the entire first cycle of Universal Periodic Reviews (UPRs) in the Human Rights Council (HRC) up to the year 2011, Pacific Island States experienced below average numbers of comments from other States – half as many comments as several other UN Member States. The common themes of the comments focused on the desirability of their more extensive engagement with the international human rights system (for example, through increased ratification of core treaties) and a need for them to realize international human rights domestically. Although each Pacific Island State had a written (and comparatively modern) constitution document and the constitution of most of these States did contain reference to human rights, none incorporated all the core human rights, partly because none had ratified all the core human rights treaties. One area of legislative need was non-discrimination laws, especially against women. The need to combat violence against women and

---

[191] Baik, *Emerging Regional Human Rights Systems in Asia* 86–9.
[192] Ibid 70–72, 97–102.
[193] Ibid 260–70.
[194] Ibid 255–7.

violence against children, including corporal punishment, was raised in respect of all Pacific Island States.[195] The latest UPR sessions on the Pacific Island States occurred during the 2014–16 period and similar major concerns were reiterated.[196]

The human rights situations in the Pacific Island States in 2018 were summarized by the UN High Commissioner for Human Rights in his lecture at the University of the South Pacific in Fiji on 10 February 2018 as follows. Only Fiji and Samoa had established national human rights institutions. Fiji had recently abolished the death penalty. In many States there had been significant legal reforms, including to improve respect for the rights of persons with disabilities and to end torture and ill-treatment of people in detention. In Fiji, Nauru, Samoa and Vanuatu, work was underway to train judges in human rights law and train police forces to respect human rights. While there was a growing openness to the voices of civil society, there were discrimination and violence against so many women across this region. In several States, women lacked equal property rights and their rights to customary land were curtailed. Women were much less likely to be able to get adequate jobs and much less likely to be able to make their own choices about their lives than men were. Women's access to health-care was limited. Girls were less likely to be in school. The plight of women trafficked in the region for purposes of labour or sexual exploitation remained very disturbing. Representation of women in parliaments, and in decision-making positions in government and business, was exceedingly low and domestic violence was shockingly high. Over two-thirds of women in Papua New Guinea, Fiji and Kiribati had suffered domestic violence and sexual offences, according to some studies – four out of ten in Samoa and one in four in Palau. Cook Islands, Kiribati, Papua New Guinea, Samoa, Solomon Islands, Tonga and Tuvalu still criminalized consenting relationships between adults of the same sex, and violence and abuse targeting lesbian, gay, bisexual, transsexual and intersexual persons regularly occurred in most Pacific Island States. For those in detention, the situation was particularly acute.[197]

---

[195] Rhona KM Smith, 'The Pacific Island States: Themes Emerging from the United Nations Human Rights Council's Inaugural Universal Periodic Review?' (2012) 13 Melbourne JIL 1, 6–26.

[196] See Asia-Pacific Human Rights Information Centre, 'Pacific Island States: Human Rights Issues' (2017) 89 FOCUS, https://www.hurights.or.jp/archives/focus/section3/2017/09/pacific-island-states-human-rights-issues.html, accessed 19 July 2019. See further, Pacific Community, *Human Rights in the Pacific – A Situational Analysis* (Quality Print 2016).

[197] 'Human Rights in the Pacific: Navigating New Challenges with the Universal Declaration of Human Rights', Lecture by UN High Commissioner for Human Rights

There is an element of irony to the allegation that women in Pacific Island States face serious discrimination. A relatively high percentage of Pacific Island State diplomats accredited to the UN in New York, including those of the rank of permanent representatives/ambassadors, are women. When female diplomats from the South Pacific are assigned by their regional or subregional group to coordinate multilateral issues, they are second to none in terms of the quality of their contribution.

There may be some good reasons why human rights in the Pacific region are still subject to criticisms. First and foremost, Pacific Island States have limited financial and human resources and therefore have to allocate them according to the priorities set by the respective States. Economic development, climate change, especially the adverse effects of sea-level rise, and nuclear weapon tests' environmental fallouts are among their top priorities in international forums. It is not unusual to find most of their seats at UN conference rooms left empty when these priorities are not on an active agenda since each permanent mission from the South Pacific comprises merely a few diplomats, normally two or three. These States coordinate their positions at regular Pacific Island States' meetings and assign one or two diplomats to speak on their behalf on non-prioritized issues. Some permanent missions have students or NGO members who volunteer to follow various UN meetings and report to them but these volunteers do not normally have influence over their decision making. It should be noted that Fiji, Marshall Islands, Nauru, Solomon Islands and Vanuatu are the only Pacific Island States with permanent missions to the UN at Geneva, where the HRC meets and various UN agencies entrusted with human rights-related mandates are based. Second, becoming party to a human rights treaty entails responsibilities, including several reforms at home, where the priorities lie elsewhere – in economic development, especially by getting foreign investment in their respective territories and exporting their domestic products. Third, the peoples of the Pacific have been living their way of life, which is culturally different from, say, Western societies, and they need to be assured that international human rights obligations to be assumed by them are compatible with their way of life and values. On the whole, it is not lack of political will or good faith that has subjected Pacific Island States to criticisms in relation to their respective human rights records.

As of this writing, ratification by these States of core human rights treaties has improved slightly. All Pacific Island States are party to the CRC. Palau and Tonga are the only two Pacific Island States not party to CEDAW. The Solomon Islands and Tonga are the only two that are not party to the CRPD.

Zeid Ra'ad Al Hussein, 10 Feb 2018, https://www.ohchr.org/EN/NewsEvents/Pages/DisplayNews.aspx?NewsID=22649&LangID=E, accessed 19 July 2019.

However, only the Marshall Islands, Papua New Guinea, Samoa and Vanuatu are party to the ICCPR. The Marshall Islands, Papua New Guinea and the Solomon Islands are the only three Pacific Island States party to the ICESCR.

5. International human rights treaty obligations: is everyone protected?

At the same time as the adoption of the Universal Declaration of Human Rights (UDHR)[1] on 10 December 1948, the UN General Assembly (UNGA) requested the Economic and Social Council (ECOSOC) to entrust the Commission on Human Rights to give priority to the preparation of a draft covenant on human rights so as to transform exhortatory provisions of the UDHR into binding treaty obligations. In early 1952 the UN agreed to have two, instead of one, covenants on human rights to reflect the viewpoint of Western nation States that economic and social rights were essentially goals to be progressively attained whereas civil and political rights had to be upheld immediately and without any reservations. Although the Commission completed its work in 1954, the two Covenants – the 1966 International Covenant on Civil and Political Rights (ICCPR)[2] and the 1966 International Covenant on Economic, Social and Cultural Rights (ICESCR)[3] – were not adopted by the UNGA until 1966, when the political climate was ripe. It was developing States that pressured the recalcitrant Western and the socialist States to approve the outcome of the protracted negotiating process for the conclusion of the two Covenants.[4] This episode bears testimony to the fact that while States may agree to pay lip service to non-binding declarations to show their good will, they are not as willing to accept binding international human rights obligations, even though the latter may exactly or almost exactly mirror the former. Furthermore, although the general ideas of human rights treaties originate in the West or are heavily influenced by Western norms, several of these treaties have been initiated by developing States hoping to improve rights within their respective borders, with outside support to achieve this objective.[5] In the case of the 1979 Convention on the Elimination of All Forms of Discrimination against Women

---

[1]   Doc A/RES/217(III).
[2]   999 UNTS 171.
[3]   993 UNTS 3.
[4]   Christian Tomuschat, 'International Covenant on Civil and Political Rights', Audio Visual Library of International Law, http://legal.un.org/avl/ha/iccpr/iccpr.html, accessed 12 Aug 2019.
[5]   Eric A Posner, *Twilight of Human Rights Law* (OUP 2014) 22.

(CEDAW),[6] for instance, there was solidarity among delegates across religious, cultural and ideological divides working together for a robust women's rights treaty.[7] Support from African States for the right to self-determination of peoples helped secure its inclusion in the ICCPR and the ICESCR, was instrumental in the adoption of the 1965 International Convention on the Elimination of All Forms of Racial Discrimination (CERD)[8] and helped inspire the adoption of the 1973 International Convention on the Suppression and Punishment of the Crime of Apartheid.[9]

The US posture in relation to the ICCPR is a case in point. The UDHR was drafted under the leadership of Eleanor Roosevelt and with palpable US influence. In order to become party to the ICCPR, as well as to any treaty, Congressional approval is necessary and Congress was not easily ready and willing to approve the ICCPR, which would require many significant changes to the existing US law. The USA was able to sign the ICCPR only in October 1977, during the first year of Jimmy Carter's Presidency, when the US Government was placing human rights at the forefront of the US domestic agenda and foreign policy. It would be ironic if the USA itself were not party to the ICCPR, which aims at protecting and promoting civil and political rights. However, the US ratification of the ICCPR did not materialize until June 1992, during George HW Bush's presidency, almost 26 years after its adoption by the UNGA in December 1966 and almost 16 years after the ICCPR's entry into force in March 1976. Becoming party to the ICCPR was eventually possible thanks to reservations entered by the US Government, many of which have been objected to by other States Parties,[10] as will be seen later in this chapter.

Article 2(d) of the 1969 Vienna Convention on the Law of Treaties (VCLT)[11] defines 'reservation' as 'a unilateral statement, however phrased or named, made by a State, when signing, ratifying, accepting, approving or acceding to a treaty, whereby it purports to exclude or to modify the legal effect of certain provisions of the treaty in their application to that State'. The VCLT does not define 'declarations' or 'understandings' frequently made by States party to treaties. In practice, a declaration expresses the position of the declaring party as to how it will implement the treaty without excluding or

---

[6]   1249 UNTS 13.
[7]   Shaheen Sardar Ali, *Modern Challenges to Islamic Law* (CUP 2016) 164.
[8]   660 UNTS 195.
[9]   1015 UNTS 243. See Frans Viljoen, *International Human Rights Law in Africa* (2nd edn, OUP 2012) 48.
[10]   See, generally, Kristina Ash, 'U.S. Reservations to the International Covenant on Civil and Political Rights: Credibility Maximization and Global Influence' (2005) 3 Northwestern J Int'l Hum Rts 1.
[11]   1155 UNTS 331.

modifying the legal effect of the treaty provision referred to in the declaration. An understanding signifies how the party interprets the treaty provision referred to in the understanding without also excluding or modifying the legal effect of the treaty provision. Declarations and understandings are often used synonymously and indicate how the parties concerned intend to implement certain treaty provisions within their respective national legal systems. What is in fact a reservation may be labelled by the party making it as a declaration or an understanding. It is, therefore, a question of fact to be considered on a case-by-case basis whether a written statement entered by the party when signing, ratifying, accepting, approving or acceding to a treaty is a reservation or otherwise. Pursuant to Article 20(5) of the VCLT, unless the treaty provides to the contrary, a reservation is considered to have been accepted by a State if it shall have raised no objection to the reservation by the end of a period of 12 months after it was notified of the reservation or by the date on which it expressed its consent to be bound by the treaty, whichever is later.[12]

Instead of analysing every one of the human rights treaties, the chapter will focus on the nine 'core' treaties monitored by the ten existing international human rights treaty bodies. They are the ICCPR; the ICESCR; CERD; CEDAW; the 1984 Convention against Torture and Other Cruel, Inhuman or Degrading Treatment or Punishment (CAT);[13] the 1989 Convention on the Rights of the Child (CRC);[14] the 1990 International Convention on the Protection of the Rights of All Migrant Workers and Members of their Families (CMW);[15] the 2006 Convention on the Rights of Persons with Disabilities (CRPD);[16] and the 2006 Convention for the Protection of All Persons from Enforced Disappearance (CED).[17]

The reservations referred to in this chapter are not exhaustive. They are chosen either because of their controversial nature or because they are permissible despite their intention to allow a certain degree of cultural, religious or other relativism in the implementation of human rights treaty obligations.

---

[12] See further Vassilis Pergantis, *The Paradigm of State Consent in the Law of Treaties: Challenges and Perspectives* (Edward Elgar Publishing 2017) ch. 6.
[13] 1465 UNTS 85.
[14] 1577 UNTS 3.
[15] 2220 UNTS 3.
[16] 2515 UNTS 3.
[17] 2716 UNTS 3.

1.   INTERNATIONAL COVENANT ON CIVIL AND POLITICAL RIGHTS[18]

Civil and political rights comprise the rights of physical and spiritual autonomy, rights of fair treatment and rights to participate meaningfully in the political process. Within these three broad categories are the rights to life and freedom from torture, inhuman or degrading treatment or punishment; the freedom of movement; the right to privacy; the freedom of religion, belief and thought; the right to a fair trial; equal protection of the law; the freedom from discrimination; the right to vote and to stand for election; and the freedoms of assembly and association, to name but a few.[19]

The ICCPR entered into force on 23 March 1976. As of this writing, it has 173 parties, including four of the five permanent members of the UN Security Council (UNSC) (that is, France, Russia, UK and USA) and the State of Palestine. China, the only permanent member of the UNSC that is not party to the ICCPR, is governed by a one-party system under the leadership of the Communist Party of China and, as such, it is impractical to implement several provisions of the ICCPR. For example, although the freedom of religious belief is recognized in Article 36 of the Chinese Constitution of 1982, that provision distinguishes 'normal religious activities' to be protected by the State from those that are not normal. It prohibits using religion 'to engage in activities that disrupt public order, impair the health of citizens or interfere with the educational system of the State' and stipulates that religious bodies and religious affairs are not subject to 'any foreign domination'.[20] China, according to one study, has a 'tripartite model of religious freedom'. First, there is 'conditional freedom of religion' whereby full religious freedom is conditional on a religion being registered with the government authorities and affiliated with the five national religious associations funded by the Chinese Government under the leadership of the Chinese Communist Party. Secondly, there is 'limited freedom of religion' for followers of a religion that has not been so registered and thus has no legal status under Chinese law. The Chinese Government adopts a tolerant attitude towards such religions to alleviate the

---

[18]   See Sarah Joseph and Melissa Castan, *The International Covenant on Civil and Political Rights: Cases, Materials and Commentary* (3rd edn, OUP 2013); Sarah Joseph, 'Civil and Political Rights' in Mashood A Baderin and Manisuli Ssenyonjo (eds), *International Human Rights Law: Six Decades after the UDHR and Beyond* (Ashgate 2010) 89.

[19]   Joseph, 'Civil and Political Rights' 90.

[20]   XIANFA, Art 36, ch. II (1982), quoted in Shucheng Wang, 'Tripartite Freedom of Religion in China: An Illiberal Perspective' (2017) 39 Hum Rts L Quarterly 783, 787.

tension between the Government and the religions' adherents and to maintain social stability in China's geographical regions. Religious followers can have freedom of religion as long as their religious activities are on a small scale and kept low profile. Thirdly, there is no freedom of religion for followers of an unregistered religion whose religious activities are on a large scale and perceived as a threat to the Chinese Government or the public, thereby warranting a national crackdown and criminal prosecution in courts of law.[21]

The other States that have not yet become party to the ICCPR are Bhutan, Brunei, Comoros, Cuba, Kiribati, Malaysia, Micronesia, Myanmar, Oman, Nauru, Palau, Saint Kitts and Nevis, Saint Lucia, Saudi Arabia, Singapore, Solomon Islands, South Sudan, Tonga, Tuvalu and the UAE. The Marshall Islands, Qatar, Fiji, and Antigua and Barbuda are the four newest States Parties to the ICCPR, having acceded to it on 12 March 2018, 21 May 2018, 16 August 2018 and 3 July 2019, respectively. Most of the small island developing States that are not party to the ICCPR are usually not party to other multilateral treaties either, unless the treaties are of immediate interest to them, such as the 1982 UN Convention on the Law of the Sea.[22] Iran has been party to the ICCPR since 1975, before the Islamic Revolution in February 1979, and has not entered any reservation.

The Human Rights Committee entrusted with interpreting the ICCPR sometimes concedes cultural differences in applying ICCPR rights. For example, in *Aumeeruddy-Cziffra et al v Mauritius*, the Committee considers the rights of family protection in Article 23(1) to 'vary from country to country and depend on different social, economic, political and cultural conditions and traditions'.[23] The Committee also interprets that the age of majority for the purposes of Article 24, the right of a child to protection, is to be determined by each State in accordance with 'relevant social and cultural conditions'.[24] However, in general, the Committee rules that the requirement under Article 2(2) of the ICCPR for its parties to take steps to give effect to the ICCPR rights is unqualified and of immediate effect and that a failure to comply with this obligation cannot be justified by reference to political, social, cultural or economic considerations within the State.[25]

---

[21]   Wang, 'Tripartite Freedom of Religion in China' 808–9.

[22]   1833 UNTS 397.

[23]   *Aumeeruddy-Cziffra et al v Mauritius*, CCPR/C/12/D/35/1978, 9 Apr 1981, §9.2(b)2(ii)1, cited in Joseph, 'Civil and Political Rights' 96.

[24]   General Comment No 17: Article 24 (Rights of the Child), Thirty-Fifth Session, 7 Apr 1989 §4, UN Doc HRI/GEN/1/Rev.9 (vol 1) at 193 (27 May 2008), cited in Joseph, 'Civil and Political Rights' 96.

[25]   General Comment No 31 on the Nature of the General Legal Obligation of States Parties to the Covenant, CCPR/C/21/Rev.1/Add.13 (26 May 2004) §14.

Another contentious point among States Parties to the ICCPR is the death penalty. There is no universal consensus on the death penalty. A conflict exists between the abolition of the death penalty for the sake of the right to life and delivering justice to victims by providing them with revenge and closure.[26] It could be argued that revenge may compound justice by sowing seeds of hatred and is part of a perpetual cycle of violence. It is also questionable whether the death penalty can actually provide victims with a sense of closure, as relatively little research has been conducted on this. In any case, international criminal tribunals are not authorized by their respective constituent statutes to impose a death penalty.[27]

Of the nine human rights treaties covered by this chapter, the ICCPR has been subject to the highest number of reservations, declarations or understandings[28] lodged by its parties.

Several States Parties to the ICCPR[29] have made reservations to Article 20(1), stipulating that any propaganda for war shall be prohibited by law, because they consider this provision might endanger the freedom of expression referred to in Article 19. A number of them[30] have made reservations on the application of specific ICCPR provisions due to the limited financial resources or facilities required for the implementation of such provisions, as in the case of Article 10(2)(b) and (3) requiring juveniles who are detained to be accommodated separately from adults.

Article 6(5) of the ICCPR provides that 'sentence of death shall not be imposed for crimes committed by persons below eighteen years of age and shall not be carried out on pregnant women'. Nevertheless, in one of its reservations, the USA has reserved 'the right, subject to its Constitutional constraints, to impose capital punishment on any person (other than a pregnant woman) duly convicted under existing or future laws permitting the imposition of capital punishment, including such punishment for crimes committed by persons below eighteen years of age'. Belgium has raises an objection, considering this US reservation incompatible with the provision and intent of

---

[26] Eg Chloe Cheeseman, 'The Death Penalty as Addressed by Regional and International Human Rights Bodies: Exploring Jurisprudential Cross-Fertilisation and Harmonisation' in Carla M Buckley, Alice Donald and Philip Leach (eds), *Towards Convergence in International Human Rights Law Approaches of Regional and International Systems* (Brill Nijhoff 2016) 68.

[27] Caleb H Wheeler, 'Rights in Conflict: The Clash between Abolishing the Death Penalty and Delivering Justice to the Victims' (2018) 18 Int'l Crim L Rev 354, 368–74.

[28] The most up-to-date information is available from the website of the UN Treaty Collection (https://treaties.un.org).

[29] Denmark, Finland, Iceland, Netherlands, Switzerland and USA.

[30] Eg Ireland, Netherlands, New Zealand, Norway, Trinidad and Tobago, UK and USA.

Article 6 of the ICCPR, which, as is made clear by Article 4(2), establishes minimum measures to protect the right to life. However, Belgium adds that this objection does not constitute an obstacle to the entry into force of the ICCPR between Belgium and the USA. Similar objections to this US reservation have been made by Denmark, Finland, France, Greece, Italy, Netherlands, Norway, Portugal, Spain and Sweden.

In addition, the USA has entered its reservation to Article 7 of the ICCPR, which reads: 'No one shall be subjected to torture or to cruel, inhuman or degrading treatment or punishment. In particular, no one shall be subjected without his free consent to medical or scientific experimentation.' The USA considers itself bound by Article 7 to the extent that 'cruel, inhuman or degrading treatment or punishment' means the cruel and unusual treatment or punishment prohibited by the Fifth, Eighth and/or Fourteenth Amendments to the US Constitution. Denmark, Finland, Germany, Italy, Netherlands, Norway, Portugal, Spain and Sweden have objected to this US reservation. According to Denmark, Norway and Spain, which have objected to the US reservations to Articles 6 and 7, Article 4(2) of the ICCPR provides that there shall be no derogation from a number of fundamental Articles, including Articles 6 and 7, even in times of public emergency which threatens the life of the nation; hence, the US reservations to these two provisions are incompatible with the ICCPR's object and purpose. For Finland and Portugal, pursuant to the general principle of treaty interpretation a party may not invoke the provisions of its internal law as justification for failure to perform a treaty. For Germany and Italy, such reservation does not affect obligations assumed by States Parties to the ICCPR on the basis of Article 2 requiring them to respect and to ensure to all individuals within their territory and subject to their jurisdiction the rights recognized in the ICCPR.

In one of its understandings as regards the ICCPR, the USA contends that its Constitution and laws guarantee all persons equal protection of the law and provide extensive protections against discrimination. The USA understands distinctions based upon race, colour, sex, language, religion, political or other opinion, national or social origin, property, birth or any other status – as those terms are used in Article 2(1) and Article 26 of the ICCPR – to be permitted when such distinctions are, at minimum, rationally related to a legitimate governmental objective. The USA further understands the prohibition in Article 4(1) on discrimination, in time of public emergency, based 'solely' on the status of race, colour, sex, language, religion or social origin, as not barring distinctions that may have a disproportionate effect upon persons of a particular status. Finland and Sweden have objected to this US understanding, which they deem to be reservations. In Sweden's opinion, the US reservations, including this one, are reservations to essential and non-derogable ICCPR provisions. Reservations of this nature contribute to undermining the basis of international treaty law since all States Parties share a common interest in the respect for the object and purpose of the treaty to which they have chosen to become parties.

The USA has also declared that Articles 1 through 27 of the ICCPR are not self-executing. There is no objection to this US declaration, probably because no other State Party could have foreseen what would transpire in the *LaGrand* and *Avena* cases, in which the USA has yet to implement the judgments of the International Court of Justice (ICJ) because of the non-executing nature of treaty obligations within the US domestic legal system. It could be argued, though, that the USA is required by Article 2(2) of the ICCPR to undertake to take the necessary steps, in accordance with its constitutional processes and with the ICCPR, to adopt such laws or other measures as may be necessary to give effect to the rights recognized in the ICCPR that are not already provided for by existing legislative or other measures.

Some Muslim-majority States have made reservations based on Sharia. Bahrain's reservation reads, inter alia,

> Bahrain interprets the provisions of Articles 3 [equal rights of men and women], 18 [freedom of thought, conscience and religion] and 23 [the protection of the family, right to marriage and the equality of rights and responsibilities of spouses as to marriage, during marriage and at its dissolution] as not affecting in any way the prescriptions of the Islamic Sharia.

The Maldives' reservation to Article 18 reads: 'The application of the principles set out in Article 18 … shall be without prejudice to the Constitution of the Republic of Maldives.' Mauritania has made reservations to Article 18 by stating that its application 'shall be without prejudice to the Islamic Sharia' and to Article 23(4) on the rights and responsibilities of spouses as to marriage as 'not affecting in any way the prescriptions of the Islamic Sharia'.

Bahrain's reservations are objected to by Latvia and the Netherlands. Latvia notes that this reservation was submitted to the Secretary General on 4 December 2006 but the consent to be bound by the ICCPR by accession was expressed on 20 September 2006. In accordance with Article 19 of the VCLT, reservations may be made upon signature, ratification, acceptance, approval or accession. Therefore, in Latvia's opinion, Bahrain's reservation is without legal effect. This is also the view of the Netherlands, which adds that the reservation with respect to Articles 3, 18 and 23, which subject their application to Islamic Sharia, is a reservation incompatible with the ICCPR's object and purpose. No other ICCPR States Parties have objected to Bahrain's reservations, possibly because they consider the reservations to have no legal effect as they were made too late.

Australia objects to the Maldives' reservation with respect to Article 18 as it is incompatible with the ICCPR's object and purpose and because a party may not invoke the provisions of its internal law as justification for its failure to perform a treaty. Moreover, Australia recalls that according to Article 4(2), no derogation of Article 18 is permitted. Australia hopes that the Maldives will soon be able to withdraw its reservation in the light of the ongoing process of a revision of the Maldivian Constitution. Australia concludes that its objection shall not preclude the entry into force of the ICCPR between Australia and the Maldives. Similar objections to the Maldives' reservation have been made by Austria, Canada, Czech Republic, Estonia, Finland, France, Greece, Hungary, Ireland, Latvia, Netherlands, Portugal, Spain, Sweden and UK.

Finland has objected to Mauritania's reservation on the grounds that a reservation which consists of a general reference to religious or other national law without specifying its contents does not clearly define to other ICCPR States Parties the extent to which the reserving State commits itself to the ICCPR and this creates serious doubts as to the commitment of the reserving State to fulfil its obligations under the ICCPR. Such reservations are, furthermore, subject to the general principle of treaty interpretation according to which a party may not invoke the provisions of its domestic law as justification for a failure to perform its treaty obligations. The reservations made by Mauritania, addressing some of the most essential provisions of the ICCPR and aiming to exclude the obligations under those provisions, are in contradiction with the ICCPR's object and purpose. Finland adds that its objection does not preclude the entry into force of the ICCPR between Mauritania and Finland, but Mauritania shall not benefit from its reservations/declarations. A similar objection to Mauritania's reservation has been made by France, Greece, Latvia, Netherlands, Poland, Portugal, Sweden and UK.

Qatar has entered a long list of what are in effect reservations to the ICCPR upon its accession in May 2018. Qatar does not consider itself bound by Article 3 with regard to provisions related to the inheritance of power for it contravenes the provisions of Article 8 of the Constitution of Qatar, and Article 23(4) for it contravenes the Islamic Sharia. In addition, Qatar shall interpret the term 'punishment' in Article 7 in accordance with the applicable legislation of Qatar and the Islamic Sharia; Article 18(2) on the understanding that it does not contravene the Islamic Sharia; the term 'trade unions' and all related matters, in Article 22, in line with the Labour Law and national legislation of Qatar; Article 23(2) in a manner that does not contravene the Islamic Sharia; and Article 27 to the effect that professing and practising one's own religion require that they do not violate the rules of public order and public morals, the protection of public safety and public health or the rights and basic freedoms of others. Austria, Belgium, Canada, Czech Republic, Estonia, Finland, Germany, Greece, Hungary, Ireland, Italy, Latvia, Netherlands, Norway,

Poland, Portugal and Switzerland have objected to Qatar's reservations that they consider to be incompatible with the ICCPR's object and purpose.

At first, Pakistan made reservations to several ICCPR provisions by expressing its willingness to apply them 'to the extent they are not repugnant to the provisions of the Constitution of Pakistan and the Sharia laws'. Pakistan has subsequently withdrawn such reservations after objections by numerous States Parties to the ICCPR. On 20 May 2016 Kuwait withdrew its reservation to Article 25(b), which it made on the grounds that Article 25(b) conflicted with the Kuwaiti electoral law that restricts the right to stand and vote in elections to males.

Declarations or reservations on the basis of religious laws are not unique to Muslim-majority States. The only reservation to the ICCPR made by Israel, a non-Muslim-majority State, is with regard to Article 23 (the protection of the family, right to marriage and the equality of rights and responsibilities of spouses as to marriage, during marriage and at its dissolution) and 'any other provision of the ICCPR that may be relevant', to the effect that 'matters of personal status are governed in Israel by the religious law of the parties concerned' and that to the extent that such law is inconsistent with Israel's obligations under the ICCPR, Israel reserves the right to apply that law. No objection has been made to this reservation by Israel. This signifies that ICCPR States Parties do recognize religious relativism, in this case giving protection under 'the religious law of the parties concerned', provided that the ICCPR's object and purpose are not thereby defeated.

Laos, one of the States still embracing communism, has declared that Article 18 shall not be construed as authorizing or encouraging any activities, including by economic means, by anyone which, directly or indirectly, coerce or compel an individual to believe or not to believe in a religion or to convert his or her religion or belief. Laos also considers all acts creating division and discrimination among ethnic groups and among religions to be incompatible with Article 18. This reservation has not met with any objection.

2. INTERNATIONAL COVENANT ON ECONOMIC, SOCIAL AND CULTURAL RIGHTS[31]

According to a renowned Soviet international lawyer, if the ICCPR basically mirrors similar legislative norms of capitalist and socialist States, the ICESCR

---

[31] See Ben Saul, David Kinley and Jacqueline Mowbray, *The International Covenant on Economic, Social and Cultural Rights: Commentary, Cases and Materials* (OUP 2016); Maniuli Ssenyonjo, 'Economic, Social and Cultural Rights' in Baderin and Ssenyonjo (eds), *International Human Rights Law* 49; Eibe Riedel, Gilles Giacca

reflects norms of Soviet legislation, many of which had been rejected by the West-dominated majority in the UNGA at the time of the adoption of the UDHR, thereby leading to the Soviet bloc's abstention in the voting on the adoption of the UDHR.[32]

The 1993 Vienna Declaration and Programme of Action[33] recognizes economic, social and cultural rights as one of the two pillars of international human rights law (IHRL) alongside civil and political rights and that all human rights are universal, indivisible, interdependent and interrelated. This Declaration somewhat tears down the historical, but unrealistic, separability of the rights under the ICCPR and those under the ICESCR.[34]

Workers' rights evolved separately thanks to the emergence of the international labour movement in the nineteenth century, culminating in the establishment of the International Labour Organization (ILO) in 1919. The ILO's human rights standards applicable to the labour force are more specific and detailed than those stipulated in other international human rights instruments.[35]

The ICESCR proceeds on the basis that while civil and political rights could be implemented immediately, economic and social rights could be progressively implemented by each State Party taking steps, individually and through international assistance and cooperation, especially in the economic and technical fields, to the maximum of its available resources.[36]

While the ICCPR sets up three global monitoring mechanisms (State reporting, individual communications and State complaint procedures), the ICESCR only provides for State reporting. It was only through a resolution of ECOSOC, and not by virtue of any provision of the ICESCR, as in the case of the Human Rights Committee of the ICCPR, which is set up by the ICCPR itself, that the Committee on Economic, Social and Cultural Rights (CESCR) was established to monitor the implementation of the ICESCR by its States Parties. The Optional Protocol to the ICESCR of 2008, in force in May 2013,

---

and Christophe Golay (eds), *Economic, Social and Cultural Rights in International Law: Contemporary Issues and Challenges* (OUP 2014).

[32] GI Tunkin, *Theory of International Law* (William E Butler tr, George Allen & Unwin 1974) 79–82.

[33] UN Doc A/CONF.157/23.

[34] For the interdependence of these rights, see Ioana Cismas, 'The Intersection of Economic, Social and Cultural Rights and Civil and Political Rights' in Riedel et al (eds), *Economic, Social and Cultural Rights in International Law* 448, 452–72.

[35] Janelle M Diller, 'Social Justice, Rights and Labour' in Dinah Shelton (ed.), *The Oxford Handbook of International Human Rights Law* (OUP 2013) 295.

[36] Committee on the ICESCR (UN Doc E/1991/23, annex III (1991) 86); *Government of the Republic of South Africa and Others v Grootboom and Others* [2000] Constitutional Court CCT11/00, [2000] ZACC 19; Charles R Beitz, *The Idea of Human Rights* (OUP 2009) 25–6.

allows individuals and groups to file complaints about violations of economic, social and cultural rights before the CESCR.

The ICESCR entered into force on 3 January 1976. There are 170 parties to the ICESCR as of this writing, including all the five permanent members of the UNSC and the State of Palestine. China, Myanmar and the Solomon Islands, which are not party to the ICCPR, are party to the ICESCR. The States that have not yet become party to either the ICCPR or the ICESCR are Bhutan, Brunei, Comoros, Cuba, Kiribati, Malaysia, Micronesia, Oman, Nauru, Palau, Saint Kitts and Nevis, Saint Lucia, Saudi Arabia, Singapore, South Sudan, Tonga, Tuvalu and UAE. The newest States Parties to the ICESCR are the Marshall Islands, Qatar, Fiji, and Antigua and Barbuda, which acceded to it on 12 March 2018, 21 May 2018, 16 August 2018 and 3 July 2019, respectively. Interestingly, South Africa, which is a relatively wealthy African State, ratified the ICESCR only in January 2015, although it ratified the ICCPR long before that – in December 1998.

There are fewer reservations and declarations/understandings regarding the ICESCR than the ICCPR. The followings are some of the controversial ones.

Bangladesh declares, inter alia, that it will implement Article 2 (guaranteeing the rights enunciated in the ICESCR without discrimination of any kind) and Article 3 (the equal right of men and women to the enjoyment of all economic, social and cultural rights set forth in the ICESCR) 'insofar as they relate to equality between man and woman, in accordance with the relevant provisions of its Constitution and in particular, in respect to certain aspects of economic rights viz. law of inheritance'. Bangladesh declares that it will apply Article 7 (the right of everyone to the enjoyment of just and favourable conditions of work) and Article 8 (trade union rights) 'under the conditions and in conformity with the procedures established in the Constitution and the relevant legislation of Bangladesh'.

China declares that the application to China of the right of everyone to form trade unions and join the trade union of his choice, subject only to the rules of the organization concerned, for the promotion and protection of his economic and social interests pursuant to Article 8(1)(a) of the ICESCR 'shall be consistent with the relevant provisions of China's Constitution, Trade Union Law and Labour Law'.

Kuwait makes an 'interpretative declaration' regarding Article 2(2) and Article 3, stating that although Kuwait endorses the principles embodied in these provisions 'as consistent with the provisions of the Kuwait Constitution in general and of its Article 29 in particular, it declares that the rights to which the Articles refer must be exercised within the limits set by Kuwaiti law'. Kuwait's 'interpretative declaration' regarding Article 9 (the right of everyone to social security, including social insurance) provides that while Kuwaiti legislation safeguards the rights of all Kuwaiti and non-Kuwaiti workers, social security provisions apply only to Kuwaitis. Its reservation concerning Article 8(1)(d) on the right to strike in conformity with the laws of the particular country states bluntly that Kuwait reserves the right not to apply this provision of the ICESCR.

Myanmar, which has been confronting separatist rebellions for decades, declares that, consistent with the 1993 Vienna Declaration and Programme of Action, the term 'the right of self-determination' in Article 1 of the ICESCR does not apply to any section of people within a sovereign independent State and cannot be construed as authorizing or encouraging any action which would dismember or impair, totally or in part, the territorial integrity or political unity of a sovereign and independent State. In addition, the term shall not be applied to undermine section 10 of the 2008 Constitution of Myanmar.

Austria objects to Myanmar's declaration, which Austria considers to be tantamount to a reservation of a general and indeterminate scope as it aims at applying a provision of the ICESCR only in conformity with the Constitution of Myanmar. Finland objects to Bangladesh's, Kuwait's and Myanmar's declarations. Objecting to Bangladesh's reservation, France asserts that economic conditions and development prospects should not affect the freedom of consent of intended spouses to enter into marriage, non-discrimination for reasons of parentage or other conditions in the implementation of special measures of protection and assistance on behalf of children and young persons or the freedom of parents or legal guardians to choose schools for their children. In France's view, economic difficulties or problems of development cannot free a State Party entirely from its obligations under the ICESCR. Germany joins in objecting to the declarations by Kuwait and Myanmar. Ireland opposes Myanmar's declaration, whereas Italy objects to Kuwait's, Latvia to Myanmar's and the Netherlands to Myanmar's and Kuwait's. This pattern of objection continues with Norway, Portugal, Slovakia, Spain, Sweden and UK objecting to one or more of these reservations/declarations that they deem to be reservations that are incompatible with the ICESCR's object and purpose. Norway and Sweden object to China's declaration, which they consider to amount to a reservation to implement the ICESCR consistent with relevant provisions of national legislation.

According to Algeria's 'interpretative declaration', it interprets Article 23(4) of the ICESCR regarding the rights and responsibilities of spouses as to marriage, during marriage and at its dissolution as in no way impairing the essential foundations of the Algerian legal system. The Netherlands and Portugal object to this declaration, which they consider to be a reservation that is incompatible with the ICESCR's object and purpose.

Qatar entered a reservation on its accession to the ICESCR in May 2018, stipulating that it does not consider itself bound by the provisions of Article 3, 'for they contravene the Islamic Sharia with regard to questions of inheritance and birth'. Qatar also reserves the right to implement Article 8 on the understanding that what is meant by 'trade unions' and their related issues stated in Article 8 is in line with the provisions of the Labour Law and national legislation of Qatar. Austria, Belgium, Canada, Czech Republic, Estonia, Finland, Germany, Greece, Hungary, Ireland, Italy, Latvia, Netherlands, Norway, Poland, Portugal, Moldova, Romania, Switzerland and UK have lodged their objection to Qatar's reservations, which they consider to be incompatible with the ICESCR's object and purpose.

3.   CONVENTION ON THE ELIMINATION OF ALL FORMS OF RACIAL DISCRIMINATION

CERD entered into force on 4 January 1969 and there are 181 parties thereto, including the Holy See and the State of Palestine. The States not party to either the ICCPR or the ICESCR but that are party to CERD are Comoros, Cuba, Oman, Singapore, Saint Kitts and Nevis, Saint Lucia, Saudi Arabia, Tonga and UAE. The Marshall Islands and Dominica are the newest parties, having acceded to CERD in April and May 2019, respectively. The States that are not party to CERD are Angola, Bhutan, Brunei, Kiribati, Malaysia, Micronesia, Myanmar, Nauru, North Korea, Palau, Samoa, South Sudan, Tuvalu and Vanuatu.

Most of the reservations made by CERD States Parties relate to Article 22, pursuant to which any dispute between two or more States Parties with respect to the interpretation or application of CERD is, at the request of any of the parties to the dispute, to be referred to the ICJ for decision, unless the disputants agree to another mode of settlement.

Thailand's controversial 'interpretative declaration' states that it does not interpret and apply CERD's provisions as imposing upon Thailand 'any obligation beyond the confines of the Constitution and the laws of the Kingdom of Thailand'. France has objected to this 'reservation of such a general and indeterminate scope that it is not possible to ascertain which changes to obligations under the Convention it is intended to introduce', thereby making CERD's provisions completely ineffective. So have Germany, Romania, Sweden and the UK.

Saudi Arabia is the only one making a reservation based on Sharia, declaring that it will implement the provisions of CERD, provided these 'do not conflict with the precepts of the Islamic Sharia'. This has met with objections from Austria, Finland, Germany, Netherlands, Norway, Spain and Sweden.

4.   CONVENTION ON THE ELIMINATION OF ALL FORMS OF DISCRIMINATION AGAINST WOMEN

CEDAW came into force on 3 September 1981 and as of this writing there are 189 parties thereto, including the Cook Islands and the State of Palestine. The States that have not yet become party to either the ICCPR or the ICESCR but are party to CEDAW are Antigua and Barbuda, Bhutan, Brunei, Comoros, Cuba, Kiribati, Malaysia, Micronesia, Oman, Nauru, Saint Kitts and Nevis, Saint Lucia, Saudi Arabia, Singapore, South Sudan, Tuvalu and UAE. The newest parties are the State of Palestine and South Sudan, acceding to CEDAW in April 2014 and April 2015, respectively. Iran, Palau, Somalia, Sudan, Tonga and USA are not party to CEDAW.

That the USA is the only Western nation State not party to CEDAW is rather surprising in view of the prominence of generations of feminist activism in the USA. The USA signed CEDAW in July 1980. Because of strong opposition among conservatives in Congress, US ratification of CEDAW has not materialized. CEDAW's opponents in the USA assail CEDAW's purported vagueness and broadness, which might permit, inter alia, legalized abortion, a highly controversial issue in US society or at least let in an unwelcomed foreign interference in this morally and legally sensitive issue. Their concern revolves around Article 12(1), which requires States Parties to take all appropriate measures to eliminate discrimination against women in the field of health care in order to ensure, on a basis of equality of men and women, access to health-care services, including those related to family planning. Their concern has increased after the CEDAW Committee suggested, in 1999, that, pursuant to Article 12, CEDAW States Parties should 'prioritize the prevention of unwanted pregnancy through family planning and sex education and reduce maternal mortality rates through safe motherhood services and prenatal assistance' and, 'when possible, legislation criminalizing abortion should be amended, in order to withdraw punitive measures imposed on women who undergo abortion'.[37] In addition, the CEDAW Committee considers that CEDAW States Parties should require all health services to be consistent with the human rights of women, including the rights to autonomy, privacy, confidentiality, informed consent and choice.[38] Another provision of concern to CEDAW's opponents in the USA is Article 6 obliging States Parties 'to take all appropriate measures, including legislation, to suppress all forms of traffic

---

[37]   CEDAW General Recommendation No 24: Article 12 of the Convention (Women and Health), 1999, A/54/38/Rev.1, ch. I §31(c).

[38]   Ibid §31(e).

in women and exploitation of prostitution of women'. In their view, this might be tantamount to an obligation to legalize prostitution so that sex workers would be protected from trafficking and exploitation.[39]

According to Algeria's reservations to CEDAW, it will apply Article 2 (the obligation to pursue a policy of eliminating discrimination against women) on condition that it does not conflict with the provisions of the Algerian Family Code. Algeria declares that the provisions of Article 15(4), concerning the right of women to choose their residence and domicile, should not be interpreted in such a manner as to contradict the provisions of chapter 4 (Article 37) of the Algerian Family Code. In addition, the provisions of Article 16 of CEDAW concerning equal rights for men and women in all matters relating to marriage, both during marriage and at its dissolution, should not contradict the provisions of the Algerian Family Code. Algeria's reservations are opposed by Germany, Netherlands and Norway.

Bahrain enters reservations to Article 2 concerning the obligation to pursue a policy of eliminating discrimination against women, Article 9(2) concerning women's equal rights with men with respect to the nationality of their children, Article 15(4) concerning the right of women to choose their residence and domicile and Article 16 on the elimination of discrimination against women in all matters relating to marriage and family relations. Bahrain will implement these provisions provided this is 'without breaching the provisions of the Islamic Sharia'. Bahrain's reservations are objected to by Austria, Canada, Denmark, Finland, France, Germany, Greece, Netherlands, Sweden and UK.

Bangladesh does not consider as binding upon itself the provisions of Article 2 and Article 16(1)(c), the latter concerning the equality of women and men during marriage and at its dissolution, as they conflict with Sharia law based on the Holy Quran and Sunna. Bangladesh's reservation is opposed by Mexico, Netherlands and Sweden.

Brunei expresses its reservations regarding those provisions of CEDAW that may be contrary to the Constitution of Brunei and to the beliefs and principles of Islam, the official religion of Brunei. Without prejudice to the generality of the said reservations, Brunei expresses its reservations regarding Article 9(2) concerning women's equal rights with men with respect to the nationality of their children. The following CEDAW States Parties object to Brunei's reservations: Austria, Belgium, Canada, Czech Republic, Denmark, Estonia, Finland, France, Germany, Greece, Hungary, Ireland, Italy, Latvia, Netherlands, Norway, Poland, Portugal, Romania, Slovakia, Spain, Sweden and UK.

---

[39] Saleh Al Shraideh, 'CEDAW in the Eyes of the United States' (2017) 18 J Legal Studies 18, 22–5.

Egypt is willing to comply with Article 2 of CEDAW on condition that such compliance does not run counter to the Islamic Sharia. Egypt also enters a reservation to Article 16, without prejudice to the Islamic Sharia's provisions whereby women are accorded rights equivalent to those of their spouses so as to ensure a just balance between them. Egypt explains that this is out of respect for the sacrosanct nature of the firm religious beliefs which govern marital relations in Egypt and which may not be called into question and in view of the fact that one of the most important bases of these relations is 'an equivalency of rights and duties so as to ensure complementary [*sic*] which guarantees true equality between the spouses'. The provisions of Sharia stipulate that the husband shall pay bridal money to the wife and maintain her fully and shall also make a payment to her upon divorce, whereas the wife retains full rights over her property and is not obliged to spend anything on her keep. Sharia therefore restricts the wife's rights to divorce by making it contingent on a judge's ruling, whereas no such restriction is laid down in the case of the husband. Germany, Mexico and Sweden have objected to Egypt's reservations.

Iraq enters reservations to Article 16(2)(f) on the equal rights of women and men with regard to guardianship, wardship, trusteeship and adoption of children or similar institutions and to Article 16(2)(g) protecting the same personal rights as husband and wife, including the right to choose a family name, a profession and an occupation. Iraq's application of the said provision of CEDAW 'shall be without prejudice to the provisions of the Islamic Sharia according women rights equivalent to the rights of their spouses so as to ensure a just balance between them'. Iraq's reservations are objected to by Sweden.

Jordan does not consider itself bound by Article 9(2), concerning women's equal rights with men with respect to the nationality of their children and Article 16(1)(c), (d)[40] and (g). Sweden has objected to Jordan's reservations.

Kuwait reserves its right not to implement the provision contained in Article 9(2), inasmuch as it runs counter to the Kuwaiti Nationality Act, which stipulates that a child's nationality shall be determined by that of his father. Kuwait also declares that it does not consider itself bound by the provision contained in Article 16(f) inasmuch as it conflicts with the provisions of the Islamic Sharia, Islam being Kuwait's official religion. Kuwait's reservations are objected to by Finland, Germany, Greece, Netherlands, Norway and Sweden.

Lebanon enters reservations regarding Article 9(2) and Article 16(1)(c), (d), (f) and (g) (regarding the right to choose a family name). Lebanon's reservations are objected to by Austria, Netherlands and Sweden.

---

[40] Art 16(d) accords women and men the same rights and responsibilities as parents, irrespective of their marital status, in matters relating to their children.

According to Libya's reservations, Article 2 shall be implemented with due regard for the peremptory norms of the Islamic Sharia relating to determination of the inheritance portions of the estate of a deceased person, whether female or male; whereas the implementation of Article 16(c) and (d) shall be without prejudice to any of the rights guaranteed to women by the Islamic Sharia. The following CEDAW States Parties have objected to Libya's reservations: Denmark, Finland, Germany, Mexico, Norway and Sweden.

Malaysia's accession to CEDAW is subject to the understanding that the provisions of CEDAW do not conflict with the provisions of the Islamic Sharia law and the Federal Constitution of Malaysia. In particular, Malaysia does not consider itself bound by the provisions of Articles 9(2), 16(1)(a),[41] (c), (f) and (g) of CEDAW. The following CEDAW States Parties have objected to Malaysia's reservations: Austria, Germany, Finland, Netherlands and Norway.

The Maldives reserves its right to apply Article 16 concerning the equality of men and women in all matters relating to marriage and family relations without prejudice to the provisions of the Islamic Sharia, which govern all marital and family relations of the 100 per cent Muslim population of the Maldives. The Maldives' reservations are objected to by Austria, Canada, Finland, Germany, Netherlands, Norway and Portugal.

Mauritania enters reservations to Article 13(a), concerning the equal right of women and men to family benefits and Article 16. These reservations are met with objections from Austria, Denmark, Finland, Germany, Netherlands, Norway, Portugal, Sweden and UK.

Niger expresses reservations with regard to Article 2(d) and (f), concerning the taking of all appropriate measures to abolish all customs and practices which constitute discrimination against women, particularly in respect of succession. It also enters a reservation to Article 5(a) with regard to the modification of social and cultural patterns of conduct of men and women. As for Article 15(4), Niger declares it can be bound by the provisions of this paragraph, particularly those concerning the right of women to choose their residence and domicile, only to the extent that these provisions refer only to unmarried women. Niger expresses reservations to Article 16(1)(c), (e) and (g), particularly those concerning the same rights and responsibilities during marriage and at its dissolution, the same rights to decide freely and responsibly on the number and spacing of their children and the right to choose a family name. Lastly, Niger declares that the provisions of Article 2(d) and (f), Article 5(a) and (b), Article 15(4) and Article 16(1)(c), (e) and (g), concerning family relations, cannot be applied immediately as they are contrary to existing customs and practices which, by their nature, can be modified only with the

---

[41] Art 16(1)(a) accords women and men the same right to enter into marriage.

passage of time and the evolution of society and cannot, therefore, be abolished by an act of authority. Niger's reservations are objected to by Denmark, Finland, Norway and Sweden.

Oman expresses reservations to all CEDAW provisions that are not in accordance with the Islamic Sharia and legislation in force in Oman; Article 9(2), which provides that States Parties shall grant women equal rights with men with respect to the nationality of their children; Article 15(4), which requires States Parties to accord to men and women the same rights with regard to the law relating to the movement of persons and the freedom to choose their residence and domicile; and Article 16, requiring States Parties to take all appropriate measures to eliminate discrimination against women in all matters relating to marriage and family relations and in particular subparagraphs (a), (c) and (f) (regarding adoption). The following CEDAW States Parties have objected to Oman's reservations: Austria, Belgium, Czech Republic, Denmark, Estonia, Finland, France, Germany, Greece, Hungary, Ireland, Italy, Latvia, Netherlands, Poland, Portugal, Romania, Slovakia, Spain, Sweden and UK.

Pakistan declares that its accession to CEDAW is subject to the provisions of Pakistan's Constitution. Austria, Finland, Netherlands and Norway have objected to Pakistan's reservation.

Qatar enters reservations to Article 2(a) in connection with the rules of the hereditary transmission of authority as it is inconsistent with the provisions of Article 8 of the Constitution of Qatar; Article 9(2) as it is inconsistent with Qatar's law on citizenship; Article 15(1), in connection with matters of inheritance and testimony, as it is inconsistent with the provisions of Islamic law; Article 15(4) as it is inconsistent with the provisions of family law and established practice; Article 16(1)(a) and (c) as they are inconsistent with the provisions of Islamic law; and Article 16(1)(f) as it is inconsistent with the provisions of Islamic law and family law. Qatar declares that all of its relevant national legislation is conducive to the interest of promoting social solidarity. Qatar also declares that it accepts Article 1 of CEDAW[42] on condition that, in accordance with the provisions of Islamic law and Qatari legislation, the phrase 'irrespective of their marital status' is not intended to encourage family relationships outside legitimate marriage. In addition, Qatar declares that the question of the modification of 'patterns' referred to in Article 5(a) of CEDAW – which requires States Parties to take all appropriate measures to

---

[42]   Art 1: 'For the purposes of the present Convention, the term 'discrimination against women' shall mean any distinction, exclusion or restriction made on the basis of sex which has the effect or purpose of impairing or nullifying the recognition, enjoyment or exercise by women, irrespective of their marital status, on a basis of equality of men and women, of human rights and fundamental freedoms in the political, economic, social, cultural, civil or any other field.'

modify the social and cultural patterns of conduct of men and women, with a view to achieving the elimination of prejudices and customary and all other practices which are based on the idea of the inferiority or the superiority of either of the sexes or on stereotyped roles for men and women – must not be understood as encouraging women to abandon their role as mothers and their role in child rearing, thereby undermining the structure of the family. The following States Parties to CEDAW have objected to Qatar's reservations: Austria, Belgium, Czech Republic, Estonia, Finland, Hungary, Ireland, Italy, Netherlands, Norway, Poland, Romania, Slovakia and Sweden.

For Saudi Arabia, in case of contradiction between any provision of CEDAW and the norms of Islamic law, Saudi Arabia is not under obligation to observe the contradictory terms of CEDAW. Saudi Arabia does not consider itself bound by Article 9(2) concerning women's equal rights with men with respect to the nationality of their children. Saudi Arabia's reservations are objected to by Austria, Denmark, Finland, France, Germany, Ireland, Netherlands, Norway, Portugal, Spain, Sweden and UK.

Syria enters reservations to Article 2; Article 9(2), concerning the grant of a woman's nationality to her children; Article 15(4), concerning freedom of movement and of residence and domicile; Article 16(1)(c), (d), (f) and (g), concerning equal rights and responsibilities during marriage and at its dissolution with regard to guardianship, the right to choose a family name, maintenance and adoption; and Article 16(2), concerning the legal effect of the betrothal and the marriage of a child, inasmuch as this provision is incompatible with the provisions of the Islamic Sharia. Syria's reservations are objected to by Austria, Denmark, Estonia, Finland, France, Germany, Greece, Italy, Netherlands, Spain, Norway, Romania, Spain, Sweden and UK.

The UAE makes reservations to Articles 2(f), 9, 15(2), 16 and 29(1) as follows. The UAE considers Article 2(f) to violate the rules of inheritance established in accordance with the precepts of Sharia. Regarding Article 9, the UAE considers the acquisition of nationality an internal matter that is governed, and the conditions and controls of which are established, by national legislation. The UAE considers Article 15(2) to be in conflict with the precepts of the Sharia regarding legal capacity, testimony and the right to conclude contracts. The UAE will abide by Article 16 insofar as it is not in conflict with the principles of Sharia. The UAE considers that the payment of a dower and of support after divorce is an obligation of the husband and the husband has the right to divorce, just as the wife has her independent financial security and her full rights to her property and is not required to pay her husband's or her own expenses out of her own property. Sharia makes a woman's right to divorce conditional on a judicial decision in a case in which she has been harmed. Austria, Latvia, Netherlands, Norway, Poland, Portugal, Spain, Sweden and UK object to the UAE's reservations.

Morocco will implement Article 2 on condition that this is without prejudice to the constitutional requirement that regulates the rules of succession to the throne of the Kingdom of Morocco and that it does not conflict with the provisions of the Islamic Sharia. Morocco adds that certain of the provisions contained in the Moroccan Code of Personal Status granting women rights that differ from the rights conferred on men may not be infringed upon or abrogated because they derive primarily from the Islamic Sharia, which strives, among its other objectives, to strike a balance between the spouses in order to preserve the coherence of family life. With regard to Article 15(4) of CEDAW, Morocco declares that it can only be bound by the provisions of this paragraph, in particular those relating to the right of women to choose their residence and domicile, to the extent that they are not incompatible with Articles 34 and 36 of the Moroccan Code of Personal Status. No State Party has objected to Morocco's aforesaid reservations.

It should be noted that Morocco used to enter a reservation to Article 9(2) requiring States Parties to grant women equal rights with men with respect to the nationality of their children as this provision was incompatible with Morocco's then Law of Moroccan Nationality. Morocco also made a reservation with regard to Article 16, requiring States Parties to take all appropriate measures to eliminate discrimination against women in all matters relating to marriage and family relations, particularly those relating to the equality of men and women, in respect of rights and responsibilities on entry into and at dissolution of marriage. Equality of this kind was considered by Morocco to be incompatible with the Islamic Sharia, which guarantees to each of the spouses rights and responsibilities within a framework of 'equilibrium and complementary [*sic*] in order to preserve the sacred bond of matrimony', obliging the husband, and not the wife, to provide a nuptial gift upon marriage, support the family, pay maintenance at dissolution of marriage and so forth. The Netherlands was the only State Party objecting to Morocco's reservations. Nonetheless, Morocco has withdrawn these reservations since 8 April 2011 after enacting a new Personal Status Code in 2004 and enshrining it in the 2011 Moroccan Constitution.

There are a few non-Islamic reservations based on religious practice or local custom.

Micronesia reserves the right not to apply the provisions of Articles 2(f), 5 and 16 to the succession of certain well-established traditional titles and to marital customs that divide tasks or decision making in purely voluntary or consensual private conduct. Finland, Sweden and the UK object to Micronesia's reservations.

Israel expresses its reservation with regard to Article 7(b) concerning the appointment of women to serve as judges of religious courts where this is prohibited by the laws of any of the religious communities in Israel. Israel also enters its reservation with regard to Article 16 to the extent that the laws on personal status which are binding on the various religious communities in Israel do not conform with the provisions of Article 16. No objection to these reservations is entered by any CEDAW State Party. Once again, this proves that religious relativism is permissible insofar as it does not defeat the object and purpose of the treaty in question. In fact, all religious communities in Israel are equally protected by Israel's reservations.

5.   CONVENTION AGAINST TORTURE

CAT entered into force on 26 June 1987 and as of this writing has 167 parties including the State of Palestine. The States that have not yet become party to the ICCPR but are party to CAT are Antigua and Barbuda, China, Comoros, Cuba, Nauru, Saudi Arabia, South Sudan and UAE.

Several States Parties have reserved their right not to accept third-party dispute settlement, with South Africa being the only one expressly declaring that it recognizes the competence of the ICJ to settle a dispute between two or more State Parties regarding the interpretation or application of CAT.

Like its reservations to the ICCPR, the USA makes reservations to CAT stating, inter alia, that the USA considers itself bound by the obligation under Article 16 of CAT to prevent 'cruel, inhuman or degrading treatment or punishment', only insofar as the term 'cruel, inhuman or degrading treatment or punishment' means the cruel, unusual and inhumane treatment or punishment prohibited by the Fifth, Eighth and/or Fourteenth Amendments to the US Constitution. It is also the US understanding that international law does not prohibit the death penalty and does not consider CAT to restrict or prohibit the USA from applying the death penalty consistent with the Fifth, Eighth and/or Fourteenth Amendments to the US Constitution, including any constitutional period of confinement prior to the imposition of the death penalty. Finland, Netherlands and Sweden have objected to the said US reservations for the same reasons they have objected to the reservation entered by the USA with regard to Article 7 of the ICCPR.

On 20 September 2011, after receiving so many objections from other, mostly Western European, States Parties to CAT, Pakistan withdrew its reservations to, inter alia, Articles 4, 6, 12, 13 and 16 of CAT, whereby Pakistan declared that these provisions 'shall be so applied to the extent that they are not repugnant to the provisions of the Constitution of Pakistan and the Sharia laws'. Likewise, on 14 March 2012, Qatar effected the withdrawal of the reservation to any interpretation of CAT's provisions 'that is incompatible with the precepts of Islamic law and the Islamic religion'.

6.   CONVENTION ON THE RIGHTS OF THE CHILD

The CRC came into force on 2 September 1990 and has 196 parties. It is the only international human rights treaty that has achieved universality of ratification/accession by all the 193 UN Member States plus the Cook Islands, the Holy See and the State of Palestine.

China, which has strictly enforced a one-child-per-family policy, enters a reservation to the effect that China shall fulfil its obligations under Article 6[43] 'under the prerequisite that [the CRC] accords with the provisions of Article 25 concerning family planning of the Constitution of the People's Republic of China and in conformity with the provisions of Article 2 of the Law of Minor Children of the People's Republic of China'. No CRC State Party has objected to China's reservation.

France declares that the CRC, particularly Article 6, cannot be interpreted as constituting any obstacle to the implementation of the provisions of French legislation relating to the voluntary interruption of pregnancy. No CRC State Party has objected to France's reservation.

India declares that certain of the rights of the child, namely those pertaining to the economic, social and cultural rights, can only be progressively implemented in developing countries subject to the extent of available resources and within the framework of international cooperation. India recognizes the right of the child to be protected from exploitation of all forms including economic exploitation. It also recognizes that, for several reasons, children of different ages do work in India. Therefore, having prescribed minimum ages for employment in hazardous occupations and in certain other areas; having made regulatory provisions regarding hours and conditions of employment and being aware that it is not practical immediately to prescribe minimum ages for admission to each and every area of employment in India, India undertakes to take measures to progressively implement the provisions of Article 32, particularly paragraph 2(a) on a minimum age or minimum ages for admission to employment, in accordance with its national legislation and relevant international instruments to which it is a State Party. No CRC State Party has objected to India's declaration.

There are a number of reservations to the CRC that are grounded in Sharia.

Afghanistan expresses reservations on all CRC provisions that are 'incompatible with the laws of Islamic Sharia and the local legislation in effect'. Bangladesh enters reservations to Article 14(1), which obliges CRC States

---

[43]   Art 6: '1. States Parties recognize that every child has the inherent right to life. 2. States Parties shall ensure to the maximum extent possible the survival and development of the child.'

Parties to respect the right of the child to freedom of thought, conscience and religion and Bangladesh will apply Article 21 on the adoption of a child 'subject to the existing laws and practices in Bangladesh'. Brunei expresses its reservations on the CRC provisions that may be contrary to the Constitution of Brunei and to the beliefs and principles of Islam, the State religion of Brunei. Without prejudice to the generality of the said reservations, Brunei particularly expresses its reservations to Article 14, Article 20(3),[44] and the inter-country adoption under Article 21(b), (c), (d) and (e) of the CRC. Iran reserves the right not to apply any provisions or Articles of the CRC that are incompatible with Islamic laws and the international legislation in effect. Iraq enters a reservation in respect to Article 14(1) concerning the child's freedom of religion as allowing a child to change his or her religion runs counter to the provisions of the Islamic Sharia. Jordan does not consider itself bound by Articles 14, 20 and 21, which grant the child the right to freedom of choice of religion and concern the question of adoption, since they are at variance with the precepts of the tolerant Islamic Sharia.

Malaysia expresses reservations to Article 2 prohibiting discrimination against the child on any ground, Article 7 on child registration, Article 14 concerning the child's freedom of religion, Article 28(1)(a) on making primary education compulsory and available free to all and Article 37 concerning, inter alia, the prohibition of subjecting the child to torture or other cruel, inhuman or degrading treatment or punishment as well as, where the child is under 18, to capital punishment or life imprisonment without possibility of release. Malaysia declares the said provisions applicable only if they are in conformity with the Constitution, national laws and national policies of the Government of Malaysia.

According to the Maldives, since the Islamic Sharia is one of the fundamental sources of Maldivian Law and since Islamic Sharia does not include the system of adoption among the ways and means for the protection and care of children contained in Sharia, the Maldives expresses its reservation to all the clauses and provisions relating to adoption in the CRC. It also expresses its reservation to Article 14(1) since the Constitution and the laws of the Maldives stipulate that all Maldivians should be Muslims.

---

[44] Art 20(3): '[Alternative care for a child temporarily or permanently deprived of his or her family environment or in whose own best interests cannot be allowed to remain in that environment] could include, inter alia, foster placement, kafalah of Islamic law, adoption or if necessary placement in suitable institutions for the care of children. When considering solutions, due regard shall be paid to the desirability of continuity in a child's upbringing and to the child's ethnic, religious, cultural and linguistic background.'

In signing the CRC, Mauritania expresses its reservations to Articles or provisions which may be contrary to the beliefs and values of Islam, the religion of the Mauritanian people and State. Equally sweeping are Saudi Arabia's reservations to all such Articles of the CRC as are in conflict with the provisions of Islamic law. Kuwait expresses reservations to all CRC provisions that are incompatible with the laws of Islamic Sharia and the local statutes in effect. Kuwait also declares in relation to Article 21 that Kuwait, adhering to the provisions of the Islamic Sharia as the main source of legislation, strictly bans abandoning the Islamic religion and does not therefore approve adoption. For its part, Syria enters reservations to the CRC's provisions that are not in conformity with Syrian legislation and with the Islamic Sharia's principles, in particular Article 14 of the CRC regarding the right of the child to the freedom of religion.

Somalia does not consider itself bound by Articles 14, 20, 21 and any other CRC provisions 'contrary to the General Principles of Islamic Sharia'.

The UAE makes reservations to Articles 7, 14, 17 and 21. Regarding Article 7, the UAE considers the acquisition of nationality an internal matter and one that is regulated and whose terms and conditions are established by national legislation. The UAE considers itself bound by Article 14 'to the extent that it does not conflict with the principles and provisions of Islamic law'. While the UAE appreciates and respects the functions assigned to the mass media by Article 17, the UAE shall be bound by the provision of that Article in the light of the requirements of the UAE's domestic statutes and laws and, in accordance with the recognition accorded them in the preamble to the CRC, in such a manner that the UAE's traditions and cultural values are not violated. As for Article 21, given its commitment to the principles of Islamic law, the UAE does not permit the system of adoption. According to Oman's reservation, it is not committed to Article 14, which gives the child the right to freedom of religion, until he reaches the age of maturity.

The 'Sharia-based reservations' have been objected to by several non-Muslim-majority States Parties to the CRC. Austria has objected to the reservations made by Brunei, Malaysia, Somalia and Saudi Arabia. Belgium, Bulgaria, Czech Republic, France, Hungary, Latvia, Moldova, Poland, Romania, Sweden, Switzerland and UK have objected to Somalia's reservation. Denmark has objected to Brunei's and Saudi Arabia's reservations. Finland has objected to Syria's, Malaysia's, Qatar's, Oman's, Somalia's and Iran's reservations. Germany has objected to the reservations made by Syria, Malaysia, Qatar, Iran and Somalia. Ireland has lodged its objection to the Sharia-based reservations made by Bangladesh, Jordan, Iran, Malaysia, Saudi Arabia, Somalia and Kuwait. Italy has objected to the reservations by Brunei, Qatar, Somalia, Syria and UAE. The Netherlands has objected to the reservations by Iran, Malaysia, Oman, Somalia, Syria and UAE. Norway has objected to the reservations by Brunei, Iran, Malaysia, Oman, Saudi Arabia, Somalia and Syria. Lastly, Portugal has objected to the reservations of Bangladesh, Brunei, Iran, Kuwait, Malaysia and Somalia.

No State Party to the CRC has objected to either Algeria's or Morocco's declaration, however. Algeria declares that Article 14(1)(2) of the CRC shall be interpreted in compliance with the basic foundations of the Algerian legal system, in particular the Constitution, which stipulates in its Article 2 that Islam is the State religion and in its Article 35 that 'there shall be no infringement of the inviolability of the freedom of conviction and the inviolability of the freedom of opinion'. Besides, Algeria's Law No 84-11 of 9 June 1984, comprising the Family Code, stipulates that a child's education is to take place in accordance with the religion of its father. For its part, Morocco makes a relatively liberal declaration, stating that it interprets Article 14(1) of the CRC in the light of the Constitution of 7 October 1996 and the other relevant provisions of its domestic law. Article 6 of the Moroccan Constitution provides that Islam, the State religion, shall guarantee freedom of worship for all. Article 54(6) of Act 70-03 (the Family Code) stipulates that parents owe their children the right to religious guidance and education based on good conduct. By this declaration, Morocco reaffirms its attachment to universally recognized human rights and its commitment to the purposes of the CRC.

This means that objections are lodged against reservations by Muslim-majority States not because the reserving States are Muslim-majority States or because the reservations are related to Islam, but because the reservations in question are so sweepingly broad and/or vague that they defeat the object and purpose of the human rights treaty at issue.

With respect to non-Islamic cultural reservations, Kiribati considers that a child's rights as defined in the CRC, in particular the rights defined in Articles 12 through 16, shall be exercised with respect for parental authority, in accordance with the Kiribati customs and traditions regarding the place of the child within and outside the family. Austria has objected to Kiribati's reservation.

Thanks to objections by so many States Parties to Pakistan's general reservation to the CRC, on 23 July 1997 Pakistan withdrew its reservation, stating that the CRC's provisions 'shall be interpreted in the light of the principles of Islamic laws and values'. This was also the case concerning Djibouti's reservation. On 7 December 2009 Djibouti withdrew its reservation stating that 'the Government of Djibouti shall not consider itself bound by any provisions or articles that are incompatible with its religion and its traditional values'. Also thanks to objections by several other CRC States Parties, Qatar has withdrawn its general reservation to the CRC based on Sharia. The remaining reservation by Qatar relates to Article 14(2), which requires CRC States Parties to respect the rights and duties of the parents and, when applicable, legal guardians, to provide direction to the child in the exercise of his or her right in a manner consistent with the evolving capacities of the child. No CRC State Party has objected to Qatar's only remaining reservation.

7. CONVENTION ON THE PROTECTION OF THE RIGHTS OF ALL MIGRANT WORKERS

The CMW entered into force on 1 July 2003. With only 54 parties, it is the international human rights treaty with a monitoring treaty body that has the fewest parties. Parties to the CMW are mainly States with a large number of migrant workers working overseas, such as Indonesia and the Philippines. None of the States hosting a sizable number of foreign migrant workers is party to CMW.

Some CMW States Parties have made declarations or reservations. There is only one objection, by Mexico to Venezuela's declaration. Mexico considers the declaration to constitute a reservation designed to exclude the legal effects of Article 26(1) by abrogating the right of members of the families of migrant workers to join freely any trade union or association.

8. CONVENTION ON THE RIGHTS OF PERSONS WITH DISABILITIES

The CRPD entered into force on 3 May 2008 and has 179 parties, including the EU since the EU shares competence with EU Member States as regards action to combat discrimination on the ground of disability, among others. Kyrgyzstan and Chad became the latest State Parties, ratifying it in May and June 2019, respectively.

Brunei expresses its reservation regarding those provisions of the CRPD that 'may be contrary to' its Constitution and to the beliefs and principles of Islam, the official religion of Brunei. Iran declares it does not consider itself bound by any provisions of the CRPD, 'which may be incompatible with its applicable rules [*sic*]'. Libya declares that it interprets Article 25(a), concerning the provision of health-care services without discrimination on the basis of disability, 'in a manner that does not contravene the Islamic Sharia and national legislation'.

Kuwait enters reservations to Article 18(1)(a), concerning the right of the disabled to acquire and change a nationality and the right not to be deprived of nationality arbitrarily or on the basis of disability, and Article 23(2), concerning the rights and responsibilities of persons with disabilities, with regard to guardianship, wardship, trusteeship, adoption of children or similar institutions. It also makes 'interpretative declarations' to the effect that the enjoyment of legal capacity under Article 12(2) shall be subject to the conditions applicable under

Kuwaiti law. In addition, Article 19(a) shall not be interpreted to permit illicit relations outside legitimate marriage, and the care referred to in Article 25(a) shall not imply recognition of illicit relations outside legitimate marriage.

Malaysia makes a reservation that it does not consider itself bound by Articles 15 (freedom of persons with disabilities from torture or cruel, inhuman or degrading treatment or punishment) and 18 (the rights of persons with disabilities to liberty of movement, to freedom to choose their residence and to a nationality on an equal basis with others).

Israel expresses its reservation with regard to the provisions concerning marriage in Article 23(1)(a), to the extent that the laws on personal status, which are binding on the various religious communities in Israel, do not conform with these provisions.

France, Latvia and Mexico have objected to the reservation made by Iran. Norway, Peru and the UK have objected to the reservation made by Brunei. Poland and Romania have objected to the reservations by Brunei and Libya. The Czech Republic has objected to the reservations by Iran and Brunei. Finland has objected to Libya's reservation. Austria and Germany have objected to the reservations by Brunei, Iran, Libya and Malaysia. Hungary and Sweden have objected to the reservations by Brunei and Malaysia. Slovakia has objected to Malaysia's reservation. Belgium, Ireland, Netherlands, Portugal and Switzerland have objected to the reservations by Brunei, Iran and Malaysia.

9. CONVENTION FOR THE PROTECTION OF ALL PERSONS FROM ENFORCED DISAPPEARANCE

CED entered into force on 23 September 2010 and has only 60 parties, 17 of which are in Africa and 16 of which are in Latin America and the Caribbean. Given that this human right for a person not to be forced to disappear is closely related to civil and political rights under the ICCPR, it is interesting to note that Cuba is the only State not party to the ICCPR that is party to CED. Neither Israel nor the State of Palestine is party to CED. Of the five permanent members of the UNSC, only France is party to CED.

There are very few declarations or reservations made by States Parties to CED. Most of them relate to the non-acceptance of the jurisdiction of third-party dispute settlement mechanisms.

10. RESERVATIONS TO HUMAN RIGHTS TREATIES AND THEIR PROPER CONTEXTS

There is no explanation why a State Party objects to some reservations but not to others that are identical or nearly identical. One possibility is that the

State has some special interest in or concern about the human rights situation in the State Party whose reservation it opposes. Nordic States, Austria and Switzerland have registered their objections the most often owing to their unwavering positions to uphold international human rights and probably because these States do not rely so much on bilateral trade with and/or direct investments in the States entering the reservations they deem unacceptable. In any event, the Sharia-based reservations have been objected to the most, but mainly by Western States.

In Muslim-majority States, the principal area of substantive law still influenced by Islamic law is the area of personal status – marriage, divorce, inheritance and child custody.[45] Islamic law does not recognize the status of children born out of wedlock as it forbids fornication and adultery.[46] Proselytizing of Muslims by members of other religions is a criminal offence in several Muslim-majority States.

Although the Organisation of Islamic Cooperation's (OIC) Cairo Declaration on Human Rights in Islam[47] is criticized for its purported departure from Islam's perspective on rights as people's duties and obligations to each other, to those in authority above them, to those subordinate to them and, above all, to God,[48] the Declaration leaves ample room for Sharia to be applied by providing in Article 24 that all the rights and freedoms stipulated in the Declaration are subject to the Islamic Sharia. Article 25 of the Cairo Declaration affirms the Islamic Sharia as the only source of reference for the explanation or clarification of any of the Articles of this Declaration.

A majority of Muslim-majority States in the Middle East and Africa have become party to the ICCPR and the ICESCR. There is also a widespread ratification among these States of CERD, CEDAW and CAT. As the CRC is universally ratified/acceded to, these States have no justifiable diplomatic excuse not to be party thereto, although several have entered as many reservations as they can. A smaller number of them have become party to other international human rights treaties such as the CMW and the CRPD. Although

---

[45] Anver M Emon, Mark Ellis and Benjamin Glahn (eds), *Islamic Law and International Human Rights Law* (OUP 2012) 6.

[46] Mashood A Baderin, *International Human Rights and Islamic Law* (OUP 2003) 196–9.

[47] UN Doc A/CONF.157/PC/62/Add.18 (1993).

[48] Ali Allawi, 'Islam, Human Rights and the New Information Technologies' in Monroe Price and Nicole Stremlau (eds), *Speech and Society in Turbulent Times* (CUP 2018) 19, 26–7. Cf Baderin, who considers the Cairo Declaration to have adopted a 'theocentric approach' to human rights, as opposed to the 'anthropocentric approach' of the ICCPR (Baderin, *International Human Rights and Islamic Law* 51).

most provisions of human rights treaties are compatible with Islamic law,[49] the reservations or declarations made conditional and subject to domestic law or to be interpreted on the basis of Sharia law are of particular concern.[50]

Muslim-majority States' reservations to human rights treaties may need to be considered in the context of 'the comparative historical dimensions of human rights'.[51] The Western separation of the Church (religion) and the secular State is alien to the jurisprudence and political philosophy of the Islamic tradition, except in Turkey. So is the Western tradition of individualism, which is alien to Islam's patriarchal tradition, Islam's treatment of the family as society's primary unit and Islam's emphasis on group rights as opposed to individual rights. The West's emphasis on rights over duties as the basis of interpersonal relationships; legalism over reconciliation, repentance or education as the way to deal with deviance; and secularism over religion in public life are also alien to most Islamic societies.[52] One study concludes, however, that Sharia is not the only motivating factor behind reservations to human rights treaties by Muslim-majority States and that where Sharia is invoked as a justification there is incoherence in the practice of the States concerned when adhering to these treaties.[53] It is therefore suspected that such reservations are at times used as subterfuges for the States to maintain or increase their margin of power under the 'legitimate' cover of 'sacred' Islamic considerations or as a tactic to lessen the impact of international human rights standards at the domestic level in deference to national public sentiment or culturally or religiously sensitive matters.[54]

Article 5(a) of the Cairo Declaration recognizes the family as 'the foundation of society and marriage [as] the basis of making a family'; hence, the duty of 'parents' to every child stipulated in Article 7 of the Declaration must be understood as the duty of wed parents. This is incompatible with Article 23 of

---

[49]   Baderin, *International Human Rights and Islamic Law* 49–53, 67–9, 75–117, 125–32, 169–218.

[50]   Joshua Castellino and Kathleen A Cavanaugh, *Minority Rights in the Middle East* (OUP 2013) 55–67; Kathleen Cavanaugh, 'Narrating Law' in Emon et al (eds), *Islamic Law and International Human Rights Law* 18, 35–42.

[51]   Yasuaki Onuma, *International Law in a Transcivilizational World* (CUP 2017) 418.

[52]   Benjamin Gregg, *Human Rights as Social Construction* (CUP 2012) 27–32, 142.

[53]   Nisrine Abiad, *Sharia, Muslim States and International Human Rights Treaty Obligations: A Comparative Study* (British Institute of International and Comparative Law 2008) 98.

[54]   Ibid 84–5, 91, 171. Also, Baderin, *International Human Rights and Islamic Law* 11.

the ICCPR, which recognizes the various forms of family, including unmarried couples and their children and single parents and their children.[55]

CEDAW and the CRC have been subject to the most Sharia-based reservations.

The reservations to CEDAW on the grounds of the Islamic law or Sharia are mostly in relation to Articles 2, 9, 15 and 16 on marriage and family matters as well as on those alien to the 'patrimonial lens' through which women's position is perceived within the family.[56] The Quran's presumption of superiority of the male over the female can, plausibly, be seen in the context of the Islamic appreciation of role differentiation within the family in a patriarchal society, with the male accorded a higher degree of responsibility than the female.[57] Although Article 6 of the Cairo Declaration specifically recognizes the equality between women and men in terms of human dignity, as well as the rights and duties of women, including their own civil entity and financial independence, it also emphasizes the responsibility of the husband for the support and welfare of the family. However, this does not explain why a Muslim woman is prohibited under Islamic law from marrying a non-Muslim man, but a Muslim man is not so prohibited from marrying a non-Muslim woman and it is conceded that this is one area where achieving equality between Islamic law and IHRL is difficult.[58] Also, under Islamic law the male heir generally receives twice the share of the female heir, probably due to the varied financial responsibilities of the two genders in the family of a patriarchal society. A question may be asked whether in a modern family of the present era in which a female member is the family breadwinner the female heir and the male heir should be given an equal share in the family inheritance, as was the case of the Iraqi Personal Status Act of 1959, which was repealed in 1963 owing to its unpopularity, or even a greater share should be given to a female heir.[59] In any event, the Human Rights Committee has ruled that Article 3 of the ICCPR requires equality during marriage, which implies equal participation of husband and wife in terms of responsibility and authority within the family.[60]

---

[55]   Human Rights Committee General Comment No 28 (2000): Article 3 (The Equality of Rights between Men and Women) 29 Mar 2000, CCPR/C/21/Rev.1/Add.10 §27.

[56]   Ali, *Modern Challenges to Islamic Law* 173–5; Baderin, *International Human Rights and Islamic Law* 62; Cavanaugh, 'Narrating Law' 40.

[57]   Baderin, *International Human Rights and Islamic Law* 133–6.

[58]   Ibid 144–5. Human Rights Committee General Comment No 28 §24 specifically chastises this as violating Art 3 of the ICCPR.

[59]   Baderin, *International Human Rights and Islamic Law* 146–9.

[60]   Human Rights Committee General Comment No 28 (2000) §25.

Article 25 of the ICCPR provides unequivocally, among other things, for the right and opportunity of every citizen, male or female, to participate in voting and public affairs without unreasonable restrictions.[61] Furthermore, Article 7(a) of CEDAW requires its States Parties to take all appropriate measures to eliminate discrimination against women in the political and public life of the country and, in particular, to ensure to women, on equal terms with men, the right to vote in all elections and public referenda and to be eligible for election to all publicly elected bodies. Nothing in the Quran or Islamic law restricts the right to be eligible for election and to vote to males only.[62]

By virtue of Article 51(2) of the CRC, a reservation incompatible with the object and purpose of the CRC is prohibited. Some Muslim-majority States have declared that Article 14 of the CRC concerning a child's freedom of religion could potentially conflict with their domestic law. Reservations have been made to Article 7 of the CRC, subjecting a child's nationality to domestic law. Many Muslim-majority States have made reservations to the CRC on the grounds of Islamic law or Sharia in relation to the issue of adoption. Sharia provides for a guardianship system (*kafalah*) to provide alternative family care for children deprived of natural parental care and Article 20(3) of the CRC itself expressly recognizes child care provided by 'kafalah of Islamic law'.[63] This kind of reservation, therefore, does not seem incompatible with the CRC.

The latest reservations, by Qatar at the time of its accession to the ICCPR and the ICESCR in May 2018, follow the pattern adopted by numerous other Muslim-majority States in relation to Sharia. Qatar enters its reservations on gender equality provisions in marriage, divorce and child custody because they contravene Sharia. Qatar's personal status law requires a male guardian to approve women's marriage. It accords men a unilateral right to divorce their wives whereas women have to apply to a court of law for divorce and on limited grounds. Wives are also required by law to obey their husbands. After divorce and even where the mother has custody over her child, the father still retains guardianship over their child. In most cases, boys live with their mother until the age of 13 and girls until the age of 15, when they automatically move to their father's custody unless the court rules otherwise or extends the custody in the best interest of the child. Women, but not men, lose custody if they remarry. Under Qatar's inheritance law, female siblings receive half the amount their brothers get. Qatar also declares, inter alia, that it will construe several provisions of the two Covenants in accordance with Sharia, including those on defining cruel, inhuman or degrading punishment; minimum mar-

---

[61] This is also highlighted in ibid §29.
[62] Baderin, *International Human Rights and Islamic Law* 160–62.
[63] Ibid 154–5.

riage ages and freedom of religion. In other words, Qatar will retain capital and corporal punishment. Qatar's interpretation of the right to profess and practise one's own religion is in order not to violate the rules of public order and public morals, the protection of public safety and public health or the rights and basic freedoms of others. While people of other religious faiths can practise their religion in Qatar, Qatar's penal code prohibits them from proselytizing.

Considered in a more positive light, declarations or reservations to human rights treaties give breathing space for the Muslim-majority States concerned to cautiously find ways of fulfilling the human rights treaty obligations that are nationally sensitive matters, and many of them have, in the long run, achieved reforms in line with what is expected of them by other States Parties. Some examples of such reforms include the reform to Morocco's Family Code in 2004 and Algeria's new Family Code adopted in January 2004. With respect to Saudi Arabia, it adopted the Basic Law of Government in 1993 with a specific chapter on rights and duties, a Law of Procedure before the Sharia Courts in 2000 and a Human Rights Commission Regulation in 2005, establishing a Human Rights Commission 'to protect and enhance human rights according to international standards for human rights in all aspects and to promote public awareness thereof and participate in ensuring implementation of the same in light of the provisions of Sharia'. Since 24 June 2018 at midnight local time, women have been permitted to drive cars on their own in Saudi Arabia. Before then, Saudi Arabia was the only State in the entire world where women were legally required to be driven by chauffeurs or travel with male family members. As of 2 August 2019, Saudi Arabia has granted women over the age of 21 the right to apply for a passport without authorization from a male guardian; all women the right to register a birth, marriage or divorce; and all citizens the right to work without facing any discrimination based on gender, disability or age. By becoming party to CEDAW after a complex legal and political decision and interaction between government authorities and the public, Pakistan performs a balancing act before international and domestic audiences with differing expectations and demands. Internationally, most States Parties to CEDAW expect and demand that the obligations under CEDAW be adhered to. Domestically, there are opposing forces, pitching some religio-political parties resisting the women's rights encapsulated in CEDAW against those individuals, NGOs and others demanding that CEDAW be faithfully implemented.[64] It should be noted that some Muslim-majority States have subsequently withdrawn their reservations to human rights treaties previously entered on the grounds of traditional historical interpretations of Islamic law. To add one more example to the ones already mentioned, thanks

---

[64]   Ali, *Modern Challenges to Islamic Law* 174, 193–5, 203–5.

to the objections from certain CEDAW States Parties, on 17 April 2014 Tunisia withdrew its declaration with regard to Article 15(4) and reservations to Articles 9(2), 16(c), (d), (f), (g) and (h) of CEDAW.

Nevertheless, many Muslim-majority States still punish apostasy with death under traditional Islamic law. The civil law of several Muslim-majority States also restricts the rights of apostates, such as by suspending their rights to dispose of property pending their repentance, automatically annulling a marriage contract upon the apostasy of one or both partners, and exclusion of apostates from the right to inheritance.[65] Apostasy is 'expressions of unbelief' by words or conduct, expressly or implicitly or (in some cases) the mere intention to disbelieve what is known to be a generally accepted part of Islam, presumably as determined by a judge or court and attested by at least two witnesses testifying that the words of the accused demonstrate apostasy. However, if a person confesses that he or she has committed apostasy, that confession suffices for the conviction of the person.[66] The law of apostasy in Islam as enforced in a number of Muslim societies and Muslim-majority States through a great variety of measures is criticized as standing in stark contrast to modern understanding of human rights and religious liberty.[67]

Islamic human rights instruments generally guarantee non-discrimination based on religion. Article 1(a) of the Cairo Declaration and Article III(c) of the Universal Islamic Declaration of Human Rights,[68] adopted in September 1981 by the London-based Islamic Council of Europe, prohibit discrimination by reason of religious belief.[69] Article 3(1) of the 2004 Arab Charter on Human Rights[70] obligates its States Parties to undertake to ensure that all individuals within their territory and subject to their jurisdiction have the right to and freedom of religion. However, the Arab Charter provides in Article 30(1) that the right to freedom of thought, belief and religion shall be subject to such limitations as are prescribed by law. Additionally, while Article 25 of the Arab Charter recognizes the right of persons belonging to minorities to enjoy their own culture, to use their own language and to profess and practise their own religion, the exercise of this right shall be governed by law.

---

[65]   Abdullah Saeed, 'Pre-Modern Islamic Legal Restrictions on Freedom of Religion, with Particular Reference to Apostasy and its Punishment' in Emon et al (eds), *Islamic Law and International Human Rights Law* 226, 229–31.

[66]   Ibid 227–8.

[67]   Patrick Sookhdeo, *Freedom to Believe: Challenging Islam's Apostasy Law* (Isaac Publishing 2009) *passim* and 100.

[68]   https://www.lawschool.cornell.edu/womenandjustice/upload/League-of-Arab -States-Universal-Islamic-Declaration-of-Human-Rights.pdf, accessed 12 Jan 2019.

[69]   Cf SI Strong, *Transforming Religious Liberties: A New Theory of Religious Rights for National and International Legal Systems* (CUP 2018) 41–2, 61–6.

[70]   (2005) 12 Int'l Hum Rts Rep 893.

Whereas Article 18 of the UDHR recognizes the freedom to change one's religion or belief, there was strong opposition from Saudi Arabia and some other Muslim-majority States to incorporating this freedom into the ICCPR, which is a legally binding treaty, lest, in Saudi Arabia's words, 'pressure, proselytism, … errors and heresies' could induce men to change their religion due to their 'weakness or credulity'.[71] A compromise wording in the ICCPR proposed by Brazil, the Philippines and the UK ('freedom to have or to adopt a religion or belief of [one's] choice') was unanimously adopted instead. Opposition from a number of Muslim-majority States in the UNGA to the right to change one's religion led to the amendment of draft Article 1 of the 1981 UN Declaration on the Elimination of All Forms of Intolerance and of Discrimination Based on Religion or Belief,[72] with express reference to the right to change religion removed. The finally adopted Article 1 of the Declaration reads:

1. Everyone shall have the right to freedom of thought, conscience and religion. This right shall include freedom to have a religion or whatever belief of his choice and freedom, either individually or in community with others and in public or private, to manifest his religion or belief in worship, observance, practice and teaching.
2. No one shall be subject to coercion which would impair his freedom to have a religion or belief of his choice.
3. Freedom to manifest one's religion or beliefs may be subject only to such limitations as are prescribed by law and are necessary to protect public safety, order, health or morals or the fundamental rights and freedoms of others.

A provision that has become Article 8 of the 1981 UN Declaration adds that nothing in that Declaration shall be construed as restricting or derogating from any right defined in the UDHR, the ICCPR and the ICESCR. Article 8 thus allows those who insist on the right to change religion to argue that, as this right is already protected by Article 18 of the hortatory UDHR and Article 18 of the legally binding ICCPR, the 1981 UN Declaration does not detract from that. On the other hand, for those States that have consistently expounded that Article 18 of the ICCPR does not protect the right to change religion, Article 1 of the 1981 UN Declaration vindicates their position.[73]

---

[71] UN Docs A/C.3/SR. 1021 §11 and A/C.3/SR. 1022, §27 (1960) quoted in Baderin, *International Human Rights and Islamic Law* 119. See also Abiad, *Sharia, Muslim States and International Human Rights Treaty Obligations* 60–63.

[72] UN Doc A/RES/36/55 (25 Nov 1981).

[73] Urfan Khaliq, 'Freedom of Religion and Belief in International Law: A Comparative Analysis' in Emon et al (eds), *Islamic Law and International Human Rights Law* 183, 195–6.

Insofar as there is no unified interpretation of Islamic law, the proscription of apostasy can be interpreted in a variety of ways depending on how strictly or broadly one interprets the scope of the freedom of expression in the Quran.[74] For example, as the Cairo Declaration itself provides in Article 10 that it is prohibited 'to exercise any form of compulsion on man or to exploit his poverty or ignorance in order to convert him to another religion or to atheism', it could be argued that if there is no such compulsion or exploitation then there is no wrong.[75] Alternatively, moderate Islamic scholars posit that apostasy must be understood in the proper historical context of Muslims denouncing their Islamic faith to join with enemies to take up arms against their Muslim-majority State, thereby committing a political offence of treason or rebellion against the State.[76] The punishment of apostasy in Islamic law is largely based on certain reported sayings of the Prophet (*hadith*)[77] but the Prophet never sentenced anyone to death for apostasy although some of his companions considered it a sin punishable within the legislative discretion of the Muslim-majority State.[78] Some moderate Muslim-majority States like Malaysia resort to deporting foreigners charged with proselytizing and barring them from re-entry instead of prosecuting them.[79]

11. EFFECTS OF RESERVATIONS TO HUMAN RIGHTS TREATIES

In 1951 the ICJ rendered its advisory opinion in reply to the question posed by the UNGA concerning reservations to the 1948 Convention on the Prevention and Punishment of the Crime of Genocide,[80] which was the first-ever multilateral convention on human rights after the establishment of the UN. By a narrow majority of seven votes to five, the ICJ opines that a State which has made and maintained a reservation objected to by one or more of the parties to the Convention but not by others can be regarded as being a party to the Convention if the reservation is compatible with the object and purpose of the Convention. Otherwise, that reserving State cannot be regarded as being

---

[74] Hossein Esmaeili, Irmgard Marboe and Javid Rehman, *The Rule of Law, Freedom of Expression and Islamic Law* (Hart 2017) ch. 5; Abiad, *Sharia, Muslim States and International Human Rights Treaty Obligations* 25–6.

[75] Baderin, *International Human Rights and Islamic Law* 122–3.

[76] Saeed, 'Pre-Modern Islamic Legal Restrictions on Freedom of Religion' 241–2.

[77] Ibid 234–5.

[78] Baderin, *International Human Rights and Islamic Law* 123–4.

[79] 'Malaysia to deport 4 Finns for distributing Christian items', *Bangkok Post* (27 Nov 2018) https://www.bangkokpost.com/news/asean/1583270/malaysia-to-deport-4 -finns-for-distributing-christian-items, accessed 16 Jan 2019.

[80] 78 UNTS 277.

a party to the Convention. Furthermore, if a party to the Convention objects to a reservation it considers incompatible with the object and purpose of the Convention, it can in fact consider that the reserving State is not a party to the Convention. If, on the other hand, a party accepts the reservation as being compatible with the object and purpose of the Convention, it can in fact consider that the reserving State is a party to the Convention. The core rationale behind permitting States to make reservations to human rights treaties is that such treaties aim at universality of States Parties for the sake of 'the authority of the moral and humanitarian principles' underpinning the treaties.[81]

Subsequent to that advisory opinion, the UNGA entrusted the UN International Law Commission (ILC) with codifying the law of treaties, culminating in the diplomatic conference that adopted the VCLT in 1969.[82] A reservation to a treaty allows a State to become party to the treaty even when the State is not yet ready to fulfil all the obligations thereunder and, by virtue of becoming party, it is placed under scrutiny of the other States Parties and the treaty monitoring body, if any, for it to take the necessary steps to fulfil the entire treaty obligations and withdraw the reservation in due course.[83] Yet the integrity of such treaties must also be preserved. Article 19(c) of the VCLT prohibits a reservation that is 'incompatible with the object and purpose of the treaty'. Article 20(4) of the VCLT permits the possibility of a State objecting to a reservation made by another State. Pursuant to Article 21, a reservation precludes the operation, as between the reserving and other States party to the treaty in question, of the provision subject to the reservation, and an objection thereto makes the reservation applicable as between the reserving State and the objecting State only to the extent that it has not been objected to by the latter.

Human rights treaties fall into the category of treaties where reciprocal fulfilment or non-fulfilment of treaty obligations may not serve as a useful mechanism to force another State Party to perform its treaty obligations.[84] Rather than regulating inter-State conduct, human rights treaties regulate States' domestic behaviour, with individuals and domestic communities as the

---

[81] *Reservations to the Convention on the Prevention and Punishment of the Crime of Genocide* (Advisory Opinion) [1951] ICJ Rep 15, 24. See also Alain Pellet and Daniel Müller, 'Reservations to Human Rights Treaties: Not an Absolute Evil …' in Ulrich Fastenrath, Rudolf Geiger, Daniel-Erasmus Khan, Andreas Paulus, Sabine von Schorlemer and Christoph Vedder (eds), *From Bilateralism to Community Interest: Essays in Honour of Judge Bruno Simma* (OUP 2011) 521, 527–30.

[82] See Draft Articles on the Law of Treaties with commentaries, ILC Yearbook, 1966, ii, 202–9.

[83] Pellet and Müller, 'Reservations to Human Rights Treaties' 530.

[84] Frédéric Mégret. 'Nature of Obligations' in Daniel Moeckli, Sangeeta Shah and Sandesh Sivakumaran (eds), *International Human Rights Law* (3rd edn, OUP 2018) 86, 105 and cf Pellet and Müller, 'Reservations to Human Rights Treaties' 533–5.

case may be as beneficiaries of the treaties.[85] If a State Party fails to perform its human rights treaty obligations, another State Party cannot reciprocate by not performing the same obligations as this non-performance by the latter State would deprive the individuals the treaty aims to protect of their human rights protection. It would be a 'race to the bottom' scenario.

As a result, most States Parties objecting to reservations to human rights treaties have indicated that their objection does not preclude the entry into force of the treaty between the States making the reservations and the objecting States. This is the usual practice of States objecting to reservations to the human rights treaties studied in this chapter despite their insistence that several of the impugned reservations are incompatible with the object and purpose of the treaties in question. This State practice appears to be at variance with the rationale explicated in the ICJ's aforesaid advisory opinion that an objection to a minor reservation should not completely exclude the State making such minor reservation from its participation in the treaty, but 'the very object [and purpose]' of the treaty should not be sacrificed 'in favour of a vain desire to secure as many participants as possible'.[86]

One plausible reason behind the aforesaid State practice is that the objecting States prefer to have as many States as possible being party to human rights treaties. Another, and probably the most important, reason is that there is little practical effect in objecting to a reservation since the reciprocity between States Parties is mostly absent in human rights treaties; therefore, objections by other States Parties have primarily symbolic importance.[87] It would be preferable to keep as many States as possible in human rights treaty regimes and maintain dialogues with them and prod them to change their laws and practice referred to in their reservations and eventually withdraw the reservations.[88] Otherwise, the objecting States would not vote for their candidacies to the Human Rights Council or some other international organs, would not grant them preferential treatment in bilateral relations, and so forth.

However, the Human Rights Committee entrusted with monitoring the implementation of the ICCPR causes some considerable confusion in making

---

[85]   Yvonne Donders, 'Cultural Pluralism in International Human Rights Law: The Role of Reservations' in Ana Filipa Vrdoljak (ed.), *The Cultural Dimension of Human Rights* (OUP 2013) 205, 210–12, 220. Also, Riedel et al, 'The Development of Economic, Social and Cultural Rights in International Law' 13.

[86]   [1951] ICJ Rep 15, 24.

[87]   Donders, 'Cultural Pluralism in International Human Rights Law' 227–8.

[88]   Ekaterina Yahyaoui Krivenko, 'Revisiting the Reservations Dialogue: Negotiating Diversity while Preserving Universality through Human Rights Law' in Machiko Kanetake and André Nollkaemper (eds), *The Rule of Law at the National and International Levels: Contestations and Deference* (Hart 2016) 289, 298–317.

its General Comment No 24, adopted on 2 November 1994, expressing its conviction that the VCLT provisions on the role of State objections in relation to reservations are 'inappropriate to address the problem of reservations to human rights treaties'. Such treaties and the ICCPR specifically, are 'not a web of inter-State exchanges of mutual obligations'; they concern 'the endowment of individuals with rights' where the principle of inter-State reciprocity has no place, save perhaps in the limited context of reservations to declarations on the Human Rights Committee's competence under Article 41 of the ICCPR. Furthermore, States have often not seen any legal interest in or need to object to reservations, but the absence of protest by States cannot imply that a reservation is either compatible or incompatible with the ICCPR's object and purpose. Objections have been occasional, made by some States but not others and on grounds not always specified, and when an objection is made it often does not specify a legal consequence or sometimes even indicates that the objecting party nonetheless does not regard the ICCPR as not in effect as between the parties concerned. The Committee concludes that 'the pattern is so unclear that it is not safe to assume that a non-objecting State thinks that a particular reservation is acceptable'. In all, owing to the special characteristics of the ICCPR as a human rights treaty, it is open to question what effect objections have between States among themselves, although an objection to a reservation made by States may provide some guidance to the Committee in its interpretation as to its compatibility with the ICCPR's object and purpose.[89] The Committee considers it is competent to determine whether a specific reservation is compatible with the ICCPR's object and purpose, partly because it is an inappropriate task for States Parties in relation to human rights treaties and partly because it is a task that the Committee cannot avoid in the performance of its functions.[90] This General Comment is strongly opposed by the UK, USA and France.[91]

The ILC's Guide to Practice on Reservations to Treaties,[92] finalized in 2011, is the outcome of dialogue among various stakeholders – States, human rights

---

[89]   Human Rights Committee, General Comment No 24 (52), General comment on issues relating to reservations made upon ratification or accession to the Covenant or the Optional Protocols thereto or in relation to declarations under Article 41 of the Covenant, UN Doc CCPR/C/21/Rev1/Add6 (1994) §17.

[90]   Ibid §18.

[91]   Report of the Human Rights Committee, UNGA Official Records, 50th Session, Supp No 40, Doc A/50/40, i, Annex VI (UK and USA) and ibid, 51st Session, Supp No 40 (A/51/40), i, Annex VI (France).

[92]   Report of the ILC on the Work of its 63rd session, UNGA Official Records, 66th Session, Supplement No 10, Addendum 1, Doc A/66/10/Add. 1.

bodies and human rights activists. The Guide does not give human rights treaties special treatment separate from other categories of treaties.

The treaty reservation regime under the VCLT is considered by the ILC to be well balanced, flexible and adaptable, striking the right balance between the need for universality and the preservation of the integrity of all categories of treaties. Although human rights treaties are largely non-reciprocal, this is also true with regard to treaties concluded in other fields, such as environmental protection and the maintenance of peace. There are some concerns with respect to the problems related to the so-called 'Sharia reservation' and those concerning reservations on provisions reflecting a peremptory norm (*jus cogens*). It transpires that the problems related to the so-called 'Sharia reservation' are by no means Sharia by itself but the unacceptable specificities of *certain* reservations based on Sharia of unlimited scope and undefined character that is not permissible irrespective of its religious origin or otherwise – its vagueness renders it impossible to assess its compatibility with the object and purpose of the treaty. So are reservations based on national law without identifying the provisions in question or specifying whether they are to be found in the reserving State's constitution or its civil or criminal code. With respect to the admissibility of reservations to treaty provisions reflecting a norm of *jus cogens*, the ILC eventually opted not to formulate a Guideline on this issue as such, but subsumed it under the Guideline on reservations to a provision reflecting a customary rule.[93]

The pertinent provisions of the Guide to Practice on Reservations to Treaties[94] are as follows.

Where the treaty envisages formulation of specified reservations without defining their content, a reservation may be formulated by a State or an international organization only if it is not incompatible with the object and purpose of the treaty.[95] A reservation is incompatible with the object and purpose of the treaty if it affects an essential element of the treaty that is necessary to its general tenor, in such a way that the reservation impairs the *raison d'être* of the treaty itself. The object and purpose of the treaty must be determined in good faith, taking account of the terms of the treaty in their context, in particular the title and the preamble of the treaty. Recourse may also be had to

---

[93] Alain Pellet, 'The ILC Guide to Practice on Reservations to Treaties: A General Presentation by the Special Rapporteur' (2013) 24 EJIL 1061. See also Ineta Ziemele and Lāsma Liede, 'Reservations to Human Rights Treaties: From Draft Guideline 3.1.12 to Guideline 3.1.5.6' (2013) 24 EJIL 1135.

[94] International Law Commission, Guide to Practice on Reservation to Treaties, Guideline 3.1.5.1 (Determination of the object and purpose of a treaty), ILC Report, Sixty-third session (26 Apr–3 June and 4 July–12 Aug 2011) UN Doc A/66/10/Add.1.

[95] Guideline 3.1.4 (Permissibility of specified reservations).

the preparatory work of the treaty and the circumstances of its conclusion and, where appropriate, the subsequent practice of the parties. A reservation must be worded in such a way as to allow its meaning to be understood, in order to assess in particular its compatibility with the object and purpose of the treaty.[96]

The fact that a treaty provision reflects a rule of customary international law does not in itself constitute an obstacle to the formulation of a reservation to that provision.[97] However, a State or an international organization may not formulate a reservation to a treaty provision concerning rights from which no derogation is permissible under any circumstances, unless the reservation in question is compatible with the essential rights and obligations arising out of that treaty. In assessing that compatibility, account shall be taken of the importance conferred by the parties on the rights at issue by making them non-derogable.[98]

The ILC take note of reservations to exclude or modify the legal effect of certain provisions of a treaty or of the treaty as a whole with a view to preserving the integrity of specific rules of internal law of the reserving State or of specific rules of the reserving organization in force at the time of the formulation of the reservations. Such reservations may be formulated only insofar as they affect neither an essential element of the treaty nor its general tenor.[99]

In order to assess the compatibility of a reservation with the object and purpose of a treaty containing numerous interdependent rights and obligations, account shall be taken of that interdependence as well as the importance that the provision subject to the reservation has within the general tenor of the treaty and the extent of the impact that the reservation has on the treaty.[100]

A reservation to a treaty provision concerning dispute settlement or the monitoring of the implementation of the treaty is not, in itself, incompatible with the object and purpose of the treaty, provided that it does not breach either of the following two conditions. First, the reservation must not purport to exclude or modify the legal effect of a provision of the treaty essential to its *raison d'être*. Second, the reservation must not have the effect of excluding the reserving State or international organization from a dispute settlement or treaty implementation monitoring mechanism with respect to a treaty provision it has

---

[96] Guideline 3.1.5 (Incompatibility of a reservation with the object and purpose of the treaty).

[97] Guideline 3.1.5.3 (Reservations to a provision reflecting a customary rule).

[98] Guideline 3.1.5.4 (Reservations to provisions concerning rights from which no derogation is permissible under any circumstances).

[99] Guideline 3.1.5.5 (Reservations relating to internal law).

[100] Guideline 3.1.5.6.

previously accepted, if the very purpose of the treaty is to put such a mechanism into effect.[101]

The following entities may assess, within their respective competences, the permissibility of reservations to a treaty formulated by a State or an international organization: contracting States or contracting organizations; dispute settlement bodies; and treaty monitoring bodies. Treaty monitoring bodies have the necessary competence to assess the permissibility of reservations made to the treaty whose implementation they are responsible for overseeing. The legal force of their findings in that regard has no greater legal value than that accorded by their constitutive instrument. When equipping bodies with the competence to monitor the application of treaties, States or international organizations should specify, where appropriate, the nature and the limits of the competence of such bodies to assess the permissibility of reservations. In addition, States and international organizations that have formulated reservations to a treaty establishing a treaty monitoring body shall give consideration to that body's assessment of the permissibility of the reservations. Furthermore, when a treaty establishes a treaty monitoring body, the competence of that body is without prejudice to the competence of the contracting States or contracting organizations to assess the permissibility of reservations to that treaty or to that of dispute settlement bodies competent to interpret or apply the treaty. When a dispute settlement body is competent to adopt decisions binding upon the parties to a dispute and the assessment of the permissibility of a reservation is necessary for the discharge of such competence by that body, such assessment is, as an element of the decision, legally binding upon the parties.[102]

The status of the author of an invalid reservation in relation to the treaty depends on the intention expressed by the reserving State or international organization on whether it intends to be bound by the treaty without the benefit of the reservation or whether it considers that it is not bound by the treaty. Unless the author of the invalid reservation has expressed a contrary intention or such an intention is otherwise established, it is considered a contracting State or a contracting organization without the benefit of the reservation. Notwithstanding the foregoing, the author of the invalid reservation may express at any time its intention not to be bound by the treaty without the benefit of the reservation. If a treaty monitoring body expresses the view that a reservation is invalid and the reserving State or international organization intends not to be bound by the treaty without the benefit of the reservation, it

---

[101] Guideline 3.1.5.7.
[102] Guideline 3.2.

should express its intention to that effect within a period of 12 months from the date at which the treaty monitoring body made its assessment.[103]

Article 20 of the VCLT regulates acceptance of and objection to reservations. A reservation expressly authorized by a treaty does not require any subsequent acceptance by the other contracting States unless the treaty so provides. When it appears from the limited number of the negotiating States and the object and purpose of a treaty that the application of the treaty in its entirety between all the parties is an essential condition of the consent of each one to be bound by the treaty, a reservation requires acceptance by all the parties. In cases not falling under the preceding situations and unless the treaty otherwise provides, there are three possibilities. First, acceptance by another contracting State of a reservation makes the reserving State a party to the treaty in relation to that other State if or when the treaty is in force for those States. Secondly, an objection by another contracting State to a reservation does not preclude the entry into force of the treaty as between the objecting and reserving States unless a contrary intention is definitely expressed by the objecting State. Thirdly, an act expressing a State's consent to be bound by the treaty and containing a reservation is effective as soon as at least one other contracting State has accepted the reservation. Where subsequent acceptance by the other contracting parties of a reservation to a treaty is required and unless the treaty otherwise provides, a reservation is considered to have been accepted by a State if it shall have raised no objection to the reservation by the end of a period of 12 months after it was notified of the reservation or by the date on which it expressed its consent to be bound by the treaty, whichever is later.

Assessing the reservations, especially the Sharia reservations, to the various human rights treaties in the light of the ILC Guide to Practice on Reservations to Treaties leads to the following conclusions. Where a competent treaty body determines such reservations to be incompatible with the object and purpose of the treaty in question, the reserving States Parties are bound by the treaty obligations, but without the benefit of their reservations. Where other States Parties to the treaty object to such reservations and the competent treaty body has not yet determined whether the reservations are in fact incompatible with the treaty's object and purpose, the objecting States Parties treat the reserving States Parties as being bound by the treaty but without the benefit of the reservations. In practice, the objecting States Parties will act as 'opinion leaders' in the Human Rights Council, the Third Committee of the UNGA and other human rights-related forums for the international community to put pressure on the reserving States Parties to faithfully comply with and implement the treaty without the benefit of these reservations.

---

[103] Guideline 4.5.3.

It should not be lightly assumed that States Parties making 'Sharia reserva-tions' do not accept the legally binding force of the treaties to which they are party. As already pointed out, they must have made reservations for several reasons, including allowing them some elbow room to reform their domes-tic legal system of human rights protection as well as to put an end to local customs or traditions practised in many localities within their borders that are popularly believed to be grounded in Sharia but are not in fact so grounded. A number of reserving Muslim-majority States have subsequently withdrawn their Sharia reservations or pared down the indeterminable scope of such res-ervations. Several positive changes in the reserving States Parties have mate-rialized. One observer even remarks that while States in the Middle East have been openly critical of the international human rights regime for its alleged politicization/double standards, they have accepted even the most intrusive of the UN's monitoring mechanisms, such as visits from thematic rapporteurs, and often with surprising levels of engagement.[104]

On the whole, while States become party to human rights treaties with res-ervations, the interplay between international law and diplomacy helps ensure that all peoples are increasingly protected by IHRL.

---

[104] Castellino and Cavanaugh, *Minority Rights in the Middle East* 70–73.

6. Complying with and enforcing international human rights law: can the bad guys get away with it?

Kathryn Sikkink of Harvard University has suggested six policy tools to address human rights violations:

> 1) diminish war and seek non-violent solutions to conflict; 2) promote democracy and enhance the quality of existing democracies; 3) guard against dehumanizing and exclusionary ideologies, whether about race, religion, gender, class or any other status; 4) encourage States to ratify existing human rights treaties and work to enforce human rights laws and norms through non-violent means; 5) end impunity, by supporting domestic and international accountability that can deter future crime and 6) support, expand and protect domestic and international mobilization on behalf of human rights.[1]

Successes and failures in upholding international human rights law (IHRL) thus depend on a combination of factors prevailing at a specific time and in particular circumstances.

Nation States desiring to fully belong to the international community tend to behave in conformity with their counterparts that form their reference group, abiding by certain practices and norms of behaviour of that group. The social pressure to conform in order to achieve social assimilation, legitimacy and status within the group is a major reason for States, including those with repressive regimes, to join international human rights treaties.[2]

Change of government can also lead to a change of position regarding human rights. For example, the UN Declaration on the Rights of Indigenous Peoples was adopted in 2007 by an affirmative vote of 143 States in favour, four against and 11 abstentions.[3] The four States voting against its adoption subsequently officially declared their acceptance of the Declaration after

---

[1]   Kathryn Sikkink, *Evidence for Hope: Making Human Rights Work in the 21st Century* (Princeton University Press 2017) 183.

[2]   Cf the acculturation analysis in the context of human rights promotion in Ryan Goodman and Derek Jinks, *Socializing States: Promoting Human Rights through International Law* (OUP 2013) 25–9, 187–8.

[3]   A/RES/61/295 (2 Oct 2007). Thirty-four were recorded as being absent.

a change of government in their respective States – Australia in April 2009, New Zealand in April 2010, Canada in November 2010 and the USA in December 2010.[4]

1.   COMPLIANCE

Article 26 of the 1969 Vienna Convention on the Law of Treaties (VCLT)[5] codifies the rule of customary international law of *pacta sunt servanda* – 'Every treaty in force is binding upon the parties to it and must be performed by them in good faith.' The principle of the sanctity of the contract has been upheld by all civilizations from time immemorial.[6] To Muslims, for example, the principle also has a religious basis, with the Quran stipulating in several places that Muslims must abide by the obligations they have undertaken 'in the sight of Allah' who is their 'Witness'.[7] The International Court of Justice (ICJ) has ruled that Article 26 of the VCLT combines two elements of equal importance – the binding force of every treaty in force upon the parties to it and the performance by these parties in good faith. The principle of good faith obliges the parties to apply the treaty in a reasonable way and in such a manner that its purpose can be realized.[8]

Article 27 of the VCLT stipulates unequivocally: 'A party may not invoke the provisions of its internal law as justification for its failure to perform a treaty. This rule is without prejudice to Article 46.' Article 46, in turn, provides that a State may not invoke the fact that its consent to be bound by a treaty has been expressed in violation of a provision of its internal law regarding competence to conclude treaties as invalidating its consent unless that violation was manifest and concerned a rule of its internal law of fundamental importance. A violation is manifest if it would be objectively evident to any State conducting itself in the matter in accordance with normal practice and in good faith.

The obligation to fulfil a treaty obligation may be one of conduct or one of result. An obligation of conduct is synonymous with the obligation of due diligence, requiring the State concerned to deploy adequate means, to exercise

---

[4]   Siegfried Wiessener, 'Culture and the Rights of Indigenous Peoples' in Ana Filipa Vrdoljak (ed.), *The Cultural Dimension of Human Rights* (OUP 2013) 117, 141–2.

[5]   1155 UNTS 331.

[6]   Hans Wehberg, 'Pacta Sunt Servanda' (1959) 53 AJIL 775.

[7]   Ibid.

[8]   *Gabčikovo-Nagymaros Project (Hungary/Slovakia)* [1997] ICJ Rep 7, 78–9 [142].

best possible efforts, to do the utmost, to obtain the envisaged result.[9] An obligation of result, on the other hand, is one that requires the State concerned to attain a specific outcome within a reasonable period of time.[10]

However, as the Committee on Economic, Social and Cultural Rights (CESCR) explains in its General Comment No 3, there are significant similarities between the obligation of conduct and that of result. For instance, Article 2(1) of the 1966 International Covenant on Economic, Social and Cultural Rights (ICESCR)[11] requires each State Party 'to take steps, individually and through international assistance and cooperation, especially economic and technical, to the maximum of its available resources, with a view to achieving progressively the full realization of the rights recognized in the [ICESCR] by all appropriate means, including particularly the adoption of legislative measures'. In the CESCR's view, while the ICESCR provides for progressive realization and acknowledges the constraints due to the limits of available resources, it also imposes various obligations of immediate effect. The undertaking in Article 2(1) 'to take steps', in itself, is not qualified or limited by other considerations. Thus, while the full realization of the relevant rights may be achieved progressively, steps towards that goal must be taken within a reasonably short time after the ICESCR's entry into force for the States concerned and such steps should be deliberate, concrete and targeted as clearly as possible towards meeting the ICESCR's obligations. The principal 'obligation of result' reflected in Article 2(1) is to take steps 'with a view to achieving progressively the full realization of the rights recognized' in the ICESCR. The concept of progressive realization constitutes a recognition of the fact that full realization of all economic, social and cultural rights will generally not be able to be achieved in a short period of time. In this sense, the obligation differs significantly from that contained in Article 2 of the 1966 International Covenant on Civil and Political Rights (ICCPR),[12] which embodies an immediate obligation to respect and ensure all of the relevant rights. Nevertheless, the fact that realization over time, or progressively, is foreseen under the ICESCR should not be misinterpreted as depriving the obligation of all meaningful content. It is a necessary flexibility device, reflecting the realities of the real world and the difficulties involved for any ICESCR State Party in ensuring full realization

---

[9]   International Tribunal for the Law of the Sea, Case No 21, *Request for Advisory Opinion submitted by the Sub-Regional Fisheries Commission, Advisory Opinion*, 2 Apr 2015 [2015] ITLOS Rep 4, 39–40 [128]–[129].

[10]   *Request for Interpretation of the Judgment of 31 March 2004 in the Case concerning Avena and Other Mexican Nationals (Mexico v United States of America) (Mexico v United States of America)* [2009] ICJ Rep 3, 12 [27].

[11]   993 UNTS 3.

[12]   999 UNTS 171.

of economic, social and cultural rights. At the same time, the phrase must be read in the light of the ICESCR's overall objective, indeed the *raison d'être*, to establish clear obligations for States Parties in respect of the full realization of the rights in question. It thus imposes an obligation to move as expeditiously and effectively as possible towards that goal. Moreover, any deliberately retrogressive measures in that regard would require the most careful consideration and would need to be fully justified by reference to the totality of the ICESCR rights and in the context of the full use of the maximum available resources. Even where the available resources are demonstrably inadequate, the obligation remains for a State Party to strive to ensure the widest possible enjoyment of the relevant rights under the prevailing circumstances.[13]

Notwithstanding the CESCR's aforesaid General Comment, the drafting history, negotiations, and current practice and debates show that Article 2(1) of the ICESCR merely envisages international assistance and cooperation as one of the possible means to achieve the realization of the ICESCR rights and not as a separate substantive legal obligation. In other words, Article 2(1) informs States Parties to the ICESCR *how* to perform the substantive obligations under the ICESCR, but is not a legally binding duty in terms of transfer of resources to another State.[14]

Regarding the obligation of result, Chapter 2 has explained how the ICJ has ruled in *Avena* that although the obligation at issue is one of result to be performed unconditionally by the USA, the USA is left to choose the means of implementation, not excluding the introduction within reasonable time of appropriate legislation, if deemed necessary under US domestic constitutional law and that the USA has not complied with the obligation incumbent upon it. The ICJ judge of Mexican nationality who sat in the *Avena* case deplores the fact that the ICJ inexplicably failed to call the USA to account for its failure to discharge its international obligations. The judge laments that the ICJ ignored the need to adjudge the consequences of the internationally wrongful acts of a State as well as the need to determine the remedial action required in such circumstances, thereby rendering the obligations of result a mere abstraction, devoid of any legal substance.[15]

---

[13] CESCR General Comment No 3 on the nature of States Parties obligations (Art 2, para 1 of the Covenant): 14/12/90, Doc E/1991/23.

[14] Takhmina Karimova and Ioana Cismas, 'The Nature and Meaning of "International Assistance and Cooperation" under the International Covenant on Economic, Social and Cultural Rights' in Eibe Riedel, Gilles Giacca and Christophe Golay (eds), *Economic, Social and Cultural Rights in International Law: Contemporary Issues and Challenges* (OUP 2014) 163, 169–83, 189–92.

[15] [2009] ICJ Rep 3, 30, 34–5 [13]–[14] (Dissenting Opinion of Judge Sepúlveda-Amor).

Mexico has pursued this matter through multilateral diplomacy, culminating, on 20 December 2018, in the UN General Assembly (UNGA) Resolution 257 entitled 'Judgment of the International Court of Justice of 31 March 2004 concerning Avena and Other Mexican Nationals: Need for Immediate Compliance',[16] with 69 votes in favour, four against (Israel, Liberia, Marshall Islands and USA) and 66 abstentions. The Resolution makes an urgent call for the full and immediate application of the ICJ's judgment in *Avena*. According to the US representative's explanation before the vote, the US negative vote should not be interpreted as a repudiation of US international obligations regarding consular notification and access, which the US Government continues to take very seriously. The US Government notes that the US Supreme Court held, in *Medellín v Texas*,[17] that the ICJ's *Avena* decision does not constitute directly enforceable federal law and that US obligations could be discharged through the adoption of federal legislation. Accordingly, legislation that would facilitate actions consistent with the ICJ's *Avena* judgment in the USA was included in the US President's Fiscal Year 2019 budget request and the US Department of State has engaged directly with relevant state authorities in the USA, urging them to take the necessary steps to give effect to the ICJ's *Avena* decision.

The US Executive branch might have been trying its best to comply with the ICJ's rulings, thereby showing good faith in the performance of the obligations as ordered by the ICJ. However, why did not the US Government introduce the said legislation sooner? In this respect, the USA has fallen short of the obligation under Article 27 of the VCLT, which codifies a rule of customary international law. The Permanent Court of International Justice (PCIJ), the ICJ's predecessor, has ruled that 'a State which has contracted valid international obligations is bound to make in its legislation such modifications as may be necessary to ensure the fulfilment of the obligations undertaken'[18] and that a State 'cannot adduce as against another State its own Constitution with a view to evading obligations incumbent upon it under international law or treaties in force'.[19]

Regionally, the human rights protection under the 1950 European Convention on Human Rights (ECHR)[20] is the most developed of all. ECHR States Parties have the primary responsibility to protect the human rights enshrined in the

---

[16] A/73/257 (23 Jan 2019).

[17] 552 US 491 (2008).

[18] *Exchange of Greek and Turkish Populations*, Advisory Opinion, 1925, PCIJ, Ser B, No 10, p 20.

[19] *Treatment of Polish Nationals and Other Persons of Polish Origin or Speech in the Danzig Territory*, Advisory Opinion, 1932, PCIJ, Ser A/B, No 44, p 24.

[20] ETS 5.

ECHR and they may exceed their ECHR obligations by according more or better protection of human rights under their respective domestic regimes.

On the positive side, domestic courts of ECHR States Parties have given effect to judgments of the European Court of Human Rights (ECtHR) and at times they rely on these judgments to safeguard against constitutional changes by the government that would lower national human rights protection and/or reviews.[21] The ECtHR judgments have even led to a reconsideration of constitutional interpretation by a domestic court and to law reform.[22]

Nonetheless, the ECtHR receives tens of thousands of new cases every year, causing a backlog of more than 113,000 cases in 2012, for example, and with only 58 per cent of the judgments rendered between 1960 and 2005 being resolved or closed, and merely a 48 per cent compliance rate.[23] Several problematic cases relate mainly to a limited number of States that persistently refuse to comply with the judgments.[24] In the case of Russia, there are on average more than 1,000 non-executed judgments pending.[25] The most notable of these cases is the ECtHR's judgment in 2014 in the *Yukos* case, in which the ECtHR ordered Russia to pay €1.9 billion in pecuniary damages, the largest ever ordered by the ECtHR, to the former shareholders of the now-defunct Yukos oil company for Russia's violation of their rights under the ECHR.[26] The Russian Constitutional Court's judgment in January 2017 rules that Russia does not have to pay the damages since that ECtHR's judgment violates the Russian Constitution.[27]

---

[21]   Jacek Chlebny, 'How a National Judge Implements Judgments of the Strasbourg Court' in Anja Seibert-Fohr and Mark E Villiger (eds), *Judgments of the European Court of Human Rights – Effects and Implementation* (Nomos 2014) 237; Andreas Paulus, 'From Implementation to Translation: Applying the ECtHR Judgments in the Domestic Legal Orders' in ibid 267.

[22]   Thomas Giegerich, 'The Struggle by the German Courts and Legislature to Transpose the Strasbourg Case Law on Preventive Detention into German Law' in Seibert-Fohr and Villiger (eds), *Judgments of the European Court of Human Rights* 207.

[23]   Eric A Posner, *Twilight of Human Rights Law* (OUP 2014) 48–9.

[24]   Giselle Gori, 'Compliance' in Dinah Shelton (ed.), *The Oxford Handbook of International Human Rights Law* (OUP 2013) 893, 910.

[25]   Bill Bowring, 'Russia's Cases in the ECtHR and the Question of Implementation' in Lauri Mälsoo and Wolfgang Benedek (eds), *Russia and the European Court of Human Rights: The Strasbourg Effect* (CUP 2017) 188.

[26]   *OAO Neftnayana Kompaniya Yukos v Russia*, App No 14902/04, Judgment (Just Satisfaction) of 31 July 2014 (2014) 59 EHRR SE12.

[27]   Constitutional Court of the Russian Federation Judgment No 1-P of 19 Jan 2017, http://www.ksrf.ru/en/Decision/Judgments/Documents/2017_January_19_1-P.pdf, accessed 21 Aug 2018.

Another oft-cited case of non-compliance is the UK's refusal to comply with the ECtHR's judgment in *Hirst v United Kingdom (No 2)*[28] holding the UK's blanket ban on British prisoners exercising the right to vote in elections to be incompatible with the ECHR. Terminating the ban would be deeply unpopular in the UK – something the UK Government preferred to avoid.[29] The UK's reluctance in this matter was cited by some other ECHR States Parties as grounds for not enforcing other judgments of the ECtHR, thereby undermining the sanctity of the judgments. A compromise solution, what the UK called 'an effective package to ensure compatibility with the *Hirst* judgment', was reached between the UK and the Council of Europe (CoE) in December 2017. The UK has promised to change the warrant of committal to prison to ensure that prisoners are individually notified of their disenfranchisement. In addition, the UK has promised to change its policy and guidance to prisons to make clear that prisoners can register to vote, and can vote, while released on temporary licence. Most prisoners eligible to vote under this solution would likely be on short sentences and would have been granted temporary release, primarily for employment-related reasons. Inmates entitled to vote would include those on remand, committed to prison for contempt of court or for default in paying fines or released on temporary licence or home detention curfew. The UK contends that making voting accessible to prisoners released on temporary licence fits with the UK's proportional system, where those prisoners on home detention curfew and remand can also vote. The number of prisoners so enfranchised is around 100.[30] The compromise was made possible after the Grand Chamber of the ECtHR's 2012 judgment in *Scoppola v Italy (No 3)*.[31] In *Scoppola*, the Grand Chamber confirms the *Hirst (No 2)* judgment by holding that general, automatic and indiscriminate disenfranchisement of all serving prisoners, irrespective of the nature or gravity of their offences, is incompatible with Article 3 (right to free elections) of Protocol No 1 to the ECHR.[32] However, it accepts the argument that each State has a wide discretion as to how to regulate the ban, both as regards the types of offence that should result in the disenfranchisement of the right to vote and as to whether disenfranchisement should be ordered by a judge in an individual case or should result from general application of a law. The Grand Chamber rules that the disenfranchise-

---

[28]   (2006) 42 EHRR 41.

[29]   Courtney Hillebrecht, *Domestic Politics and International Human Rights Tribunals: The Problem of Compliance* (CUP 2014) 109–11.

[30]   'Council of Europe accepts UK compromise on prisoner voting rights', *The Guardian* (7 Dec 2017) https://www.theguardian.com/politics/2017/dec/07/council-of-europe-accepts-uk-compromise-on-prisoner-voting-rights, accessed 21 Aug 2018.

[31]   *Scoppola v Italy* (2013) 56 EHRR 19.

[32]   ETS No 9.

ment of convicted prisoners provided for under Italian law is not tantamount to the general, automatic and indiscriminate measure that has led it to find a violation of Article 3 of Protocol No 1 in *Hirst (No 2)* since the Italian law in question takes care to adapt the measure to the particular circumstances of a case, particularly the length of the sentence.

An in-depth study, published in 2014, of the problem of governments' non-compliance with the rulings of the Inter-American Court of Human Rights (IACtHR) and the ECtHR has reached the following conclusions. Compliance with international human rights courts' rulings is inherently a domestic affair since the rulings are not self-executing but need to be implemented by the State concerned. The Executive and the other domestic agencies responsible for the implementation of the rulings use compliance to advance their domestic policy objectives, such as signalling a commitment to human rights, particularly to domestic audiences; advancing and legitimizing domestic human rights reform; and providing political safeguards against contentious or politically divisive policies. On average, the ECtHR has a 48 per cent compliance rate in respect of the total of 2,614 rulings under study, whereas the newer IACtHR has a 34 per cent compliance rate in respect of the total 359 rulings under study. Ireland has the highest compliance rate of 80 per cent with the ECtHR's rulings, followed by the Netherlands at 78 per cent and the UK and Sweden at 71 per cent each, with Croatia having the lowest compliance rate at 22 per cent. Russia has a compliance rate of 41 per cent and an in-depth analysis shows that it has little to lose as well as little to gain from non-compliance. With respect to the IACtHR, Chile has the highest rate of compliance with its rulings – at 81 per cent – followed by Bolivia at 75 per cent, leaving the other States far behind. Moreover, States pick and choose among the types of obligations they are demanded by the courts to comply with, with reparations being the obligations States have complied with the most, followed somewhat down the road by the States providing symbolic redress through the acknowledgement of their responsibility and honouring the victims. The most obvious way to improve compliance is to focus on the domestic politics behind compliance and by a two-step process. First, look for governments' motivation for compliance so that such motivation can be supported by the relevant stakeholders for governments to achieve their objectives. Second, focus on domestic institutional capacity building to handle human rights issues domestically by strengthening the rule of law and providing redress for human rights abuses. All stakeholders should be made aware of the rulings so that they can participate in these two steps appropriately.[33]

---

[33] Hillebrecht, *Domestic Politics and International Human Rights Tribunals* 3, 11–18, 29–40, 48–9, 114–21, 133, 135–7, 155–7. See also Gori, 'Compliance' 893.

Another empirical study on the phenomenon of non-compliance with the ECtHR's judgments, published in 2019, concludes that the ECtHR should adopt a more assertive approach to damages and adopt punitive damages since the choice of remedy affects compliance, and aggravated or punitive damages appear to be an ideal option to prod States into compliance. However, the current case law of the ECtHR presents several obstacles to the introduction of punitive damages, thereby making the ECtHR fail to incentivize States to change their behaviour to comply with its judgments. Only in one decision – *Cyprus v Turkey*[34] – have the awards been sufficiently high and unpredictable, as well as having been openly labelled as punitive, to fulfil the criteria of punitive damages. The Grand Chamber of the ECtHR awarded the Cypriot Government aggregate sums of €30 million for non-pecuniary damage suffered by the surviving relatives of 1,456 missing persons, and €60 million for non-pecuniary damage suffered by the enclaved residents of the Karpas peninsula whose human rights were violated by Turkey. Although Turkey has refused to pay the damages as of this writing, within a few months of the 2014 decision, Turkey started putting in place a domestic scheme for restitution, exchange or compensation for those deprived of property. Turkey has also begun to provide access for experts to military zones so that the excavations of those missing can be started as well as to archives to determine the location of remains and so forth. This suggests that unpredictable, high-value judgments may nudge States to begin to redress the underlying violation. Although, in a system that relies on voluntary compliance by States, such damages are unlikely to be paid out, they may nevertheless encourage States to conduct a cost–benefit analysis and conclude that it is in their best interest to get rid of structural/systemic problems hindering compliance with judgments of the ECtHR rather than to continue the violation.[35]

The Copenhagen Declaration adopted by the High Level Conference of the 47 CoE Member States in April 2018[36] sums up the problem of non-compliance in the ECHR system as one of ineffective national implementation of the ECHR, particularly in relation to serious systemic and structural human rights problems,[37] and calls upon ECHR States Parties to fulfil their responsibility to implement and enforce the ECHR at the national level.[38]

In a global human rights treaty context, in 1999 a study was undertaken in collaboration with the Office of the High Commissioner for Human Rights

[34]   App No 25781/94, Judgment of 12 May 2014.
[35]   Veronika Fikfak, 'Changing State Behaviour: Damages before the European Court of Human Rights' (2019) 29 EJIL 1091.
[36]   https://rm.coe.int/copenhagen-declaration/16807b915c, accessed 1 Sept 2018.
[37]   Ibid §12.
[38]   Ibid §15.

to investigate the influence of human rights treaties and their supervisory mechanisms in ensuring the realization of the norms these treaties espouse in States Parties thereto and to make recommendations for their reform. The six treaties studied were the 1965 International Convention on the Elimination of All Forms of Racial Discrimination (CERD);[39] the ICESCR; the ICCPR and its First Optional Protocol;[40] the 1979 Convention on the Elimination of All Forms of Discrimination against Women (CEDAW);[41] the 1984 Convention against Torture and Other Cruel, Inhuman or Degrading Treatment or Punishment (CAT);[42] and the 1989 Convention on the Rights of the Child (CRC).[43] The four States from each of the five UN regions selected for this study were Australia, Brazil, Canada, Colombia, Czech Republic, Egypt, Estonia, Finland, India, Iran, Jamaica, Japan, Mexico, Philippines, Romania, Russia, Senegal, South Africa, Spain and Zambia.[44]

The study shows that, according to all the available evidence, these treaties had an enormous influence in shaping the worldwide understanding among stakeholders of basic human rights and their limits imposed by the conditions under which the treaties operated. The international system had its greatest impact where treaty norms had been made part of domestic law more or less spontaneously (for example as part of constitutional and legislative reform), and not as a result of norm enforcement (through reporting, individual complaints or confidential inquiry procedures). As regards international norm enforcement, its influence was very unevenly spread among the States studied. International enforcement mechanisms used by the treaty bodies had had a very limited demonstrable impact thus far, partly due to their inefficiencies (backlogs, overlaps, vagueness in findings and so forth). However, even focused and relevant concluding observations and views were routinely ignored. Strengthening the monitoring mechanisms had to be supplemented by creative efforts to ensure that treaty norms were internalized in the domestic legal and cultural system and that they were enforced on the domestic level.[45] Special attention should be paid to regions and States that had low engagement with treaty bodies, and technical assistance with reporting should be given to them.[46]

---

[39]   660 UNTS 195.
[40]   999 UNTS 302.
[41]   1249 UNTS 13.
[42]   1465 UNTS 85.
[43]   1577 UNTS 3.
[44]   Christoff Heyns and Frans Viljoen, 'The Impact of the United Nations Human Rights Treaties on the Domestic Level' (2001) 23 Hum Rts Quarterly 483, 484–6.
[45]   Ibid 487–9.
[46]   Ibid 535.

It should be noted in this connection that one study on UN human rights treaty bodies published in 2018 concludes that domestic courts of States Parties to the ICCPR and, where applicable, the Optional Protocol thereto, have frequently taken into account the Human Rights Committee's general comments and recommendations, which inform domestic judges of the substance of the applicable law of the ICCPR while allowing flexibility to these judges in implementing them at the domestic level. By contrast, the Committee's concluding observations and comments addressed to a particular State Party are occasionally challenged and deliberately avoided by domestic courts of that State. So are findings on the Committee's individual communications or petitions pursuant to the Optional Protocol. These latter two outcomes of the Committee's deliberations are usually considered by the domestic courts on a case-by-case basis, with the courts scrutinizing their persuasiveness as well as the Committee's impartiality as perceived by these courts.[47]

The 1999 study discovers factors limiting the impact of the treaties as including governmental resistance to international supervision, recommendations and views. In many instances, the widespread ignorance of the treaty system in government circles, among lawyers and in civil societies around the world, effectively impeded any impact that the treaties might otherwise have had. So did the absence of a domestic human rights culture and socio-economic factors such as illiteracy of the population and poverty. Some customs, traditions and religious practices also limited the impact of the system. Political instability and association of treaties with unpopular political causes undermined the treaty impact. Lack of independence of the judiciary, poor national human rights institutions and lack of coordination among stakeholders were some of the negative factors against the impact of the treaties. The UN human rights system was seen as toothless, slow, distant and lacking a domestic profile. Human rights were sometimes seen as a tool of Western imperialism (as in the case of Iran) or viewed at least as disproportionately Western oriented (as in the case of Japan). In Egypt the work of human rights organizations was discounted because of their foreign funding. Sometimes the lack of impact might be ascribed (at least partially) to the nature of the treaty itself, as in the case of the ICESCR, widely seen as a treaty that sets goals but does not impose legal obligations.[48]

Factors found by the study of 1999 to enhance the impact of the human rights treaties were a strong domestic constituency, be it governmental or

---

[47] Machiko Kanetake, 'UN Human Rights Treaty Monitoring Bodies before Domestic Courts' (2018) 67 ICLQ 201, 207–31.

[48] Heyns and Viljoen, 'The Impact of the United Nations Human Rights Treaties on the Domestic Level' 517–22.

non-governmental (including NGOs and the media), and a certain minimum level of commitment to human rights norms in the domestic system. Where the granting of membership of a strong regional trade network was conditional on a State's human rights record, the impact of the treaties would be strengthened as effective international human rights protection often followed trade patterns.[49]

According to one academic analysis published in 2002, (1) nation States with worse human rights records appear to ratify treaties at a higher rate than those with better records; (2) treaty ratification is associated with worse human rights practices than expected; (3) enforcement procedures reduce non-compliance; and (4) ratification of a treaty is associated with better practices in full-fledged democracies.[50] It maintains that some States ratify human rights treaties as a symbolic gesture of their commitment to human rights and, consequently, reduce international political pressure for them to promote human rights at home. These States purportedly get away with adverse consequences of non-compliance with the treaties since unenforced treaty rules do not require any actual changes in State practice. Therefore, contends the analysis, ratification of human rights treaties by such States actually provides an incentive for them to increase human rights violations as pressure for real improvement in human rights has been relieved after the ratification.[51] This line of thinking is shared by critics of the usefulness of human rights treaties. A question is raised as to why serious violations of human rights continue to persist in States party to the relevant human rights treaties and 'even the most humane and liberal European countries have violated the human rights of migrants and other non-citizens'.[52]

The conclusions of the 2002 analysis are strongly disputed by another analysis, published in 2003.[53] The latter reasons that the incorporation of human rights norms into the domestic sphere is a process in which treaty law plays an important role. Ratification might essentially represent the initiation, culmination or reconfiguration of a domestic political struggle. A government's decision to ratify might be preceded by other actions of international legal significance (such as affirming the treaty's fundamental principles, pledging to join the treaty and signing the treaty) and followed by others (such as adopting implementing legislation and withdrawing reservations that would effectively

[49]   Ibid 522–4.

[50]   Oona A Hathaway, 'Do Human Rights Treaties Make a Difference?' (2002) 112 Yale LJ 1935, 1999.

[51]   Ibid 2005–7.

[52]   Posner, *Twilight of Human Rights Law* 5 and also 2–4, 7, 59–66, 78.

[53]   Ryan Goodman and Derek Jinks, 'Measuring the Effects of Human Rights Treaties' (2003) 14 EJIL 171.

dilute the treaty obligations). The most important moment in the incorporation process for any given State might be the decision of some other States with similar human rights stances to follow suit. In addition, any analysis must account for strategies governments often adopt in response to improved enforcement of a human rights norm. For example, in Latin America in the late 1970s and early 1980s, levels of torture, political imprisonment and unfair trials declined but they were replaced with forced 'disappearances', which human rights groups and victims eventually succeeded in reducing as well. Measuring one area of human rights should, therefore, also concurrently measure the other areas of human rights. Another statistical difficulty is that analyses usually only measure recorded and reported human rights violations, not actual violations. By improving human rights conditions, access to information on the extent of human rights violations correspondingly increases and, for many governments, the decision to ratify indicates their willingness to increase access to information on and dialogue about domestic human rights practices. Human rights treaty ratification also increases the salience and legitimacy of human rights concepts as well as greater legitimacy and prominence of human rights NGOs in their struggle against the repressive regime of the State that ratifies the relevant human rights treaty. Individuals likewise become more informed of their human rights, especially where treaty ratification enables them to initiate individual legal claims based on the treaty's substantive guarantees. An assessment of the consequences of ratification may be biased if it is based on biased data/information, such as biased official reports by a foreign government with vested interests in the State concerned. Furthermore, if treaty ratification is virtually costless, why has or have there been non-ratification or various forms of qualified participation (such as ratification with reservations or formal notices of derogation) of various human rights treaties? Conversely, why have some States with bad human rights records ratified human rights treaties at all, given that joining the treaties would formally signal these States' acceptance of the human rights principles embodied in the treaties which the 'signalled States' and other stakeholders expect the ratifying/signalling States to uphold? This analysis of 2003 concludes that broad ratification of human rights treaties plays an important role in the process of building national and international human rights cultures.

One example of the seriousness of a decision by a State to become or not to become party to a human rights treaty is Malaysia's decision related to CERD, to which the Human Rights Commission of Malaysia wants Malaysia to become party. The newly elected Malaysian Government at first appeared to support this idea but had to back off after facing strong opposition from Malay–Muslim civil society groups and the two largest Malay opposition parties, who feared that by becoming party to CERD Malaysia would be bound to curtail certain privileges enjoyed by ethnic Malays as enshrined in Article

153 of the Constitution of Malaysia. Malaysia and Brunei are the only two out of the 57 Member States of the Organisation of Islamic Cooperation that are not yet party to CERD.[54]

According to another empirical study, human rights in a State improve after the State becomes party to key human rights treaties with which the government in that State is under pressure to comply. Human rights norms are invoked to resolve conflicts within a society and courts can play only a secondary role to the political process as their judgments are respected most enthusiastically when public opinions agree.[55] Gross human rights violations, such as apartheid in South Africa, have been brought to an end not by court judgments but by non-judicial means of international pressure.[56]

An analysis published in 2017 drawing on experimental governance (EG) theory supports the optimistic conclusions regarding the working of the human rights treaty system. EG has five key features: (1) initial reflection and identification of a broadly shared perception of a common problem across diverse participating units of States; (2) the articulation of a framework understanding with open-ended goals; (3) implementation of these broadly articulated goals by contextually situated or 'lower level' actors, entailing the active participation of key stakeholders with knowledge of local conditions and discretion to adapt the framework norms to these different contexts; (4) continuous provision of feedback to the 'centre' from local contexts and by relevant stakeholders, allowing for reporting and monitoring across a range of contexts, with results subject to non-hierarchical or peer review; and (5) periodic and routine re-evaluation/revision of the original goals and the existing practices in the light of the results of the ongoing review and of the shared purposes. At times, EG operates behind measures undertaken to incentivize cooperation such as conditional aid to, or boycott of goods from, the targeted

---

[54] Shannon Teo, 'Thousands in KL for street protest against UN rights convention; rally ends peacefully', *New Straits Times* (8 Dec 2018) https://www.straitstimes .com/asia/se-asia/thousands-gather-for-kl-rally-against-un-rights-convention, accessed 12 Aug 2019.

[55] Michael Haas, *International Human Rights: A Comprehensive Introduction* (2nd edn, Routledge 2014) 516. Also, Samantha Besson, 'The Legitimate Authority of International Human Rights Law: On the Reciprocal Legitimation of Domestic and International Human Rights' in Andreas Føllesdal, Johan Karlsson Schaffer and Geir Ulfstein (eds), *The Legitimacy of International Human Rights Regimes: Legal, Political and Philosophical Perspectives* (CUP 2014) 32, 76–7; Cf Beth A Simmons, *Mobilizing for Human Rights: International Law in Domestic Politics* (CUP 2009) 4–5, 12–14, 59–65, 68–108, 112–55.

[56] David P Forsythe, *Human Rights in International Relations* (4th edn, CUP 2018) 16.

State.[57] Applying EG to assess the qualitative and quantitative results of States becoming party to CEDAW, the CRC and the CRPD, respectively, leads to the conclusion that the human rights treaty system does work. Positive impacts of the treaty system include an increased degree of political liberalization even in repressive States, promoting a reasonably active domestic civil society strongly engaged with the UN treaty reporting system, which can be a catalyst for reform through an iterative process pushing for and promoting change, and facilitating genuinely two-way interaction and engagement between locally situated stakeholders and internationally situated actors and institutions such as the UN International Children's Emergency Fund or international NGOs.[58]

On the whole, there is reason to believe that the perception that the world is worse off in terms of human rights derives from the fact that we care more and know more about human rights than ever before and human beings tend to be 'cognitive misers' who pay more attention to prominent negative or miserable information.[59] The outcomes of IHRL assessment among human rights scholars differ depending on whether they use empirical comparisons or comparison to the ideal of human rights.[60] In this light, global human rights trends may be far more positive than pessimists would have us believe, with less violence and fewer human rights violations than in the past. For example, in 1977 there were merely 16 States that had abolished the death penalty, compared with 140 States in 2017 and famine has declined proportionately.[61]

One method to pre-empt the issue of complying with IHRL obligations is by not giving access to human rights mandate holders, or UN special rapporteurs on particular human rights issues, to visit the nation State in question. A very small minority of States consistently decline approaches by the special rapporteurs for a visit. In general, a State tends to accord importance to the 'comfort level' it has with regard to the human rights issue entrusted to the requesting special rapporteur as well as the person of the special rapporteur himself or herself. The State subject of the request may consider some special rapporteurs, as evidenced by their past records, to be partial, biased or prone to write unbalanced reports after their visits. The State in question also balances the gains it expects from the visit by a special rapporteur, on the one hand, and any risk of the visit ending up tarnishing its human rights image even further, on the other hand. Such a visit is, at least, of symbolic significance, bearing witness to the visited State's willingness to show transparency and accounta-

---

[57]   Gráinne de Búrca, 'Human Rights Experimentalism' (2017) 111 AJIL 277, 281–2.

[58]   Ibid, 279–80, 298–314.

[59]   Sikkink, *Evidence for Hope* 14, 159–66.

[60]   Ibid 31–2, 44.

[61]   Ibid 141–51, 179.

bility by opening up for international human rights scrutiny. Civil society as well as the national human rights institution in the State in question must help convince the government of that State how the gains ensuing from the visit far outweigh all the combined potential risks arising therefrom.

National human rights institutions have a vital role to play in monitoring human rights in the State. As of 2017 there were almost 120 such institutions across the globe. They need formal institutional safeguards in order to perform their task efficiently even in authoritarian regimes. Those with the mandate to receive complaints from aggrieved individuals enjoy broad bases of support in the society where they operate. At the same time, national human rights institutions need to be subject to international peer review to ensure that they perform their functions without coming under the undue influence of the authorities they are supposed to keep in check from abusing human rights.[62]

Realization of human rights goes beyond compliance with human rights treaties as it involves a comprehensive societal process in domestic societies. The following factors are especially relevant: the independent and actual functioning of domestic courts; the status and power of the domestic judiciary in the national power structures; political systems and realities on the ground together with economic conditions associated with the realization of human rights, especially socio-economic rights; religions; and cultures and the power and influences of various stakeholders, including NGOs.[63]

UNGA Resolution 60/251 setting up the Human Rights Council (HRC) specifically acknowledges in a preambular paragraph an important role played by non-governmental organizations at the national, regional and international levels, in the promotion and protection of human rights. NGOs have their views heard through the submission in one of the three formal reports for the HRC's universal periodic review of each State. Moreover, NGOs have played significant roles in regional as well as international courts or tribunals relating to human rights.[64] As of 2016, there were 40,673 human rights NGOs across the globe, 21,276 of which were based in Europe, 10,257 in North

---

[62] Katerina Linos and Tom Pegram, 'What Works in Human Rights Institutions?' (2017) 111 AJIL 628, *passim* and 641, 686–7; Gauthier de Beco and Rachel Murray, *A Commentary on the Paris Principles on National Human Rights Institutions* (CUP 2015) 62–90, 135–47; Allison Corkery and Duncan Wilson, 'Building Bridges: National Human Rights Institutions and Economic, Social and Cultural Rights' in Riedel et al (eds), *Economic, Social and Cultural Rights in International Law* 473.

[63] Yasuaki Onuma, *International Law in a Transcivilizational World* (CUP 2017) 408–9, 417. See further, Forsythe, *Human Rights in International Relations* ch. 7. Simmons (*Mobilizing for Human Rights: International Law in Domestic Politics* 378) stresses the significance of 'domestic ownership' in human rights advocacy.

[64] Heidi Nichols Haddad, *The Hidden Hands of Justice: NGOs, Human Rights and International Courts* (CUP 2018) *passim*.

America, 3,836 in Asia, 2,396 in Africa, 1,049 in Oceania (of which 819 were in Australia alone) and 1,859 in Latin America and the Caribbean.[65] Although the precise impact of greater presence of human rights NGOs in targeting of States within global human rights forums remains uncertain,[66] these NGOs' concerted efforts internationally and domestically as part of the human rights movement can play a crucial role in exerting influence in international law making and the crystallization of new rights, and act as watchdogs to help ensure that States do comply with their human rights obligations.[67]

2.   ENFORCEMENT

When States do not comply with their international human rights obligations, enforcing IHRL, like enforcing other areas of international law, is quite different from enforcing domestic law. Officially, there is no world police to enforce international law, including IHRL, and, in reality, the more powerful a nation State, the more likely it can escape punishment for violation of international law.[68]

Where a State Party to a human rights treaty is aggrieved by another State Party's violation of the treaty, the former may sue the latter before a competent international court or tribunal. Nevertheless, there is usually an inordinately high number of States Parties making reservations to the acceptance of compulsory jurisdiction of such court or tribunal. Even where the parties to a dispute have not entered such reservations, they must fulfil preconditions stipulated in the human rights treaty in question before the court or tribunal can take up the case. As the ICJ observed in *Application of the International Convention on the Elimination of All Forms of Racial Discrimination (Georgia v Russian Federation)*, at the time when CERD was being elaborated, the idea of submitting to the compulsory settlement of disputes by the ICJ was not readily acceptable to a number of States. While States could make reservations to the compulsory dispute settlement provisions of CERD, additional limitations to resort to judicial settlement in the form of prior negotiations and

[65]   Marlies Glasius and Doutje Lettinga, 'Global Civil Society and Human Rights' in Michael Goodhart (ed.), *Human Rights: Politics and Practice* (3rd edn, OUP 2016) 147, 151.
[66]   Christine Chinkin, 'Human Rights and the Politics of Representation: Is There a Role for International Law?' in Michael Byers (ed.), *The Role of Law in International Politics: Essays in International Relations and International Law* (OUP 2000) 131, 145.
[67]   Aryeh Neier, *The International Human Rights Movement: A History* (Princeton University Press 2012) *passim*, esp ch. 10; Sikkink, *Evidence for Hope* 247.
[68]   Cf Rosa Freedman, *Failing to Protect: The UN and the Politicisation of Human Rights* (C Hurst & Co 2014) 1–19, 34–5, 87–93.

other settlement procedures without fixed time limits were provided for with a view to facilitating wider acceptance of CERD by States.[69] In that particular case, the ICJ found that Georgia had made no genuine attempts to negotiate matters in respect of a dispute concerning 'actions [by Russia] on and around the territory of Georgia' in breach of CERD. As such, Georgia failed to fulfil a precondition of prior negotiations before the seisin of the ICJ as required by Article 22 of CERD.

On 11 June 2018 Qatar instituted proceedings against the UAE at the ICJ with regard to alleged violations of CERD, to which both States are parties. Qatar submits that the UAE has enacted and implemented a series of discriminatory measures directed at Qataris based expressly on their national origin. According to Qatar, on and following 5 June 2017, the UAE expelled all Qataris within its borders; prohibited them from entering or passing through the UAE, closed the UAE's airspace and seaports to Qatar and Qataris, interfered with the rights of Qataris who own property in the UAE, limited the rights of Qataris to any speech deemed to be in support of or opposed to the actions against Qatar, and shut down the local offices of Al Jazeera Media Network and blocked the transmission of Al Jazeera and other Qatari media outlets. Qatar claims that those measures interfere with a number of rights, including the right to marriage and choice of spouse; result in violations of the rights to freedom of opinion and expression, the right to education and the right to work; and impact the rights of Qataris to own property and enjoy equal treatment before tribunals.[70] Qatar has entered no reservation to CERD, whereas the UAE has made a reservation that its accession to CERD 'shall in no way amount to recognition of nor the establishment of any treaty relations with Israel'. As of this writing, the ICJ has yet to deliver its judgment on this case.

Apart from the possibility of a directly injured State Party to a human rights treaty to sue the injuring State Party before a competent international court or tribunal, the right of any State to take legal action in vindication of a public interest (*actio popularis*) at the international level is quite limited. In *South West Africa (Second Phase)*, the ICJ rules that neither Liberia nor Ethiopia has legal standing to challenge the apartheid policy implemented by South Africa in South West Africa (Namibia) in disregard of the League of Nations Mandate entrusted to South Africa to promote the material and moral well-being and the social progress of the inhabitants of South West Africa. The ICJ rejects the principle of 'sacred trust of civilization' cited by Liberia and Ethiopia as

---

[69] [2011] ICJ Rep 70, 129 [147].
[70] *Application of the International Convention on the Elimination of All Forms of Racial Discrimination (Qatar v United Arab Emirates), Provisional Measures* ICJ Order of 23 July 2018.

a basis of their legal standing, treating it as a mere moral political ideal. The ICJ affirms that international law as it stood in 1966 did not know 'an *actio populari*s, or right resident in any member of the international community in vindication of a public interest'.[71]

This hardly changes even after the reference to the concept of *erga omnes* in an oft-cited dictum of the ICJ in *Barcelona Traction* that, in view of the importance of certain rights, all States have a legal interest in their protection. Such obligations of a State towards the international community as a whole are obligations *erga omnes* and derive, for example, from the outlawing of acts of aggression and of genocide, as also from the principles and rules concerning the basic rights of the human person, including protection from slavery and racial discrimination. Some of the corresponding rights of protection have entered into the body of general international law; others are conferred by international instruments of a universal or quasi-universal character.[72]

The ICJ has subsequently narrowed down the scope of obligations *erga omnes*. In *Case Concerning East Timor (Portugal v Australia)*, Portugal submits, inter alia, that Australia has acted unlawfully by concluding an agreement on maritime areas lying between Australia and East Timor, then occupied by Indonesia, in disregard of the right of the East Timorese to self-determination. The case was dismissed because Indonesia did not consent to the ICJ's jurisdiction. The ICJ notes that Portugal's assertion that the right of peoples to self-determination has an *erga omnes* character is irreproachable, and that the principle of self-determination of peoples has been recognized by the UN Charter and in the ICJ's jurisprudence and is one of the essential principles of contemporary international law. The ICJ holds, however, that the *erga omnes* character of a norm and the rule of consent to jurisdiction are two different things – whatever the nature of the obligations invoked, be they ones of *erga omnes* or otherwise, the ICJ cannot rule on the lawfulness of the conduct of a State when its judgment would imply an evaluation of the lawfulness of the conduct of another State not a party to the case. Where this is so, the Court cannot act, even if the right in question is a right *erga omnes*.[73] In essence, the ICJ has ruled that even if one State has legal standing because of the *erga omnes* nature of the rights being violated, it cannot take the offending State to the ICJ if the latter State does not consent to the ICJ's jurisdiction in that particular case. This rationale is followed in the ICJ's judgment in *Armed Activities on the Territory of the Congo (New Application: 2002) (Democratic*

---

[71]   *South West Africa Cases (Ethiopia v South Africa; Liberia v South Africa)* (Second Phase) [1966] ICJ Rep 6, 34–5 [52]–[54], 47 [88].

[72]   *Barcelona Traction, Light and Power Company Limited (Belgium v Spain)* Second Phase [1970] ICJ Rep 3, 32 [33]–[34].

[73]   [1995] ICJ Rep 90, 102 [29].

Republic of the Congo v Rwanda), Jurisdiction and Admissibility,[74] where DR Congo argues, inter alia, that Rwanda's reservation to Article IX of the 1948 Convention on the Prevention and Punishment of the Crime of Genocide,[75] as well as to other similar provisions and compromissory clauses, seeks to prevent the ICJ from fulfilling its mission of safeguarding peremptory norms, including the prohibition of genocide, and must therefore be regarded as null and void.[76] This contention is rejected outright by the ICJ, reiterating its ruling in *East Timor*. The ICJ adds that the fact that a dispute relates to compliance with a norm having a peremptory character (*jus cogens*), which is assuredly the case with regard to the prohibition of genocide, cannot of itself provide a basis for the jurisdiction of the ICJ to entertain that dispute without the consent of the parties.[77]

Only those States honestly convinced that their conduct does not fall foul of international law would be willing to submit themselves to this kind of scrutiny by the ICJ.[78]

The ECHR, the world's most developed regional human rights regime, provides in Article 46 that its States Parties shall undertake to abide by the final judgments of the ECtHR in any case where they are parties. The Article entrusts the Committee of the Ministers of the Council of Europe to supervise the execution by States of the ECtHR's judgments.[79] In December 2017 the Committee of the Ministers instituted the first-ever infringement proceedings for non-implementation of a judgment of the ECtHR – against Azerbaijan concerning the *Mammadov* case.[80] Previously, the Committee, being a political body composed of representatives from each CoE Member State, was either unwilling to use this mechanism or never attained the requisite two-thirds majority to refer to the ECtHR the question whether a CoE Member State had fulfilled its obligation to comply with the ECtHR's judgment in a case to which the State was a party.

---

[74] [2006] ICJ Reports 6.

[75] 78 UNTS 277.

[76] [2006] ICJ Reports 6, 50 [121].

[77] Ibid 32 [64] and 52 [125]. See also Farid Turab Ahmadov, *The Right of Actio Popularis before International Courts and Tribunals* (Brill Nijhoff 2018).

[78] Cf Maurizio Rogazzi, *The Concept of International Obligations Erga Omnes* (Clarendon Press 1997) ch. 10.

[79] See further, Linos-Alexander Sicilianos, 'The Role of the European Court of Human Rights in the Execution of its Own Judgments: Reflection on Article 46 ECHR' in Seibert-Fohr and Villiger (eds), *Judgments of the European Court of Human Rights* 285.

[80] *Ilgar Mammadov v Azerbaijan* App No 15172/13 (ECHR 22 May 2014); *Ilgar Mammadov v Azerbaijan (No 2)* App No 919/15 (ECHR 16 Nov 2017).

In two judgments, the ECtHR rules that Azerbaijan has violated the ECHR in relation to, inter alia, its arrest on 4 February 2013 on charges of inciting mass violence and pre-trial detention of Ilgar Mammadov, a prominent Azerbaijani opposition politician who was planning to run for president in 2013, without any evidence to reasonably suspect him of having committed a criminal offence. Mammadov was sentenced to seven years' imprisonment in 2014. The reasons why the Committee instituted this infringement proceeding for the first time, after the CoE's repeated calls to Azerbaijan to comply with the ECtHR's judgments, could be because Mammadov is an internationally well-known political figure who has support from the EU, the CoE and human rights NGOs. Besides, Azerbaijan is a relatively easier State to target than other non-complying CoE Member States in Western Europe, Turkey and Russia, infringement proceedings against which might further alienate them away from accepting the ECtHR's judgments. Finally, determining Azerbaijan's non-compliance would not be complicated – since the ECtHR has already concluded that the charges against Mammadov were unfounded and the criminal proceedings against him unfair, releasing him from prison would be the only available remedy. Unfortunately, this kind of infringement proceeding does not entail any legal sanction. Should the Grand Chamber of the ECtHR determine that Azerbaijan has not complied with its judgments, the ECtHR would have to refer the case back to the Committee for consideration of the measures to be taken, as provided in Article 46(5) of the ECHR.[81] On 13 August 2018, the Shaki Court of Appeals in Azerbaijan had his sentence reviewed and replaced the two remaining years of Mammadov's seven-year imprisonment with a suspended sentence. Mammadov was released from prison on that same day. Amnesty International has called on the Azerbaijani authorities to immediately overturn his conviction and ensure his access to adequate reparations, including compensation, for his unlawful imprisonment.[82]

In addition to the Committee of the Ministers of the CoE, the Parliamentary Assembly of the Council of Europe (PACE), comprising 324 members from the national parliaments of CoE Member States, is entrusted with enforcing human rights in the Member States. Although it has no power to pass binding

---

[81]   Julie-Enni Zastrow and Andreas Zimmermann, 'Council of Europe's Committee of Ministers Starts Infringement Proceedings in Mammadov v Azerbaijan: A Victory for the International Rule of Law?', *EJIL Talk!* (5 Feb 2018) https://www.amnesty.org/en/latest/news/2018/08/azerbaijan-prisoner-of-conscience-ilgar-mammadovs-early-release-is-long-overdue/, accessed 21 Aug 2018.

[82]   Amnesty International, 'Azerbaijan: Prisoner of conscience Ilgar Mammadov's early release is long overdue' (13 Aug 2018) https://www.amnesty.org/en/latest/news/2018/08/azerbaijan-prisoner-of-conscience-ilgar-mammadovs-early-release-is-long-overdue/, accessed 24 Dec 2018.

laws, PACE holds a constant dialogue with governments, national parliaments, other international organizations and civil society on human rights issues. PACE elects judges of the ECtHR from a list of three candidates nominated by each of the States Parties to the ECHR. PACE has the authority to demand action from 47 European governments, who must jointly reply; conduct probes to uncover new facts about human rights violations; question Presidents and Prime Ministers of the Member States on any topic it chooses; observe elections and send delegations to mediate in crisis hot spots; negotiate the terms on which States may join the CoE; inspire new national laws by proposing and giving opinions on treaties; request legal opinions on the laws and constitutions of Member States; and sanction a Member State by recommending its exclusion or suspension. Among PACE's most important accomplishments are: adopting a blueprint of what has subsequently become the ECHR; ending the death penalty in Europe by making it an accession condition; after 1989, helping ex-Communist States move towards democracy; and inspiring a host of national laws by pressing for new conventions and serving as a forum for debating controversial social or political issues.

An interesting development in relation to the enforceability of decisions of human rights treaty bodies has occurred in Spain, one of the States in the 1999 study. In July 2018 the Spanish Supreme Court ruled[83] that the decision of the CEDAW Committee in 2014, finding Spain in violation of certain rights of one Spanish national under CEDAW,[84] is binding on Spain. The Court consequently ordered Spain to pay €600,000 in compensation to the complainant Ángela González for the responsibility of its authorities in relation to the death of her daughter, murdered by her father in an unsupervised visit authorized by a judge. After exhausting local remedies in Spain, the complaint was brought before the CEDAW Committee, which concluded that Spain had failed to act with due diligence in a particularly tragic case of gender-based violence and this amounted to discrimination and the violation of the complainant's human rights under CEDAW. She then sought to enforce the decision of the CEDAW Committee in Spain. The Spanish Government argued that, unlike the ECtHR, there was no administrative mechanism in place to enforce treaty body decisions. The Spanish Supreme Court disagrees. It reasons that although neither CEDAW nor its Optional Protocol establishes the directly enforceable character of decisions on individual complaints, Article 24 of CEDAW

---

[83]   Judgment 1263/2018, 17 July 2018. The present author benefits from the summary and comments on the case by Koldo Casla, 'Supreme Court of Spain: UN treaty body individual decisions are legally binding', *EJIL Talk!* (1 Aug 2018) https://www.ejiltalk.org/supreme-court-of-spain-un-treaty-body-individual-decisions-are-legally-binding/, accessed 24 Aug 2018.
[84]   Communication No 47/2012, Doc CEDAW/C/58/D/47/2012, 15 Aug 2014.

requires States Parties to adopt all necessary measures at the national level to achieve the full realization of the rights recognized therein, while Article 7(4) of the Optional Protocol stipulates that States Parties 'shall give due consideration to the views of the Committee'. Besides, Article 96 of the 1978 Spanish Constitution provides that international treaties form part of the internal legal order in Spain and, pursuant to Article 10(2) of the Constitution, the constitutional bill of rights shall be interpreted in accordance with IHRL. Complying with treaty body decisions is a matter of rule of law and not doing so would breach the principles of legality and legal hierarchy proclaimed in Article 9(3) of the Spanish Constitution, as well as constituting a breach of a legal and constitutional mandate by Spain.

There are, indeed, numerous non-judicial mechanisms, either individually or in combination, to enforce human rights. A State may be held *accountable* before an international body, such as a treaty body with competent jurisdiction, although the binding force of the decisions does vary from one body to another. The State could be *induced* to comply with its human rights obligations in return for conditional foreign aid. The State may be given unconditional foreign *aid* in order to build its capacity to fulfil human rights obligations, especially economic rights. *Domestic* movements may *pressure* the government of the State to be more responsive to human rights within that State. The State may find it necessary to *adapt* itself *to external factors* such as the policies of foreign States and/or non-State actors like international organizations in order to protect its people's human rights. The most drastic form of enforcement is the use of *coercive means* such as economic sanctions or the use of force by a foreign State or group of States in the name of 'humanitarian intervention' against the State accused of serious violations of human rights. Most of the international efforts to promote and defend human rights are perceived to be political rather than legal in nature, owing to the absence of mechanisms for the appellate review of findings of human rights violations or for sanctions against such violations.[85] Some measures seem altruistic, as in the case of the EU's Everything But Arms (EBA) scheme, which allows those classified as the world's least developed States to export anything, apart from armaments, to the EU duty- and quota-free, on conditions that include requiring the States benefiting from the EBA not to be engaged in serious and systematic violation of principles laid down in fundamental human rights and labour rights conventions. Yet it is the EU itself that determines whether such violation has occurred.

---

[85]   Charles R Beitz, *The Idea of Human Rights* (OUP 2009) 33–42; Christian Tomuschat, *Human Rights: Between Idealism and Realism* (3rd edn, OUP 2014) 326–7.

In the field of human rights, if one is in a position to make a difference in preventing their violations or in upholding such rights, there is 'a universal ethical demand' for one to do just that. The choice of actions must permit variation, depending on the choice of priorities, weights and other relevant factors. For instance, in a repressive regime that does not allow open public discussion or free access to information about the outside world, international monitoring and naming and shaming can be an effective means to convince the regime to conform to international human rights norms.[86]

Sanctions against human rights abuses are often piecemeal and not always sustained. For example, the USA pushed for the UN Security Council (UNSC) referring the situation in Darfur, Sudan, to the International Criminal Court for the purpose of prosecution of the Sudanese leadership under the then President Al-Bashir, accused of having perpetrated genocide, war crimes and crimes against humanity in Darfur. The USA has also imposed a series of economic sanctions on Sudan, starting from 1997.[87] In October 2017 the USA lifted a number of economic sanctions on Sudan in response to what the US Government considered to be Sudan's sustained positive actions in the preceding six months, which had largely alleviated human suffering for the people concerned, countered the threats of serious human rights violation by a notorious paramilitary group called the Lord's Resistance Army, and addressed the threat of terrorism.[88] In addition, the US Government supported its decision to ease economic sanctions on Sudan on the grounds that the USA needed to rely on its bilateral relationship with the Sudanese Government to fully implement all UNSC resolutions on North Korea, 'a critically important issue for US national security'.[89] This may seem a selfish reason. A closer look might reveal the US Government's need to appease any possible resistance from its domestic constituencies to the partial lifting of the economic sanctions against Sudan by pointing out another unrelated reason, but one that is of direct interest to the home constituencies – the North Korean threat to US national security. In any event, the USA has not normalized its relations with Sudan as Sudan is still on the US list of States sponsoring terrorism and subject to various UNSC resolutions against it.

---

[86]   Amartya Sen, *The Idea of Justice* (Penguin 2010) 373–4, 387.

[87]   Executive Order No 13067, 62 Fed Reg 59989 (3 Nov 1997), subsequently expanded by Executive Order No 13400, 71 Fed Reg 25483 (26 Apr 2006) and Executive Order No 13412, 71 Fed Reg 61369 (13 Oct 2006).

[88]   Executive Order No 13761, 82 Fed Reg 5331 (13 Jan 2017) conditionally authorizes the future rollback of certain sanctions on Sudan in the light of Sudan's positive actions over the previous six months.

[89]   Ibid.

One study, published in 2013, concludes that enforcing human rights through economic sanctions works when a combinations of factors are at play. First, the sanction is the best tool available and is used for a clearly specified policy goal and broader policy interests. Secondly, there is a framework for continued dialogue between the sanctioning and the targeted States. Thirdly, the sanction should not be utilized solely to punish or isolate the targeted State. Fourthly, the targeted State must understand that unless it complies with the goal of the sanction, it will face more stern measures that will put it in a worse position than it is in now. Finally, the sanction may be commodity specific (such as targeting 'blood diamonds') and/or may target enablers of human rights violations as well (such as smugglers of blood diamonds).[90]

'Humanitarian intervention' by means of the use of force against the State abusing human rights within its border has been subject to extensive debate.[91] Criticisms of humanitarian intervention are grounded on the double standards as well as ensuing setbacks and traps because decisions for such intervention are normally made not with purely humanitarian motives and they frequently entail unintended adverse consequences for the State and its people who are the targets of the intervention.[92]

Some purportedly 'humanitarian' interventions have been criticized as 'pro-democratic [armed] invasions', as in the case of the US armed intervention in Nicaragua in 1982–1984, Panama in 1989 and Haiti in 1994, the aftermath of which is democracy being downgraded in deference to stability.[93] Phrased differently, proponents of democratic and human rights principles at

---

[90] George A Lopez, 'Enforcing Human Rights through Economic Sanctions' in Shelton (ed.), *The Oxford Handbook of International Human Rights Law* 772, 788–91.

[91] Eg, Edward Kwakwa, 'Internal Conflicts in Africa: Is There a Right of Humanitarian Action' (1994) 2 African YBIL 9, 12–22; Fernando R Téson, *Humanitarian Intervention: An Inquiry into Law and Morality* (2nd edn, Transnational Publishers 1997); Simon Chesterman, *Just War or Just Peace?: Humanitarian Intervention and International Law* (OUP 2001); JL Holzgrefe and Robert O Keohane (eds), *Humanitarian Intervention: Ethical, Legal and Political Dilemmas* (CUP 2003); Anne Orford, *Reading Humanitarian Intervention: Human Rights and the Use of Force in International Law* (CUP 2003); Aidan Hehir, *Humanitarian Intervention: An Introduction* (2nd edn, Palgrave Macmillan 2013); Alan J Kuperman, 'Humanitarian Intervention' in Goodhart (ed.), *Human Rights* 370; Christine Chinkin and Mary Kaldor, *International Law and New Wars* (CUP 2017) 175–226; Christine Gray, *International Law and the Use of Force* (4th edn, OUP 2018) 40–64.

[92] Samuel Moyn, *Human Rights and the Uses of History* (Verso 2014) ch. 3; Simmons, *Mobilizing for Human Rights* 374.

[93] Hilary Charlesworth, 'Democracy and International Law' (2014) 371 Hague Recueil 43, 89–92, 131–2. See further, Tom Ruys, Olivier Corten and Alexandra Hofer (eds), *The Use of Force in International Law: A Case-Based Approach* (OUP 2018) chs 11, 29, 32, 36; Gray, *International Law and the Use of Force* 64–8.

home may be prepared to sacrifice the same overseas in order to advance the foreign policy and interests of their own State.[94]

A combination of factors decide whether foreign armed intervention is a preferred choice to end serious human rights abuses in a particular State. The West found a worthy cause to intervene by large-scale use of force in the former Yugoslavia to save besieged Bosnian Muslim civilians after the worst massacre of civilians in Europe since the Second World War, perpetrated by the paramilitary Bosnian Serb Army of Republika Srpska (VRS) under Ratko Mladić's command in Srebrenica in July 1995 and the market bombing in Sarajevo the following month. Western economies were booming then while the Soviet Union had just collapsed and China was still not the international superpower it now is. By contrast, the West has been reluctant to intervene on a comparable and sustained scale in the ongoing wars in Syria after a series of fiascos of US-led interventions in Iraq, Afghanistan and Libya, which put these States in a worse position than before the interventions and which bogged down the interveners in seemingly endless nation-building undertakings in these States, whose causes are not popularly shared by economically struggling Western societies.[95] As regards the armed conflict in the Democratic Republic of the Congo, it ranks among the bloodiest conflicts since the 1940s, with an estimated death toll of between 1 and 5 million during 1998–2003. Yet it has been largely ignored by the majority of States, which consider DR Congo, whose population is approximately 200 million, 43 million of whom were internally displaced in 2017, a faraway African nation with no discern-

---

[94] Forsythe, *Human Rights in International Relations* 6. Cf Jack Donnelly, *International Human Rights* (3rd edn, Westview Press 2007) 115–47; Olivier Roy and Pasquale Annicchino, 'Human Rights between Religions, Cultures and Universality' in Ana Filipa Vrdoljak (ed.), *The Cultural Dimension of Human Rights* (OUP 2013) 13, 19–20. For a view supporting humanitarian intervention in international law, see Marc Weller, 'Forcible Humanitarian Action in IL', *EJIL Talk!* (Parts I and II), 17–18 May 2017, https://www.ejiltalk.org/forcible-humanitarian-action-in-international-law-part-i/ and https://www.ejiltalk.org/forcible-humanitarian-action-in-international-law-part-ii/, accessed 21 Aug 2018.

[95] Michael Ignatieff, 'Bosnia and Syria: Intervention Then & Now' in Nader Hashemi and Danny Postel (eds), *The Syria Dilemma* (MIT Press 2013) 45, 46–7, 50–4, 57; Michael Barnett, *Empire of Humanity: A History of Humanitarianism* (Cornell University Press 2011) 174–94; Neier, *The International Human Rights Movement* 311–16; Elizabeth O'Shea, 'Responsibility to Protect (R2P) in Libya: Ghosts of the Past Haunting the Future' (2012) 1 Int'l Hum Rts L Rev 173; Christian Tams, 'Prospects for Humanitarian Use of Force' in Antonio Cassese (ed.), *Realizing Utopia: The Future of International Law* (OUP 2012) 359–74; Manisuli Ssenyonjo, 'Unilateral Military Action in the Syrian Arab Republic: A Right to Humanitarian Intervention or a Crime of Aggression?' (2013) 2 Int'l Hum Rts L Rev 323; David Rieff, 'The End of Human Rights?', Foreign Policy (Apr 2018).

ible effect on the global economy or geopolitics as well as too complex and intractable for external intervention.[96] It is pragmatism or realism that reigns supreme in these scenarios.[97]

The late UN Secretary-General Kofi Annan, writing in 2000, posits that human rights under the UN Charter belong to peoples, not governments, which are mere servants of their citizens, not vice versa. Therefore, in April 1991 the UNSC acted to intervene in Iraq's internal affairs to save the Kurds as no government has the right to hide behind the veil of national sovereignty and violate human rights or fundamental freedoms of its people.[98] 'Internal' conflict generally does not stay 'internal' for very long due to spillover effects into neighbouring States and beyond, including mass influx of refugees. The UN is frequently paralysed by deadlocks in the UNSC preventing the collective implementation of the relevant provisions of the UN Charter and driving States to take unilateral action not authorized by the Charter. For instance, in 1971 India used force to intervene to end the civil war in East Pakistan, leading to the independence of Bangladesh; in 1978 Vietnam used force to invade Cambodia to overthrow the Khmer Rouge regime and in 1979 Tanzania invaded Uganda to overthrow Idi Amin's dictatorship regime. The refugee flow across the border was invoked as the reason for the interventions. However, what appeared to legitimize the three incidents of intervention in global public opinion was the oppressive nature of the targeted regimes. The intervention/invasion was 'a lesser evil than allowing massacre and extreme oppression to continue'.[99] The UN failed to take collective action as required by the UN Charter during the Rwandan genocide in 1994. NATO's armed intervention in Kosovo in 1999 without the UNSC's prior authorization echoed the tragic failure of the international community to reconcile the two equally compelling interests – universal legitimacy versus effectiveness in defence of human rights. In Annan's opinion, the UN Charter as a living document can curtail the strictly traditional notion of sovereignty when this notion can no longer do justice to the human rights of peoples.

---

[96]   'Africa's great war reignites', *The Economist* (17–23 Feb 2018) 11, 22–6.
[97]   This would reflect the position taken by 'pragmatic liberals' in Forsythe, *Human Rights in International Relations* 44, 363. See also Michael P Scharf, *Balkan Justice: The Story behind the First International War Crimes Trial since Nuremberg* (Carolina Academic Press 1997); Kingsley Moghalu, *Rwanda's Genocide: The Politics of Global Justice* (Palgrave Macmillan 2005) 18–22; Posner, *Twilight of Human Rights Law* 127–34; Ruys et al (eds), *The Use of Force in International Law*, ch. 41.
[98]   Kofi Annan, 'Human Rights and Humanitarian Intervention in the Twenty-First Century' in Samantha Power and Graham Allison (eds), *Realizing Human Rights: Moving from Inspiration to Impact* (St Martin's Press 2000) 309.
[99]   Ibid 314.

Kofi Annan proposes four principles of intervention to resolve future conflicts. First, intervention is to be defined as broadly as possible to allow actions along a wide continuum, from the most pacific to the most coercive. Emphasis should be placed on preventive capabilities, including early warning, preventive diplomacy, preventive deployment, preventive disarmament and deterrence for future atrocities as in the case of the setting up of ad hoc international criminal tribunals like the International Criminal Tribunal for the former Yugoslavia and that for Rwanda. Secondly, the conception of collective interest of the global community should replace that of national interest. Thirdly, the UNSC must be reformed and revitalized by becoming more representative, reflecting the modern-day realities rather than those of 1945 and must improve the quality and speed of its decisions. Finally, there must be post-conflict commitment to peace, with the UN given the means and support to provide peacekeeping and peace-building missions to assist post-conflict States. Annan concludes by opining that the UN must not stand aside and its intervention must be based on legitimate and universal principles if it is to command the sustained support of the world's peoples.[100]

The world's leaders, meeting at the UN Headquarters in New York from 14 to 16 September 2005, agreed on a series of measures to tackle global challenges. The 2005 World Summit Outcome endorsed by the UNGA on 16 September 2005 contains a section on 'Responsibility to protect populations from genocide, war crimes, ethnic cleansing and crimes against humanity'. Its pertinent paragraphs read:

138. Each individual State has the *responsibility to protect* its populations from genocide, war crimes, ethnic cleansing and crimes against humanity. This responsibility entails the prevention of such crimes, including their incitement, through appropriate and necessary means. We accept that responsibility and will act in accordance with it. The international community should, as appropriate, encourage and help States to exercise this responsibility and support the United Nations in establishing an early warning capability.

139. The international community, through the United Nations, also has the *responsibility* to use appropriate diplomatic, humanitarian and other peaceful means, in accordance with Chapters VI and VIII of the Charter, to help *to protect* populations from genocide, war crimes, ethnic cleansing and crimes against humanity. *In this context, we are prepared to take collective action, in a timely and decisive manner, through the Security Council, in accordance with the Charter, including Chapter VII, on a case-by-case basis and in cooperation with relevant regional organizations as appropriate, should peaceful means be inadequate and national authorities are manifestly failing to protect their populations from genocide, war crimes, ethnic cleansing and crimes against humanity.* We stress the need for the General Assembly to continue consider-

---

[100] Ibid 310–19.

ation of the *responsibility to protect* populations from genocide, war crimes, ethnic cleansing and crimes against humanity and its implications, bearing in mind the principles of the Charter and international law. We also intend to commit ourselves, as necessary and appropriate, to helping States build capacity to protect their populations from genocide, war crimes, ethnic cleansing and crimes against humanity and to assisting those which are under stress before crises and conflicts break out.[101]

Paragraphs 138 and 139 encapsulate three pillars of the responsibility to protect (R2P) – prevention, capacity building and collective action in accordance with the UN Charter, respectively. These are reaffirmed by the UNSC.[102]

To date, States generally have no problems with the first two pillars, but are wary of the third one.[103] Since 2018, the UNGA has held an annual plenary meeting on R2P and the *prevention* of genocide, war crimes, ethnic cleansing and crimes against humanity. The meeting focuses on taking effective preventive action and timely responses to the risks of as well as accountability for those responsible for these atrocities.[104] Some States – including Cuba, North Korea, Pakistan, Russia, Sudan, Syria and Venezuela – have questioned the *application* of R2P in practice. The vital role of the UNSC in the context of R2P is often emphasized, especially in relation to its inability to adequately respond to mass atrocities in Syria and Yemen. None has specifically suggested that the UNSC exercise its mandate under Chapter VII of the UN Charter to authorize the use of force for the purpose of R2P, however.[105] The Group of Friends of R2P[106] has also continuously emphasized the link between

---

[101]   UN Doc A/60/1, 24 Oct 2005 (emphasis added).

[102]   UN Doc S/RES/1674 (2006) 28 Apr 2006 §4.

[103]   James Pattison, *Humanitarian Intervention and the Responsibility to Protect: Who Should Intervene?* (OUP 2010); Ramesh Thakur, *The Responsibility to Protect: Norms, Laws and the Use of Force in International Politics* (Routledge 2011); Charles Samford and Ramesh Thakur (eds), *Responsibility to Protect and Sovereignty* (Ashgate 2013); Ramesh Thakur, 'The Use of International Force to Prevent or Halt Atrocities: From Humanitarian Intervention to the Responsibility to Protect' in Shelton (ed.), *The Oxford Handbook of International Human Rights Law* 815; Richard Barnes and Vassilis P Tzevelekos (eds), *Beyond Responsibility to Protect: Generating Change in International Law* (Intersentia 2016); Alex Bellamy and Tim Dunne (eds), *The Oxford Handbook on the Responsibility to Protect* (OUP 2016).

[104]   See also, eg, Report of the Secretary-General, 'Responsibility to protect: lessons learned from prevention', UN Doc A/73/898–S/2519/463 (10 June 2019).

[105]   Eg, Global Centre for the Responsibility to Protect, 'Summary of the UN General Assembly Plenary Meeting on the Responsibility to Protect' (July 2019) http://www.globalr2p.org/media/files/2019-summary-of-unga-plenary-on-r2p.pdf, accessed 7 Aug 2019.

[106]   As of this writing, the Group of Friends of R2P comprises the following UN Member States as well as the EU: Argentina, Australia, Bangladesh, Belgium, Bosnia

R2P and Geneva-based human rights mechanisms and institutions, especially the HRC, to apply preventive measures in situations where early warning signs of possible atrocities arise.

Not long after the World Summit Outcome, R2P was reportedly invoked by France in 2008 after cyclone Nargis had caused the worst-ever natural disaster in Myanmar, implying that humanitarian aid might have to be brought in by force if the Government of Myanmar kept on resisting large-scale international aid.[107] However, contrary to mainstream Western media reports, according to several colleagues of the present author who were involved in arranging foreign humanitarian assistance for Myanmar, the Myanmar Government agreed to accept foreign humanitarian assistance two or three days after Nargis had wreaked devastation upon Myanmar. Thailand and China were the first and second foreign States whose assistance Myanmar accepted.[108] A tripartite committee was subsequently set up comprising Myanmar, ASEAN and the UN to coordinate disaster relief efforts. Myanmar, nonetheless, did not agree to having foreign personnel accompany the assistance, perhaps for fear that they might intervene in its domestic affairs or even harbour an ulterior motive of orchestrating a regime change in Myanmar. That was why Myanmar had serious concerns regarding France's wish to use Myanmar's air and naval bases in Pathein on the bank of a tributary of the Ayeyarwady delta, which was the worst affected area, to support its relief operations and regarding the US offer to send an aircraft carrier to provide disaster relief. The official explanation by the Myanmar Government was that it had enough human resources to handle the disaster relief efforts.

When the UN International Law Commission (ILC) was working on its Draft Articles on the protection of persons in the event of disasters, the issue of R2P came up several times during the debate within the ILC and the incident relating cyclone Nargis was often referred to by the present author, who was then an ILC member. The ILC's decision to exclude the R2P concept from the scope of application of the Draft Articles was endorsed by China, Colombia,

---

and Herzegovina, Botswana, Canada, Chile, Costa Rica, Cote d'Ivoire, Croatia, Czech Republic, Denmark, Finland, France, Germany, Ghana, Guatemala, Hungary, Italy, Japan, Liberia, Liechtenstein, Luxembourg, Mali, Mexico, Morocco, Mozambique, Netherlands, New Zealand, Nigeria, Norway, Panama, Peru, Qatar, Republic of Korea, Rwanda, Romania, Senegal, Sierra Leone, Singapore, Slovakia, Slovenia, South Sudan, Spain, Sweden, Switzerland, Tanzania, UK, USA and Uruguay.

[107] 'Responsibility to protect: The lessons of Libya', *The Economist* (19 May 2011) https://www.economist.com/international/2011/05/19/the-lessons-of-libya, accessed 21 Aug 2018.

[108] Nargis made landfall in Myanmar on the evening of Friday 2 May 2008 and the Myanmar Government accepted Thailand's offer to provide disaster relief assistance on Monday 5 May 2008 at 10 am.

Cuba, Czech Republic, Ghana, Ireland, Iran, Israel, Japan, Myanmar, Russia, Spain, Sri Lanka, Thailand and Venezuela. Conversely, Poland was of the view that the R2P concept should apply to disaster situations. Hungary, Finland (on behalf of the Nordic States) and Portugal suggested that R2P 'be kept in mind' in the situations covered in the Draft Articles. Austria, while acknowledging that the ILC had excluded the relevance of R2P from the Draft Articles, observed that it was conceivable that international law could evolve.[109]

The final version of the Articles on the protection of persons in the event of disasters adopted by the ILC in 2016[110] proceeds on the basis that R2P has no place in this kind of situation. Article 10 of the Articles provides that the affected State has the duty to ensure the protection of persons and provision of disaster relief assistance in its territory or in territory under its jurisdiction or control, and that the affected State has the primary role in the direction, control, coordination and supervision of such relief assistance. To the extent a disaster manifestly exceeds the national response capacity of the affected State, Article 11 imposes a duty on the affected State to seek external assistance from, as appropriate, other States, the UN and other potential assisting actors. Paragraph 8 of the Commentary to Article 11 explains that the phrase 'as appropriate' is adopted by the ILC to emphasize the discretionary power of the affected State to choose from among States, the UN and other potential assisting actors the assistance that is most appropriate to its specific needs and this duty does not imply that the affected State is obliged to seek assistance from every source listed in Article 11. According to Article 13, the provision of external assistance requires the consent of the affected State, which shall not be withheld arbitrarily, and when an offer of external assistance is made in accordance with the present Articles, the affected State shall, whenever possible, make known its decision regarding the offer in a timely manner. As clarified by paragraph 8 of the Commentary to Article 13, the determination of whether the withholding of consent is arbitrary must be determined on a case-by-case basis although as a general rule several principles can be adduced. For example, withholding consent to assistance from one external source is not arbitrary if an affected State has accepted appropriate and sufficient assistance from elsewhere. Conversely, where an offer of assistance is made in accordance with the Articles and no alternate sources of assistance are available, there would be a strong inference that a decision to withhold consent is arbitrary. Article 14 gives the affected State the right to condition assistance

---

[109] Special Rapporteur's eighth report on the protection of persons in the event of disasters, Doc A/CN.4/697 (17 Mar 2016) 11 [10].

[110] Report of the ILC on the work of its sixty-eighth session (2 May–10 June and 4 July–12 Aug 2016) UN Doc A/71/10 ch. IV.

so as to deny unwanted or unneeded assistance and to determine what assistance is appropriate and when.

Chapter VII of the UN Charter permits the UNSC to take action with regard to a threat to peace, breach of the peace or act of aggression. The UNSC's Resolution 1970 (2011), adopted under Chapter VII, expresses grave concern at the situation in Libya and condemns the violence and use of force against civilians, including the repression of peaceful demonstrators and the deaths of civilians, which constituted deplorably gross and systematic violation of human rights and might amount to crimes against humanity, with the incitement to hostility and violence against the civilian population being made from the highest level of the Libyan Government. It recalls the Libyan authorities' responsibility to protect its population and imposed a series of sanction measures against the individuals allegedly involved in the human rights violations.[111] Less than a month later, the UNSC adopted Resolution 1973 (2011), also under Chapter VII of the Charter, reiterating the responsibility of the Libyan authorities to protect the Libyan population, the operative paragraph 4 of which stipulates:

> *Authorizes* Member States that have notified the Secretary-General, acting nationally or through regional organizations or arrangements and acting in cooperation with the Secretary-General, to take all necessary measures ... to protect civilians and civilian populated areas under threat of attack in the Libyan Arab Jamahiriya, including Benghazi, while excluding a foreign occupation force of any form on any part of Libyan territory and requests the Member States concerned to inform the Secretary-General immediately of the measures they take pursuant to the authorization conferred by this paragraph which shall be immediately reported to the Security Council.

This authorization was duly used by the NATO-led military alliance to conduct air strikes against military targets in Libya that threatened the lives and safety of civilians. This intervention was instrumental to the eventual regime change in Libya, the capital city of which fell to the rebels at the end of August 2012, but widespread instability has continued to permeate the whole country.[112]

After the alleged chemical attacks against civilians in Syria by the Syrian Government in April 2013, US President Barak Obama declared, 'All of us, not just the United States, but around the world, have to recognize how we cannot stand by and permit the systematic use of weapons like chemical

---

[111] UN Doc S/RES/1970 (2011) 26 Feb 2011.

[112] Debora Valentina Malito, 'The Responsibility to Protect What in Libya?' (2017) 29 Peace Review: A Journal of Social Justice 289. Also, Erfaun Norooz, 'Responsibility to Protect and its Applicability in Libya and Syria' (2015) 9(3) ICL Journal – Vienna J on Int'l Constitutional L 1.

weapons on civilian populations.'[113] The Arab League's Foreign Ministers demanded that the UN and the international community 'assume their responsibilities in line with the UN Charter and international law' by taking the necessary deterrent measures against the Syrian regime over its alleged use of chemical weapons.[114] Diplomatic efforts eventually prevailed, culminating in the UNSC unanimously adopting Resolution 2118 on 27 September 2013 for Syria to destroy its chemical weapons arsenal by mid 2014.[115]

However, after the Syrian Government had purportedly used chemical weapons in April 2017 and April 2018, the USA, joined by the UK and France, launched air strikes to punish the Syrian Government. US President Donald Trump did not allude to humanitarian intervention or R2P and his Administration focused on the argument that the use of force against Syria protected vital US national security interests to prevent and deter the spread and use of deadly chemical weapons. Unlike its US counterpart, the UK Government invoked humanitarian intervention, defending 'the legality of UK military action to alleviate the extreme humanitarian suffering of the Syrian people by degrading the Syrian regime's chemical weapons capability and deterring their further use, following the chemical weapons attack in Douma on 7 April 2018'. The UK explained that the Syrian regime had been killing its own people for seven years and its use of chemical weapons, which had exacerbated the human suffering, was a serious breach of the customary international law prohibition on the use of chemical weapons and amounted to a war crime and a crime against humanity. The UK contended that it was permissible under international law, on an exceptional basis, 'to take measures in order to alleviate overwhelming humanitarian suffering'. The legal basis for the use of force by the UK was 'humanitarian intervention', which required three conditions to be met. First, there was 'the existence of convincing evidence, generally accepted by the international community as a whole, of extreme humanitarian distress on a large scale, requiring immediate and urgent relief'. Secondly, it was 'ojectively clear' that there was no practicable alternative to the use of force if lives were to be saved. Thirdly, the use of force was 'necessary and proportionate to the aim of relief of humanitarian suffering'

---

[113] 'Barak Obama warns Syria chemical arms a "game changer"', *BBC News* (26 Apr 2013) https://www.bbc.com/news/world-middle-east-22318749, accessed 16 Dec 2018.

[114] 'Arab League urges UN-backed action against Syria', *Al Jazeera* (2 Sept 2013) https://www.aljazeera.com/news/middleeast/2013/09/20139118235327617.html, accessed 16 Dec 2018.

[115] S/RES/2118 (2013).

and 'strictly limited in time and in scope to this aim (that is, the minimum necessary to achieve that end and for no other purpose)'.[116]

The legality of invoking humanitarian intervention or R2P to support unilateral use of force against Syria without the UNSC's authorization in the aforesaid circumstances remains controversial.[117] Russia, China, Iran, Iraq, Belarus, Brazil, Bolivia and Venezuela are among those opposed to the unilateral use of force against Syria, although several other States, the EU and NATO appear to generally support these military actions. There is no unified position among the veto-wielding UNSC permanent members on how to balance human rights protection with the sovereignty of a close strategic ally whose government seriously abuses human rights. After the chemical attacks in Syria in April 2017, France, the UK and the USA circulated a draft UNSC resolution to condemn the chemical attacks and demand a full investigation, but Russia vetoed it on the grounds that the draft resolution attributed blame to the Syrian Government before any independent investigation had been undertaken. After the April 2018 chemical attacks, Russia failed to get the UNSC to adopt a resolution condemning the unilateral use of force by certain States against Syria.[118]

Russia's resolute position in this matter echoes the view of President Vladimir Putin, expressed in February 2012 when he was Prime Minister and former President of Russia, that although human rights are more important than national sovereignty and crimes against humanity should be punished by an international court,

> if this principle is used as an excuse for a presumptuous violation of national sovereignty and if human rights are protected by foreign forces and selectively and if, while 'protecting' those rights, they violate the rights of many other people, includ-

---

[116] Prime Minister's Office, Position Paper on Syria action – UK Government Legal Position, 14 Apr 2018.

[117] Eg, Jack Goldsmith and Oona A Hathaway, 'The Downsides of Bombing Syria', *Just Security* (10 Apr 2013) https://www.justsecurity.org/54698/; Oona A Hathaway and Scott J Shapiro, 'On Syria, a UN Vote Isn't Optional', *NY Times* (3 Sept 2013) https://www.nytimes.com/2013/09/04/opinion/on-syria-a-un-vote-isnt-optional.html; Mary Ellen O'Connell, 'Unlawful Reprisal to the Rescue against Chemical Attacks?', *EJIL Talk!* (12 Apr 2018) https://www.ejiltalk.org/unlawful-reprisals-to-the-rescue -against-chemical-attacks/; Marc Weller, 'Syria air strikes: Were they legal?', *BBC News* (14 Apr 2018) https://www.bbc.com/news/world-middle-east-43766556; Monica Hakimi, 'The Attack on Syria and the Contemporary Jus ad Bellum' *EJIL Talk!* (15 Apr 2018) https://www.ejiltalk.org/the-attack-on-syria-and-the-contemporary-jus-ad -bellum/; Marko Milanovic, 'The Syria Strikes: Still Clearly Illegal' ibid (15 April 2018) https://www.ejiltalk.org/the-syria-strikes-still-clearly-illegal/, all accessed 16 Dec 2018.

[118] 'Security Council rejects Russian request to condemn airstrikes in Syria', *UN News* (14 Apr 2018).

ing the most fundamental and sacred right, the right to life, this is no longer a noble effort. This is merely demagoguery.[119]

The use of force by foreign States in the name of humanitarian intervention to protect human rights in Syria without prior UNSC authorization has turned Syria into a battleground of proxy wars between some of the world's major military powers, with no end in sight for human rights abuses allegedly committed by both the Syrian Government and its armed opposition groups. As of 3 January 2019, more than 68,000 Russian soldiers, led by 460 Russian generals, were conducting military operations in Syria to support Syria's Assad Government, an increase from around 63,000 soldiers in August 2018. The Russian Ministry of Defence was quoted as disclosing that all leaders of Russian military departments, leaders of infantry, air force and air defence armies and leaders of military divisions and 96 per cent of brigade commanders, had been posted in Syria. Eighty-seven per cent of the tactical flight crews, 91 per cent of army flight crews, 97 per cent of military transport crews and 60 per cent of strategic flight crews had developed their military operations experience during operations carried out in Syria. The Ministry reportedly said that before the Russian military intervention in September 2015, 92 per cent of Syria was outside the control of the regime,[120] compared with about 25 per cent by the end of December 2018.[121]

Although the third pillar of R2P has yet to crystallize into a norm of customary international law,[122] States have obligations to prevent genocide and some other gross human rights violations under the relevant treaties binding upon

---

[119] Vladimir Putin, 'Russia and the Changing World', *RT News* (27 Feb 2012) reproduced in *Global Research* (22 Sept 2015) https://www.globalresearch.ca/vladimir -putin-russia-and-the-changing-world/5477500, accessed 4 Jan 2019.

[120] 'Russia Reveals Number of its Soldiers Supporting Assad', *Syrian Observer* (4 Jan 2019) quoting *Russia Today*, https://syrianobserver.com/EN/news/47756/russia -reveals-number-of-its-soldiers-supporting-assad.html, accessed 5 Jan 2019.

[121] Layal Abou Rahal and Rouba El Husseini, 'As Assad nears victory, Arab world readies to bring him back into fold', *Times of Israel* (30 Dec 2018) https://www .timesofisrael.com/as-assad-nears-victory-arab-world-readies-to-bring-him-back-into -fold/, accessed 31 Dec 2018.

[122] Or, as Wolfrum puts it, 'there is not yet conclusive evidence that R2P has already been accepted in all its facets' (Rüdiger Wolfrum, 'Solidarity' in Shelton (ed.), *The Oxford Handbook of International Human Rights Law* 400, 415). *Contra*: Jordan Paust, 'R2P and Protective Intervention' (2017) 31 Temple Int'l & Comp LJ 109, esp 121, where Paust asserts that 'it is evident that R2P protective intervention against atrocities committed by a government against its own people or another people within its territory can be justified as self-determination assistance or collective self-defense at the request of a victimized people'.

them.[123] Here are three examples: Article I of the 1948 Genocide Convention expressly stipulates the obligation of its Contracting Parties to prevent and punish genocide.[124] Similarly, Article 2 of CAT obligates each State Party to take effective measures to prevent acts of torture in any territory under its jurisdiction. Article I(c) of the 1994 Inter-American Convention on the Forced Disappearance of Persons[125] requires its States Parties to cooperate with one another in helping to prevent, punish and eliminate the forced disappearance of persons. The challenge is to realize such obligation. The case of genocide is a good example.

The ICJ has held the prohibition of genocide to be a peremptory norm of international law (*jus cogens*),[126] and the obligation to prevent genocide to be 'both normative and compelling'.[127] Yet, France, the UK and the USA repeatedly put pressure on the other UNSC members not to propose draft resolutions in the UNSC on the Rwanda genocide in 1994, thereby amounting to a de facto veto on any such resolutions that might have prevented or at least abated the genocide.[128] These States were at that time preoccupied with debates about military intervention and non-intervention in the Balkan wars in Europe, and what was happening in Rwanda, a State of little geostrategic importance and in Africa, was of relatively remote interest to them.[129]

---

[123] Andrea Gattini, 'Breach of the Obligation to Prevent and Reparation Thereof in the ICJ's Genocide Judgment' (2007) 18 EJIL 695; Andreas Zimmermann, 'The Obligation to Prevent Genocide: Towards a General Responsibility to Protect?' in Ulrich Fastenrath, Rudolf Geiger, Daniel-Erasmus Khan, Andreas Paulus, Sabine von Schorlemer and Christoph Vedder (eds), *From Bilateralism to Community Interest: Essays in Honour of Judge Bruno Simma* (OUP 2011) 629, 633–7; Serena Forlati, 'The Legal Obligation to Prevent Genocide: Bosnia v Serbia and Beyond' (2011) 31 Polish YBIL 189; Etienne Ruvebana, *Prevention of Genocide under International Law* (Intersentia 2014); Etienne Ruvebana and Marcel Brus, 'Before It's Too Late: Preventing Genocide by Holding the Territorial State Responsible for Not Taking Preventive Action' (2015) 62 Netherlands ILR 25.
[124] See *Application of the Convention on the Prevention and Punishment of the Crime of Genocide (Bosnia and Herzegovina v Serbia and Montenegro)* (Judgment) [2007] ICJ Rep 43, 220–3 [428]–[432].
[125] (1994) 33 ILM 1429.
[126] *Armed Activities on the Territory of the Congo (New Application: 2002) (Democratic Republic of the Congo v Rwanda)*, Jurisdiction and Admissibility, Judgment [2006] ICJ Reports 6, 31–2 [64].
[127] *Bosnia and Herzegovina v Serbia and Montenegro* [2007] ICJ Reports 43, 220 [427].
[128] John Heieck, 'The Responsibility Not to Veto Revisited. How the Duty to Prevent Genocide as a *Jus Cogens* Norm Imposes a Legal Duty Not to Veto on the Five Permanent Members of the Security Council' in Barnes and Tzevelekos (eds), *Beyond Responsibility to Protect: Generating Change in International Law* 103, 121.
[129] Moghalu, *Rwanda's Genocide* 18–22.

Efforts by some States, especially the Czech Republic, New Zealand and Nigeria, to engage the UN in stopping or at least containing the ongoing genocide in Rwanda did not succeed. For its part, the USA was still being haunted by the military disaster in Somalia in 1993 in which 18 US soldiers participating in a peacekeeping operation under US command were ambushed and killed, entailing widespread public and Congressional outrage at home. The consequential US Presidential Decision Directive (PDD) 25 of 3 May 1994 lists 16 factors to determine whether the USA will support/participate in peacekeeping operations abroad. They include the potential that such operations will advance US interests, low likelihood of US casualties, domestic and Congressional support and a clear exit strategy.[130] The US Government moved to prevent the UN from branding the massacres in Rwanda 'genocide' by blocking, with the support of the UK and China, the UNSC Presidential Statement on 30 April 1994 that would have called the massacres 'genocide'.[131] Consequently, the UNSC Presidential Statement merely

> condemns all these breaches of international humanitarian law in Rwanda, particularly those perpetrated against the civilian population and recalls that persons who instigate or participate in such acts are individually responsible. In this context, the Security Council recalls that the killing of members of an ethnic group with the intention of destroying such a group in whole or in part constitutes a crime punishable under international law.[132]

The Statement deliberately avoids mentioning that such killing actually constitutes a crime of genocide under international law, as codified in Article II(a) of the 1948 Genocide Convention. The USA also rejected UN proposals to jam the broadcasts by Rwanda's national radio station inciting genocide, heeding the US Department of Defense's recommendation that it would cost US$8,500 an hour to position a jamming aircraft over Rwanda and that such jamming would violate Rwanda's sovereignty.[133]

The present ongoing movement for the reform of the UNSC therefore encompasses proposals to prevent any of the five permanent members of the UNSC from abusing their veto power in the face of threats or occurrence of gross

---

[130] PDD 25 – Reforming Multilateral Peace Operations. 'The Clinton Administration's Policy on Reforming Multilateral Peace Operations', Dept of State Publication 10161 (May 1994) ES1. Discussed in Donald CF Daniel, *US Perspectives on Peacekeeping: Putting PDD25 in Context* (Occasional Paper of the Center for Naval Warfare Studies, Strategic Research Dept Research Memorandum 3–94, US Naval War College, 1994).

[131] Moghalu, *Rwanda's Genocide* 19–20.

[132] UN Doc S/PRST/1994/21, 30 April 1994, 3rd preambular paragraph.

[133] Moghalu, *Rwanda's Genocide* 19–21.

atrocities of international concern such as genocide.[134] The Accountability, Coherence and Transparency (ACT) Group, comprising 27 UN Member States working to improve the working methods of the UNSC, proposed, in July 2015, a one-page 'Code of Conduct regarding UNSC action against genocide, crimes against humanity and war crimes'. The Code is not only for the permanent members of the UNSC, but also for the UNSC non-permanent members as well as for any UN Member State that may, at some point in time, become a UNSC member. It comprises a general and positive pledge to support the UNSC's action to prevent or end the crimes covered by the Code that the UN Secretary-General has brought to the UNSC's attention. This general and positive pledge is complemented by a more specific pledge to be made by all 15 members of the UNSC not to vote against any credible draft resolution aiming at preventing or halting these crimes.

In that same year, France and Mexico presented a one-page 'Political Statement on the suppression of the veto in case of mass atrocities', open to signature by UN Member States to propose a collective and voluntary agreement among the UNSC permanent members to the effect that the latter would refrain from using the veto in case of mass atrocities. The Political Statement proceeds on the basis that the UNSC 'should not be prevented by the use of veto from taking action with the aim of preventing or bringing an end to situations involving the commission of mass atrocities', with the veto being considered not as a privilege but as 'an international responsibility'. As of 27 March 2017, 112 States have supported the Code of Conduct, whereas 98 States supported the Political Statement and 90 States supported both initiatives. Of the five UNSC permanent members, the UK supports the Code of Conduct, while France supports both the Code of Conduct and the Political Statement.[135] Silence by the other three UNSC permanent members does not bode well for the future realization of either the Code or the Political Statement.

Frustration with the UNSC permanent members' veto power is deep rooted. In November 1950 the UNGA adopted the 'Uniting for Peace Resolution' by 52 votes to five (Byelorussia SSR, Czechoslovakia, Poland, Soviet Union and Ukrainian SSR), with two abstentions (Argentina and India) after the Soviet Union's veto since August 1950 against all UNSC resolutions to deal with the then ongoing crisis in the Korean peninsula after North Korea's armed invasion of South Korea on 25 June 1950. In its pertinent part, the Resolution

---

[134] John Heieck, *A Duty to Prevent Genocide: Due Diligence Obligations among the P5* (Edward Elgar Publishing 2018); Andreas S Kolb, *The UN Security Council Members' Responsibility to Protect* (Springer 2018) 1–47, 525–9.

[135] Source: International Coalition for the Responsibility to Protect. According to the Global Centre for the Responsibility to Protect, as of 1 June 2018 the Code had been signed by 115 UN Member States and two observers.

resolves that if the UNSC, because of lack of unanimity of the permanent members, fails to exercise its primary responsibility for the maintenance of international peace and security in any case where there appears to be a threat to the peace, breach of the peace or act of aggression, the UNGA shall consider the matter immediately with a view to making appropriate recommendations to members for collective measures. Such measures may include, in the case of a breach of the peace or act of aggression, the use of armed force, when necessary, to maintain or restore international peace and security.[136]

Practice subsequent to the Resolution is quite limited and the relevant subsequent UNGA resolutions do not always cite the Uniting for Peace Resolution. In the Korean War context itself, UNGA Resolution 498(V) of 1 February 1951 did not refer specifically to the Uniting for Peace Resolution but noted in its preamble that the lack of unanimity of the UNSC permanent members had led to the failure of the UNSC to exercise its primary responsibility for the maintenance of international peace and security. UNGA Resolution 498(V) then proceeded to, inter alia, find that the People's Republic of China engaged in aggression in Korea and call on all States and authorities to continue to render every assistance to the UN action in Korea.[137] Since the Uniting for Peace Resolution, approximately ten to twelve emergency special sessions have been convened according to the conditions laid down in that Resolution, the first being on the occasion of the 1956 war between Israel and Egypt and the British–French attack on the Suez Canal zone. The tenth special session, first convened in 1997, deals with the Israeli occupation of Palestinian territory – the session has not yet come to its end as of this writing.[138]

There is practically not much hope in resorting to the Uniting for Peace Resolution mechanism to avert or alleviate serious human rights violations. It was not used to deal with the imminent and the ongoing genocide in Rwanda in 1994 after the UNSC had failed to act. The same has been repeated in relation to the unrest and subsequent armed conflicts in Syria since March 2011 where gross violations of human rights are rampant and well documented. After the alleged chemical attacks by the Syrian Government against civilians in Syria,

---

[136] UNGA Res A/RES/377 (3 Nov 1950).
[137] UNGA Res A/RES/498 (1 Feb 1951).
[138] Security Council Report, 'Security Council Deadlocks and Uniting for Peace: An Abridged History', https://www.securitycouncilreport.org/atf/cf/%7B65BFCF9B -6D27-4E9C-8CD3-CF6E4FF96FF9%7D/Security_Council_Deadlocks_and_Uniting _for_Peace.pdf, accessed 22 Oct 2019; Christina Binder, 'Uniting for Peace Resolution (1950)' in *Max Planck Encyclopedia of Public International Law* (May 2017); Christian Tomuschat, 'Uniting for Peace: General Assembly Resolution 377(V)', UN Audio Visual Library of International Law, http://legal.un.org/avl/ha/ufp/ufp.html, accessed 24 Nov 2018.

the UNSC failed to adopt a resolution to deal with the situation due to the lack of unanimity of its permanent members and the UNGA did not resort to the Uniting for Peace Resolution mechanism to deal with it, either. It may be recalled that the legality of the consequential unilateral use of force by France, the UK and the USA against Syria without appropriate authorization from the UN is disputed. The best the UNGA can achieve in relation to human rights abuses in Syria is the establishment of the 'International, Impartial and Independent Mechanism to Assist in the Investigation and Prosecution of Those Responsible for the Most Serious Crimes under International Law Committed in the Syrian Arab Republic since March 2011' (or 'IIIM') under the auspices of the UN.[139] The IIIM will work closely with the Independent International Commission of Inquiry on the Syrian Arab Republic

> to collect, consolidate, preserve and analyse evidence of violations of international humanitarian law and human rights violations and abuses and to prepare files in order to facilitate and expedite fair and independent criminal proceedings, in accordance with international law standards, in national, regional or international courts or tribunals that have or may in the future have jurisdiction over these crimes, in accordance with international law.[140]

Nevertheless, with the Russian-backed Bashar Assad Government in Syria regaining its control over almost two-thirds of the Syrian territory from opposing forces by the end of 2018, several States are looking forward to reopening their embassies in Damascus, Syria's capital city, as well as exploring the possibility of ending the Arab League's suspension of Syria since November 2011. A group of States in the Middle East and Israel reportedly want to wean Syria away from Iran, which has been providing Assad with military support during Syria's civil war, as well as to counter Turkey, which has military presence in northern Syria to quell the Kurdish-led militia Turkey considers to be 'terrorists' jeopardizing Turkey's national security.[141] As in the cases of the prosecution of former Peruvian President Alberto Fujimori in Peru and former Guatemalan President General Efrian Ríos Montt in Guatemala, to name but a few, Assad and his lieutenants might be called to account for human rights abuses they have been accused of only after a regime change in Syria.

---

[139] UNGA Res 248 (2017) UN Doc A/RES/71/248 (11 Jan 2017) adopted on 21 Dec 2016 with 105 votes in favour to 15 against and 52 abstentions.

[140] Ibid §4. See also Kriangsak Kittichaisaree, *The Obligation to Extradite or Prosecute* (OUP 2018) 334–7.

[141] David Hearst, 'REVEALED: How Gulf States hatched plan with Israel to rehabilitate Assad', *Middle East Eye* (8 Jan 2019) https://www.middleeasteye.net/news/saudi-uae-egypt-israel-syria-khashoggi-1467976694, accessed 9 Jan 2019.

International human rights law and diplomacy

In the final analysis, it has to be admitted that 'human rights cannot be promoted by the force of arms', but through confidence building and persuasion, however tedious and slow the process may be.[142] There may be extreme circumstances where recalcitrant States that persistently defy universally recognized human rights have to be subjected to other measures, including coercion and ultimately use of force, provided that these measures are in compliance with the UN Charter. Any necessary coercion should be used to execute arrest warrants against perpetrators of gross human rights violations rather than as unilateral military intervention to cope with mass atrocities.[143]

Punishing individuals responsible for gross human rights violations is a most effective way to ensure that human rights are respected. This can be done at the domestic level before national criminal courts repressing human rights violations as criminal offences or by a competent international criminal tribunal/court where it has jurisdiction over the case. At the international level, such individuals bear individual criminal responsibility because, as the post-Second World War Nuremberg Tribunal has held, '[c]rimes against international law are committed by men, not by abstract entities and only by punishing individuals who commit such crimes can the provisions of international law be enforced'.[144]

The crimes subject to the jurisdiction of modern-day international criminal tribunals are largely confined to genocide, crimes against humanity, war crimes and, in the case of the International Criminal Court, the crime of aggression as well. A State may exercise criminal jurisdiction to prosecute an offender before its domestic court where the offence is committed in its territory, the offender or the victim is its national or the offender's conduct abroad threatens the State's national security or interferes with the operation of its government functions. Some States assert 'universal jurisdiction' over a crime that has no such connection (*nexus*) with them at all.[145]

According to a survey by Amnesty International published in September 2012, the law of 147 UN Member States (that is, approximately 76.2 per cent of the total 193 UN Member States) has provided for universal jurisdiction over one or more of the following 'crimes under international law' that are of the gravest concern to the international community: genocide, crimes against humanity, war crimes and torture. Another 16 States (or 8.29 per cent of the total) can exercise universal jurisdiction over conduct constituting such

---

[142] Tomuschat, *Human Rights* 431.

[143] Cf Sikkink, *Evidence for Hope* 192.

[144] *Trials of German Major War Criminals*, Proceedings of the International Military Tribunal Sitting at Nuremberg, Germany (1947) 41 AJIL 172, 222.

[145] See further, Kittichaisaree, *The Obligation to Extradite or Prosecute* 204–30; Devika Hovell, 'The Authority of Universal Jurisdiction' (2018) 29 EJIL 427.

a crime under international law, but only as an ordinary crime under their respective national laws. Ninety-one States (or approximately 47.1 per cent) have provided for universal jurisdiction over ordinary crimes, even when the conduct does not amount to a crime under international law.[146]

Another study, published in 2011, finds that from the trial of the notorious Nazi officer Adolf Eichmann in Israel in 1961 up to August 2010 there were only 32 defendants actually tried in domestic courts around the world on the basis of universal jurisdiction. Eight were tried in Belgium; five in the Netherlands; four in Germany; two each in Canada, France, Israel, Switzerland and the UK; and one each in Australia, Austria, Denmark, Norway and Spain. Twenty-four of the 32 were Nazis, former Yugoslavs accused of committing serious international crimes during and in the aftermath of the disintegration of the former Yugoslavia, or Rwandans connected with the commission of international crimes in Rwanda in 1994. All of these 24 defendants were the type of defendants that the international community has most clearly agreed should be prosecuted and punished and their own States of nationality have not bothered to defend them. For five out of the eight remaining defendants (four Afghans and one Congolese), their respective States of nationality did not protest their prosecution in foreign courts on the basis of universal jurisdiction. Two of the remaining three defendants included a Mauritanian and a Tunisian who were tried *in absentia* and did not serve any sentence. The other remaining defendant was an Argentine tried in Spain in spite of the protests of Argentina. Five of the 32 were acquitted, 17 convicted and ten acquitted on some charges. These statistics have to be considered in the light of the total number of 1,051 criminal complaints or cases based on universal jurisdiction brought on motions of public authorities. Spain had the largest number of such complaints at 259, followed by Germany (at 235), Canada (at 216), the UK (at 85), Australia (at 70) and Belgium (at 63), with the other States receiving from one to 17 such complaints each. Most of these States were in Western Europe. Turkey received 17 complaints, Israel received three, New Zealand received one, Senegal received one and South Africa received two, respectively.[147]

With the mass influx of people coming from war-torn States like Syria, new criminal complaints have been lodged with Germany, Sweden, Finland, Switzerland, Norway, Netherlands, Spain and France, among others, for these States to exercise universal jurisdiction to prosecute asylum seekers accused of

---

[146] Amnesty International, *Universal Jurisdiction – A Preliminary Survey of Legislation around the World – 2012 Update* (Amnesty International 2012) 2, 12 and Annexes I and II.

[147] Máximo Langer, 'The Diplomacy of Universal Jurisdiction: The Political Branches and the Transnational Prosecution of International Crimes' (2011) 105 AJIL 1, 2, 7–9, 42–4.

committing war crimes and/or crimes against humanity in their States of origin before their arrival in Europe as well as individuals in their States of origin accused of the same.[148]

The legitimacy of the exercise of universal jurisdiction has not been definitively settled by an international court or tribunal. In the *Arrest Warrant* case between the Democratic Republic of the Congo and Belgium, decided by the ICJ in 2002,[149] DR Congo challenged the legality of the arrest warrant issued by a Belgian investigating judge in the exercise of his purported universal jurisdiction for the arrest of the then incumbent Minister of Foreign Affairs of DR Congo, charged with war crimes punishable under Belgian law concerning the punishment of serious violations of international humanitarian law. DR Congo at first invoked two separate grounds of challenge: Belgium's claim to exercise universal jurisdiction and the alleged violation of the immunities of the Minister. It later withdrew the first ground of challenge, leaving the ICJ to address the issue of immunities without having to decide whether the exercise of universal jurisdiction was lawful under international law.

Although the ICJ abstains from deciding on the issue of universal jurisdiction in *Arrest Warrant*, some of the ICJ judges touch upon it in their separate or dissenting opinion. ICJ President Guillaume opines that traditionally customary international law recognizes universal jurisdiction over piracy at sea; whereas in modern days universal jurisdiction is conferred by treaties over offences covered in the respective treaties committed abroad by foreigners against foreigners, but only where the perpetrator of such an offence is present in the territory of the State exercising universal jurisdiction.[150] The Joint Separate Opinion of Judges Higgins, Kooijmans and Buergenthal goes much further. The three judges consider that while there is no rule of international law specifically authorizing the right to exercise universal jurisdiction, there is no rule of international law that prohibits it and the growing international consensus on the need to punish the most serious crimes indicates that Belgium's arrest warrant did not as such violate international law.[151] If a State chooses to exercise universal jurisdiction *in absentia*, it must ensure that certain safe-

---

[148] For some useful links to news about these cases, see Human Rights Watch, 'Q&A: First Cracks to Impunity in Syria, Iraq: Refugee Crisis and Universal Jurisdiction in Europe' (20 Oct 2016) https://www.hrw.org/news/2016/10/20/qa-first-cracks-impunity-syria-iraq, accessed 13 Dec 2018. See also Isabelle Hassfurther, 'Will There Be "Justice for Syria"?: The Assad Regime in German Courts' (2017) 60 German YBIL 731.

[149] *Arrest Warrant of 11 April 2000 (DR Congo v Belgium)* [2002] ICJ Rep 3.

[150] Ibid 37–40 [5]–[9] (Separate Opinion of President Guillaume).

[151] Ibid 75–9 [44]–[52] (Joint Separate Opinion of Judges Higgins, Kooijmans and Buergenthal).

guards are put in place, as these safeguards are 'absolutely essential to prevent abuse and to ensure that the rejection of impunity does not jeopardize stable relations between States'.[152] Judge ad hoc Van den Wyngaert, appointed by Belgium in that case, goes the furthest, positing that international law does not prohibit States from enacting legislation to permit themselves to exercise prescriptive extraterritorial jurisdiction to investigate and prosecute war crimes and crimes against humanity committed abroad. In her view, international law allows and even encourages the exercise of universal jurisdiction to end impunity for such crimes, even *in absentia* although there may be some good political or practical reasons not to exercise universal jurisdiction *in absentia* (for example, because of international relations costs and the difficulty in obtaining the evidence in trials of extraterritorial crimes).[153] At the opposite extreme, Judge ad hoc Bula-Bula appointed by DR Congo considers universal jurisdiction 'variable geometry' jurisdiction, selectively exercised against some States to the exclusion of others.[154]

Criminal complaints mostly in Western States about alleged serious human rights violations elsewhere have led to proceedings for arrest warrants to be issued against the suspects or alleged offenders, many of whom are or have been high-ranking government officials, such as presidents, prime ministers, cabinet ministers and so on. Several of the targeted suspects or alleged offenders are Africans, like the Minister of Foreign Affairs of DR Congo in the *Arrest Warrant* case.

In November 2008 the African Union (AU) and the European Union set up the AU–EU Technical ad hoc Expert Group on the Principle of Universal Jurisdiction in response to the AU's concern over 'abusive applications' of this principle. The Expert Group comprised three distinguished international lawyers from Africa[155] and three highly regarded international law experts from Europe.[156] The report issued by the Expert Group in April 2009 states unequivocally:

> International law, both customary and conventional, regulates States' assertion of universal criminal jurisdiction. States by and large accept that customary international law permits the exercise of universal jurisdiction over the international crimes of genocide, crimes against humanity, war crimes and torture, as well as over piracy. In addition, numerous treaties oblige States Parties to empower their criminal justice

---

[152] Ibid 79–83 [56]–[65].
[153] Ibid 165–77 [44]–[67] (Dissenting Opinion of Judge ad hoc Van den Wyngaert).
[154] Ibid 133 [104] (Separate Opinion of Judge ad hoc Bula-Bula).
[155] Former ICJ President Mohammed Bedjaoui (Algeria), Chaloka Beyani (Zambia) and Chris Maina Peter (Tanzania).
[156] Antonio Cassese (Italy), Pierre Klein (Belgium) and Roger O'Keefe from Australia who teaches public international law in the UK.

systems to exercise universal jurisdiction over the crimes defined in those treaties, although their obligation extends only to the exercise of such jurisdiction when a suspect is subsequently present in the territory of the forum State.[157]

The report recommends that when exercising universal jurisdiction, priority is to be given to a State having a significant link with the crime in question, especially the territorial State where the crime is committed. States wishing to exercise universal jurisdiction should bear in mind the need to avoid impairing friendly international relations. National criminal justice authorities considering exercising this jurisdiction should consider refraining from taking steps that might publicly and unduly expose the suspects, thereby discrediting and stigmatizing them, curtailing their rights to be presumed innocent until found guilty by a court of law and hampering the discharge of their official functions. The national authorities considering exercising this jurisdiction must take into consideration all the immunities to which foreign State officials may be entitled under international law. Where *either* the State in whose territory the crime is committed *or* the State of nationality of the victim or the suspect/accused seems manifestly unwilling or unable to prosecute the suspect/accused, the national criminal justice authorities considering exercising universal jurisdiction over the suspect/accused who is a foreign State official exercising a representative function on behalf of his/her State should seek and issue a summons to appear before the court or an equivalent measure, rather than an arrest warrant, for the suspect/accused to appear before the court and to produce, with the assistance of counsel, any exculpatory evidence.

Also in April 2009 the Non-Aligned Movement Ministerial Meeting held in Cuba adopted a resolution that, realizing 'the negative effects on international relations of the abuse of the Principle of Universal Jurisdiction', calls upon States 'to refrain from such abuse' and urges them to discuss this matter in the UNGA 'aiming at identifying the scope and limits of this Principle and establish a mechanism to monitor such implementation and to prevent its abuse in the future'.[158] The UNGA has included on its agenda the topic 'The scope and application of the principle of universal jurisdiction' since the second half of 2009 at the request of the African Group of States at the UN, New York, acting on behalf of the AU. The Sixth (Legal) Committee of the UNGA is entrusted

---

[157] Report of the AU–EU Technical ad hoc Expert Group on the Principle of Universal Jurisdiction dated 15 April 2009, Annexed to the Council of European Union Doc 8672/1/09 dated 16 Apr 2009 §9 (footnotes omitted).

[158] Final Document of the Ministerial Meeting of the Non-Aligned Movement Coordinating Bureau, Havana, Cuba, 27–30 Apr 2009 (Doc NAM 2009/MM/Doc1/Rev1 of 30 Apr 2009) §17.3.

with this matter, without prejudice to the consideration of related issues in other UN forums.[159]

In 2011 the AU proposed to the UN Secretary-General that the UN set up an international commission on universal jurisdiction as a subsidiary body of the UNGA to act as a regulatory body on the exercise of universal jurisdiction by verifying the validity, legality and factual basis of indictments and warrants issued by judges in individual States before they can be approved for execution outside their own respective territories.[160] Having met with strong opposition in the UN as it would undermine the independence of the national judiciary, this proposal is no longer being pursued by the AU.

The Working Group on the Scope and Application of the Principle of Universal Jurisdiction was set up by the Sixth Committee of the UNGA in October 2011, with its establishment renewed annually by the Sixth Committee. As of this writing, the Working Group has not made substantive progress beyond agreeing on abstract principles such as the need to fight impunity while avoiding abuse/misuse of universal jurisdiction.[161] Some African States have questioned who would decide whether a State is unable or unwilling to prosecute a person who has committed a serious human rights violation so that another State could step in to exercise universal jurisdiction to prosecute the person. China and India insist that piracy at sea is the only crime subject to universal jurisdiction under customary international law – a regression from the conclusion of the AU–EU Technical ad hoc Expert Group on the Principle of Universal Jurisdiction in April 2009. The Working Group has not taken up what has already been done by the AU–EU Technical ad hoc Expert Group or developed the well-balanced Princeton Principles of Universal Jurisdiction,[162] adopted in January 2001 by a group of eminent jurists from around the world, including Africa and Asia, which suggest several in-built safeguards against potential abuses of the exercise of universal jurisdiction.

Every year, delegates in the Sixth Committee of the UNGA reiterate what they have previously said about universal jurisdiction in the preceding years. As regards the scope of universal jurisdiction, delegations note that consensus on the *ratione materiae* of the crimes subject to the principle of universal jurisdiction has yet to emerge. A number of delegations consider universal jurisdiction to apply to the most serious international crimes and provide

---

[159]   UN Doc A/RES/64/117 (15 Jan 2010).

[160]   Report of the Secretary-General, 'The scope and application of the principle of universal jurisdiction', UN Doc A/66/93 (20 June 2010) §168.

[161]   See a summary of the progress of the Working Group's work in Kittichaisaree, *The Obligation to Extradite or Prosecute* 213–17.

[162]   Stephen Macedo (ed.), *The Princeton Principles on Universal Jurisdiction* (Princeton University Press 2001).

various examples of such crimes. Some delegations observe that the principle applies to certain serious crimes under international treaties, while some other delegations note that customary international law also permits the exercise of universal jurisdiction over certain crimes. While some delegations warn against the establishment of an exhaustive list of crimes subject to universal jurisdiction, some others stress that the crimes to which the principle applies should be identified. With respect to the application of universal jurisdiction, delegations reaffirm their concern over potential abuse or manipulation of the principle. Several delegations emphasize that the principle must be applied in accordance with the UN Charter and international legal norms, including the sovereign equality of States, territorial integrity and the non-interference in the internal affairs of States.[163]

Several States, such as Liechtenstein, Switzerland, Czech Republic and Morocco, wish to have the ILC – a body comprising 34 international law experts elected by the UNGA for a five-year term and mandated to codify and progressively develop international law – undertake the study on universal jurisdiction. These States consider the ILC more independent and free from politics as ILC members are not representatives of States, unlike State delegates in the Sixth Committee. They suggest that the discussions in the current forum are at an impasse and that a study by the ILC can provide substantive elements for future debates. This proposal to refer the topic to the ILC has not received general approval in the Sixth Committee. A number of States prefer to keep the topic on the Sixth Committee's annual agenda without a final outcome or solution likely to be attained in the near future. The formula adopted in successive annual UNGA resolutions on the 'Scope and application of the principle of universal jurisdiction' typically recognizes the diversity of views expressed by States, including concerns about the abuse or misuse of the principle of universal jurisdiction and the need to continue discussion on the scope and application of this principle in the Sixth Committee. It reiterates the commitment to fight impunity and notes the views expressed by States that the legitimacy and credibility of the use of universal jurisdiction are best ensured by its responsible and judicious application consistent with international law.[164] The resolutions do not indicate what that international law says however. For its part, the ILC has included the topic 'Universal criminal jurisdiction' in its

---

[163] Eg, the summary of the debate on this topic during the 72nd Session of the Sixth Committee in 2018, http://www.un.org/en/ga/sixth/72/universal_jurisdiction.shtml, accessed 17 Jan 2019.

[164] Eg, the fifth preambular paragraph of UNGA resolution A/RES/71/120 (18 Dec 2017) and the fourth preambular paragraph of draft res A/C.6/73/L.16 (6 Nov 2018) adopted by the Sixth (Legal) Committee of the UNGA without a vote on 13 Nov 2018.

long-term programme of work since 2018[165] but is likely to heed the Sixth Committee's indication as to when the ILC may start working on this topic.

In the meantime, an attempt by a State to exercise universal jurisdiction will be challenged by States most affected or potentially affected by it, contending that since the international community (that is, the Sixth Committee) has not yet agreed on the scope and application of the principle of universal jurisdiction, any unilateral exercise of universal jurisdiction is politically motivated and unlawful. Yet, as observed by a legal scholar, the actual trials based on the exercise of universal jurisdiction concentrate on defendants who impose little or no cost on prosecuting States – primarily defendants whom the international community agrees should be prosecuted and punished – and that the political branches of individual States concerned have the incentive to keep using universal jurisdiction in just this rather limited way.[166]

Where a human rights violator is present in a foreign State and that State does not exercise universal jurisdiction to prosecute the person, it may use its immigration law to deport the person back to his or her State of origin[167] or use its extradition law to extradite the person to stand trial in the State where the person has committed an offence that violates human rights. However, there are extradition requirements under the national law of most States. For example, some States cannot extradite a person to another State without a treaty between them that specifically authorizes extradition. Other States cannot extradite a person to States having the death penalty for the crime of which the person being sought for extradition is accused. In such circumstances, the State having custody of the human rights violator should extradite the person to a third State that, for some reason, has concurrent jurisdiction over the case, is able and willing to prosecute the person and can fulfil the extradition conditions set by the law of the extraditing State. The third State may have legal bases for prosecuting the person, for example because one of the person's victims is a national of that third State.

Amnesties are usually considered as serious impediments to the bringing of human rights abusers to justice. However, there are several types of justice. Retributive justice demands proportionate punishment as a morally justifiable response to crime so that the victim of the crime can find satisfaction

---

[165] Report of the ILC on the work of its seventieth session (30 Apr–1 June and 2 July–10 Aug 2018) UN Doc A/73/10 Annex A.

[166] Langer, 'The Diplomacy of Universal Jurisdiction' 49.

[167] As in the case of Leon Mugesera, deported from Canada back to Rwanda to face charges of inciting genocide and crimes against humanity arising from an incendiary anti-Tutsi speech he gave in 1992 ('Canada deports Rwanda genocide suspect Leon Mugesera', *BBC News* (24 Jan 2012) https://www.bbc.com/news/world-us-canada -16694130, accessed 14 Dec 2018).

and society can be saved by the deterrence of further commission of crime. Restorative justice, also known as reparative justice, emphasizes the needs of victims and perpetrators of crimes, whereby the latter are to acknowledge and take responsibility for their conduct by giving reparation to their victims after having dialogue with them.[168] Restorative justice overlaps conceptually with transitional justice and can be a catalyst for the latter. A truth and reconciliation commission set up after the end of the apartheid regime in South Africa is an example of both restorative justice and transitional justice resorted to in lieu of prosecuting hundreds of thousands of individuals accused of implementing apartheid, which would be costly, time consuming and disruptive to national reconciliation and harmony. Transitional justice in post-conflict situations in a nation State usually involves balancing prosecution of large-scale serious violations of human rights, on the one hand, and the need to achieve national reconciliation, on the other hand.[169]

The ECtHR remarks that while there is a 'growing tendency in international law' against amnesties for grave breaches of fundamental human rights as they are incompatible with the unanimously recognized obligation of States to prosecute and punish such crimes, amnesties may be possible in other circumstances, such as a reconciliation process and/or a form of compensation to victims.[170] Article 6(5) of the Protocol Additional to the Geneva Conventions of 12 August 1949 and relating to the protection of victims of non-international armed conflicts[171] even encourages the granting of 'the broadest possible amnesty' at the end of an internal armed conflict or civil war to 'persons who have participated in the armed conflict, or those [interned or detained] for reasons related to the armed conflict'.

As a rule of thumb, blanket amnesties issued by those who themselves are alleged to have committed mass atrocities are self-serving efforts to circumvent the rule of law and should not be recognized as legally or constitutionally

---

[168] Kathleen Daly, 'Restorative Justice versus Retributive Justice' (2005) 60 Crim Justice Matters 28; Wesley Cragg, *The Practice of Punishment: Towards a Theory of Restorative Justice* (Routledge 1992) 15.

[169] On transitional justice, see Nicola Palmer, Phil Clark and Danielle Granville (eds), *Critical Perspectives in Transitional Justice* (Intersentia 2012); Moses Chrispus Okello, Chris Dolan, Undine Whande, Nokukhanya Mncwabe, Lewis Onegi and Stephen Oola (eds), *Where Law Meets Reality: Forging African Transitional Justice* (Pambazuka Press 2012); Noha Aboueldahab, *Transitional Justice and the Prosecution of Political Leaders in the Arab Region: A Comparative Study of Egypt, Libya, Tunisia and Yemen* (Hart 2017).

[170] *Marguš v Croatia* [GC], No 4455/10 §139, 27 May 2014. Cf Miles Jackson, 'Amnesties in Strasbourg' (2018) 38 Oxford J Legal Studies 451, 462–3.

[171] 1125 UNTS 609.

valid.[172] Amnesties granted by a subsequent government with overriding political objectives but without due regard to the rights of the victims of human rights abuses should suffer the same fate. A clear example is the amnesty granted in 1986 to former Guatemalan President Ríos Montt and his aides by the army general who staged a *coup d'état* to overthrow Ríos Montt in 1983. On 1 March 2012 a Guatemalan court ruled the 1986 amnesty to be invalid as it was contrary to the provisions of the 1948 Genocide Convention, to which Guatemala had become party in 1950 and which was implemented in Guatemala's domestic law in 1973. Ríos Montt was therefore not entitled to amnesty or immunity from the charges, brought in January 2012, of ordering 1,771 murders, 1,400 human rights violations, including rapes and tortures and displacement of 29,000 indigenous Guatemalans in a 'scorched earth' campaign to eliminate the support for a left-wing guerrilla movement during his regime in 1982–83. Even more interesting is the ruling of the IACtHR in 2011 refusing to recognize and even condemning Uruguay's amnesty law, which had been confirmed in a plebiscite. According to the IACtHR, the fact that a law has been approved in a democratic regime and ratified or supported by the public does not automatically or by itself grant legitimacy under international law. It reasons that the democratic legitimacy of specific facts in a society is limited by the norms of protection of human rights recognized in international treaties, such as the 1969 American Convention on Human Rights,[173] in such a form that the existence of one true democratic regime is determined by both its formal and substantial characteristics and therefore, particularly in cases of serious violations of non-revocable norms of international law, the protection of human rights constitutes 'an impassable limit to the rule of the majority'.[174] In another example, on 3 October 2018 the Peruvian Supreme Court invalidated the pardon on health grounds granted by the then President of Peru on 24 December 2017 to the 79-year-old former Peruvian President Alberto Fujimori, who had been convicted and sentenced in 2009 to 25 years' imprisonment for ordering, when he was President from 1990 to 2000, the killings of 25 people by a government-backed death squad.

In the final analysis, the decision whether to resort to which type of justice for the victims of human rights violations involves prioritizing the competing goals of: (i) preventing violations of human rights; (ii) ending impunity for past violations; (iii) maintaining and restoring international peace and security;

---

[172] José E Alvarez, 'Alternative to International Criminal Justice' in Antonio Cassese (ed.), *The Oxford Companion to International Criminal Justice* (OUP 2009) 25, 36; Jackson, 'Amnesties in Strasbourg' 472–3.

[173] 1144 UNTS 123.

[174] *Gelman v Uruguay*, Merits and reparations, IACtHR (2011) Ser C, No 110, 24 Feb 2011 §§238–9.

(iv) providing closure or redress for victims of human rights violations; (v) expressing condemnation of atrocities; (vi) fostering post-conflict reconciliation; and (vii) retribution.[175] Above all, the granting of amnesty by one State has no direct effect on prosecution in another State with concurrent jurisdiction over the case or on prosecution by a competent international criminal court or tribunal with jurisdiction over the case.

A potent tool against impunity for human rights violations is the inapplicability of the statute of limitations. There is widespread practice in both States' practice and the legal literature that core crimes proscribed by *jus cogens* are not subject to the statute of limitations.

The 1968 Convention on the Inapplicability of the Statute of Limitations to War Crimes and Crimes against Humanity,[176] in force on 11 November 1970 and binding on 55 States Parties as of this writing, prohibits the applicability of the statute of limitations to the crimes covered by this Convention. One of its preambular paragraphs expresses the conviction of the parties to the Convention that the effective punishment of war crimes and crimes against humanity is an important element in, inter alia, the prevention of such crimes and the protection of human rights and fundamental freedoms. Article 29 of the Rome Statute of the International Criminal Court (ICC),[177] binding on 122 States Parties as of this writing, provides unequivocally that the crimes against humanity, war crimes, genocide and aggression within the ICC's jurisdiction shall not be subject to any statute of limitations. The International Committee of the Red Cross posits that the inapplicability of the statute of limitations to war crimes in both international and non-international armed conflicts is a norm of customary international law thanks to well-established State practice in this regard.[178] The Revitalized Agreement on the Resolution of the Conflict in the Republic of South Sudan,[179] signed on 12 September 2018 by all the parties to the conflict in South Sudan, provides that the Hybrid Court for South Sudan shall be established by the African Union Commission to investigate and prosecute individuals responsible for the crimes of genocide, crimes against humanity, war crimes and other serious crimes under international law and relevant laws of South Sudan including gender-based crimes and sexual

---

[175] Stuart Ford, 'A Hierarchy of the Goals of International Criminal Courts' (2018) 27 Minnesota JIL 179.

[176] 754 UNTS 73.

[177] 2187 UNTS 3.

[178] Jean-Marie Henckaerts and Louise Doswald-Beck, *International Committee of the Red Cross: Customary International Humanitarian Law* (CUP 2009) vol I (Rules), 614–18.

[179] https://www.dropbox.com/s/6dn3477q3f5472d/R-ARCSS.2018-i.pdf?dl=0, accessed 17 Jan 2019.

violence, committed from 15 December 2013 through the end of the transitional period. The Agreement expressly stipulates that the Court shall not be impeded or constrained by any statute of limitations or the granting of pardons, immunities or amnesties.[180]

It is not unusual for justice for victims of human rights violations to be *temporarily* suspended for the sake of national peace and reconciliation or during the transition from an authoritarian regime to a full-fledged democracy. However, this justice must be 'reactivated' when the time is ripe and it is politically safe for a truly independent and impartial domestic court to sit in judgment of former dictators, autocrats and their ilk for their past human rights violations. This is a most effective avenue to enforce IHRL in the long run.

In any case, human rights violations in one State may be subject to civil actions for damages before a domestic court of another State, as in *Cathleen Colvin et al v Syrian Arab Republic*,[181] decided by the US District Court for the District of Columbia on 31 January 2019. It arises out of an intense artillery assault on the Baba Amr Media Centre in Homs, Syria, that killed Marie Colvin, an American war journalist for *The Sunday Times* who was there covering the war between the Syrian Government and rebel groups. In their complaint, the plaintiffs assert that Colvin was the victim of a targeted government policy to surveil, capture and even kill journalists to prevent reporting on the Syrian Government's suppression of the political opposition. The plaintiffs, who are Colvin's relatives, assert that her death constitutes an extrajudicial killing in violation of the Foreign Sovereign Immunities Act.[182] Under the Act, a court may not enter default judgment against a foreign State 'unless the claimant establishes his claim or right to relief by evidence satisfactory to the court'.[183] Given the considerations of sovereign immunity that pertain notwithstanding the default, a court must carefully scrutinize the plaintiff's allegations and may not unquestioningly accept a complaint's unsupported allegations as true. Under the Act, a foreign State is presumptively immune from the jurisdiction of US courts and, unless a specified exception applies, a federal court lacks subject-matter jurisdiction over a claim against a foreign State. This case falls within the exception of the Act stipulating that a foreign State shall not be immune from the jurisdiction of US courts in which money damages are sought against the foreign State for personal injury or death caused by an act of torture, extrajudicial killing, aircraft sabotage, hostage taking or the provision of material support or resources for such an act if such

---

[180] Art 5.3 of the Agreement.
[181] 363 F.Supp.3d 141 (2019).
[182] 28 U.S.C. §§1602–1611.
[183] Ibid §1608(e).

act or provision of material support or resources is engaged in by an official, employee or agent of such foreign State while acting within the scope of his or her office, employment or agency.[184] The Court notes in this connection that media activists and journalists became high-priority targets of the Syrian Government because it was through the media that demonstrators could organize protests against the Government, and that murder of journalists acting in their professional capacity could have a chilling effect on reporting such events worldwide. The Act lists a set of additional conditions that must be met before a federal district court may hear a claim: (i) the foreign State must be designated a State sponsor of terrorism at the time of the act giving rise to the claim, (ii) the claimant or the victim must be a US national, a member of the armed forces or a government employee at the time of the act, and (iii) the claimant must have afforded the foreign State a reasonable opportunity to arbitrate the claim in accordance with the accepted international rules of arbitration.[185] Because the Plaintiffs have demonstrated all of these elements, the Court finds that Syria is not immune from suit.

After finding that it has both personal and subject-matter jurisdiction and that the Plaintiffs have demonstrated with a satisfactory amount of evidence that Syria is liable for Colvin's death by extrajudicial killing, the Court grants the Plaintiffs' motion for default judgment and enter judgment in the amount of US$302,511,836, comprising US$300 million in punitive damages, US$2.5 million in compensation to Colvin's sister and US$11,836 in funeral expenses. In awarding the punitive damages, the Court refers to Section 1605A(c) of the Act, which authorizes punitive damages to be assessed against foreign State sponsors of terrorism in order to punish and deter defendants for their bad acts. In this respect, courts shall calculate punitive damages by considering the following four factors: (1) the character of the defendants' act, (2) the nature and extent of harm to the plaintiffs that the defendants caused or intended to cause, (3) the need for deterrence and (4) the wealth of the defendants. The Court remarks, in particular, that 'a targeted murder of an American citizen, whose courageous work was not only important, but vital to our understanding of war zones and of wars generally, is outrageous and therefore a punitive damages award that multiples the impact on the responsible state is warranted'.

The main hurdle thereafter for the Plaintiffs in *Cathleen Colvin et al v Syrian Arab Republic* is to enforce the award. The judgment will form the grounds for a legal claim to seize Syria's overseas assets, provided that the assets can be proved to belong to the nation State of Syria or the Syrian Government and not Syrian individuals or entities who are not holders of the assets as agents or on

---

[184] Ibid §1605A(a)(1).
[185] Ibid §1605A(a)(2).

behalf of the Syrian State or Government. In any event, the Plaintiffs may avail themselves of compensation from the fund set up under the Justice for United States Victims of State Sponsored Terrorism Act,[186] which compensates eligible US persons who hold a final judgment issued by a US district court awarding them compensatory damages arising from acts of international terrorism for which a foreign State sponsor of terrorism was found not immune from the jurisdiction of US courts under the Foreign Sovereign Immunities Act.

---

[186] 34 U.S.C §20144.

7. Universalization of international human rights norms: reassessment

Given that the 1948 Universal Declaration of Human Rights (UDHR)[1] has been embraced by diverse peoples all over the world, these peoples must be able to contribute to the development and realization of international human rights norms from their own perspectives beyond the traditional confine of Western liberalism underpinning the development of human rights in past centuries.[2] What matters for non-Westerners would be a dialogue for the inclusion of their traditions as well as their State practices previously disregarded by the West during the crystallization of human rights norms before and after the Second World War and the alleviation of human suffering in the global South that impedes the capacity of the States in the southern hemisphere to fulfil the duty of upholding human rights expected of them.[3]

The universalism-versus-relativism debate is a complex one. It might be argued that human rights can be 'universal' in a 'morally' significant sense only if they are acceptable from all moral and cultural points of view.[4] Yet it is inconceivable for every human rights norm to be universally embraced by all ideologies. For Marxists, for example, Karl Marx identifies the limited potential of realizing human rights in bourgeois societies where there exist institutional arrangements made and enforced by a class of owners of capital in the market against the working class.[5] Marxists also insist that the 'essential aim' of the 'modern' doctrine of customary international law developed near

---

[1]   Doc A/RES/217(III).

[2]   Cf Makau W Mutua, 'Politics and Human Rights: An Essential Symbiosis' in Michael Byers (ed.), *The Role of Law in International Politics: Essays in International Relations and International Law* (OUP 2000) 149, 173–5.

[3]   Ali Allawi, 'Islam, Human Rights and the New Information Technologies' in Monroe Price and Nicole Stremlau (eds), *Speech and Society in Turbulent Times* (CUP 2018) 19, 23; Gavin W Anderson, 'Human Rights and the Global South' in Tom Campbell, KD Ewing and Adam Tomkins (eds), *The Legal Protection of Human Rights: Sceptical Essays* (OUP 2011) 347, 350, 354–7.

[4]   As pointed out by Charles R Beitz, *The Idea of Human Rights* (OUP 2009) 5; Rosa Freedman, *Failing to Protect: The UN and the Politicisation of Human Rights* (C Hurst & Co 2014) 39.

[5]   BS Chimni, *International Law and World Order: A Critique of Contemporary Approaches* (CUP 2017) 534–41.

the end of the Cold War while the 'neoliberal globalization process' was gathering momentum – when there was rapid development in such fields as international human rights law (IHRL), international humanitarian law and international criminal law – is 'the generation of norms that safeguard the systemic interests of the global capitalist system'. Customary international law, in Marxists' view, is an undemocratic source of international law due to, among other things, the absence and neglect of practice of Third World States, the paucity of writing of publicists from the Third World, the lack of adequate weight given to the qualifying resolutions of international organizations and the non-recognition of the practices of the global civil society.[6]

However, it could be contended that for human rights to be effective they need not be universal, and yet 'it is difficult to imagine a human rights regime in a multicultural world that is completely devoid of culture, provided, of course, that it is not used as an excuse by authoritarian regimes to abuse the rights of their nationals'.[7] Even so, for human rights to be universally adopted and respected, they need to be universally justifiable. Universalism or universality is not synonymous with uniformity, nonetheless.[8]

International human rights norms can be flexible in the sense that the State's good faith restrictions on human rights for legitimate purposes as permitted by IHRL allow the State to adapt universal human rights norms to specific local conditions and priorities in fulfilling the State's human rights obligations within the means and resources available to it.[9] One of the most serious shortcomings in the flexibility in enforcing legal rules is the inherent risk of arbitrariness or perceived bias of the person or body entrusted with their

---

[6]   Id, 'Customary International Law: A Third World Perspective' (2018) 112 AJIL 1, esp 16–17, 20–27 and 44–6. Cf Samuel Moyn, *Not Enough: Human Rights in an Unequal World* (Harvard University Press 2018); Terrence E Paupp, *Redefining Human Rights in the Struggle for Peace and Development* (CUP 2014) 4 and *passim*; Paul O'Connell, 'Brave New World? Human Rights in the Era of Globalization' in Mashood A Baderin and Manisuli Ssenyonjo (eds), *International Human Rights Law: Six Decades after the UDHR and Beyond* (Ashgate 2010) 195, 210.

[7]   Edwin Egede and Peter Sutch, *The Politics of International Law and International Justice* (Edinburgh University Press 2013) 183. See also Benjamin Gregg, *Human Rights as Social Construction* (CUP 2012) 3; Rein Müllerson, 'Human Rights Are neither Universal nor Natural' (2018) 17 Chinese JIL 925; Sabine C Carey, Mark Gibney and Stern C Poe, *The Politics of Human Rights: The Quest for Dignity* (CUP 2010) 27.

[8]   Cf Hurst Hannum, *Rescuing Human Rights: A Radically Moderate Approach* (CUP 2019) 97–118.

[9]   Cf id, 'Reinvigorating Human Rights for the Twenty-First Century' (2016) 16 Hum Rts L Rev 409, 439–43.

enforcement.[10] The most common argument for relativity relates to cultures that differ, often dramatically, across time and space.[11] There are several concerns about cultural relativism in the field of human rights. For example, it risks falsely assuming that each culture is morally infallible, immutable and not susceptible to adaptation. More importantly, cultures may represent values of bygone eras that do not necessarily reflect realities of the present days.[12]

In 1998 the proposal by the then President Mohammad Khatami of the Islamic Republic of Iran that the UN organize the Dialogue among Civilizations led to the UN General Assembly (UNGA) proclaiming the year 2001 as the UN Year of Dialogue among Civilizations. The initiative intends to project a new paradigm of international relations favouring dialogue instead of confrontation among States with different ideologies and systems of government.[13] As Khatami himself explains, '[i]n order to provide natural unity and harmony in form and content for global culture to prevent anarchy and chaos, all the parties concerned should engage in a dialogue in which they can exchange knowledge, experience and understanding in diverse areas of culture and civilization'.[14] The initiative has no substantive bearing on international human rights and any credence to cultural relativistic claims deriving from such dialogue might, arguably, be susceptible to its potential abuse to justify human rights violations in the name of cultural relativism.[15]

It may be recalled that conflicts between Sharia and IHRL as generally understood in the non-Muslim world are manifest in relation to the status of women, family matters, restrictions on religious liberty and corporal

---

[10]   Eg, Art 53(1)(c) and (2)(c) of the 1998 Rome Statute of the International Criminal Court (2187 UNTS 3) allowing the ICC Prosecutor discretion not to proceed with investigating or prosecuting a crime within the ICC's jurisdiction as it would not be in the 'interests of justice' to do so. See Talita de Souza Dias, '"Interests of Justice": Defining the Scope of Prosecutorial Discretion in Article 53(1)(c) and (2)(d) of the Rome Statute of the International Criminal Court' (2017) 30 Leiden JIL 731.

[11]   Jack Donnelly, 'International Human Rights: Universal, Relative or Relatively Universal?' in Baderin and Ssenyonjo (eds), *International Human Rights Law* 31, 43.

[12]   Ibid 44–5.

[13]   Giandomenico Picco, 'A Dialogue among Civilizations' (Winter/Spring 2000) Seton Hall J Diplomacy & Int'l Relations 3; Fabio Petito, 'Khatami's Dialogue among Civilizations as International Political Theory' (2004) 11 J Humanities 11; Akbar Ahmed and Brian Forst, *After Terror: Promoting Dialogue among Civilizations* (Polity 2005).

[14]   UNESCO, *Dialogue among Civilizations: The Round Table on the Eve of the United Nations Millennium Summit* (UNESCO 2001) 25.

[15]   Mishana Hosseinioun, *The Human Rights Turn and the Paradox of Progress in the Middle East* (Palgrave Macmillan 2018) 135–6; Jack Donnelly, 'Human Rights and the Dialogue among Civilizations', personal blog, https://mysite.du.edu/~jdonnell/papers/dialogue.pdf, accessed 2 Sept 2018.

punishment. The Cairo Declaration on Human Rights in Islam[16] adopted by the Organisation of Islamic Cooperation (OIC) in August 1990 may be seen as Islamic conservatives' push against a neo-Western 'crusade' or cultural imperialism, whereas liberal Muslims strive, through the Cairo Declaration, for pragmatic reconciliation between the Islamic understanding of human rights and that of the non-Islamic world. Such pragmatic reconciliation might be possible where there exists 'overlapping consensus', with international norms being adapted to fit different cultural and religious communities as well as political realities.[17] Such 'overlapping consensus' may involve finding agreement on basic norms while accepting disagreement on their underlying justifications if that makes agreement on the norms possible.[18] The question is how to achieve this. Recognizing cultural relativism to the full, or even half way, might unnecessarily undermine international human rights norms.[19] One suggestion is to centre attention on areas where international human rights norms are approaching Islamic ones in order to find the consensus,[20] or where there is common ground between IHRL and Islamic law.[21] A possible methodology is to search for the purpose of the Quran that is the same as or similar to the one shared in the non-Islamic world where this would negate Islamic traditions and practices not actually sanctioned by the Quran. This is, arguably, the case of the status of women in Islamic society (including their rights in relation to divorce, polygamy and inheritance), which the Quran intends to elevate and not subjugate as is commonly believed and practised in many Islamic societies today.[22] Another view considers that law reform within the framework of Sharia is possible and necessary to reflect the constantly evolving norms of modern society, even in Iran, which is a constitutionally Islamic republic.[23] In addition, Sharia courts, where they exist, are jurisprudentially flexible as they

---

[16]   UN Doc A/CONF.157/PC/62/Add.18 (1993).
[17]   Heiner Bielefeldt, 'Muslim Voices in the Human Rights Debate' (1995) 7 Hum Rts L Quarterly 587.
[18]   Jeffrey Flynn, *Reframing the Intellectual Dialogue on Human Rights* (Routledge 2014) 66, 143.
[19]   Mashood A Baderin, *International Human Rights and Islamic Law* (OUP 2003) 27.
[20]   Jason Morgan-Foster, 'A New Perspective on the Universality Debate: Reverse Moderate Relativism in the Islamic Context' (2003) 10 Int'l L Students Assoc J of Int'l & Comp Law 25, 66–7.
[21]   Ahmed M El Demey, *The Arab Charter of Human Rights: A Voice for Sharia in the Modern World* (Council on International Law and Politics 2015) 8.
[22]   Niaz A Shah, 'Women's Human Rights in the Quran: An Interpretative Approach' (2006) 28 Hum Rts L Quarterly 863.
[23]   Nisrine Abiad, *Sharia, Muslim States and International Human Rights Treaty Obligations: A Comparative Study* (British Institute of International and Comparative Law 2008) 119–21.

can change their jurisprudence without having to abide by precedents, and this is the case even in the most orthodox Islamic legal system in Saudi Arabia.[24]

However, a view has been expressed that there is little prospect of accommodation by Muslim-majority States on gender matters concerning polygamy, divorce and inheritance rights and some forms of capital punishment.[25] Yet, thanks to a general acknowledgement of the significance of IHRL by Muslim-majority States, most of these States have been cautiously moving to bridge the existing gap between traditional interpretations of Sharia and the implementation of their IHRL obligations, whereas some treaty bodies have taken cognizance of and used Islamic jurisprudential arguments against hard-line positions adopted by certain Muslim-majority States on particular issues.[26]

One proposed avenue to reconcile Islamic law with IHRL is a *genealogical* approach or 'clearing ground' by examining how Islamic law and IHRL are legitimately formed, interpreted and applied, most importantly by focusing on instances in which freedoms in both traditions may be legitimately limited. The fundamental question according to this approach is 'What does it mean to legitimately limit a particular freedom and what do those limits signify about the legal system under consideration?'[27] The idea is to create a space that Islamic law and international law can both occupy, though neither one of them holds the territory entirely on its own terms.[28] However, no ideal model of reconciliation is suggested by the proponents of this approach. They would merely emphasize the need to avoid taking one set of principles as the universal norms transcending culture and political power to which other values must be assimilated or acculturated, and the need to relativize, instead, both sets of values by trying to grasp their meaning and social significance within specific historical formations of politics, place and power.[29]

The most touted route to reconciliation between the Islamic understanding of human rights norms and that of the non-Islamic world is through the adaptation of the margin of appreciation doctrine developed by the European Court of Human Rights (ECtHR), according to which Islamic cultures/values and legal

---

[24]   Ibid 160–71. Cf Eli Grossman, 'The Human Dimension of Shari'a Law' (2018) 50 NYU J Int'l L & Pol 1021, 1027, 1036, 1040–49.

[25]   Mashood A Baderin, 'A Macroscopic Analysis of the Practice of Muslim-Majority States Parties to International Human Rights Treaties: Conflict or Congruence?' (2001) 1 Hum Rts L Rev 265, 301.

[26]   Ibid.

[27]   Anver M Emon, Mark Ellis and Benjamin Glahn (eds), *Islamic Law and International Human Rights Law* (OUP 2012) 4–5.

[28]   Robin A Lovin, 'Epilogue – Common Ground or Clearing Ground' in Emon et al (eds), *Islamic Law and International Human Rights Law* 379, 381.

[29]   Ibid 384–6.

traditions should be interpreted as compatible with international human rights norms and vice versa, as much as practicable.[30] According to this view, Islam is compatible with IHRL since the sources and methods of Islamic law share the principles of good governance and human welfare with IHRL although the Muslim world may need to adapt its understanding of Islamic law to positively suit the societal changes that have taken place since ancient times while, at the same time, IHRL needs to adopt a multicultural or cross-cultural approach so as to realize an inclusive universalism.[31] In other words, Islamic law and IHRL are to be 'accommodative and complementary' to one another, combining 'the best in both systems for all humanity',[32] while, at the same time, providing elbow room to avoid confrontation between the two systems.[33]

Proponents of the application of margin of appreciation to reconcile the difference between Islamic law and IHRL concede that while the ECtHR often applies it the Human Rights Committee has not officially adopted this doctrine.[34] The Human Rights Committee has alluded to it in *Hertzberg et al v Finland*, holding that there is no violation of the right to hold opinions without interference and the right to freedom of expression under Article 19 of the 1966 International Covenant on Civil and Political Rights (ICCPR)[35] because public morals differ so widely that there is no universally applicable common standard; hence, 'a certain margin of discretion' needed to be accorded to the responsible national authorities.[36] However, in *Länsman et al v Finland* a decade later, the Human Rights Committee, while finding no violation of the rights of minorities under Article 27 of the ICCPR, rules that the scope of a State Party's conduct is not to be assessed by reference to 'a margin of appreciation', but to its obligations under Article 27.[37]

---

[30] Baderin, 'A Macroscopic Analysis of the Practice of Muslim-Majority States Parties to International Human Rights Treaties' 302–3; id, *International Human Rights and Islamic Law* 6, 167–8, 199, 218–21, 231–5; El Demey, *The Arab Charter of Human Rights* 121–9, esp 126–9. *Contra*: Eric A Posner, *Twilight of Human Rights Law* (OUP 2014) 97–102.
[31] Baderin, *International Human Rights and Islamic Law* 12–14, 28, 40–43, 46.
[32] Ibid 221.
[33] Ibid 235.
[34] Ibid 231–3.
[35] 999 UNTS 171.
[36] Communication No 61/1979 Finland: 2/4/82, UN Doc CCPR/C/15/D/61/1979 (2 Apr 1982) §10.3.
[37] Communication No 511/1992 Finland: 08/11/942, UN Doc CCPR/C/52D/511/1992 (8 Nov 1994) §9.4. One author considers that the Human Rights Committee in that case 'has mistaken the way in which a margin of appreciation operates' (Andrew Legg, *The Margin of Appreciation in International Human Rights Law: Defence and Proportionality* (OUP 2012) 34–5).

Supporters of the doctrine of margin of appreciation point out, nevertheless, that States have continued to make the case for deference before the Human Rights Committee while avoiding employing the terminology of the 'margin of appreciation'.[38] For example, in *Bryhn v Norway*,[39] the Human Rights Committee upheld Norway's submission for a 'certain margin with regard to the implementation of the right to review' under Article 14(5) of the ICCPR. The Committee ruled that in the circumstances of the case, notwithstanding the absence of an oral hearing, the totality of the reviews by Norway's Court of Appeal satisfies the requirements of Article 14(5) of the ICCPR. In *Vjatšeslav Borzov v Estonia*,[40] the Committee in effect accepted Estonia's submission for the Committee 'to defer, as a question of fact and evidence, to the assessment of the [applicant's] national security risk made by the Government and upheld by the courts [of Estonia]'. That assessment by Estonia deprives the applicant, a Russian army retiree residing in Estonia, of Estonian citizenship on national security grounds even though he is married to a naturalized Estonian. According to the Committee, while it cannot leave it to the unfettered discretion of a State Party to the ICCPR whether reasons related to national security exist in an individual case, it recognizes that its own role in reviewing the existence and relevance of such considerations depends on the circumstances of the case and the relevant provision of the ICCPR. This, arguably, implies the Committee's deference to the State's assessment of the national security risks, depending on the 'circumstances of the case' and the ICCPR provision at issue. Be that as it may, a question may be asked: to what extent can the discretion given to the States in the two cases just mentioned be applied generally to accommodate cultural or religious differences in the understanding of international human rights norms?

Another counter-argument concerning the Human Rights Committee's de facto application of the doctrine of margin of appreciation is that the Committee gives some leeway to States by taking cognizance of 'the factors and difficulties, if any, affecting the implementation of the [ICCPR]', as provided in Article 40(2) of the ICCPR. Most often, such factors and difficulties are economic difficulties, ongoing armed conflicts, political transition and instability, geographic and natural obstacles and traditional practices and customs. Yet, human rights treaty bodies generally stress the obligation of the States to overcome these obstacles and fulfil their treaty obligations.[41]

---

[38] Legg, *The Margin of Appreciation in International Human Rights Law* 35–6.
[39] CCPR/C/67/D/789/1997 (HRC) §§4.4 and 7.2.
[40] CCPR/C/81/D/1136/2002 (HRC) §§4.11 and 7.3.
[41] Eva Brems, *Human Rights: Universality and Diversity* (Martinus Nijhoff 2001) 346–80.

Even the liberal interpreters of Islamic law concede that reconciliation between Islamic law and IHRL is not possible in all areas or aspects. For example, the prohibition of torture as well as inhuman or degrading treatment or punishment under Article 7 of the ICCPR and Article 1(1) of the 1984 Convention against Torture and Other Cruel, Inhuman or Degrading Treatment or Punishment (CAT)[42] is hard to reconcile with the severity of some criminal punishment under Islamic law, such as amputations, beheading, stoning and other severe corporal punishment meted out by some Muslim-majority States.[43] One plausible solution is for these States to resort to legally valid means of procedural safeguard under Islamic law, such as Pakistan's strict adherence to high procedural evidential onuses in cases involving the harshest form of punishment under Islamic law.[44]

As regards the rights of children born out of wedlock, one proposal is to consider that since Islamic law also gives importance to the need to protect the best interest of the child, there is room for the application of the doctrine of margin of appreciation for Muslim-majority States to recognize the rights of children born out of wedlock as well.[45] It remains to be seen whether this proposal is acceptable to some, or most or all Muslim-majority States. In this connection, in a landmark decision, Malaysia's Court of Appeal unanimously ruled on 27 July 2017 that a child conceived out of wedlock can take on his or her father's surname despite the National Fatwa Committee's edict (*fatwa*) in 2003 that a child conceived out of wedlock cannot carry the name of the person who claims to be the father of the child if the child was born less than six months after the marriage. The Court reasons the jurisdiction of the National Registration Department director-general is a civil one and is confined to the determination of whether the father has fulfilled the requirements of section 13A(2) of the Births and Deaths Registration Act[46] for any decisions relating to a child's surname, irrespective of whether a child conceived out of wedlock is a Muslim or a non-Muslim. The director-general is therefore not obligated to apply, and is not legally bound by, a *fatwa* issued by a religious body such as the National Fatwa Committee since a fatwa does not have the force of law, unless the fatwa has been made or adopted as federal law by an Act of Parliament. One of the judges of the Court of Appeal in that case explains that,

---

[42] 1465 UNTS 85.
[43] Baderin, *International Human Rights and Islamic Law* 75–81.
[44] Ibid 84.
[45] Ibid 198–9, 218.
[46] This provision stipulates that the surname to be entered in respect of an illegitimate child may, at the joint request and respective signatures of the child's mother and the person acknowledging to be the father of the child, be the surname of the person acknowledging to be the father of that child.

besides legal technicalities, the issue implicates the child's human rights to be free from any stigma in the form of humiliation, embarrassment and public scorn for the rest of his or her life.[47]

A hurdle to the reconciliation between Islamic law and IHRL is the uncertainty about the authoritativeness of those Islamic legal scholars engaged in the 'apologetic' discourse on the issue. They may be considered too 'liberal' or too 'progressive' in their interpretation of Islamic law to be acceptable to the mainstream Islamic lawyers in Muslim-majority States in general.[48] Although Muslim-majority States allied themselves with the Asian human rights view at the 1993 Vienna Conference on Human Rights, the Islamic critique is the one that comes closest among all human rights critiques to a rejection of the universality or universalism of human rights.[49] The most important impediment to reconciliation is the religious nature of the claims for relativism of human rights. Compared with cultural relativism, religion-based relativism is more radical. As one commentator cogently puts it, '[o]nce the content of the religious rule is established in an authoritative manner, there is very little flexibility: it has to remain intact, because theoretically at least human beings cannot alter divine commandments'.[50]

Critics of the application of the doctrine of margin of appreciation to accommodate cultural or religious relativism also doubt whether there exists 'a core cluster of universal rights' acceptable to all, and who would be entrusted with identifying these core rights.[51] There is no uniform practice in domestic courts of various States when a defendant or a plaintiff raises the 'cultural defence' by arguing that his or her conduct in question is determined or influenced by his or her culture – it seems that all depends on the particular circumstances of the case and whether the elements of the offence charged, especially the mental element, are proven.[52] On the international plane, there is no uniform catalogue

---

[47]   Hafiz Yatim, 'COA: Child conceived out of wedlock can bear father's surname', *Malaysiakini* (27 July 2017) https://www.malaysiakini.com/news/389958, accessed 8 May 2019.

[48]   Cf Brems, *Human Rights* 185–288, 322; El Demey, *The Arab Charter of Human Rights* 450.

[49]   Brems, *Human Rights* 285, 288.

[50]   Ibid 290.

[51]   Federico Lenzerini, *The Culturalization of Human Rights Law* (OUP 2014) 29. For an argument for the application of the doctrine of margin of appreciation in the Asian context, see Tae-Ung Baik, *Emerging Regional Human Rights Systems in Asia* (CUP 2012) 55–61, 290–91. Baik cautions that if this doctrine is applied, its boundary should be monitored, supervised and kept in check by democracy, constitutionalism and the rule of law in the Asian State concerned.

[52]   See Lenzerini, *The Culturalization of Human Rights Law* 228–9 and cases cited in the accompanying footnotes 44–6.

of non-derogable human rights.[53] The non-derogable rights even in time of war or other public emergency threatening the life of the nation as enumerated in Article 15 of the 1950 European Convention on Human Rights (ECHR)[54] are the right to life (except in respect of deaths resulting from lawful acts of war), freedom from torture and inhuman or degrading treatment or punishment, freedom from slavery or servitude, and protection from punishment without law. The 2004 Arab Charter on Human Rights[55] lists in Article 4 the following non-derogable rights even in time of public emergency which threatens the life of the nation: the rights and special guarantees concerning the prohibition of torture and degrading treatment, return to one's country; political asylum, trial, inadmissibility of retrial for the same act; and the legal status of crime and punishment. The African Charter on Human and Peoples' Rights[56] has no comparable provision on non-derogable rights and its Article 27(2) even provides sweepingly that '[t]he rights and freedoms of each individual shall be exercised with due regard to the rights of others, collective security, morality and common interest'. In the case of the International Covenant on Economic, Social and Cultural Rights, it has no derogation provision; hence, no list of non-derogable rights.[57]

If one is to permit encroachment into international human rights norms to accommodate cultural or religious relativism provided that the encroachment is proportional, the operational modality of the principle of proportionality varies so much in the case law of human rights bodies and courts/tribunals as to be a general principle worthy of universal application.[58]

The lowest common denominator for all cultures, religions and geographical regions appears to be that any leeway, or margin of appreciation, must not violate the peremptory norms of general international law (*jus cogens*) from which no derogation is permitted.[59] However, the list of such norms as uni-

---

[53]   Ibid 240.

[54]   ETS 5.

[55]   (2005) 12 Int'l Hum Rts Rep 893.

[56]   (1982) 21 ILM 58.

[57]   See also Martin Scheinin, 'Core Rights and Obligations' in Dinah Shelton (ed.), *The Oxford Handbook of International Human Rights Law* (OUP 2013) 527; Gui-mei Bai, 'Are There Any Hierarchies of Human Rights in International Law?' in Peter R Bauer, Fried van Hoof, Liu Nanlai, Tao Zhenghua and Jacqueline Smith (eds), *Human Rights: Chinese and Dutch Perspectives* (Martinus Nijhoff 1996) 133.

[58]   Cf Yutaka Arai-Tanahashi, 'Proportionality' in Shelton (ed.), *The Oxford Handbook of International Human Rights Law* 446, 448–51.

[59]   Cf Lenzerini, *The Culturalization of Human Rights Law* 240–42; Mark Ellis, 'Islamic and International Law: Convergence or Conflict?' in Emon et al (eds), *Islamic Law and International Human Rights Law* 91; Antonio Cassese, 'For an Enhanced Role of *Jus Cogens*' in Antonio Cassese (ed.), *Realizing Utopia: The Future of International*

versally understood is presently narrow, being confined to the prohibition of aggression against another State, genocide, crimes against humanity, serious violations of the law and customs of war (war crimes), racial discrimination, slavery and slave-related practices and torture, as well as the protection of the right to self-determination.[60] There is some discrepancy in the list of peremptory norms among different human rights mechanisms, though, thereby making it difficult to find universality in this respect. For instance, whereas the ECtHR has recognized torture as an act proscribed by *jus cogens*,[61] the Inter-American Court of Human Rights goes even further by including, inter alia, the prohibition of cruel, inhuman or degrading treatment or punishment,[62] extrajudicial killing,[63] as well as the principle of equality and non-discrimination[64] among peremptory norms. Above all, every nation State is bound not to violate *jus cogens* norms in any circumstances anyway.

It is, therefore, doubtful whether the doctrine of margin of appreciation applied by the ECtHR in the context of relatively culturally and religiously homogeneous European societies can be meaningfully adapted to apply to the heterogeneous communities/societies across the globe.

In order to transform IHRL to be truly universal, those nation States having difficulties with some of the IHRL norms should progressively and gradually realize these norms insofar as practicable in the light of prevailing circumstances, especially domestic opposition from conservatives or traditionalists. Some leeway may be given to them where the 'local' situations impeding the said realization are beyond the normal power of the State, which must act in good faith to eradicate the situations and integrate IHRL norms to be upheld in the State.[65]

Law (OUP 2012) 158, 160–62; Willem van Genugten, 'The Universalization of Human Rights' in Steven van Hoogstraten (ed.), *New Challenges to International Law: A View from The Hague* (Brill Nijhoff 2018) 100, 109.

[60]   Report of the International Law Commission, Fifty-third session, 2001, GAOR, Fifty-sixth session, Supp No 10 (A/56/10) 208 [5]; Kriangsak Kittichaisaree, *The Obligation to Extradite or Prosecute* (OUP 2018) 99–107; Pavel Šturma, 'Jus Cogens and International Law of Human Rights' in Wagner Menezes (ed.), *Bulletin of the Brazilian Society of International Law – Centenary Commemorative Edition* (Arraes Editores 2017) 875, 878–80.

[61]   *Al-Adsani v UK* App No 35763/97, 21 Nov 2001 §§88–89; *Demir and Baykara v Turkey* App No 34503/97, 12 Nov 2008 §73.

[62]   *Caesar v Trinidad and Tobago*, Merits and Reparations (2005) Ser C, No 123, 11 Mar 2005 §70 and §100.

[63]   *Hermanos Gómez Paquiyauri v Peru*, Merits and Reparations (2004) Ser C, No 110, 8 July 2004 §112.

[64]   *Condición jurídica y derechos de los migrantes indocumentados*, Advisory Opinion (2003) Ser A, No 18, 17 Sept 2003 §§100–101.

[65]   Cf Brems, *Human Rights* 496, 499, 501–3.

Honour killing, female genital mutilation (FGM), dowry demands and caste-based discrimination, to name just a few, are founded on traditional beliefs and practices, not religions. Article 15(1) of the Indian Constitution itself provides that the State shall not discriminate against any citizen on the grounds only of religion, race, caste, sex, place of birth or any of them. Traditional practices may run counter to religious teachings. For instance, although both Article 12 of the ICCPR and the Quran (Quran 67:15; Quran 4: 97; Quran 6:11; Quran 27:69 and so forth) recognize the right to freedom of movement, women in some Muslim-majority States are required to be accompanied by a male relative on a journey, for their own safety, based on a Muslim tradition. However, contemporary Islamic scholars concur that where there is no threat to their safety the women can go on a journey unaccompanied by a male relative.[66] Although different cultures produce different values and practices, this does not mean that all of them must be tolerated where they are tantamount to abuses of human rights.[67]

Some Islamic practices are not considered by all Muslim-majority States as immutable Islamic law. One example is the dissolution of marriage or divorce by means of unilateral repudiation by the husband and without any need for justification whatsoever (*talaq*), which has now been modified in several Muslim-majority States, including Iran, in such a way as to protect the rights of the wife.[68] Restriction of employment of women is also a custom in some Muslim-majority States that has no justification under Islamic law.[69]

The Human Rights Committee has condemned the 'social attitudes' which tend to marginalize women victims of rape and put pressure on them to agree to marriage. It has likewise condemned laws that allow the rapist to have his criminal responsibility extinguished or mitigated if he marries the victim. States Parties to the ICCPR should indicate whether marrying the victim extinguishes or mitigates criminal responsibility and, in the case in which the victim is a minor, whether the rape reduces the marriageable age of the victim, particularly in societies where rape victims have to endure marginalization from society.[70]

---

[66] Baderin, *International Human Rights and Islamic Law* 93–5.

[67] Marie-Bénédicte Dembour, 'Critiques' in Daniel Moeckli, Sangeeta Shah and Sandesh Sivakumaran (eds), *International Human Rights Law* (3rd edn, OUP 2018) 41, 51.

[68] Baderin, *International Human Rights and Islamic Law* 149–53.

[69] Ibid 218.

[70] Human Rights Committee General Comment No 28 (2000): Article 3 (The Equality of Rights between Men and Women) 29 Mar 2000, CCPR/C/21/Rev.1/Add.10 §24.

The 1989 Convention on the Rights of the Child (CRC)[71] provides in Article 30 that in States where there are ethnic, religious or linguistic minorities or persons of indigenous origin, a child belonging to such a minority or who is indigenous shall not be denied the right, in community with other members of his or her group, to enjoy his or her own culture, to profess and practise his or her own religion or to use his or her own language. The Committee on the Rights of the Child has made it clear that such cultural practices must be exercised in accordance with other provisions of the CRC and under no circumstances may be justified if deemed prejudicial to the child's dignity, health and development. It adds that should harmful practices be present as in the cases of, inter alia, early marriages and FGM, the CRC State Party should work together with indigenous communities to ensure their eradication and the CRC Committee strongly urges States Parties to develop and implement awareness-raising campaigns, education programmes and legislation aimed at changing attitudes and to address gender roles and stereotypes that contribute to harmful practices.[72]

FGM, the coming-of-age ritual cutting or removal of some or all of the external female genitalia in the belief that it would curb women's sexuality, is torture pure and simple, with no known medical benefits whatsoever.[73] An estimated 200 million women in no fewer than 30 nation States around the world, mainly in Africa, have undergone FGM. It is also practised in some parts of Asia and the Middle East as well as in a few non-Muslim-majority States, such as in some villages in Russia's mainly Muslim region of Dagestan in the North Caucasus. This is despite the condemnation of FGM by a senior mufti in Russia's Spiritual Administration of Muslims as something 'alien to Islamic theology'.[74]

Some immigrants who have settled in the West surreptitiously practise FGM although proscribed by the law of their host States. For example, the Female Genital Mutilation Act 2003[75] in force in England and Wales and Northern Ireland criminalizes FGM, assisting a girl to mutilate her own genitalia, assisting a non-UK person to mutilate overseas a girl's genitalia and failing to protect a girl from the risk of genital mutilation. The maximum sentence under the Act is 14 years' imprisonment. The Act also imposes a duty on

---

[71]　1577 UNTS 3.

[72]　General Comment No 11 (2009): Indigenous children and their rights under the Convention [on the Rights of the Child] 12 Feb 2009, CRC/C/GC/11 §22.

[73]　Freedman, *Failing to Protect* 45. See also Brems, *Human Rights* 170–77.

[74]　'Russia furore over FGM in mainly Muslim Dagestan', *BBC News* (18 Aug 2016) https://www.bbc.com/news/world-europe-37115746, accessed 30 Nov 2018.

[75]　2003 c 31, in force on 3 Mar 2004. Scotland has its own Prohibition of Female Genital Mutilation Act (Scotland) Act 2005 (2005 asp 8), in force on 1 Sept 2005.

a person who works in a regulated profession in England and Wales to notify the authorities if, in the course of his or her work in the profession, the person discovers that an act of FGM appears to have been carried out on a girl who is aged under 18. As of this writing, there have been four cases brought under the Act, resulting in acquittals in three cases and conviction in the other case.[76]

In the USA, the Female Genital Mutilation Act of 1996[77] criminalizes performing FGM on anyone under the age of 18. However, in November 2018, in *United States v Jumana Nagarwala et al*,[78] the first federal case involving the violation of this Act, the Act was struck down as unconstitutional by the US District Court for the Eastern District of Michigan, Southern Division. The Court reasoned that that FGM was a 'local criminal activity' for the federal states to regulate, not a commercial activity to be regulated by Congress under the Commerce Clause or the Necessary and Proper Clause of the US Constitution. The Court therefore ordered that the charges under that Act be dropped against eight people who had mutilated the genitals of at least nine girls between the ages of eight and 13.[79] The medical doctor in that case denied she had done anything illegal since she had merely performed a religious custom on girls from her Muslim sect, the India-based Dawoodi Bohra, which has a small community in Detroit. On 30 March 2019 the US Justice Department decided not to appeal against the judgment but urged Congress to change the federal law so as not to be in conflict with the US Constitution, bearing in mind that an estimated half a million women and girls in the USA had already suffered or were at risk of being subjected to FGM in the future.[80]

One piece of research finds evidence of a huge and significant decline in the prevalence of FGM among 208,195 children aged 0–14 years in 29 States spread across Africa and two States in Western Asia over the period 1990–2017. The percentage decline was highest in East Africa, followed by North and West Africa. The prevalence decreased from 71.4 per cent in 1995 to 8.0 per cent in 2016 in East Africa. In North Africa the prevalence decreased

---

[76] Criminal Case No 17-CR-20274.

[77] 18 U.S.C. §116.

[78] https://content-static.detroitnews.com/pdf/2018/US-v-Nagarwala-dismissal -order-11-20-18.pdf, accessed 2 Feb 2019.

[79] On 14 Jan 2018, the same court and the same judge had dismissed the charge of transporting minors intending that they engage in 'sexual activity' as it would stretch the law against FGM too far (*United States v D-1, Jumana Nagarwala*, https://www .casemine.com/judgement/us/5a619fe6add7b0300e293caf, accessed 20 Aug 2019).

[80] Ed White, 'Physician Jumana Nagarwala, Accused of Several Counts of Female Genital Mutilation, Freed by Fed', *India West* (23 Apr 2019) https://www.indiawest .com/news/global_indian/physician-jumana-nagarwala-accused-of-several-counts-of -female-genital/article_1464ef54-6539-11e9-ba88-e72311683d7c.html, accessed 20 Aug 2019.

from 57.7 per cent in 1990 to 14.1 per cent in 2015. In West Africa the prevalence decreased from 73.6 per cent in 1996 to 25.4 per cent in 2017.[81]

In Sudan 87 per cent of girls have been subject to FGM, often in the most severe form. However, some 30 years ago, one family in a village decided not to circumcise its women as the elder of the family believed that FGM was against Islam. Islamic religious leaders in that village gradually agreed and FGM is now entirely eradicated in the village. The Sudanese Government is hoping to end FGM nationwide by 2030, with the help of £15 million British financial aid over five years from 2018.[82] The British Government's financial aid to Sudan for this purpose directly serves the UK's own objective. Through this diplomatic manoeuvre, the British Government ensures that those who have emigrated to the UK from Sudan and other States where FGM is still practised understand that FGM is not acceptable in any society.

As for child marriage, according to the Malaysian Government's data, there were 5,362 applications for child marriage to Sharia courts in Malaysia in the years 2013–17. In the federal state of Sabah, 2,130 out of 2,191 applications by children aged 14 and 15 to marry were granted during that same period. After her eight-day fact-finding mission to Malaysia in September 2018, the UN Special Rapporteur on the sale and sexual exploitation of children concludes that the root cause of child marriage is not poverty but 'patriarchal structure and attitude' in Malaysia, whereby 'girls and women are simply disposed of as commodities'. The Special Rapporteur suggests the need for standard operating procedures on child marriage and that all of Malaysia's federal states follow Malaysia's state of Selangor in amending Sharia laws to raise the legal marriage age for Muslims to 18. The Malaysian Government, which has the necessary political will to end child marriage, is recommended to reach out to religious authorities and talk to community leaders who practise customary Islamic law to end the said patriarchal structure and attitude.[83]

The fact that followers of Islam generally oppose lesbian, gay, bisexual, transsexual and intersexual rights is not unique. Conservative Christian

---

[81]   Nganga-Bakwin Kandala, Martinsixtus C Ezejimofor, Olaketan A Uthman and Paul Komba, 'Secular Trends in the Prevalence of Female Genital Mutilation/Cutting among Girls: A Systematic Analysis' (2018) 3 BMJ Global Health 1.

[82]   'The village that's eradicated FGM', *BBC News* (23 Nov 2018) https://www.bbc.com/news/av/world-africa-46309516/the-village-that-s-eradicated-fgm, accessed 23 Nov 2018.

[83]   Boo Su-Lyn, 'Child marriage rules? Just raise minimum age to 18, says UN rights expert', *Malay Mail* (1 Oct 2018) https://www.malaymail.com/s/1678225/child-marriage-rules-just-raise-minimum-age-to-18-says-un-rights-expert, accessed 3 Oct 2018.

Churches, such as the Russian Orthodox Church, are also against such rights.[84] However, in May 2018 Pakistan's Parliament enacted the Transgender Persons (Protection of Rights) Act. Guaranteeing basic rights for transgender people, the Act allows Pakistani citizens to self-identify as male, female or a mixture of both and to have that identity recorded on official documents, including passports and identity cards. The Act proscribes discrimination against transgender persons in public places and accords them the right to vote in elections as well as to run for public office and the right to inheritance. Government safe houses are to be set up for citizens at risk of violence and psychological counselling shall be provided to those who need it. Separate rooms shall be provided in prisons where transgender persons are detained.[85] In April 2019 Brunei imposed the death penalty on those convicted of having gay sex but this punishment has been suspended since May 2019 after strong international opposition, led by the UN High Commissioner for Human Rights, the Commonwealth Secretary-General, as well as a number of politicians in many nations and international celebrities, some of whom called for a boycott of hotels owned by the Sultan of Brunei.

Blasphemy overlaps with apostasy because an act of blasphemy of a Muslim is also apostasy. A rational solution would be to criminalize incitement to religious hatred without having to rely on anti-blasphemy law.[86] Article 22 of the Cairo Declaration recognizes the right of everyone to express his opinion freely in such manner not contrary to the principles of Sharia, as well as the right to advocate what is right and propagate what is good and warn against what is wrong and evil according to the norms of the Islamic Sharia. However, information may not be exploited or misused in such a way as may violate the sanctity and the dignity of Prophets, undermine moral and ethical values or disintegrate, corrupt or harm society or weaken its faith. It is also not permissible to arouse nationalistic or doctrinal hatred or to do anything that may be an incitement to any form of racial discrimination. It should be noted that in Europe the ECtHR in *Otto-Preminger-Institut v Austria* upheld Austria's seizure and prevention of distribution of a film and charging the person behind its intended screening with the offence of 'disparaging religious doctrines'

---

[84] Pasquale Annicchino, 'The Past Is Never Dead: Christian Anti-Interventionism and Human Rights' in Martti Koskenniemi, Mónica García-Salmones Rovira and Paolo Amorosa (eds), *International Law and Religion: Historical and Contemporary Perspectives* (OUP 2017) 178, 183, 186.

[85] https://www.pinknews.co.uk/2018/05/10/pakistan-passes-historic-transgender-law/, accessed 11 May 2018.

[86] Hossein Esmaeili, Irmgard Marboe and Javid Rehman, *The Rule of Law, Freedom of Expression and Islamic Law* (Hart 2017) ch. 6; Baderin, *International Human Rights and Islamic Law* 128.

proscribed under section 188 of the Austrian Criminal Code. In the film, God was presented both in image and in text as a senile, impotent idiot, Christ as a cretin and the Virgin Mary as a wanton lady with a corresponding manner of expression, and the Eucharist was ridiculed. The ECtHR ruled that the film's merit as a work of art or as a contribution to public debate in Austrian society does not outweigh those features which make it essentially offensive to the general public, especially in Tyrol where the overwhelming majority of the population are Roman Catholics. In seizing the film, the Austrian authorities did not violate Article 10 (freedom of expression) of the ECHR since Austria acts to respond to a pressing social need to preserve religious peace in that region and to prevent some people from feeling the object of attacks on their religious beliefs in an unwarranted and offensive manner.[87]

A similar approach could be pursued by Muslim-majority States in relation to blasphemy of Islam. The resolutions on defamation of religions initiated by the OIC were adopted annually by the Commission on Human Rights and its successor, the Human Rights Council (HRC), from 1999 to 2010, with increasingly diminishing support. The West, led by EU Member States, Canada and the USA, together with human rights special rapporteurs and NGOs, considered proscribing defamation of religions to be incompatible with IHRL, in particular the freedom of expression and the criteria for permissible exceptions to that freedom as provided in Article 19(2) and (3)[88] and Article 20(2)[89] of the ICCPR as well as freedom of religion or belief protected by various IHRL instruments. A compromise was reached in 2011, thanks partly to the Arab Spring uprisings, to challenge human rights violations, including restrictions on the freedom of speech and political freedom, in several Arab States that convinced the OIC not to press for another annual and repetitious resolution on defamation of religions in the circumstances.[90] The unanimously adopted HRC resolution 16/18 of 12 April 2011 is entitled 'Combating intolerance,

---

[87] (1994) 19 EHRR 34.

[88] Art 19(2): 'Everyone shall have the right to freedom of expression; this right shall include freedom to seek, receive and impart information and ideas of all kinds, regardless of frontiers, either orally, in writing or in print, in the form of art or through any other media of his choice.'

Art 19(3): 'The exercise of the rights provided for in paragraph 2 of this article carries with it special duties and responsibilities. It may therefore be subject to certain restrictions, but these shall only be such as are provided by law and are necessary: (a) For respect of the rights or reputations of others; (b) For the protection of national security or of public order (*ordre public*) or of public health or morals.'

[89] Art 20(2): 'Any advocacy of national, racial or religious hatred that constitutes incitement to discrimination, hostility or violence shall be prohibited by law.'

[90] Sejal Parmar, 'Uprooting "Defamation of Religions" and Planting a New Approach to Freedom of Expression at the United Nations' in Tarlach McGonagle

negative stereotyping and stigmatization of, and discrimination, incitement to violence and violence against, persons based on religion or belief'.[91] Instead of referring to defamation of religions, the resolution, in its preamble, expresses the HRC's deep concern about 'incidents of intolerance, discrimination and violence against persons based on their religion or belief in all regions of the world' and deplores 'any advocacy of discrimination or violence on the basis of religion or belief'. The focus of the resolution's condemnation is not defamation of religions as such, but 'any advocacy of religious hatred against individuals that constitutes incitement to discrimination, hostility or violence', and the resolution urges States to take effective measures consistent with their obligations under IHRL to address and combat such incidents of incitement.[92]

The Human Rights Committee's General Comment No 34[93] affirms this understanding of the HRC's resolution. Specifically, the Committee makes it clear that since any restriction on freedom of expression constitutes a serious curtailment of human rights, it is not compatible with the ICCPR for a restriction to be based on traditional, religious or other such customary law.[94] In addition, laws restricting the rights enumerated in Article 19(2) of the ICCPR must not only comply with the strict requirements of Article 19(3), but must also themselves be compatible with the ICCPR's provisions, aims and objectives. Laws must not violate the ICCPR's non-discrimination provisions and must not provide for penalties incompatible with the ICCPR, such as corporal punishment.[95] The Human Rights Committee pronounces unequivocally that 'prohibitions of displays of lack of respect for a religion or other belief system, including blasphemy laws, are incompatible with the [ICCPR]', except in the specific circumstances envisaged in Article 20(2) thereof. Article 20(2) stipulates in no uncertain terms that 'any advocacy of national, racial or religious hatred that constitutes incitement to discrimination, hostility or violence shall be prohibited by law'. Such prohibitions must also comply with the strict requirements of Article 19(3) – that they must be provided by law and are necessary for respect of the rights or reputations of others or for the protection of

---

and Yvonne Donders (eds), *The United Nations and Freedom of Expression and Information: Critical Perspectives* (CUP 2015) 373, 374–412.
[91] A/HRC/RES/16/18.
[92] Ibid §§2 and 3.
[93] General Comment No 34 (Art 19: Freedoms of opinion and expression), CCPR/C/GC/34 (12 Sept 2011).
[94] Ibid §24.
[95] Ibid §26.

national security or of public order (*ordre public*) or of public health or morals – as well as other relevant ICCPR provisions. For example,

> it would be impermissible for any such laws to discriminate in favour of or against one or certain religions or belief systems, or their adherents over another, or religious believers over non-believers. Nor would it be permissible for such prohibitions to be used to prevent or punish criticism of religious leaders or commentary on religious doctrine and tenets of faith.[96]

With respect to the elements of proscribed incitement referred to in the HRC's resolution 16/18 and the Human Rights Committee's General Comment No 34, guidance may be found in the Rabat Plan of Action[97] adopted in October 2012 by a group of experts invited by the UN High Commissioner for Human Rights to examine legislation, jurisprudence and national policies with regard to the prohibition of national, racial or religious hatred as reflected in IHRL. To assess the severity of the hatred, possible elements may include the cruelty or intent of the statement or harm advocated and the frequency, quantity and extent of the communication. In this regard, a six-part threshold test is proposed for expressions considered as criminal offences. First, the context of the statement in question is of great importance when assessing whether it is likely to incite discrimination, hostility or violence against the target group and it may have a direct bearing on both intent and/or causation. Analysis of the context should place the speech act within the social and political context prevalent at the time the speech was made and disseminated. Secondly, the speaker's position or status in the society should be considered, especially the individual's or organization's standing in the context of the audience to whom the speech is directed. Thirdly, because Article 20 of the ICCPR anticipates intent, negligence and recklessness are not sufficient for an act to be an offence under that Article, as this Article provides for 'advocacy' and 'incitement' rather than the mere distribution or circulation of material. It thus requires the activation of a triangular relationship between the object and subject of the speech act as well as the audience. Fourthly, the content of the speech constitutes one of the key foci of judicial deliberations and is a critical element of incitement. Content analysis may include the degree to which the speech was provocative and direct, as well as the form, style and nature of arguments deployed in the speech or the balance struck between arguments deployed. Fifthly, the extent of the speech act, including such elements as the reach of the speech act, its public nature, its magnitude and the size of its audience must be taken into account. Other elements to consider include whether the speech

---

[96] Ibid §48.
[97] A/HRC/22/17/Ad.4 (11 Jan 2013) Appendix.

is public; what means of dissemination are used – for example by a single leaflet or broadcast in the mainstream media or via the Internet, the frequency, the quantity and the extent of the communications; whether the audience had the means to act on the incitement and whether the statement (or work) is circulated in a restricted environment or widely accessible to the general public. Lastly, since incitement, by definition, is an inchoate crime, the action advocated through incitement speech does not have to be committed for that speech to amount to a crime. Nevertheless, there must be a reasonable probability that the speech would succeed in inciting actual action against the target group and such causation should be rather direct.[98]

On 31 October 2018, in a judgment widely lauded as 'historic', the three-judge Supreme Court of Pakistan acquitted Asia Bibi, a female Christian, accused of blasphemy of Islam during a row in June 2009 between her and a group of Muslim women in which the latter said she should convert to Islam but she allegedly reacted by making offensive comments about the Prophet Mohammad. She was subsequently beaten up at home, allegedly confessed to blasphemy, and was arrested and prosecuted.

Bibi was the first female non-Muslim charged with blasphemy in Pakistan. The governor of Pakistan's Punjab Province was assassinated by his own devout Muslim bodyguards in January 2011 because he visited Bibi in prison, sympathized with her and expressed his wish to reform Pakistan's blasphemy law. Two months later, Pakistan's then Minister for Minority Affairs was assassinated after making similar remarks. The anti-blasphemy vigilante groups in Pakistan threatened to kill Bibi and harm the judges who would dare acquit her of the charge. In acquitting Bibi, the Supreme Court ruled the evidence against her to be unreliable and that she confessed under duress, in front of a mob threatening to kill her. The first 11 pages of the main 34-page judgment, written by Chief Justice Nisar who was due to retire in January 2019, explain what constituted blasphemy, why it ought to be punished with death, why Pakistan has incorporated laws to punish blasphemy and how Pakistan has inspired the 2009 UN resolution that declares defamation of religion as a violation of human rights. It then quotes the Quran and the Prophet Mohammad's tradition to establish sanctity and deplores the abuse of the law by individuals levelling false allegations of blasphemy, leading to the vigilante killing in Pakistan of 62 persons for blasphemy since 1990. The judgment also emphasizes the Prophet's benevolent attitude towards other religions. A separate 21 pages written by Justice Khosa, the new Chief Justice designate, quotes from the 'Charter of Privileges to Christians', which is a letter from the Prophet Muhammad to the Christian monks of St Catherine's Monastery on the Sinai

---

[98]   Ibid §29.

Peninsula in Egypt. The Charter exhorts Muslims to protect Christians, with the letter serving as a covenant for protection and other privileges granted to the Christians.[99] The Supreme Court's judgment in that case did not immediately lay the matter to rest as Bibi and her family, as well as her defence lawyer, continued to be subject to death threats from the vigilante groups and had to ask for asylum abroad. On 29 January 2019 the Pakistan Supreme Court dismissed a petition to review its judgment of October 2018, upholding its decision to overturn Bibi's conviction and quash her death sentence since the petitioners failed to show any single mistake in the judgment. In early May 2019 it was reported that Bibi had left Pakistan for Canada to join two of her daughters who are understood to have been granted asylum.[100]

At about the same time as the aforesaid judgment of the Supreme Court of Pakistan, on 25 October 2018 the ECtHR upheld the Austrian law that purportedly criminalizes blasphemy against Islam. In *E.S. v Austria* the applicant made several statements about Islam and the Prophet Muhammad at public meetings and was convicted by Austrian courts for violation of Article 188 of the Austrian Criminal Code for disparaging religious doctrines. In particular, she was found guilty of publicly disparaging an object of veneration of a domestic church or religious society, namely Muhammad, the Prophet of Islam, in a manner capable of arousing justified indignation, specifically by essentially conveying the message that Muhammad had paedophilic tendencies. She was ordered to pay the costs of the proceedings and a day-fine of €4 for a period of 120 days (amounting to €480 in total), which would result in 60 days' imprisonment in the event of default. According to the Austrian Supreme Court, the applicant had not aimed to contribute to a serious debate about Islam or the phenomenon of child marriage, but merely to defame the Prophet Muhammad by accusing him of a specific sexual preference, based on the assumption that he had had sexual intercourse with a prepubescent child, in order to show that he was not a worthy subject of worship.

The ECtHR in *E.S. v Austria* proceeds on the basis that the applicant's freedom of expression is interfered with, that the interference is prescribed by law and that it pursues a legitimate aim of preventing disorder by safeguarding religious peace and protecting religious feelings, which corresponds to the pro-

---

[99]   M Ilyas Khan, 'Asia Bibi: Pakistan Supreme Court's "Historic" ruling', *BBC* (31 Oct 2018) https://www.bbc.com/news/world-asia-46048134, accessed 4 Nov 2018.

[100]   'Asia Bibi: Christian leaves Pakistan after blasphemy acquittal', *BBC* (8 May 2019) https://www.bbc.com/news/world-asia-48198340, accessed 8 May 2019.

tection of the rights of others under Article 10(2) of the ECHR. That provision stipulates that the exercise of the freedom of expression

> may be subject to such formalities, conditions, restrictions or penalties as are pre-scribed by law and are necessary in a democratic society, in the interests of national security, territorial integrity or public safety, for the prevention of disorder or crime, for the protection of health or morals, for the protection of the reputation or rights of others, for preventing the disclosure of information received in confidence or for maintaining the authority and impartiality of the judiciary.

In determining whether the interference was necessary in a democratic society, the ECtHR concedes that matters of religious peace are particularly sensi-tive and vary from one State to another. However, the ECtHR distinguishes blasphemy law as such from the Austrian law in question by holding that 'a religious group must tolerate the denial by others of their religious beliefs and even the propagation by others of doctrines hostile to their faith, as long as the statements at issue do not incite hatred or religious intolerance'. Article 188 of the Austrian Criminal Code 'in fact does not incriminate all behaviour that is likely to hurt religious feelings or amounts to blasphemy, but addition-ally requires that the circumstances of such behaviour were able to arouse justified indignation, therefore aiming at the protection of religious peace and tolerance'.[101]

The contrast in the outcome of the judgment of the Supreme Court of Pakistan and that of the judgment in *E.S. v Austria* shows that there should be a case-by-case approach to the issue of blasphemy and that any punishment against insensitive religious statements may be legitimate provided that the relevant rules of human rights law are respected.

Chapter 5 informs readers that insofar as there is no unified interpretation of Islamic law, the proscription of apostasy can be interpreted in a variety of ways depending on how strictly or broadly one interprets the scope of the freedom of expression in the Quran. For their part, moderate Islamic scholars consider that apostasy must be defined in the proper historical context of Muslims denouncing their Islamic faith to join with enemies to take up arms against their Muslim-majority State, thereby committing a political offence against the State. To them, the punishment of apostasy in Islamic law is largely based on certain reported sayings of the Prophet (*hadith*), but the Prophet never sentenced anyone to death for apostasy.

There was a very interesting and positive development during the widely reported story of a Saudi Arabian teenage girl who ran away from her parents

---

[101] *E.S. v Austria*, App No 38450/12, https://hudoc.echr.coe.int/eng#{%22itemid %22:[%22001-187188%22]}, accessed 4 Nov 2018) *passim*, esp §52.

in defiance of the Muslim male guardianship system and renounced Islam. While in transit en route to Australia, she was detained at Bangkok international airport, Thailand, but managed to harness the power of the social media Twitter to mobilize international support to prevent her deportation from Thailand back to Saudi Arabia. While the UN High Commission for Refugees was assessing her claim to be a refugee, the Saudi Arabian Embassy in Bangkok did not demand her deportation from Thailand and it refused to intervene in this 'family affair' despite the fact that apostasy is an offence punishable by death in Saudi Arabia.[102] This might be because the Saudi Government did not want to attract more negative international attention when it was already embroiled in the controversy surrounding the murder on 2 October 2018 at the Saudi Arabian Consulate General in Istanbul, Turkey, of Jamal Khashoggi, a Saudi national who was a US resident, *Washington Post* columnist and critic of the Saudi Government, in which certain individuals at a high level of the Saudi Government were purportedly implicated. The teenager has subsequently been granted asylum by the Canadian Government. This episode reveals that when there is room for interpretation of Islamic law, a Muslim-majority State, however religiously devout it may be, can be flexible when warranted by the circumstances.

This precedent has inspired Saudi women to demand further reforms in Saudi Arabian treatment of women, including the end of the male guardianship system.[103] The immediate reaction from the Saudi Arabian Government-funded National Society for Human Rights revolves around expressing its concern about the 'incitement' by certain foreign States for 'some Saudi female delinquents to rebel against the values of their families and push them out of the country and seek to receive them under the pretext of granting them asylum'. It is also feared that the women may ultimately be 'lost and fall into the arms of brokers and human traffickers'.[104] Several weeks later, a Saudi public prosecutor is reported to have said his office would spare no efforts in protecting

---

[102] 'Rahaf al-Qunun: UN "considers Saudi woman a refugee"', *BBC News* (9 Jan 2019) https://www.bbc.com/news/world-australia-46806485; 'Saudi teen runaway in Bangkok is "legitimate refugee": UN', *Bangkok Post* (9 Jan 2019) https://www.bangkokpost.com/news/world/1608198/saudi-teen-runaway-in-bangkok-is-legitimate-refugee-un, accessed 11 Jan 2019.

[103] Joseph Hincks, '"Rehaf Is Going to Start a Revolution." Saudi Arabian Women Demanding Reforms after a Teen Fled the Country in Fear of her Life', *Time* (10 Jan 2019) http://time.com/5499106/rahaf-saudi-arabia-guardianship-system/, accessed 11 Jan 2019.

[104] 'Saudi-backed body denounces countries for "inciting" women to flee', *Bangkok Post* (14 Jan 2019) https://www.bangkokpost.com/news/world/1611014/saudi-backed-body-denounces-countries-for-inciting-women-to-flee#cxrecs_s, accessed 15 Jan 2019.

individuals, whether women, children or parents, from unfair treatment by those who abuse guardianship powers, many aspects of which derive from social customary practices rather than specific laws.[105] Eventually, the Saudi Government enacted a series of royal decrees, effective on 2 August 2019, granting women over the age of 21 the right to apply for a passport without authorization from a male guardian; all women the right to register a birth, marriage or divorce; and all citizens the right to work without facing any discrimination based on gender, disability or age.

Another positive development is the Indian Supreme Court's judgment overruling the previously entrenched Hindu custom of prejudice against women based on notions of impurity and pollution associated with menstruation. Pursuant to Rule 3(b) of the Kerala Hindu Places of Public Worship Act of 1965, women in their 'menstruating years', between the ages of 10 and 50, are not allowed to enter Sabarimala Hindu temple. The Indian Supreme Court's judgment of 28 September 2018 holds, by a majority of four to one, that this Rule is unconstitutional as it violates the right to equality and the right to worship. The majority rejects all the arguments of the temple board that the exclusion is an age-old and essential practice. Article 25 of the Indian Constitution guarantees to 'all persons', meaning every individual in society, the freedom of conscience and free profession, practice and propagation of religion. The impugned custom is considered to be a form of 'untouchability' which cannot be allowed under Article 17 of the Indian Constitution[106] as it entails the systemic humiliation, exclusion and subjugation of women. Since all individuals are created equal, to exclude women from worship by allowing the right to worship to men is to place women in a position of subordination, thereby perpetuating patriarchy. As one judge in the majority puts it eloquently, '[p]atriarchy in religion cannot be permitted to trump over elements of pure devotion borne out of faith and the freedom to practise and profess one's religion'. All the judges in the majority concur that restrictions put in place by Sabarimala temple cannot be considered essential religious practice. By contrast, the dissenting judge opines that issues of deep religious sentiments should not ordinarily be interfered with by the court, unless there is an aggrieved person from that section or religion. In her dissenting opinion, what constitutes essential religious practice is for the religious community to decide, not for the court, and a secular polity must allow heterogeneity in religion and

---

[105] 'After Bangkok drama, Saudi addresses abuse of "male guardianship"', *Bangkok Post* (5 Feb 2019) https://www.bangkokpost.com/news/general/1623510/after-bangkok -drama-saudis-address-abuse-of-male-guardianship, accessed 5 Feb 2019.

[106] Art 17 (Abolition of Untouchability): '"Untouchability" is abolished and its practice in any form is forbidden. The enforcement of any disability arising out of "untouchability" shall be an offence punishable in accordance with law.'

allow diverse forms of worship, even if irrational.[107] After several months of resisting and challenging the Supreme Court's judgment on the grounds that the entrenched tradition was not to be violated, on 6 February 2019 the board overseeing the Sabarimala Hindu temple relented, stating that it now supports allowing women of menstruating age to enter the ancient shrine and that disallowing them would be discriminatory.[108]

To recapitulate, religious relativism in relation to human rights norms may be justifiable insofar as the act inimical to human rights is not a mere tradition or custom not prescribed by the actor's religion. States must take steps in good faith, and in the light of the circumstances prevailing within their respective jurisdictions, to eradicate traditions and customs that violate IHRL. The doctrine of margin of appreciation pioneered by the ECtHR may not be able to generally reconcile the divergences among religions or cultures in the implementation of IHRL, however.

According to one view, where there are human rights violations in Muslim-majority States, the violations are often closely associated with the oppression inherent in military or authoritarian government and are not due to Sharia.[109] The preceding chapters show how critiques of relativism of human rights norms question whether governments invoking such relativism to justify their policies or measures in fact intend to suppress their opponents in the name of 'national security' and/or 'law, public order and morality' so that they can remain in power. Therefore, tyranny, not human rights relativism, is the real concern.

A universal safety valve against such tyranny can be found in the provision of Article 29(2) of the UDHR, which allows limitations on the rights and freedoms provided that such limitations are determined by law solely for the purpose of securing due recognition and respect for the rights and freedoms of others and of meeting the just requirements of morality, public order and the general welfare 'in a democratic society'.

The ECHR closely follows the UDHR's Article 29(2). Paragraph 1 of Article 6, on the right to a fair trial, provides that the press and public may

---

[107] Samanwaya Rautray, 'Women of all ages can enter Sabarimala Temple, rules Supreme Court', *Economic Times* (29 Sept 2018) https://economictimes.indiatimes.com/news/politics-and-nation/supreme-court-allows-women-to-enter-sabarimala-temple/articleshow/65989807.cms; 'In 4:1 Verdict, Supreme Court Allows Women's Entry into Sabarimala Temple', *Wire* (Sept 2018) https://thewire.in/law/sabarimala-women-temple-entry-supreme-court-verdict, accessed 23 Jan 2019.
[108] 'Sabarimala temple board reverses opposition to entry of women', *Al Jazeera* (7 Feb 2019) https://www.aljazeera.com/news/2019/02/sabarimala-temple-board-reverses-opposition-entry-women-190207020635383.html, accessed 7 Feb 2019.
[109] Abiad, *Sharia, Muslim States and International Human Rights Treaty Obligations* 174.

be excluded from all or part of the trial in the interests of, inter alia, 'morals, public order or national security in a democratic society'. Article 8(2) of the ECHR prohibits interference by a public authority with the exercise of the right to respect for one's private and family life

> except such as is in accordance with the law and is necessary in a democratic society in the interests of national security, public safety or the economic well-being of the country, for the prevention of disorder or crime, for the protection of health or morals or for the protection of the rights and freedoms of others.

By virtue of Article 9(2) of the ECHR, freedom to manifest one's religion or beliefs shall be subject only to such limitations 'as are prescribed by law and are necessary in a democratic society in the interests of public safety, for the protection of public order, health or morals or for the protection of the rights and freedoms of others'. Article 10(2) of the ECHR invoked by the ECtHR in *E.S. v Austria* is also of direct relevance. Likewise, Article 11 of the ECHR prohibits restrictions on the exercise of the right to freedom of peaceful assembly and to freedom of association with others 'other than such as are prescribed by law and are necessary in a democratic society in the interests of national security or public safety, for the prevention of disorder or crime, for the protection of health or morals or for the protection of the rights and freedoms of others'.

Paragraph 8 of the 2012 ASEAN Human Rights Declaration[110] copies almost verbatim Article 29(2) of the UDHR, adding that such limitations may be for the purpose of meeting the just requirements of 'national security' and 'in a democratic society'. The American Convention on Human Rights (ACHR)[111] provides that the exercise of the freedom to manifest one's religion and beliefs under Article 12, the freedom of thought and expression under Article 13 and the freedom of association under Article 16 'shall be subject only to such restrictions established by law as may be necessary in a democratic society, in the interest of national security, public safety or public order or to protect public health or morals or the rights and freedoms of others'. Although the ACHR neither mentions the national security exception nor includes the ter-minology 'in a democratic society', the preamble of the 2001 Inter-American Democratic Charter[112] reaffirms, inter alia, that the promotion and protection of human rights is a basic prerequisite for the existence of a democratic society. For its part, the Arab Charter on Human Rights provides in Article 4(a) that no restrictions shall be placed on the rights and freedoms recognized in the

---

[110] http://asean.org/asean-human-rights-declaration, accessed 12 Aug 2019.
[111] 1144 UNTS 123.
[112] 40 ILM 1289.

Arab Charter except where such is provided by law and deemed necessary to protect the national security and economy, public order, health or morals, or the rights and freedoms of others. The Arab Charter includes the 'national security' exception but omits any reference to the need for the suitability of human rights exceptions 'in a democratic society'. The African Charter on Human and Peoples' Rights has no provision on limitations of rights similar to those of the American Convention, the Arab Charter or the non-binding ASEAN Declaration.

The ICCPR permits restrictions on the exercise of the right of peaceful assembly under Article 21 and the right of assembly under Article 22, provided that they are 'in conformity with the law and ... are necessary in a democratic society in the interests of national security or public safety, public order (*ordre public*), the protection of public health or morals or the protection of the rights and freedoms of others'. Article 19(3) of the ICCPR is narrower, stipulating that the exercise of the right to freedom of expression may be subject to certain restrictions, but these shall only be such as are 'provided by law and are necessary'. The Human Rights Committee clarifies that pursuant to Article 19(3) the permissible restrictions must be provided by law, may only be imposed for one of the enumerated grounds and must conform to the strict tests of necessity and proportionality. The test of necessity dictates that restrictions must be applied only for those purposes for which they were prescribed and must be directly related to the specific need on which they are predicated. The proportionality test requires that the restrictions must be appropriate to achieve their protective function, the least intrusive instrument amongst those which might achieve their protective function, and proportionate to the interest to be protected. Furthermore, proportionality has to be respected not only in the law that frames the restrictions, but also by the administrative and judicial authorities in applying the law. In this regard, the Human Rights Committee recalls that the scope of the freedom of expression is not to be assessed by reference to a margin of appreciation and in order for the Committee to carry out this function, a State Party, in any given case, must demonstrate in specific fashion the precise nature of the threat to any of the enumerated grounds listed in paragraph 3 that has caused it to restrict freedom of expression.[113]

The tests of necessity and proportionality have been consistently applied in the jurisprudence of the ECtHR, which has ruled that interferences with human rights, including the right to privacy or the right to freedom of expression under Article 10 of the ECHR, must: (a) be in accordance with the law, (b) pursue a legitimate aim and be necessary to achieve that aim and (c) also be

---

[113] Human Rights Committee, General Comment No 34 (Art 19: Freedoms of opinion and expression) CCPR/C/GC/34 (12 Sept 2011) §§22, 34, 36.

reasonable and proportionate.[114] In *Belkacemi and Oussar v Belgium*[115] and *Dakir v Belgium*,[116] both decided on 11 July 2017 and concerning the Belgian ban on Islamic headscarves, the ECtHR ruled that the decision on whether or not to proscribe the wearing of full-face veils in public places is a choice of society and that the Belgian law at issue is proportionate to the aim pursued, namely the preservation of the conditions of 'living together' as an element of the protection of the rights and freedoms of others, as well as 'necessary' 'in a democratic society'. Therefore, there is no violation of either the right to respect for private or family life under Article 8 or the right of thought, conscience and religion under Article 9 of the ECHR. This reasoning is sound, considering that some Muslim-majority States themselves have banned the wearing of full-face veils. For example, Chad has banned it since June 2015 after a series of suicide bombings carried out by members of the terrorist group Boko Haram disguised as women wearing full-face veils. In July 2019, a Tunisian government decree prohibited any person with an undisclosed face from access to public headquarters, administrations or institutions. The decree cites security reasons for the ban and was issued in the wake of three bombing incidents for which the Islamic State of Iraq and the Levant (ISIL or ISIS) claimed responsibility. This brings to an end the permission in 2011 for women to wear the hijab and niqab in Tunisia after a decades-long ban on all forms of Islamic dress. It also comes after the Tunisian interior minister's instruction in February 2014 to the Tunisian police to step up supervision of the wearing of the niqab as part of anti-terrorism measures to prevent its use as a disguise.

Although the different regional human rights mechanisms vary in their approach to permissible restrictions on human rights and the ICCPR provides details of the requirements for permissible restrictions in relation to only three rights, Article 29(2) of the exhortatory UDHR is the guidance for all States. To recapitulate, it allows limitations on human rights on condition that such limitations are determined by law solely for the purpose of securing due recognition and respect for the rights and freedoms of others and of meeting the just requirements of morality, public order and the general welfare 'in a democratic society'. This must be read in conjunction with the Human Rights Committee's General Comment No 34 and the established jurisprudence of the ECtHR on the *test* to be applied in this respect so as to constitute the *best practices* for all States to measure up to, irrespective of whether they are party to the ICCPR or

---

[114] Eg, *Ahmet Yıldırım v Turkey*, App No 3111/10, ECHR 2012 and see esp the concurring opinion of Judge Paulo Pinto de Albuquerque at §§27–8.

[115] App No 37798/13 (ECHR 11 July 2017).

[116] [2017] ECHR 656.

the ECHR and whether the human rights at issue are the ones for which restrictions are expressly stipulated in the relevant human rights treaties. Whenever a State invokes human rights relativism – be it cultural, religious, value based or otherwise – as a reason not to comply with a binding human rights norm, it should have the burden of proving how the non-compliance is determined by law solely for the purpose of securing due recognition and respect for the rights and freedoms of others and of meeting the just requirements of morality, public order and the general welfare 'in a democratic society'. It would be even better if the State could also pass the tests of necessity and proportionality as required by the Human Rights Committee's General Comment No 34 and by the ECtHR's jurisprudence. Otherwise, the leadership of the government of that State may be presumed to use human rights relativism as a lame excuse to oppress the populace unless it can prove to the contrary. In a State not having democracy, it must prove that despite its undemocratic system of government any limitations on the rights of individuals or groups found within its territory, jurisdiction or effective control are determined by law solely for the purpose of securing due recognition and respect for the rights and freedoms of others and of meeting the just requirements of morality, public order and the general welfare similar to the limitations generally permissible 'in a democratic society'. Only in this way may the universalization of international human rights norms be meaningfully accomplished.

8.   Human rights in new dimensions: in cyberspace and at sea

There may be a dilemma of 'undermining old rights with new ones' by expanding the list of 'novel' human rights that may be mere subsets of the existing ones (such as the rights of African descendants, persons with albinism and human rights defenders) or those not yet finding sufficient support in the international community (for example, the right to be free from official corruption).[1] This expansion puts extra burdens on human rights monitoring and enforcement mechanisms as well as distracting from the focus on addressing existing and well-established human rights.[2] Conversely, giving priority to a narrow set of fundamental human rights would be self-defeating as it would be impossible to agree which human rights should be included in the set[3] and all human rights are somehow interrelated. Relatively recently asserted rights include lesbian/gay/bisexual/transgender/intersex rights, environmental rights and animal rights.[4] Several of the so-called 'new rights', such as the rights of children born of wartime rape, the untouchable Dalit caste in India, people living with HIV/AIDS, as well as other stigmatized minorities or marginalized groups,[5] can possibly fit in the rights already protected under the existing

---

[1]   Cf Alison Brysk and Michael Stohl (eds), *Expanding Human Rights: 21st Century Norms and Governance* (Edward Elgar Publishing 2017); Anne Peters, 'Corruption as a Violation of International Human Rights', Max Planck Institute for Comparative Public Law & International Law (MPIL) Research Paper No. 2016-18 (5 July 2016).

[2]   Eric A Posner, *Twilight of Human Rights Law* (OUP 2014) 92–4; Hurst Hannum, 'Reinvigorating Human Rights for the Twenty-First Century' (2016) 16 Hum Rts L Rev 409, 431; id, *Rescuing Human Rights: A Radically Moderate Approach* (CUP 2019) 57–79, 157–72.

[3]   Posner, *Twilight of Human Rights Law* 137–8.

[4]   Michael Haas, *International Human Rights: A Comprehensive Introduction* (2nd edn, Routledge 2014) 462–508; Frans Viljoen, 'Minority Sexual Orientation as a Challenge to the Harmonised Interpretation of International Human Rights Law' in Carla M Buckley, Alice Donald and Philip Leach (eds), *Towards Convergence in International Human Rights Law Approaches of Regional and International Systems* (Brill Nijhoff 2016) 156; John Barry and Kerri Woods, 'The Environment' in Michael Goodhart (ed.), *Human Rights: Politics and Practice* (3rd edn, OUP 2016) 405.

[5]   Theo van Boven, 'Categories of Rights' in Daniel Moeckli, Sangeeta Shah and Sandesh Sivakumaran (eds), *International Human Rights Law* (3rd edn, OUP 2018) 135, 144–5; Michael O'Flaherty, 'Sexual Orientation and Gender Identity' ibid 296.

international human rights law (IHRL). Human rights to a clean environment in the light of climate change and global warming,[6] which have attracted considerable interest recently, can be seen as building upon other already existing rights.[7]

Human rights in cyberspace and those at sea are less well-trodden terrains in the existing international legal literature and to them this chapter now turns.

1.   HUMAN RIGHTS IN CYBERSPACE[8]

'Cyberspace' may be defined as the manmade environment or space where electronic communication over interconnected networks of information and communications infrastructure, including the Internet, telecommunications networks and computer systems, occurs.[9] The phenomena of the Internet and online activities including smartphones have broken down spatial borders that divide nation States. As of 30 June 2019, there were 4,422,494,622 Internet users around the world (or more than half of the world's total population of approximately 7.72 billion). The largest number of Internet users were in Asia (49.8 per cent), followed by Europe (16.3 per cent), Africa (11.9 per cent), Latin America and Caribbean (10.1 per cent), North America (7.4 per cent), the Middle East (3.9 per cent) and Australia and Oceania (0.6 per cent).[10]

International law governing cyberspace comprises three dimensions: purely inter-State, inter-State but affecting rights of individuals in another State, and intra-State. The first dimension concerns action by one State vis-à-vis another State in the cyber realm such as waging a cyber war or cyber espionage against the government apparatus of that other State. An example of the second dimension is cyber surveillance by one State against individuals in another State. The

---

[6]   Alan Boyle, 'Human Rights and the Environment: Where Next?' (2012) 23 EJIL 613; Dinah Shelton, 'Whiplash and Backlash – Reflections on a Human Rights Approach to Environmental Protection' (2015) 13 Santa Clara JIL 11; Bridget Lewis, *Environmental Human Rights and Climate Change: Current Status and Future Prospects* (Springer 2018).

[7]   See, for example, *The State of the Netherlands (Ministry of Infrastructure and the Environment) v Urgenda Foundation*, Hague Court of Appeal (Civil Law Division) Case No 200.178.245/01, Case/cause list No C/09/456689/HA ZA 13-1396.

[8]   See also Kriangsak Kittichaisaree, *Public International Law of Cyberspace* (Springer 2017) 45–152; Eyal Benvenisti, 'Upholding Democracy amid the Challenges of New Technologies: What Role for the Law of Global Governance?' (2018) 29 EJIL 9, 55–82.

[9]   This is the all-inclusive working definition adopted by the present author in *Public International Law of Cyberspace* 2.

[10]   Internet World Stats, http://www.internetworldstats.com/stats.htm, accessed 8 Aug 2019.

third one happens when the government of a State conducts a cyber activity in relation to individuals present within its territory, jurisdiction or effective control. This chapter will deal with the latter two dimensions.

International law governing cyberspace is being shaped by States with bargaining power in cyber technologies. The USA is the world leader in cyber technologies, mostly in the hand of US multinational corporations such as Microsoft, Apple, Google, Facebook and Twitter. China and Russia are also superpowers in cyberspace thanks to their advanced cyber technological innovations. Chinese companies are still catching up with their US counterparts in terms of global market shares. However, China's population is the world's largest; hence, China has considerable leverage vis-à-vis US companies wishing to do business in the Chinese market for cyber products and services. Russia's cyber technological advance is formidable thanks to Russia's decades of research in all scientific fields that serve Russia's strategic goals in world politics.

Israel, Iran and North Korea are often in the news when cyberattacks occur. These States have developed their respective cyber capabilities to the level that they can use them offensively as well as defensively to protect their national security interests.

The remaining nation States are trying to catch up. Developing States are placed in the least advantageous position owing to their modest cyber technologies, relatively weak bargaining power and vulnerability to fake news, manipulative information, cyberattacks and cyber espionage perpetrated against them by States with superior cyber technologies. Developing States' entrenched position at both multilateral and bilateral diplomatic forums dealing with cyberspace is that they need cyber technological capacity-building assistance, and that their national interests must not be undermined by cyber activities of those States with cyber superiority.

Development of a discrete body of international law to specifically address developments in cyberspace would be too slow to catch up with the speed of the ever-changing innovations in cyberspace such as artificial intelligence (AI) and the Internet-of-Things. In any case, when there is no general consensus among States with varying national interests on new rules of international law, they have to be content with the ones already in existence insofar as the latter can be applicable to new challenges in international relations. The international community thus has to make do with existing relevant rules of international law, including IHRL, to cope with challenges, opportunities and threats in the cyber domain, lest there be chaos in cyberspace. This is affirmed by the Group of Governmental Experts on Developments in the Field of Information and Telecommunications in the Context of International Security (UNGGE), set up under the First Committee (Disarmament and International Security Committee) of the UN General Assembly (UNGA).

The UNGGE was composed of the delegations representing the five UN Security Council (UNSC) permanent members and some other UN Member States selected and rotated by their respective regional groups by consultation within each group, taking due account of the Member States' active role in cyberspace issues – whether or not they actually had the cyber technological expertise – and/or their prominent international stature. The UNGGE issued its first report on 24 June 2013. While the report observes that common understanding on how norms derived from existing international law relevant to the use of information and communications technologies (ICT) shall apply to State behaviour and the use of ICT by States requires further study and that, given the unique attributes of ICT, additional norms could be developed over time, it affirms that international law, particularly the UN Charter, is applicable. The report also emphasizes that cybersecurity must go hand in hand with respect for human rights and fundamental freedoms set forth in the 1948 Universal Declaration of Human Rights (UDHR)[11] and other pertinent international instruments.[12] In July 2015 a new UNGGE consisting of 20 Member States[13] submitted its report. In relation to international law, the report singles out the applicable principles of the UN Charter and other international law, including respect for human rights and fundamental freedoms.[14]

According to the International Group of Experts, including the present author, invited by the NATO Cooperative Cyber Defence Centre of Experience to write *The Tallinn Manual 2.0 on the International Law Applicable to Cyber Operations*, IHRL is applicable to cyber-related activities, individuals enjoy the same international human rights with respect to cyber-related activities that they otherwise enjoy and every State has obligations to respect and protect international human rights as required by relevant IHRL and treaty obligations binding on it.[15]

Application of existing public international law to cyberspace is not the same thing as applying law by analogy. Analogy involves an earlier, existing rule being followed in a later case because the later case is similar to the earlier

---

[11]   Doc A/RES/217(III).

[12]   *On the Developments in the Field of Information and Telecommunications in the Context of International Security*, UNGA Doc A/68/98 (24 June 2013) Part III. The 15 members of the Group were the five permanent members of the UNSC (China, France, Russia, UK and USA) plus Argentina, Australia (Chair), Belarus, Canada, Egypt, Estonia, Germany, India, Indonesia and Japan.

[13]   All the five permanent members of the UNSC together with Belarus, Brazil (Chair), Colombia, Egypt, Estonia, Germany, Ghana, Israel, Japan, Kenya, Malaysia, Mexico, Pakistan, South Korea and Spain.

[14]   UNGA Doc A/70/174 (22 July 2015) §§26–7.

[15]   Michael N Schmitt (ed.), *Tallinn Manual 2.0 on the International Law Applicable to Cyber Operations* (CUP 2017) 182–208.

one to which the said rule applies. By contrast, applying the relevant existing rules of public international law to cyberspace is practicable because such rules are broad enough to cover activities in cyberspace although, like any other body of law, some grey areas still remain.

Notwithstanding the foregoing, there is no universal consensus among nation States on how to apply IHRL governing cyberspace, since they interpret the law according to their respective cyber capabilities, ideologies, and strategic, economic and political interests.

The US Government's policy announced in May 2011 emphasizes as the core principles the fundamental freedoms, privacy and free flow of information. Fundamental freedoms include the freedom of expression and the freedom of association, subject to the narrow exceptions of public safety and protection of US citizens from cybercrimes. Privacy involves balancing appropriate investigative authorities for law enforcement, on the one hand, and protection of individual rights to privacy through appropriate judicial review and oversight to ensure consistency with the rule of law, on the other hand. Free flow of information aims at ensuring an open, interoperable, secure and reliable information and communications infrastructure, which also permits the freedoms of expression and association. In the US view, existing international norms for cyberspace include, inter alia, upholding fundamental freedoms of expression and association, respect for intellectual property rights, protection from arbitrary or unlawful interference with Internet users' privacy and protection from cybercrimes. Emerging norms in the field include global interoperability, network stability, reliable access, multi-stakeholder governance and cybersecurity due diligence. It defines the rule of law, cherished by the USA, as 'a civil order in which fidelity to law safeguards people and interests, brings stability to global markets and holds malevolent actors to account internationally'.[16]

China under President Xi Jinping (March 2013–) calls for universal respect for 'national cyber sovereignty', whereby each State has the right to decide how to develop and regulate its Internet and no State or group of a few States may resort to 'unilateralism' or 'cyber hegemony' or engage in activities that undermine other States' national security. China has proposed a global governance system to 'curb the abuse of information technology, oppose network surveillance and hacking and fight against a cyberspace arms race', with China playing an important role in formulating global rules for the Internet.[17]

---

[16] *International Strategy for Cyberspace: Prosperity, Security and Openness in a Networked World* (May 2011) 5, 10.

[17] His speech was delivered at the World Internet Conference held in Zhejiang province, China, in December 2015.

For its part, Russia insists on 'a firm commitment to the principles of non-interference in internal affairs of States, their equality in the process of Internet governance and the sovereign right of States to Internet governance in their national information space, to international law and to the observance of fundamental human rights and freedoms'.[18] In January 2015 Russia, together with China, Kazakhstan, Kyrgyzstan, Tajikistan and Uzbekistan, submitted a draft international code of conduct for information security to the UN Secretary-General for circulation as an official document of the UNGA. This draft code,[19] which is a revised version of the earlier one submitted in September 2011,[20] stresses that States with global dominance in the sphere of ICT shall not undermine other States' right of independent control of ICT products and services, or threaten other States' political, economic and social security. Also, it prohibits the use of ICT and information and communications networks to carry out activities which run counter to the task of maintaining international peace and security. The draft code adds a human rights aspect by providing that there be full respect for the rights and freedoms in the information space, including the right and freedom to seek, receive and impart information, taking into account the fact that Article 19 of the 1966 International Covenant on Civil and Political Rights (ICCPR)[21] attaches to such rights special duties and responsibilities, subject to certain restrictions as provided by law and as are necessary for respect for the rights or reputation of others and for the protection of national security, public order or public health or morals.

In the aftermath of Edward Snowden's disclosure, starting from May 2013, about alleged activities by certain Western governments to eavesdrop on personal data or information of private individuals at every level as well as on government agencies and corporate entities, the idea of 'cyber sovereignty', with a State or a geographical region completely isolated in cyberspace from the rest, has been broached. Concepts such as EU-only electronic networks, an EU-only cloud and a national-only cloud have been debated. A first question concerning 'cyber sovereignty' is whether it is technically realistic. Another question is whether, if it is feasible for a particular State, it will reinforce the control by censorship in cyberspace by the government of that State over its citizens and persons within its territorial borders. Whatever the answers to

---

[18] Russia's interpretative statement attached to the Initial Set of the Organization for Security and Cooperation in Europe's Confidence-Building Measures to Reduce the Risks of Conflict Stemming from the Use of Information and Communication Technologies, Organization for Security and Cooperation in Europe's Permanent Council Decision No 1106 (PC.DEC/1106) (3 Dec 2013).

[19] UNGA Doc A/69/723 (9 Jan 2015).

[20] UNGA Doc A/66/359 (14 Sept 2011).

[21] 999 UNTS 171.

these questions, national security and maintaining law and order and public morality are the most frequently cited grounds for departing from human rights protection at the national level. Moreover, effects of online communications, including via social media in the borderless world, as in the case of the Arab Spring uprisings and the incitement to commit acts of terrorism by the so-called Islamic State of Iraq and the Levant, or ISIL, have led a number of government agencies worldwide to take measures to pry on the contents of private online communications and/or even ban the use of social media.[22] For example, on 30 April 2018 Iran's Culture and Media Court ordered telecoms companies to block the Telegram app, which has about 40 million users in Iran, on the grounds that it had been threatening Iran's national security and enabling anti-establishment protesters to organize.

In the name of national security, especially the maintenance of social and political stability, China's Great Firewall initiative prevents politically sensitive information from reaching users. YouTube, Facebook, Twitter, Google and, from time to time, websites of certain Western news agencies are inaccessible in China. In April 2016 the Chinese State Administration of Press, Publication, Radio, Film and Television ordered the shutting down of Apple's iBooks store and iTunes Movie service after the promulgation of Chinese regulations in March 2016 proscribing foreign ownership of online publishing services and requiring all content shown to the Chinese in China to be stored on servers based in mainland China. On 7 November 2016 China passed the Cybersecurity Act, in force as of 1 June 2017. The legislative purpose of the Cybersecurity Act, as identified in Article 1 thereof, is 'to protect cybersecurity; to safeguard cyberspace sovereignty, national security and the societal public interest; to protect the lawful rights and interests of citizens, legal persons and other organizations and to promote the healthy development of economic and social informatization'.[23] Operators of 'key information infrastructure' – defined as information infrastructure maintained by certain industry sectors which would seriously undermine national security and the public interest if such infrastructure malfunctions, is damaged or leaks data – are subject to a data localization requirement. They must retain, within the territory of China, critical and personal information collected by them and produced during their operations in China. They may transmit such information overseas to the extent authorized under the mandatory security protection measures to be formulated by the State Council of the Chinese

---

[22] See, generally, David P Forsythe, *Human Rights in International Relations* (4th edn, CUP 2018) ch. 9.
[23] As translated and quoted in Jyh-An Lee, 'Hacking into China's Cybersecurity Law' (2018) 53 Wake Forest LR 57, 67.

Government. When such operators procure network products or services that may affect national security, a national security inspection is required. These industry sectors include public communication and information services, energy, transportation, water resources utilization, finance, public service and e-government affairs. The collection and use of personal information must comply with the requirements of notice and consent and the principles of legitimacy, rightfulness and necessity. Network operators must provide technical support and assistance to public or national security agencies when conducting an investigation of a crime. They shall also adopt technical measures to monitor and record their network operations and preserve related web logs for at least six months. Overseas entities or individuals that attack, invade, interfere with or destroy 'key information infrastructure' in China shall be legally liable and Chinese public security agencies may adopt sanctions against them, including freezing their assets.[24]

Pursuant to the Cybersecurity Act, the Chinese Internet regulatory agency imposed huge fines on China's three major Internet companies – Tencent, Baidu and Sina – for failing to properly manage their social media platforms by letting some users 'spread information of violence and terror, false rumours, pornography and other information jeopardizing national security, public safety and social order'. Likewise, the Shanghai Internet Information Office shut down, for a week, the Chinese website and mobile apps of the hotel chain Marriott International for its violation of the Cybersecurity Act and advertising regulations by listing Hong Kong, Macau, Taiwan and Tibet as separate countries in a survey distributed to Marriott's customers, thereby purportedly indicating support for secession movements and a threat to Chinese sovereignty and territorial integrity.[25] The Regulation on Internet Security Supervision and Inspection by Public Security Organs,[26] in force as of 1 November 2018, authorizes China's Ministry of Public Security to conduct in-person or remote inspections of the network security defences taken by companies operating in China, check for 'prohibited content' banned inside China, log security response plans during on-site inspections, copy any user information found on inspected systems during on-site or remote inspections, perform penetration tests to check for vulnerabilities, perform remote inspections without informing companies and share any collected data with other State agencies. The

---

[24]   'Final Cybersecurity Law Enacted in China', Hunton & Williams LLP's *Privacy & Information Security Law Blog*, 8 Nov 2016, https://www.huntonprivacyblog .com/2016/11/08/final-cybersecurity-law-enacted-china/, accessed 10 Dec 2018; Lee, 'Hacking into China's Cybersecurity Law' 70–89.

[25]   Lee, 'Hacking into China's Cybersecurity Law' 92–3.

[26]   http://www.mps.gov.cn/n2254314/n2254409/n4904353/c6263180/content.html, accessed 10 Feb 2019.

Regulation also authorizes two members of the People's Armed Police to be present during on-site inspections to enforce the procedures stipulated in this Regulation.[27]

For its part, the Russian Government submitted a draft law entitled 'Digital Economy National Programme' to Parliament in 2018 to allow Russia to construct the 'Runet', which is its own version of the Internet's domain name system, or DNS, which stores all of the domain names and corresponding Internet Protocol (IP) numbers. The envisaged 'Runet' will continue to operate even though links to the servers located outside Russia are cut off. A test was scheduled by 1 April 2019 to demonstrate that Internet service providers in Russia could direct data to Russian Government-controlled routing points in order to filter traffic so that data sent between Russians reached its destination, but any destined for foreign computers was discarded. In the long run, the Russian Government wants all domestic online traffic to pass through these domestic routing points only. This measure has caused some concern that the Russian Government would bring router points that handle data entering or exiting Russia under its control and censor what outside information people inside Russia can access.[28]

On 6 December 2018 the Australian Parliament enacted the world's first-ever law to compel technology companies to give police and government security agencies a technical function to give them access to a suspect's encrypted messages in a smartphone without the suspect's knowledge. The law's objective is to suppress acts of terrorism and crimes by getting backdoor access to circumvent end-to-end encryption that allows only the sender and recipient to view a message.[29] Laws in China, Russia and Turkey ban services offering end-to-end encryption.

Curtailing the right to privacy and the right to freedom of expression must be in accordance with IHRL.

Let us start with the right to privacy in cyberspace.

In the Americas, the General Assembly of the Organization of American States (OAS) has, since 1996, been giving importance to access to information and protection of personal data to safeguard fundamental rights and freedoms,

---

[27] Catalin Cimpanu, 'China's cybersecurity law update lets state agencies "pen-test" local companies', *Zero Day* (9 Feb 2019) https://www.zdnet.com/article/chinas-cybersecurity-law-update-lets-state-agencies-pen-test-local-companies/, accessed 10 Feb 2019.

[28] Frank Hoermann, 'Russia takes steps to survive global internet shutdown with its own web', *RT News* (12 Feb 2019) https://www.rt.com/russia/451292-russia-internet-cut-off/, accessed 13 Feb 2019.

[29] Telecommunications and Other Legislation Amendment (Assistance and Access) Act 2018.

notably the right to privacy and the right to access personal information (also known as *habeas* data), while also encouraging the flow of information and electronic commerce.[30]

The right to privacy is not expressly provided for in the African Charter on Human and Peoples' Rights.[31] In June 2014, the African Union (AU) adopted the Convention on Cyber Security and Personal Data Protection[32] whose objective includes the establishment in each State Party of a mechanism capable of combating violations of privacy that may be generated by data collection, processing, transmission, storage and use.

Paragraph 21 of the hortatory Declaration of Human Rights adopted by the Association of Southeast Asian Nations (ASEAN) in 2012[33] recognizes the right of every person to be free from arbitrary interference with his or her privacy, including personal data and the right to the protection of the law against such interference.

In the aftermath of Edward Snowden's disclosure, the UNGA,[34] the EU,[35] and the Human Rights Council (HRC)[36] adopted resolutions to affirm that the right to privacy as protected by the UDHR and other relevant human rights instruments is applicable, both online and offline, in the digital age.

The right to privacy is enshrined in most IHRL treaties, including Article 17 of the ICCPR, Article 8 of the 1950 European Convention on Human Rights (ECHR),[37] Article 7 of the 2000 EU Charter of Fundamental Rights,[38] and Articles 11 and 13 of the 1969 American Convention on Human Rights.[39]

---

[30] Draft Preliminary Principles and Recommendations on Data Protection (Protection of Personal Data), OAS Permanent Council, Committee on Juridical and Political Affairs, Doc OEA/Ser.G CP/CAJP-2921/10, 19 Nov 2010; Inter-American Juridical Committee of the OAS's report entitled *Personal Data Protection* presented to the OAS Permanent Council on 31 Mar 2015, Doc CJI/RES.186 (LXXX-O/12).

[31] (1982) 21 ILM 58.

[32] https://au.int/sites/default/files/treaties/29560-treaty-0048_-_african_union_convention_on_cyber_security_and_personal_data_protection_e.pdf, accessed 5 Jan 2019.

[33] http://asean.org/asean-human-rights-declaration, accessed 12 Aug 2019.

[34] UNGA Res 68/167, 'The right to privacy in the digital age', 18 Dec 2013.

[35] The Conclusions of the European Council (24/25 Oct 2013), EUCO 169/13 §8, http://www.consilium.europa.eu/uedocs/cms_data/docs/pressdata/en/ec/139197.pdf, accessed 2 Jan 2019.

[36] A/HRC/28/L.27 (26 Mar 2015).

[37] ETS 5.

[38] OJ C 326/391 of 26.10.2012.

[39] 1144 UNTS 123.

As early as 1988, the Human Rights Committee issued General Comment No 16 to clarify the scope of the right to privacy under Article 17 of the ICCPR[40] as follows:

> 7. As all persons live in society, the protection of privacy is necessarily relative. However, the competent public authorities should only be able to call for such information relating to an individual's private life the knowledge of which is essential in the interests of society as understood under the [ICCPR]. ...
> 8. Even with regard to interferences that conform to the [ICCPR], relevant legislation must specify in detail the precise circumstances in which such interferences may be permitted. A decision to make use of such authorized interference must be made only by the authority designated under the law and on a case-by-case basis. Compliance with Article 17 requires that the integrity and confidentiality of correspondence should be guaranteed de jure and de facto. Correspondence should be delivered to the addressee without interception and without being opened or otherwise read. Surveillance, whether electronic or otherwise, interceptions of telephonic, telegraphic and other forms of communication, wire-tapping and recording of conversations should be prohibited. Searches of a person's home should be restricted to a search for necessary evidence and should not be allowed to amount to harassment.
> ...
> 10. The gathering and holding of personal information on computers, data banks and other devices, whether by public authorities or private individuals or bodies, must be regulated by law. ... In order to have the most effective protection of his private life, every individual should have the right to ascertain in an intelligible form, whether and if so, what personal data is stored in automatic data files and for what purposes.

Article 8 of the EU Charter specifically addresses the protection of personal data of every person. On 24 October 1995 the EU adopted Directive 95/46 on the protection of individuals with regard to the processing of personal data and on the free movement of such data.[41] The Directive has been improved and replaced since 25 May 2018 by the EU General Data Protection Regulation.[42] Collection of metadata, or data that describes other data,[43] straddles the issues

---

[40] Human Rights Committee, General Comment No 16: Art 17 (Right to Privacy), The Right to Respect of Privacy, Family, Home and Correspondence and Protection of Honour and Reputation, 8 Apr 1988.

[41] Directive 95/46/EC of the European Parliament and of the Council of 24 Oct 1995 on the protection of individuals with regard to the processing of personal data and on the free movement of such data, 1995 OJ L 281/31.

[42] Regulation (EU) 2016/679 of the European Parliament and of the Council of 27 Apr 2016 on the protection of natural persons with regard to the processing of personal data and on the free movement of such data and repealing Directive 95/46/EC (General Data Protection Regulation), 2016 OJ L 119/1.

[43] For example, telephone metadata are data on the identity of the caller and the person called and the duration of the call, but not the content of the call itself.

of the right to privacy and the right to data protection. The Grand Chamber of the European Court of Justice (ECJ) in *Digital Rights Ireland Ltd* rejected the idea that metadata should attract less protection than the content of communications,[44] and the European Court of Human Rights (ECtHR) adopts the same position in *Big Brother Watch v The United Kingdom*.[45] By contrast, US courts generally draw a distinction between the content of a communication, which is protected by the Fourth Amendment against unreasonable searches and seizures,[46] and information which is not so protected because it is voluntarily shared, such as details of phone calls held by telephone companies.[47]

With regard to the right to freedom of expression, another important human right in cyberspace, it is protected under, inter alia, Article 19 of the ICCPR, Article 10 of the ECHR, Article 11 of the EU Charter, and the First Amendment of the US Constitution. However, with regard to the EU Charter the ECJ in the now famous case of *Costeja González* has upheld the 'right to be forgotten' (or more accurately, the 'right to suppression' of links to search engine results)[48] by resolving the conflict between the right to the freedom of expression and the right to privacy/protection of personal data in favour of the latter.[49] By contrast, US courts may not enforce the 'right to be forgotten' on the conditions set by the ECJ's *Costeja* judgment. In *Cox Broadcasting Corp v Cohn*, the US Supreme Court ruled that the state of Georgia's Shield Law and its common-law counterpart violated, inter alia, the First Amendment of the US Constitution, which protects the freedom of speech, since US federal states may not impose sanctions on the publication of truthful information contained in official court records open to public inspection.[50] Likewise, the Supreme Court of California in *Gates v Discovery Communications* ruled that accurate

---

[44]	*Digital Rights Ireland Ltd v Minister for Communications, Marine and Natural Resources and Others and Kärntner Landesregierung and Others*, Joined Cases C-293/12 and C-594/12, ECLI:EU:C:2014:238, §§26–7, 37. This ruling has been endorsed by the Report of the Office of the UN High Commissioner for Human Rights on the right to privacy in the digital age, A/HRC/27/37 (18 July 2014) §§19–20.
[45]	*Big Brother Watch v The United Kingdom*, App Nos 58170/13, 62322/14 and 24960/15, 13 Sept 2018, §§356–7.
[46]	*Katz v United States*, 389 US 347 (1967).
[47]	*Smith v Maryland*, 442 US 735, 744 (1979); *United States v Forrester*, 512 F.3d 500 (2008).
[48]	Christopher Kuner, 'The Court of Justice of the EU Judgment on Data Protection and Internet Search Engines: Current Issues and Future Challenges' in Burkhard Hess and Cristina M Mariottini (eds), *Protecting Privacy in Private International and Procedural Law and by Data Protection: European and American Developments* (Nomos/Brill 2015) 19.
[49]	*Google Spain SL and Google Inc. v Agencia Española de Protección de Datos (AEPD) and Mario Costeja González*, Case C-131/12, ECLI:EU:C:2014:317.
[50]	420 US 469 (1975).

news reporting of facts about a crime obtained from a public record may not be a legal ground for invasion of privacy, even almost a decade after the crime was committed and the convicted person who now sues a news reporter for invasion of privacy has been released from prison. The Court cites a long line of US Supreme Court cases, starting from *Cox Broadcasting Corp v Cohn*, to reject the argument that the passage of time could reduce the 'newsworthiness' of information in a public record and eliminate the freedom of speech protection under the First Amendment of the US Constitution for publishing it.[51]

In Europe, the ECtHR has consistently held that interferences with human rights, including the right to privacy or the right to freedom of expression, must be: (a) in accordance with the law, (b) pursue a legitimate aim and be necessary to achieve that aim, and (c) reasonable and proportionate.[52] The ECtHR's judgment in *Yildirim v Turkey*[53] adds the requirement that any law mandating Internet blocking or filtering include, at a minimum, notification of the blocking order and the grounds for it to the person or institution affected, as well as providing for a judicial appeal procedure. Any person who could be subject to a secret surveillance measure undertaken by the government or within the scope of national legislation authorizing such measure may claim to be a victim of a violation of the ECHR, even without having to allege that such measure has in fact been applied to that person. The ECtHR has held in earlier cases that the mere existence of such measure or threat of surveillance in and of itself entitles the said person to claim that he or she is a victim of a violation of the ECHR,[54] and that a victim of a violation of the ECHR may be a natural person or a legal person such as an NGO.[55]

In *Big Brother Watch v United Kingdom*, the ECtHR had to determine whether mass electronic surveillance measures by the UK violate, inter alia, Article 8 of the ECHR. The ECtHR refers to its case law on the interception of communications in criminal investigations as well as for reasons of national security. The ECtHR's case law has developed the following six minimum requirements that should be set out in law in order to avoid abuses of power: the nature of offences or national security threat which may give rise to an interception order; a definition of the categories of people liable to have their

---

[51]   101 P.3d 552 (2005).
[52]   Eg *Malone v The United Kingdom*, 2 Aug 1984, Ser A No 82; *Leander v Sweden*, 26 Mar 1987, Ser A No 116; *Uzun v Germany*, No 35623/05, ECHR 2010.
[53]   *Ahmet Yıldırım v Turkey*, No 3111/10, ECHR 2012.
[54]   *Klass and Others v Germany*, 6 Sept 1978, Ser A No 28 §§33–8; *Weber and Saravia v Germany* (dec), No 54934/00, ECHR 2006-XI §78.
[55]   *Association for European Integration and Human Rights and Ekimdzhiev v Bulgaria*, No 62540/00, 28 June 2007; *Liberty and Others v The United Kingdom*, No 58243/00, 1 July 2008 §§56–7.

communications intercepted; a limit on the duration of interception; the procedure for examining, using and storing the data obtained; the precautions to be taken when communicating the data to other parties; and the circumstances in which intercepted data may or must be erased or destroyed. However, in determining whether the impugned legislation or measure is in breach of Article 8, regard must be had to the arrangements for supervising the implementation of secret surveillance measures, any notification mechanisms and the remedies provided for by national law.[56]

In determining whether an interference is 'necessary in a democratic society' in pursuit of a legitimate aim, the ECtHR in *Big Brother Watch* has acknowledged that, when balancing the interest of the respondent State in protecting its national security through secret surveillance measures against the seriousness of the interference with an applicant's right to respect for his or her private life, the national authorities enjoy 'a certain margin of appreciation in choosing the means for achieving the legitimate aim' of protecting national security. This is subject to European supervision over both legislation and decisions applying it to ensure that there be adequate and effective guarantees against abuse. The assessment depends on all the circumstances of the case, such as the nature, scope and duration of the possible measures, the grounds required for ordering them, the authorities competent to authorize, carry out and supervise them and the kind of remedy provided by the national law. The national procedures for supervising the ordering and implementation of the restrictive measures must be such as to keep the 'interference' to what is 'necessary in a democratic society'.[57] Review and supervision of secret surveillance measures may come into play at three stages: when the surveillance is first ordered, while it is being carried out or after it has been terminated. During the first two stages, when the individual is ignorant of the surveillance due to its secrecy, the procedures established should themselves provide adequate and equivalent guarantees safeguarding his or her rights, and it is in principle desirable to entrust supervisory control to a judge, as judicial control offers the best guarantees of independence, impartiality and a proper procedure. At the third stage, the question of subsequent notification of surveillance measures is inextricably linked to the effectiveness of remedies before the courts and, hence, to the existence of effective safeguards against the abuse of monitoring powers. In principle, the individual concerned must be advised of the measures taken without his or her knowledge and thus be able to challenge their legality retrospectively. Alternatively, any person who suspects that he or she has been subject to surveillance must be able to apply to courts whose jurisdiction does not depend

---

[56] *Big Brother Watch* §307.
[57] Ibid §308.

on notification to the surveillance subject of the measures taken.[58] However, while it is desirable to entrust supervisory jurisdiction to a judge, this is not a necessary requirement in every State Party to the ECHR, provided that there exists independent oversight with adequate safeguards against abuse that can compensate for an absence of judicial supervision.[59]

The ECtHR in *Big Brother Watch* proceeds to consider the then existing case law on the bulk interception of communications. It concludes that, like other types of surveillance, the bulk interception is equally subject to the six minimum requirements plus the arrangements for supervising the implementation of secret surveillance measures, any notification mechanisms and the remedies provided for by national law.[60] The ECtHR considers the UK's impugned bulk interception proportionate for three reasons. First, terrorists, criminals and hostile foreign intelligence services have become increasingly sophisticated at evading detection by traditional means. Secondly, the nature of the global Internet means that the route a particular communication would travel has become hugely unpredictable. Thirdly, the bulk interception enables the security services to adopt a proactive approach, looking for hitherto unknown dangers rather than investigating known ones.[61] However, the ECtHR ruled that the UK violates Article 8 of the ECHR. While there is no evidence to suggest that the UK intelligence services are abusing their powers, the safeguards governing the selection of bearers for interception and the selection of intercepted material for examination are not sufficiently robust to provide adequate guarantees against abuse. Of greatest concern to the ECtHR is the absence of robust independent oversight of the selectors and search criteria used to filter intercepted communications.[62] The ECtHR in *Big Brother Watch* ordered the UK to pay €150,000 to the applicants in the first of the joined cases and €35,000 to the applicants in the second of the joined cases, both amounts to include any tax that may be chargeable to the applicants, in respect of costs and expenses.

The applicants in *Big Brother Watch* also claimed to be victims of violation of Article 8 of the ECHR occasioned by the existence of an intelligence sharing regime.[63] The interception itself did not occur within the UK's jurisdiction and

---

[58] Ibid §§309–10.
[59] Ibid §319.
[60] Ibid §§314–20.
[61] Ibid §§384–5.
[62] Ibid §§340–47, 357.
[63] On the UK–US cooperation on signals intelligence sharing, see Itamar Mann, 'The Disaggregated Law of Global Mass Surveillance' in Tanja Aalberts and Thomas Gammeltoft-Hansen (eds), *The Changing Practices of International Law* (CUP 2018) 129, 136–50.

is not attributable to the UK under international law. As the communications were intercepted by foreign intelligence agencies, their interception could only engage the responsibility of the UK if the UK were exercising authority or control over those agencies. Even when the UK authorities requested the interception of communications (rather than simply conveying the product of intercept), the interception would appear to take place under the full control of the foreign intelligence agencies who were neither placed at the disposal of the UK nor acting in exercise of elements of the governmental authority of the UK. Moreover, the UK did not aid or assist the foreign intelligence agencies in intercepting the communications, exercise direction or control over the foreign government or act in any other way that would incur State responsibility on the UK under international law. Consequently, the interference occasioned by the existence of an intelligence sharing regime would lie in the receipt of the intercepted material and its subsequent storage, examination and use by the UK intelligence services.[64]

The ECtHR decided in *Big Brother Watch* that the rules governing the acquisition of surveillance material also apply to the obtaining of such material from foreign governments. They must be 'in accordance with the law' in the sense of having some basis in domestic law, accessible to the person concerned, foreseeable as to its effects, proportionate to the legitimate aim pursued and equipped with adequate and effective safeguards against abuse. The procedures for supervising the ordering and implementation of the measures in question must be such as to keep the 'interference' to what is 'necessary in a democratic society'. As the material obtained is the product of intercept, those requirements relating to its storage, examination, use, onward dissemination, erasure and destruction must be present. A suitable safeguard will be to provide that the bulk material transferred can only be searched if all the material requirements of a national search are fulfilled and this is duly authorized in the same way as a search of bulk material obtained by the signals intelligence agency using its own techniques. In addition, the circumstances in which intercepted material can be requested from foreign intelligence services must also be set out in domestic law in order to avoid abuses of power. The circumstances in which such a request can be made must be circumscribed sufficiently to prevent – insofar as possible – States from using this power to circumvent either domestic law or their obligations under the ECHR.[65] The ECtHR, by five votes to two, found no violation by the UK of Article 8 of the ECHR in respect of the intelligence sharing regime.[66]

---

[64]   *Big Brother Watch* §§419–21.
[65]   Ibid §§422–4.
[66]   Ibid §6 of the dispositif.

The foreign government implicated in the interception of communications in *Big Brother Watch* was the US Government.

With regard to the human rights obligations of a State arising in the territory of another State, the Human Rights Committee of the ICCPR decided in *Lopez Burgos v Uruguay* that although Article 2(1) of the ICCPR obligates a State Party to respect and to ensure to all individuals within its territory and subject to its jurisdiction the rights recognized in the ICCPR, 'it does not imply that the State Party concerned cannot be held accountable for violations of rights under the [ICCPR] which its agents commit upon the territory of another State, whether with the acquiescence of the Government of that State or in opposition to it'.[67] Article 2(1) ICCPR has been interpreted by the Human Rights Committee, in General Comment No 31, to mean that a State Party must respect and ensure the rights laid down in the ICCPR to anyone within the power *or* effective control of that State Party, even if not situated within the territory of the State Party, regardless of the circumstances in which such power or effective control was obtained.[68] This includes both de jure and de facto power or effective control over persons supposedly entitled to human rights protection under the ICCPR and is a question of fact, to be considered in the light of all the circumstances. This is also the interpretation by the ECtHR concerning the exercise of authority and control over persons for the purpose of establishing a jurisdictional link between such persons and a State Party pursuant to Article 1 of the ECHR, which obligates all States Parties to secure to everyone within their jurisdiction the rights and freedoms under the ECHR.[69] The International Court of Justice has ruled that the Human Rights Committee is correct in interpreting the ICCPR as being applicable in respect of acts done by a State in the exercise of its jurisdiction outside its own territory.[70] However, some States, most notably Israel and the USA, have denied that their human rights obligations under the ICCPR apply extraterritorially.[71]

The Fourth Amendment to the US Constitution guarantees 'the right of the people to be secure in their persons, houses, papers and effects, against unreasonable searches and seizures'. This right of privacy 'shall not be

---

[67] *Lopez Burgos v Uruguay*, 29 July 1981, Communication No 25/1979 §12.3.

[68] Human Rights Committee, General Comment No 31, The nature of the general legal obligation imposed on States Parties to the Covenant, 26 May 2004, CCPR/C/21/Rev.1/Add.13 §10.

[69] *Al-Skeini and Others v The United Kingdom* [GC] App No 55721/07, ECHR 2011; *Hassan v The United Kingdom* [GC] App No 29750/09, ECHR 2014; *Jaloud v Netherlands* [GC] App No 47708/08, ECHR 2014.

[70] *Legal Consequences of the Construction of a Wall in the Occupied Palestinian Territory*, Advisory Opinion [2004] ICJ Rep 136, 178–80 [108]–[111].

[71] Ibid 177 [102]; Human Rights Committee, Concluding Observations on the fourth periodic report of the USA §4.

violated and no Warrants shall issue, but upon probable cause, supported by Oath or affirmation, and particularly describing the place to be searched, and the persons or things to be seized'.[72] Nevertheless, there are inherent distinctions under US law between citizens and aliens, although an alien's mere lawful presence in the USA creates an implied assurance of safe conduct and gives him or her certain rights.[73] The protections given by US Acts of Congress, Executive Orders and judicial decisions to protect US persons who are subject to intelligence collection are: restrictions on the types of information to be collected, retained or disseminated, and restrictions on the duration of such retention, plus the existence of oversight mechanisms.[74] Aliens not lawfully present in the USA and aliens outside the USA are not so protected. This discriminatory treatment is contrary to the conclusion in April 2014 by the Human Rights Committee of the ICCPR about the US National Security Agency's surveillance programmes. The Committee asked the US Government to 'take all necessary measures to ensure that its surveillance activities, both within and outside the United States, conform to its obligations under the [ICCPR], including Article 17' and suggested that 'measures should be taken to ensure that any interference with the right to privacy complies with the principles of legality, proportionality and necessity regardless of the nationality or location of individuals whose communications are under direct surveillance'.[75] In addition, the US Government should reform its oversight system of surveillance activities, including electronic surveillance, by, inter alia, providing for judicial involvement in the authorization or monitoring of surveillance measures and considering the establishment of strong and independent oversight mandates with a view to preventing abuses.[76] In response, the US Congress passed the Uniting and Strengthening America by Fulfilling Rights and Ensuring Effective Discipline over Monitoring Act (USA Freedom Act) of 2 June 2015[77] establishing a new process with a better safeguarding of the rights of individuals to be followed when the FBI submits an application to the Foreign Intelligence Surveillance Court for an order requiring the pro-

---

[72]   *Griswold v Connecticut*, 382 US 479 (1965); *Katz v United States*, 389 US 317 (1967); *Kyllo v United States*, 533 US 27, 31–41 (2001).

[73]   *Johnson v Eisentrager*, 339 US 763, 769, 771 (1950) (*per* Jackson J); *United States v Verdugo-Urquidez*, 494 US 259, 266, 275 (1990) (*per* Rehnquist CJ, writing for the plurality).

[74]   Daniel Severson, 'American Surveillance of Non-U.S. Persons: Why New Privacy Protections Offer Only Cosmetic Change' (2015) 56 Harvard ILJ 465, 474–6, 482.

[75]   Human Rights Committee, Concluding Observations on the fourth periodic report of the USA, 23 Apr 2014, CCPR/C/USA/CO/4 §22(a).

[76]   Ibid §22(c).

[77]   Pub L 114-23, 129 Stat 268 (2015).

duction of business records or other tangible things. It is too early as of this writing to fully evaluate whether the USA Freedom Act fully complies with international human rights standards, especially the ICCPR, which is legally binding on the USA.

A question may also be asked whether the ECtHR in *Big Brother Watch* adopts a lower standard of human rights protection than the Grand Chamber of the ECJ.

In *Digital Rights Ireland* the Grand Chamber of the ECJ had to determine whether EU Directive 2006/24/EC, which regulates Internet service providers' storage of telecommunications data that could be used to fight serious crimes in the EU, violates the EU Charter of Fundamental Rights. The Directive is intended to harmonize the different regulations in EU Member States on the retention of information concerning the source, destination and time of communications within the EU. The applicants allege that the Directive is becoming the legal basis for mass surveillance laws that violate fundamental human rights. In its judgment of 8 April 2014, the Grand Chamber holds the Directive to be invalid because of its interference with the right to private life under Article 7 and the right to the protection of personal data under Article 8 of the EU Charter. Although the Directive's aim might be legitimate, its implementation is not proportionate to the intended objective. In particular, the Directive does not stipulate clear and precise rules on the extent of the interference, for example by applying to all traffic data and all users of all modes of electronic communications for an unspecified length of time and by not requiring a nexus between the data retained and serious crimes. The Directive is also not sufficiently specific about the conditions of data storage and the obligations of both Internet service providers and security agencies accessing the data. Furthermore, the Directive has no guarantees on how telecommunications data will be kept, managed and accessed and it fails to provide that the data has to be retained within the EU. The Grand Chamber ruled that the collection and retention of data constitute an interference with Articles 7 (respect for private and family life) and 8 (protection of personal data) and affects Article 11 (freedom of expression and information) of the EU Charter.[78]

In the *Schrems* case decided on 6 October 2015,[79] the Grand Chamber of the ECJ invalidates the Safe Harbour Agreement concluded between the European Commission and the US Department of Commerce in 2000. The Agreement aimed to bridge the differences in approach to data protection and provide a streamlined means for US organizations subject to the jurisdiction

---

[78]   *Digital Rights Ireland Ltd* §§28–9.
[79]   *Maximillian Schrems v Data Protection Commissioner*, Case C-362/14, ECLI: EU:C:2015:650.

of the Federal Trade Commission or US air carriers and ticket agents subject
to the jurisdiction of the US Department of Transportation to comply with the
'adequacy' standard under the EU's Directive 95/46. The Grand Chamber
largely adopts the Advocate General's opinion that the mass, indiscriminate
access by the US intelligence services to the transferred data from the EU
constitutes an interference with the right to respect for private life and the
right to protection of personal data guaranteed by the EU Charter, contrary
to the principle of proportionality. The inability of EU citizens to be heard
on the question of the surveillance and interception of their data in the USA
amounts to an interference with the right of EU citizens to an effective remedy,
protected by the Charter. The Safe Harbour Agreement has been found not to
contain any appropriate guarantees for preventing mass and generalized access
to the transferred data and no independent authority can monitor, in the USA,
breaches of the principles for the protection of personal data committed by
public actors, such as US security agencies, in respect of the EU.[80] The Grand
Chamber's judgment alludes to the fact that US public authorities are not
themselves subject to the Safe Harbour undertaking and that US national security, public interest and law enforcement requirements prevail over the Safe
Harbour scheme. It rules that legislation permitting the public authorities to
have access on a generalized basis to the content of electronic communications
compromises the essence of the fundamental right to respect for private life.[81]
When that legislation does not provide for any possibility for an individual
to pursue legal remedies in order to have access to personal data relating to
him, or to obtain the rectification or erasure of such data, it compromises the
essence of the fundamental right to effective judicial protection, inherent in the
rule of law. The Grand Chamber interprets the adequate level of protection in
third States to mean that the protection must be essentially equivalent to that
accorded under EU law.

The ECtHR in *Big Brother Watch* is correct in appreciating that protection
of human rights in cyberspace must take cognizance of the ever-evolving
nature of cyber technologies.

The US Supreme Court's five to four majority judgment of 22 June 2018
in *Carpenter v United States*[82] involves the US Government's acquisition of
wireless carrier cell-site records revealing the location of a person's cell phone
whenever it made or received calls. This sort of digital data – personal location
information maintained by a third party – does not fit neatly under existing

---

[80] Opinion of Advocate General Bot of 23 Sept 2015, *Maximillian Schrems v Data
Protection Commissioner*, Case C-362/14 (Request for a preliminary ruling from the
High Court (Ireland)).

[81] Grand Chamber's judgment §94.

[82] *Carpenter v United States*, 585 US ____ (2018).

precedents. Requests for cell-site records lie at the intersection of two lines of cases. The first set of cases addresses a person's expectation of privacy in his physical location and movements. In a second set of decisions, the US Supreme Court has drawn a line between what a person keeps to himself and what he shares with others ('third parties') thereby relinquishing the person's legitimate expectation of privacy in information he voluntarily turns over to third parties.

The question in *Carpenter* is how to apply the constitutional protection of privacy to a new phenomenon: the ability to chronicle a person's past movements through the record of his cell phone signals. Such tracking partakes of many of the qualities of global positioning system (GPS) monitoring. Much like GPS tracking of a vehicle, cell phone location information is detailed, encyclopaedic and effortlessly compiled. At the same time, the fact that the individual continuously reveals his location to his wireless carrier implicates the third-party principle. Given the unique nature of cell phone location records, the fact that the information is held by a third party does not by itself overcome the user's claim to constitutional protection. Whether the US Government employs its own surveillance technology or leverages the technology of a wireless carrier, an individual maintains a legitimate expectation of privacy in the record of his physical movements as captured through the cell-site location information (CSLI).

The location information obtained from Carpenter's wireless carriers was held to be the product of a search. A person does not surrender all protection under the Fourth Amendment by venturing into the public sphere. To the contrary, what one seeks to preserve as private, even in an area accessible to the public, may be constitutionally protected and allowing the US Government access to cell-site records contravenes that expectation. Although such records are generated for commercial purposes, that distinction does not negate Carpenter's anticipation of privacy in his physical location. Mapping a cell phone's location over the course of 127 days provides an all-encompassing record of the holder's whereabouts. As with GPS information, the time-stamped data provides an intimate window into a person's life, revealing not only his particular movements, but through them his familial, political, professional, religious and sexual associations. In fact, historical cell-site records present even greater privacy concerns than the GPS monitoring of a vehicle. Moreover, the retrospective quality of the data here gives police access to a category of information otherwise unknowable. In the past, attempts to reconstruct a person's movements were limited by a dearth of records and the frailties of recollection. With access to CSLI, the US Government can now travel back in time to retrace a person's whereabouts, subject only to the retention policies of the wireless carriers, which currently maintain records for up to five years. Critically, because location information is continually logged for all of the 400 million devices in the USA – not just those belonging to persons who might happen to come under investigation – this newfound tracking capacity runs against everyone. Unlike with the GPS device tracking a vehicle, police need not even know in advance whether they want to follow a particular individual, or when. Whoever the suspect turns out to be, he has effectively been tailed every moment of every day for five years and the police may call upon the results of that surveillance without regard to the constraints of the US Constitution. Only the few without cell phones could escape this tireless and absolute surveillance. Given the unique nature of cell phone location information, the fact that the US Government obtained the information from a third party does not overcome Carpenter's claim to constitutional protection. The US Government's acquisition of the cell-site records was a search within the meaning of the Fourth Amendment and the US Government had to obtain a warrant supported by probable cause before acquiring such records.

To recapitulate, what the US Supreme Court's judgment in *Carpenter* decides is that the US Government cannot have unrestricted access to a wireless carrier's database of physical location information. Owing to the deeply revealing nature of CSLI, its depth, breadth and comprehensive reach, and the inescapable and automatic nature of its collection, the fact that such information is gathered by a third party does not make it any less deserving of constitutional protection. However, if law enforcement is confronted with an urgent situation, such fact-specific threats will likely justify the warrantless collection of CSLI. While police must get a warrant when collecting CSLI to assist in the mine-run criminal investigation, the rule in *Carpenter* does not limit their ability to respond to an ongoing emergency.

This judgment in *Carpenter* is a narrow one as the US Supreme Court does not express a view on matters not before it, for example other collection techniques involving foreign affairs or national security.

Despite any shortcomings, the European and US legal protection of human rights in cyberspace is more developed than the rest of the world and should serve as a yardstick for other regions and nation States to measure up to.

Human rights in cyberspace also need to be seen in the broader overall context in which cyber technologies are 'disruptive' as they reshape the pre-existing patterns of employment, commerce and industrial production. Transactions through cyberspace such as e-commerce and e-payment do away with the need for shops and banks, while AI gradually replaces the human workforce. Massive job losses caused by downsizing and restructuring in the 'age of digital economy' have ensued all over the world. Appropriate solutions must be sought to protect human rights and improve human welfare in the light of this new phenomenon connected to cyberspace.

2.   HUMAN RIGHTS AT SEA

Human rights relating to the law of the sea are multidimensional.[83] In general, as stated by the International Tribunal for the Law of the Sea, '[c]onsiderations of humanity must apply in the law of the sea, as they do in other areas of international law'.[84]

Throughout its history, the international law of the sea was made by nation States with power and influence at sea at the relevant time. The modern international law of the sea is encapsulated in the 1982 UN Convention on the Law of the Sea (UNCLOS),[85] concluded by an international diplomatic conference lasting from 1973 to 1982 and attended by all nation States existing at that time. In terms of the human rights to economic development, UNCLOS codifies the regime of the exclusive economic zone of up to 200 nautical miles offshore, unilaterally proclaimed by developing coastal States in Latin America, Asia and Africa, starting from 1947 and gaining momentum in the 1970s. The critical mass of the developing States united together as the bargaining bloc to maximize their economic benefits, especially from living resources, of the sea off their coasts was too much for the other States to resist.[86] Using their collective bargaining power at the conference, developing States also succeeded in incorporating in Part XI of UNCLOS the regime under which the resources in

---

[83]   Bernard H Oxman, 'Human Rights and the United Nations Convention on the Law of the Sea' (1997) 36 Columbia J Transnat'l L 399; Budislav Vukas, 'Droit de la mer et droits de l'homme' in Budislav Vukas (ed.), *The Law of the Sea: Selected Writings* (Martinus Nijhoff 2004) 71; Tullio Treves, 'Human Rights and the Law of the Sea' (2010) 28 Berkeley JIL 1; Irini Papanicolopulu, 'The Law of the Sea Convention: No Place for Persons?' in David Freestone (ed.), *The 1982 Law of the Sea Convention at 30: Successes, Challenges and New Agenda* (Martinus Nijhoff 2013) 193; id, 'Human Rights and the Law of the Sea' in Malgosia Fitzmaurice and Norman A Martínez Gutiérrez (eds), *The IMLI Manual on International Maritime Law* (OUP 2014) vol I, 509–33; Tafsir Malick Ndiaye, 'Human Rights at Sea and the Law of the Sea' (2019) 10 Beijing L Rev 261.

[84]   *M/V 'SAIGA' (No 2) (Saint Vincent and the Grenadines v Guinea)*, Judgment, ITLOS Reports 1999, 61–2 [155]. This echoes the pronouncement of the ICJ in *Corfu Channel* [1949] ICJ Rep 4, 22 that there are 'certain general and well recognized principles' that include 'elementary considerations of humanity', which is subsequently quoted by the ICJ in *Military and Paramilitary Activities in and against Nicaragua (Nicaragua v USA)* [1986] ICJ Rep 14, 112 [215].

[85]   1833 UNTS 3.

[86]   Jonathan I Charney, 'The Exclusive Economic Zone and Public International Law' (1985) 15 Ocean Development & IL 233; David Joseph Attard, *The Exclusive Economic Zone in International Law* (OUP 1987); Umberto Leanza and Maria Cristina Caracciolo, 'The Exclusive Economic Zone' in David J Attard, Malgosia Fitzmaurice and Norman A Martínez Gutiérrez (eds), *The IMLI Manual on International Maritime Law* (OUP 2014) vol I, ch. 7.

the 'Area' – the seabed and ocean floor and subsoil thereof, beyond the limits of national jurisdiction – are recognized as the 'common heritage of mankind', the benefits ensuing from the exploitation of which are to be allocated by the International Seabed Authority for the benefit of mankind as a whole, taking into particular consideration the interests and needs of developing States and of peoples who have not attained full independence or other self-governing status. These resources are identified as all solid, liquid or gaseous mineral resources *in situ* in the Area or beneath the seabed, including polymetallic nodules. However, due to strong opposition from industrialized States with technologies to explore and exploit such resources without whom Part XI would not be realizable, Part XI is now modified by the 1994 Agreement relating to the Implementation of Part XI of UNCLOS.[87] Bargaining power is thus crucial to the formulation of new rules in the law of the sea. This is also likely to be the case with the efforts by the developing States to have the common heritage of mankind principle emulated vis-à-vis marine genetic resources in a new international convention being negotiated multilaterally on the conservation and sustainable use of marine biological diversity of areas beyond national jurisdiction.[88]

With regard to the human right to a clean environment, Part XII of UNCLOS stipulates the obligations of States to protect and preserve the marine environment. Article 297(1)(c) of UNCLOS subjects marine environmental disputes to compulsory third-party dispute settlement proceedings entailing binding decisions when it is alleged that a coastal State has acted in contravention of specified international rules and standards for the protection and preservation of the marine environment which are applicable to the coastal State and which have been established by UNCLOS or through a competent international organization or diplomatic conference in accordance with UNCLOS.

In an oft-cited statement, the Grand Chamber of the ECtHR in *Medvedyev and Others v France* pronounces unequivocally that 'the special nature of the maritime environment ... cannot justify an area outside the law where ships' crews are covered by no legal system capable of affording them enjoyment of the rights and guarantees protected by the [ECHR] which the States have undertaken to secure to everyone within their jurisdiction'.[89]

---

[87]   1864 UNTS 3.
[88]   See Konrad Jan Marciniak, 'Marine Genetic Resources: Do They Form Part of the Common Heritage of Mankind Principle?' in Lawrence Martin, Constantinos Salonidis and Christina Hioureas (eds), *Natural Resources and the Law of the Sea: Exploration, Allocation, Exploitation of Natural Resources in Areas under National Jurisdiction and Beyond* (Juris Publishing 2017) 373.
[89]   App No 3394/03 (29 Mar 2010) §81.

The human rights of individuals at sea are protected in a number of ways. For instance, Article 99 of UNCLOS requires every State to take effective measures to prevent and punish the transport of slaves in ships authorized to fly its flag and to prevent the unlawful use of its flag for that purpose. Any slave taking refuge on board any ship, whatever its flag, shall ipso facto be free. Article 73 of UNCLOS provides several human rights protections to individuals engaged in maritime activities. First, foreign vessels and their crews arrested by the coastal State when enforcing its laws and regulations in its exclusive economic zone shall be promptly released upon the posting of reasonable bonds or other security. The International Tribunal for the Law of the Sea has held this obligation to include 'elementary considerations of humanity and due process of law'.[90] Secondly, coastal State penalties for violation of fisheries laws and regulations in the exclusive economic zone may not include imprisonment, in the absence of agreements to the contrary by the States concerned, or any other form of corporal punishment. Thirdly, in cases of arrest or detention of foreign vessels, the coastal State shall promptly notify the flag State, through appropriate channels, of the action taken and of any penalties subsequently imposed. Article 146 of UNCLOS provides, inter alia, that with respect to the activities in the Area, necessary measures shall be taken to ensure effective protection of human life.

The 2009 FAO Port State Measures Agreement to Prevent, Deter and Eliminate Illegal, Unreported and Unregulated Fishing[91] aims at denying access by vessels suspected of involvement in such fishing to ports of States Parties to the Agreement. However, Article 11(2)(a) of the Agreement provides that a party shall not deny such a vessel the use of port services essential to the safety or health of the crew or the safety of the vessel, provided these needs are duly proven. Article 8*bis* (10)(a)(i) and (ii) of the 2005 Convention for the Suppression of Unlawful Acts against the Safety of Maritime Navigation[92] stipulates that where a State Party takes measures against a ship pursuant to this Convention, it shall take due account of the need not to endanger the safety of life at sea as well as ensuring that all persons on board are treated in a manner which preserves their basic human dignity and in compliance with the applicable provisions of international law, including IHRL. The duty to

---

[90] '*Juno Trader' (Saint Vincent and the Grenadines v Guinea-Bissau)*, Prompt Release, Judgment, 18 December 2004, ITLOS Reports 2004, 38–9 [77].

[91] http://www.fao.org/fileadmin/user_upload/legal/docs/037t-e.pdf, accessed 27 Jan 2019.

[92] 1678 UNTS 221.

avoid endangering the safety of life at sea is a well-established rule of law enforcement at sea and has become a standard requirement in several treaties.[93]

The International Labour Organization (ILO) has adopted several conventions to protect the welfare of working seamen. For example, the ILO's Maritime Labour Convention of 2006,[94] in force on 20 August 2013, sets the minimum standards to ensure satisfactory conditions of employment for the world's seafarers. It brings together and updates more than 65 other ILO maritime labour instruments, while introducing a system of certification and inspection to enforce it. The ILO Work in Fishing Convention (No 188),[95] adopted in 2007 and in force on 16 November 2017, sets standards to protect workers in the fishing sector to ensure that fishers have improved occupational safety and health and medical care at sea and that sick or injured fishers receive care ashore, receive sufficient rest for their health and safety, have the protection of a work agreement and have the same social security protection as other workers. There are also measures to ensure compliance and enforcement, including possible inspection of large fishing vessels on extended voyages when docked in foreign ports, to ensure that fishers do not work under conditions that are hazardous to their safety and health.[96]

Efforts by the International Maritime Organization (IMO) to ensure the safety of fishing vessels have not come to fruition so far.[97] Its latest instrument is the Cape Town Agreement, adopted at an international conference held in Cape Town, South Africa in 2012, to bring into effect the provisions of the 1977 Torremolinos International Convention for the Safety of Fishing Vessels, as modified by the 1993 Torremolinos Protocol.[98] In ratifying the 2012 Agreement, parties also agree to the amendments to the provisions of the 1993 Protocol, so that they can come into force 12 months after at least 22 States, with an aggregate 3,600 fishing vessels of 24 metres in length and over, operating on the high seas, have expressed their consent to be bound by it. As of February 2019, 11 States had ratified the Cape Town Agreement: Belgium,

---

[93] For example, Art 17(5) of the 1988 UN Convention against Illicit Traffic in Narcotic Drugs and Psychotropic Substances (1982 UNTS 95); Art 9(1) of the Protocol against the Smuggling of Migrants by Land, Sea and Air Supplementary to the UN Convention against Transnational Organized Crime (2001) 40 ILM 348.
[94] ILO Convention No 186 (MLC).
[95] ILO Convention No 188 (C188).
[96] For a discussion of the ILO conventions applicable to seafarers, see Irini Papanicolopulu, *International Law and the Protection of People at Sea* (OUP 2018) 34–40.
[97] Irini Papanicolopulu, 'International Law and the Protection of Fishers' in Angela Del Vecchio (ed.), *International Law of the Sea: Current Trends and Controversial Issues* (Eleven International Publishing 2014) 317, 323–5.
[98] IMO, *Cape Town Agreement of 2012* (IMO Publishing 2018).

Congo, Denmark, France, Germany, Iceland, Netherlands, Norway, St Kitts and Nevis, South Africa and Spain, with a combined number of 1,413 fishing vessels of 24 metres in length or more operating on the high seas.

With hundreds or even thousands of lives lost at sea each year during Mediterranean crossings from Africa to Europe, human rights at sea have become a subject of discussion in international organizations concerned with human rights, irregular migration and refugee protection, as well as in the governments and parliaments of the affected States, the mass media and academia.[99]

What is happening in Europe used to happen elsewhere. In the late 1970s– early 1990s there were mass influxes (according to some estimates between 800,000 and 2 million) of boat people from Indochina, especially Vietnam after the collapse of South Vietnam to Communist North Vietnam. The boat people searched for safe havens in several South East Asian States, none of which (except for the Philippines – since 1981) was party to the 1951 Convention Relating to the Status of Refugees[100] and its 1967 Protocol.[101] The South East Asian States of 'first asylum', except the Philippines, rejected as a rule of customary international law binding upon them the principle of *non-refoulement* enshrined in the 1951 Convention and its 1967 Protocol, which prohibits returning asylum seekers to a State where they have a well-founded fear of persecution based on race, religion, nationality, membership of a particular social group or political opinion. However, they yielded to the pressure from the West to temporarily shelter the boat people, pending their final resettlement,

---

[99]   Marcello Di Filippo, 'Irregular Migration and Safeguard of Life at Sea. International Rules and Recent Developments in the Mediterranean Sea' in Del Vecchio (ed.), *International Law of the Sea* 9; Thomas Gammeltoft-Hansen and Jens Vedsted-Hansen (eds), *Human Rights and the Dark Side of Globalisation: Transnational Law Enforcement and Migration Control* (Routledge 2016); Paul von Mühlendahl, 'Protection of Fundamental Rights, the Principle of *Non-Refoulement* and the Law of the Sea within the Context of the European Union: An Incompatible Trio?' in Angela Del Vecchio and Fabrizio Marrella (eds), *International Law and Maritime Governance: Current Issues and Challenges for Regional Economic Integration Organizations* (Editoriale Scientifica 2016) 101; Violeta Moreno-Lax and Efthymios Papastavridis (eds), *'Boat Refugees' and Migration at Sea: A Comprehensive Approach – Integrating Maritime Security with Human Rights* (Brill Nijhoff 2017); Itamar Mann, *Humanity at Sea: Maritime Migration and the Foundations of International Law* (CUP 2017); id, 'Maritime Legal Black Holes: Migration and Rightlessness in International Law' (2018) 29 EJIL 347; Papanicolopulu, *International Law and the Protection of People at Sea*; Elaine Burroughs and Kira Williams (eds), *Contemporary Boat Migration: Data, Geopolitics and Discourses* (Rowman & Littlefield International 2018).
[100]   189 UNTS 137, in force on 22 Apr 1954.
[101]   606 UNTS 267, in force on 4 Oct 1967.

mostly in the West, in exchange for the West's support in their fight against the spread of communism into their respective States as a 'domino effect' after the fall of South Vietnam. Neither IHRL nor the law of the sea played a prominent role in this boat people episode.[102] It was international diplomacy that prevailed. The States of first asylum, except the Philippines, insisted that they persistently objected to *non-refoulement* but agreed to give temporary shelter to the boat people not because of their belief that they were bound by international law to do so, but as part of the international 'burden sharing' regarding these asylum seekers. They were at pains to explain that they were not insensitive to the plight of the boat people but were constrained by various factors, financial and otherwise. It took more than two decades for all the boat people to be resettled permanently in the States willing and ready to accept them. These States imposed quotas on how many they could resettle each year, bearing in mind their available resources, the need to gradually assimilate the asylum seekers into their new societies without also disrupting the way of life of the local community, and available employment opportunities for the new-comers that would not result in putting an inordinate number of local residents out of work.

In the early 1990s the USA faced its own boat people crisis as a State of final resettlement, and not as a State of 'first asylum' as in the aforesaid Indochinese boat people episode. It should be noted that the US Government had taken the lead in persuading South East Asian States to temporarily shelter the Indochinese boat people as South Vietnam had allied with the USA to fight North Vietnam during the Vietnam War.

Sale v Haitian Ctrs Council, Inc,[103] decided by the US Supreme Court in June 1993, concerns the direction given by the US President to the US Coast Guard to intercept vessels illegally transporting passengers from Haiti to the USA and to return those passengers to Haiti without first determining whether they might qualify as refugees. The question presented in this case is whether such forced repatriation, 'authorized to be undertaken only beyond the territorial sea of the United States', violates section 243(h)(1) of the Immigration and Nationality Act of 1952[104] and/or the prohibition of expulsion or return of

---

[102] Cf a narrative account of the boat people episode in Mann, *Humanity at Sea* 60–86.

[103] 509 US 155. For a discussion of this case and its global influence, see Mann, *Humanity at Sea* 115–47.

[104] 'The Attorney General shall not deport or return any alien (other than an alien described in section 1251(a)(4)(D) of this title) to a country if the Attorney General determines that such alien's life or freedom would be threatened in such country on account of race, religion, nationality, membership in a particular social group or political opinion.' 8 U.S.C. 1253(h)(1) (1988 edn, Supp. IV).

refugees under Article 33 of the 1951 Refugee Convention to which the USA is party.

The Supreme Court, by a majority of eight to one, ruled that neither section 243(h) nor Article 33 of the Refugee Convention limits the US President's power to order the Coast Guard to repatriate undocumented aliens intercepted on the high seas. It alludes to the fact that the mass influx of Haitian boat people was caused by the *coup d'état* on 30 September 1991 against the government of Jean Bertrand Aristide, the first democratically elected president in Haitian history, after which 'hundreds of Haitians have been killed, tortured, detained without a warrant or subjected to violence and the destruction of their property because of their political beliefs. ... [and t]housands have been forced into hiding'. During the six months after October 1991, the US Coast Guard interdicted over 34,000 Haitians. Because so many interdicted Haitians could not be safely processed on Coast Guard cutters, the US Department of Defense established temporary facilities at the US Naval Base in Guantánamo, Cuba, to accommodate them during the screening process. Those temporary facilities, however, had a capacity of only about 12,500 persons. With both the facilities at Guantánamo and available US Coast Guard cutters saturated and with the number of Haitian emigrants in unseaworthy craft increasing (many had drowned as they attempted the trip to Florida), the US Government could no longer both protect US borders and offer the Haitians even a modified screening process. It had to choose between allowing Haitians into the USA for the screening process or repatriating them without giving them any opportunity to establish their qualifications as refugees. In the judgement of the President's advisers, the first choice not only would have defeated the original purpose of the programme (controlling illegal immigration), but also would have impeded diplomatic efforts to restore democratic government in Haiti and would have posed a life-threatening danger to thousands of persons embarking on long voyages in dangerous craft. The second choice would have advanced those policies but deprived the fleeing Haitians of any screening process at a time when a significant minority of them were being screened in. On 23 May 1992 US President Bush adopted the second choice. After assuming office, President Clinton decided not to modify that order.

The majority of the US Supreme Court opines that Acts of Congress are ordinarily presumed not to apply outside US borders. Therefore, it must reasonably be concluded that Congress used the phrase 'deport or return' in section 243(h)(1) only to make the section's protection available both in proceedings to deport aliens already in the country and proceedings to exclude those already at the border. With respect to the Refugee Convention, Article 33 prohibits expulsion or return (*refoulement*) of a refugee in any manner whatsoever to the frontiers of territories where his life or freedom would be threatened on account of his race, religion, nationality, membership of a particular social group or political opinion. Article 33(1) uses the words 'expel or return ("*refouler*")' as an obvious parallel to the words 'deport or return' in section 243(h)(1). 'Expel' has the same meaning as 'deport'; it refers to the deportation or expulsion of an alien who is already present in the host country. This suggestion – that 'return' has a legal meaning narrower than its common meaning – is reinforced by the parenthetical reference to *refouler*, a French word that is not an exact synonym for the English word 'return'. Neither of two respected English–French dictionaries mentions *refouler* as one of many possible French translations of 'return'. Conversely, the English translations of *refouler* do not include the word 'return', but include words like 'repulse', 'repel', 'drive back' and even 'expel'. To the extent that they are relevant, these translations imply that 'return' means a defensive act of resistance or exclusion at a border, rather than an act of transporting someone to a particular destination. In the context of the Convention, to 'return' means to 'repulse' rather than to 'reinstate'. The majority concludes that '[t]his case presents a painfully common situation in which desperate people, convinced that they can no longer remain in their homeland, take desperate measures to escape. Although the human crisis is compelling, there is no solution to be found in a judicial remedy.'[105] The lone dissenting Judge Blackmun, by contrast, considers the duty of non-return expressed in both the Refugee Convention and the US statute is clear and unambiguous. He concludes:

> The refugees attempting to escape from Haiti do not claim a right of admission to this country. They do not even argue that the US Government has no right to intercept their boats. They demand only that the United States, land of refugees and guardian of freedom, cease forcibly driving them back to detention, abuse and death. That is a modest plea, vindicated by the treaty and the statute. We should not close our ears to it.[106]

Sale is about international refugee law applicable at sea as implemented by US domestic law. The US Government's aforesaid second option did not appear to have taken into consideration Article 12 of the 1958 Geneva Convention on the High Seas,[107] to which the USA is party. Article 12(1) obligates 'every State' to require the master of a ship sailing under its flag, insofar as he can do so without serious danger to the ship, the crew or the passengers: (a) to render assistance to any person found at sea in danger of being lost; (b) to proceed with all possible speed to the rescue of persons in distress if informed of their need of assistance, insofar as such action may reasonably be expected of him;

---

[105] 509 US 155, 188.
[106] Ibid 208.
[107] 405 UNTS 11.

and (c) after a collision, to render assistance to the other ship, her crew and her passengers and, where possible, to inform the other ship of the name of his own ship, her port of registry and the nearest port at which she will call. Paragraph 2 of that Article stipulates that 'every coastal State shall promote the establishment and maintenance of an adequate and effective search and rescue service regarding safety on and over the sea and – where circumstances so require – by way of mutual regional arrangements cooperate with neighbouring States for this purpose'.

Article 12 of the 1958 Convention now also appears as Article 98(1) of UNCLOS, to which the USA is not party but the EU and all EU Member States bordering the Mediterranean are. Additionally, Article 18(2) of UNCLOS, which has no similar provision in the 1958 Convention, allows a foreign ship exercising the right of innocent passage in the territorial sea of another State to stop and anchor if necessary for the purpose of rendering assistance to persons, ships or aircraft in danger or distress. However, this latter provision by no means signifies that ships carrying irregular migrants or asylum seekers have the right of innocent passage in the territorial sea of a coastal State.

UNCLOS applies to this matter alongside other relevant international treaties, including the 1951 Refugees Convention and its 1967 Protocol, the 1974 IMO Convention on Safety of Life at Sea (SOLAS) as amended in 2004,[108] and the 1979 International Convention on Maritime Search and Rescue (SAR Convention) as amended in 2004.[109]

SOLAS, as amended, clarifies that the obligation to provide assistance applies regardless of the nationality or status of such persons or the circumstances in which they are found. Moreover, States shall coordinate and cooperate to assist the ship's master in delivering persons rescued at sea to a place of safety with minimum further deviation from the ship's intended voyage, provided this does not further endanger the safety of life at sea. The State responsible for the search and rescue region in which such assistance is rendered shall exercise the primary responsibility for the coordination and cooperation. In addition, the owner, the charterer, the company operating the ship or any other person shall not prevent or restrict the master of the ship from taking or executing any decision which, in the master's professional judgement, is necessary

---

[108] 1184 UNTS 278, as amended by IMO Res MSC.153(78) 20 May 2004, in force on 1 July 2006.

[109] 1405 UNTS 119, as amended by IMO Maritime Safety Committee Resolution MSC.155(78) 20 May 2004, in force on 1 July 2006. See Patricia Mallia, *Migrant Smuggling by Sea: Combating a Current Threat to Maritime Security through the Creation of a Cooperative Framework* (Martinus Nijhoff 2010) 106–7; Irini Papanicolopulu, 'The Duty to Rescue at Sea, in Peacetime and in War: A General Overview' (2016) 98 Int'l Rev Red Cross 491.

for safety of life at sea and protection of the marine environment. The SAR Convention, as amended, clarifies procedures for the party responsible for the search and rescue region in which persons were rescued at sea to guarantee that they will be provided a place of safety within a reasonable time regardless of their nationality, status or circumstances in which they are found.

The actual implementation of these international instruments has been subject to controversy due to the subjective interpretation of their provisions by the parties concerned.[110] In particular, there appears to be no unequivocal definition of what constitutes 'distress', leaving it to the ship's master to determine when a vessel at sea is in need of rescue, with due regard to the safety of his own crew and ship in the light of the various perils of the high seas when answering a call for distress.[111] There is no direct obligation on States to allow rescued persons' access to their territory. For example, Malta, which has an excessively large search and rescue region, has not ratified the 2004 IMO's amendments and has insisted that the coordinating State's obligation is to disembark rescued persons at the nearest safe port of call.[112] In *Ruddock v Vadarlis*,[113] decided by the High Court of Australia in September 2001, Justice Beaumont's *obiter dictum* comments that while customary international law imposes an obligation upon a coastal State to provide humanitarian assistance to vessels in distress, it imposes no obligation upon the coastal State to resettle those rescued in the coastal State's territory. Justice Beaumont adds that this accords with the principles of the Refugee Convention, Article 33 of which stipulates that a person who has established refugee status may not be expelled to a territory where his life and freedom would be threatened for a Convention reason, but the Convention does not impose an obligation on the coastal State to resettle in its own territory.[114] But where the refugee will go after the rescue is a thorny question. This lack of clarity of the applicable

---

[110] Sophie Cacciaguidi-Fahy, 'The Law of the Sea and Human Rights' (2007) 19 Sri Lanka JIL 85, 91–101; Lisa-Marie Komp, 'The Duty to Assist Persons in Distress: An Alternative Source of Protection against the Return of Migrants and Asylum Seekers to the High Seas?' in Moreno-Lax and Papastavridis (eds), *'Boat Refugees' and Migration at Sea* 222; Jorrit J Rijpma, 'The Patrolling of the European Union's External Maritime Border: Preventing the Rule of Law from Getting Lost at Sea' in Del Vecchio (ed.), *International Law of the Sea* 77, 98; Daniel Ghezelbash, Violeta Moreno-Lax, Natalie Kline and Brian Opeskin, 'Securitization of Search and Rescue at Sea: The Response to Boat Migration in the Mediterranean and Offshore Australia' (2018) 67 ICLQ 315.
[111] Cacciaguidi-Fahy, 'The Law of the Sea and Human Rights' 94.
[112] Thomas Gammeltoft-Hansen and Tanja Aalberts, 'Search and Rescue as a Geopolitics of International Law' in Aalberts and Gammeltoft-Hansen (eds), *The Changing Practices of International Law* 188, 194–7.
[113] [2001] FCA 1329 (18 Sept 2001).
[114] Ibid §126.

international legal regime has given rise to the phenomenon of 'migration management', whereby wealthier States 'outsource' the taking of irregular migrants and asylum seekers found at sea to their less wealthy counterparts in exchange for funds, development assistance, trade privileges, labour migration quotas and other form of benefits from the former States. This is irrespective of whether the States agreeing to take these persons are able to meet the international standards expected of them in relation to the rescued persons, especially if the rescued persons do qualify as refugees under international law.[115]

Hirsi Jamaa and Others v Italy,[116] decided on 23 February 2012 by the Grand Chamber of the ECtHR, involves applications by 11 Somali nationals and 13 Eritrean nationals who were part of a group of approximately 200 individuals leaving Libya in 2009 aboard three vessels bound for the Italian coast that was intercepted, taken on board and forced back to Libya by Italian government ships pursuant to bilateral agreements between Italy and Libya to combat clandestine immigration. The Grand Chamber ruled that under international law and the Italian Navigation Code a vessel sailing on the high seas is subject to the exclusive jurisdiction of the State of the flag it is flying. In the instant case, the impugned events took place entirely on board ships of the Italian armed forces, the crews of which were composed exclusively of Italian military personnel. During the period between boarding the ships by the Italian armed forces and being handed over to the Libyan authorities, the applicants were under the continuous and exclusive de jure and de facto control of the Italian authorities. Speculation as to the nature and purpose of the intervention of the Italian ships on the high seas would not lead to any other conclusion. Therefore, the Grand Chamber held that the events giving rise to the alleged violations fall within Italy's 'jurisdiction' within the meaning of Article 1 of the ECHR.[117] It finds two violations of Article 3 of the ECHR because the applicants were exposed to the risk of torture, inhuman or degrading treatment or punishment in Libya, the receiving State, and to the risk of their arbitrary repatriation to Somalia or Eritrea, their States of origin, where they would risk ill-treatment prohibited by Article 3. The Grand Chamber also found a violation of Article 4 of Protocol No 4[118] prohibiting collective expulsion of aliens and a violation of Article 13 (the right to an effective remedy before a national

---

[115] Gammeltoft-Hansen and Aalberts, 'Search and Rescue as a Geopolitics of International Law' 201–4.

[116] App No 27765/09.

[117] Judgment §§70–82. See also Mariagiulia Giuffre, 'Access to Asylum at Sea? *Non-Refoulement* and a Comprehensive Approach to Extraterritorial Human Rights Obligations' in Moreno-Lax and Papastavridis (eds), *'Boat Refugees' and Migration at Sea* 248, 263–4.

[118] ETS 46.

authority) read in conjunction with Article 3 and Article 4 of Protocol No 4. Each applicant was awarded €15,000 in respect of non-pecuniary damage plus €1,575.74 in total in respect of costs and expenses.

On 30 October 2018 the Human Rights Committee of the ICCPR adopted General Comment No 36, paragraph 63 of which extends the spatial scope of the obligation of every State Party to the ICCPR to respect and to ensure the right to life protected by Article 6 of the ICCPR. The obligation is owed to all persons over whose enjoyment of the right to life the State Party exercises power or effective control. This includes persons located outside any territory effectively controlled by the State, whose right to life is nonetheless 'impacted' by its military or other activities in a direct and reasonably foreseeable manner. The State also has obligations under international law not to aid or assist activities undertaken by other States and non-State actors that violate the right to life. ICCPR States Parties are required to respect and protect the lives of all individuals located on marine vessels or aircraft registered by them or flying their flag, and of those individuals who find themselves in a situation of distress at sea, 'in accordance with their international obligations on rescue at sea'. Given that the deprivation of liberty brings a person within a State's effective control, States Parties must respect and protect the right to life of all individuals arrested or detained by them, even if held outside their territory.[119] It remains to be seen how this far-reaching expansion of the spatial scope of the ICCPR obligation will be implemented in practice to address the situation of irregular migrants at sea.

The complexities of the phenomenon of irregular migration by sea cannot be generalized and the circumstances surrounding each incident may need to be assessed on a case-by-case basis to accommodate competing rights. For example, how is the duty under Article 98 of UNCLOS to be enforced against stateless vessels encountering persons in distress at sea? What of the right to private property of the owner of the rescuing ship, especially when it is a merchant ship with carriage contractual obligations to perform within a specific time frame? The list may continue as new situations arise.

The phenomenon of irregular migrants or asylum seekers found at sea, or 'boat people', also has another far-reaching implication: the right to resettle permanently in another State if they prefer not to return home even after the end of upheavals back there. There could be many theories for and against this. It could be posited, for example, that people from former colonies should be entitled to resettle permanently in the States that used to colonize theirs – something in the nature of 'colonial debts' to be repaid, that is, 'X country got rich from our natural resources etc., it's now time for X to take care of us'.

---

[119] CCPR/C/GC/36 (30 Oct 2018) §63.

The duty to rescue those in peril at sea as part of the human encounter may involve a delicate issue of moral choice, too. It is difficult to find a right solution to at least one situation: when the boat people see a passing ship nearby, they deliberately sink their own vessel in the hope of being rescued and given shelter on land. This kind of deliberate action imperils the lives of the passengers of the vessel being sunk. However, if the passing ship does not 'rescue' them, the captain of that ship would be in violation of the duty of rescue. Yet, if the rescue is undertaken in such circumstances, it will act as a 'pull' factor, giving an incentive to other boat people to deliberately sink their vessels.[120]

The law of the sea as a niche area of IHRL will continue to evolve and its outcome will very much depend on the interplay between IHRL and diplomacy among affected States with diverging national interests and bargaining power.

---

[120] See Mann, *Humanity at Sea* 154–62.

Appendix: Treaty body monitoring procedures

Treaty	Institutions	Type[a] & composition	Reporting procedure	Individual complaints, applications or communications	Inter-State applications or communications	Inquiries and visits	Other procedures[b] or remarks
ECHR	ECtHR	Court: number of judges equal to that of High Contracting Parties (Art 20)		Individual applications (Art 34)	Inter-State applications (Art 33)		Advisory jurisdiction (Art 47)
	Secretary General, Council of Europe					Inquiries by the Secretary General (Art 52)	
CERD	Comm'ee on the Elimination of Racial Discrimination	Committee: 18 Experts (Art 8(1))	Reports by States Parties within 1 year after the entry into force of CERD for the State concerned & every 2 years thereafter (Art 9(1))	Individual communications, upon declaration by States Parties (Art 4(1))	Inter-State communications (Art 11(1))		
	Ad hoc conciliation comm'ns	Commission: 5 members (Art 12(1))			Unresolved inter-State communications (Art 12(1))		

Treaty	Institutions	Type[a] & composition	Reporting procedure	Individual complaints, applications or communications	Inter-State applications or communications	Inquiries and visits	Other procedures[b] or remarks
ICCPR	Human Rights Comm'ee	Committee: 18 members (Art 28(1))	Reports by States Parties within 1 year after the entry into force of CERD for the State concerned & thereafter whenever the Comm'ee so requests (Art 40 (1))		Inter-State communications, upon declaration by States Parties (Art 41(1))		
	Ad hoc conciliation comm'ns	Comm'n: 5 members (Art 42(1) and (2))			Unresolved inter-State communications (Art 42(1)(a))		
1st Protocol to ICCPR	Human Rights Comm'ee (see ICCPR)			Individual communications (Art 1)			

Treaty	Institutions	Type[a] & composition	Reporting procedure	Individual complaints, applications or communications	Inter-State applications or communications	Inquiries and visits	Other procedures[b] or remarks
ACHR	IACHR	Commission: 7 members (Art 34)	Copies of reports by States Parties to Executive Comm'ees of the Inter-American Economic & Social Council and the Inter-American Council for Education, Science & Culture (Art 42)	Individual petitions (Art 44)	Inter-State communications, upon declaration by States Parties (Art 45(1))		
	IACtHR	Court: 7 judges (Art 52(1))		Submissions by ACHR on the basis of individual petitions (Art 61(1))	Inter-State cases unresolved by ACHR, upon declaration by States Parties or by special agreement (Arts 61(1) & 62)		Advisory jurisdiction (Art 64(1) and (2))
CEDAW	CEDAW Comm'ee	Committee: 23 experts (Art 17(1))	Reports by States Parties within 1 year after the entry into force of CEDAW; thereafter at least every 4 years (Art 18(1))				

Treaty	Institutions	Type[a] & composition	Reporting procedure	Individual complaints, applications or communications	Inter-State applications or communications	Inquiries and visits	Other procedures[b] or remarks
ACHPR	African Comm'n on Human & Peoples' Rights	Commission: 11 members (Art 31(1))	Reports by States Parties every 2 years (Art 62)	Communications from entities other than States Parties (Art 55)	Inter-State communications (Art 47)		
CAT	CAT Comm'ee	Committee: 10 experts (Art 17(1))	Reports by States Parties within 1 year after CAT's entry into force; thereafter every 4 years (Art 19(1))	Individual communications, upon declaration by States Parties (Art 22(1))	Inter-State communications, upon declaration by States Parties (Art 21(1))	Confidential inquiries & visits (Art 20(2) & (3))	
CRC	CRC Comm'ee	Committee: 10 experts (Art 43(2))	Reports by States Parties within 2 years of CRC's entry into force; thereafter every 5 years (Art 44(1))				Internat'l cooperation with specialized agencies, the UN Children's Fund & other competent bodies (Art 45)

Treaty	Institutions	Type[a] & composition	Reporting procedure	Individual complaints, applications or communications	Inter-State applications or communications	Inquiries and visits	Other procedures[b] or remarks
Protocol to ACHPR on the Establishment of ACtHPR	ACtHPR	Court: 11 judges (Art 11(1))		Individual petitions and petitions from NGOs with observer status before the African Comm'n on Human & Peoples' Rights, either by submission of the African Commission (Art 5(1)(a)), or directly upon declaration by States Parties (Arts 5(3) & 34(6))	Inter-State communications (Art 5(1) & (2))		Advisory jurisdiction (Art 4(1))

Treaty	Institutions	Type[a] & composition	Reporting procedure	Individual complaints, applications or communications	Inter-State applications or communications	Inquiries and visits	Other procedures[b] or remarks
Optional Protocol to CEDAW	CEDAW Comm'ee (see CEDAW)		Info on the measures taken in response to an inquiry to be included in the report under Art 18 of CEDAW (Art 9(1))	Individual communications (Art 2)			Request to States Parties to take interim measures (Art 5(1))
Optional Protocol to CRC on sale of children, child prostitution & child pornography	CRC Comm'ee (see CRC)		Reports by States Parties within 2 years following the entry into force of the Protocol (Art 12(1)) Info re the implementation of the Protocol to be included in the reports of States Parties under Art 44 of CRC (Art 12(2)) Reports by other States Parties every 5 years (Art 12(2))				

Treaty	Institutions	Type & composition	Reporting procedure	Individual complaints, applications or communications	Inter-State applications or communications	Inquiries and visits	Other procedures[b] or remarks
Optional Protocol to CRC on the involvement of children in armed conflict	CRC Comm'ee (see CRC)		Reports by States Parties within 2 years following the entry into force of the Protocol (Art 8 (1)) Info re the implementation of the Protocol to be included in the reports of States Parties under Art 44 of CRC (Art 8(2)) Reports by other States Parties every 5 years (Art 8(2))				

Treaty	Institutions	Type[a] & composition	Reporting procedure	Individual complaints, applications or communications	Inter-State applications or communications	Inquiries and visits	Other procedures[b] or remarks
Optional Protocol to CAT	Sub-comm'ee on Prevention of Torture etc.	Sub-committee: 25 members (Arts 2(1) & 5(1))				Visits to any place where persons are/may be deprived of their liberty (Arts 4(1) & 11(a))	
	Nat'l preventive mechanism	Visiting body (Art 3)				Visits to any place where persons are/may be deprived of their liberty (Art 4(1))	

International human rights law and diplomacy

Treaty	Institutions	Type[a] & composition	Reporting procedure	Individual complaints, applications or communications	Inter-State applications or communications	Inquiries and visits	Other procedures[b] or remarks
CED	Comm'ee on Enforced Disappearance	Committee: 10 experts (Art 26(1))	Reports by States Parties within 2 years after the entry into force of CED (Art 29)	Individual communications, upon declaration by States Parties (Art 31(1))	Inter-State communications, upon declaration by States Parties (Art 32)	Inquiries and visits (Art 33)	Urgent actions (Art 30) Information to UNGA (Art 34)
Optional Protocol to CRC on a communications procedure	CRC Comm'ee (see CRC)		Follow-up procedure re any action by States Parties as regards recommendations of the Comm'ee & implementation of friendly settlements (Art 11)	Individual communications (Art 5)	Inter-State communications, upon declaration by States Parties (Art 12(1))	Inquiries and visits (Art 13(2))	Request to States Parties to take interim measures (Art 6(1))

Notes: [a] Type = committee, commission, court, assembly, meeting or conference
[b] Other procedures = urgent actions, information to assemblies, etc
Source: Memorandum by the Secretariat of the International Law Commission, 'Crimes against Humanity: Information on existing treaty-based monitoring mechanisms which may be of relevance to the future work of the International Law Commission', Doc A/CN.4/698 (18 Mar 2016), Annex II. Reproduced in accordance with the Guidelines on the Publications of Commission Documents (International Law Commission, 'Report of the International Law Commission on the work of its 59th Session' (7 May–5 June and 9 July–10 Aug 2007) UN Doc A/62/10 §381).

Index